Après-coup in Psychoanalysis

This important book argues that après-coup, a concept that has blossomed in French psychoanalytic discourse, not only allows an understanding of how repressed early memories determine adult life, and how human sexuality develops, but also allows for a richer and wider explanation of our mental structures and thinking.

The book outlines how après-coup has been understood and defined by Freud, Lacan and other authors, considers it in diverse psychoanalytic cultures and explores its resonance in dream-work, sexual drives, thought, and the experience of trauma. Bernard Chervet considers that the totality of human thought can be approached according to the theory of après-coup. It offers a metapsychological approach to the operation of après-coup, bodily erogeneity and the regeneration of libido. Chervet's compelling work argues that the phenomenon of après-coup allowed for the development of the psychoanalytic theories of causality, sexuality, temporality, memory and trauma.

Illustrated by clinical vignettes and written by one of the leading theorists on the topic, *Après-coup in Psychoanalysis* will be an invaluable resource for psychoanalysts in training and in practice.

Bernard Chervet is a Training and Supervising Psychoanalyst of the Paris Psychoanalytic Society and a former SPP President. He is a European Representative on the IPA Board of Representatives and the IPA ExCom and Scientific Director of the Congress of French-Speaking Psychoanalysts (CPLF). His numerous and distinguished publications cover a wide range of clinical and theoretical psychoanalytic topics. He was awarded the Bouvet Prize in 2017 for his work.

Après-coup in Psychoanalysis

The Fulfilment of Desire and Thought

Bernard Chervet

Translated by Andrew Weller

Routledge
Taylor & Francis Group
LONDON AND NEW YORK

Designed cover image: The Stryge. Photograph by Bernard Chervet

First published in English 2023
by Routledge
4 Park Square, Milton Park, Abingdon, Oxon OX14 4RN

and by Routledge
605 Third Avenue, New York, NY 10158

Routledge is an imprint of the Taylor & Francis Group, an informa business

© 2023 Bernard Chervet

Translated by Andrew Weller

The right of Bernard Chervet to be identified as author of this work has been asserted in accordance with sections 77 and 78 of the Copyright, Designs and Patents Act 1988.

All rights reserved. No part of this book may be reprinted or reproduced or utilised in any form or by any electronic, mechanical, or other means, now known or hereafter invented, including photocopying and recording, or in any information storage or retrieval system, without permission in writing from the publishers.

Trademark notice: Product or corporate names may be trademarks or registered trademarks, and are used only for identification and explanation without intent to infringe.

British Library Cataloguing-in-Publication Data
A catalogue record for this book is available from the British Library

ISBN: 9780367188788 (hbk)
ISBN: 9780367188795 (pbk)
ISBN: 9780429198953 (ebk)

DOI: 10.4324/9780429198953

Typeset in Times New Roman
by Deanta Global Publishing Services, Chennai, India

Printed in the United Kingdom
by Henry Ling Limited

Contents

1 The emergence of desire and thought 1

2 Semantic and semiological vicissitudes of the term
  Nachträglichkeit 14

3 The work of Freud and his followers as a clinical illustration
  of the operation of après-coup 26

4 Evolving clinical situations 71

5 Metapsychological approach to the concept of après-coup 115

6 A theory of human thought 143

7 Saturation in dreams, sessions and sciences 163

8 Après-coup and bodily erogeneity 181

9 The missing trace and feelings of lack 206

10 The foundational murder and the superego 231

   Index 263

Chapter 1

The emergence of desire and thought

Psychoanalysis is a discipline and method that attempts to promote, thanks to their links to consciousness, *desire* and *human thought* in all their forms as emergences of *psychic matter*. It proposes a theory of thought that extends its definition to all expressions of the psyche, whether they belong to the register of the verb, the image, affects, feelings and emotions, experiences, sensations, or sensuality and erotogenicity.

Beyond this extension, psychoanalysis thinks about human thought and its various expressions, bringing into play a reality that is apparently in total heterogeneity with this emergence. Initially referred to by the term "unconscious," this reality turns out in fact to be the extinctive tendency of every instinctual drive, its regressive tendency to return to an earlier state of things, even to the inorganic and "inanimate" state (Freud, 1920, p. 38). It is expressed in the session by all the forms of resistance in both senses of the term: as resistance to becoming conscious and resistance to erasure (the resistance of materials). This *extinctive regressivity* peculiar to every drive impulse cannot, by definition, be directly registered by a specific thing-presentation. There are no traces or thing-representations of lack.

It is linked to the sensory perceptions of lacks arising from destruction and loss, but above all to those arising from the sensory perception of differences. These cannot produce either traces or thing-presentations. Only the tangible realities involved in differences are representable. Extinctive regressivity can only be represented by operations of disappearance and erasure concerning representations arising from the differentiation of perceptual traces of tangible realities. These thing-presentations ground the positivity of the drives. The negative extinctive tendency of the drives has a counter-effect. It obliges expressions of thought to emerge and participates in the registration of the various drive vicissitudes. An imperative of registration is required as a counterpoint and grounds the positive registration of the drives. While this negativity is opposed to any new registrations and tends to make all the formations produced disappear, it can also be used to accomplish psychic registrations and to promote the assumption of a bonus of desire that can be cathected in the body and the world.

In psychoanalysis, the term *thought* designates all the forms of emergence of elusive psychic matter. The existence of the latter can only be deduced from its manifestations as they appear on the screen of consciousness. A generic wish is thereby fulfilled that is inherent to life itself. This wish is fulfilled through all the other wishes on the basis of which it can be recognized and interpreted. It is the wish to generate a bonus of desire that finds its ideal fulfilment in erotic life, but that can also be used for an infinite number of other achievements, so great is its plasticity. The assumption and availability of this bonus of desire is the goal of all psychic work. A teleology of psychic life can be inferred here.

All the productions that form human thought are therefore after-effects of the psychic work required by the tendency to extinction and by the imperative of registration. This work of the psychic apparatus constitutes the operation of après-coup.

Thus conceived, thinking is one of the major achievements of organic matter. That is why Freud always supported the idea that psychoanalysis belongs to the field of the natural sciences, namely the science of psychic life.

This explains why we can consider the advent of psychoanalysis as an emergence of thought, since the elaboration of desire requires the appropriation of the drives and the establishment of their vicissitudes in the form of the various forms of thought. Erotic desire is an aim whose advent requires a precise temporal order and the establishment of many other vicissitudes of thought arising from the transformations of primary instinctual drive impulses.

This detour via the advent of thought allows access to mature sexuality and requires a long process in two stages. The in-between period of latency establishes the regressive forms of thought in the making. The latter are indispensable for the future sensual regression characteristic of erotic desire, and for the formal regression of the dream-work. Erotic desire and dreams are deferred effects because they are the result of the operation of après-coup. Erotic life follows a sensual regression that requires, like dreams, a prior deployment of regressive modes of thinking.

Psychoanalytic treatment is part of this detour, and the analyst participates in the advent of thought from which he expects the advent of desire as a corollary. This additional benefit of recovery finds its specific and object-related enacted scene outside the sessions. These belong to the in-between period of latency.

With the fundamental rule, the analytic method does not require reflexive thought, but speech uttered in the presence of another person who listens to this speech as an instinctual drive vicissitude and interprets it as both a failure to speak out and a revelation of a lack at the heart of the nature of the drives. Saying everything reveals the lack inherent in speech arising from the heterogeneity that exists between language and drive. The only thing the analyst observes concretely is this enunciation and its link with psychic functioning. He does not observe the thought or desire directly. By means of this method, the instinctual vicissitudes of thought can be registered in language and in the body via two paths – affects and erotogenicity and objects and the world.

By supporting the link to consciousness through speech, the fundamental rule promotes all the instinctual vicissitudes. The latter can only be established thanks to the positive action of this imperative of registration that makes the goal of reaching an attractor and speech a vehicle of all drive vicissitudes.

The psychoanalytic conception of psychic formations takes into account not only the unconscious instinctual drive tendencies, but also the equally unconscious processual activity. Both are involved in each of them. All psychic formations participate in the fulfilment of this wish to make desire come into existence. All these manifestations are overdetermined by such negative and positive unconscious attractions. They all express the wish to experience ourselves as desiring beings, on which our joy of living depends.

Psychoanalysis, a science and a discipline

From an epistemological point of view, psychoanalysis, more than any other science, presents a close proximity between its object of study (thought), the tool used to conduct this study (the apparatus for thinking), and the method employed (thought itself); thus, an isomorphism exists between what is being studied, the person doing the study, and the study. It is a matter of *thought thinking about thinking*.

This synergy explains why psychoanalysis is better described as a *scientific discipline* rather than as a science, since it obliges anyone who takes the mind as an object of study to accept a self-discipline that consists in recognizing that they are fully engaged in a process that escapes them for the most part. It is a discipline of decentering, of being powerless to free oneself from it. An ethical duty arises from this in all psychoanalytical research. The results and theorizations proposed are always subject to interpretation retrospectively to free them from the mortgage of certain unconscious determinants. Like dreams, theories are also attempted wish-fulfilments based on temporary denials of reality. The exegetical reading of Freud's work is driven by this motivation to render psychoanalysis impersonal and universal. This theoretical ideal is asymptotic, in fact mythical and unattainable. Scientists working in the so-called exact sciences are increasingly aware of these psychic, historical and bodily implications. This explains why this reading is sometimes used, conversely, to denigrate the value of psychoanalytic thought itself.

Psychoanalysis is concerned with the infinite set of productions and achievements of which men are capable. In particular, it has participated in modifying the definition of the term *science* by including in its corpus the concepts of the unconscious and interpretation, which could not be part of traditional positivist objectivity since they are neither tangible nor measurable; nor are they identically reproducible.

Interpretation: A scientific concept

The concept of the unconscious is the result of a logical inference, which, in turn, has very concrete heuristic consequences concerning the existence of irrational infantile theories and the reasons for them.

Since the 20th century, all sciences have recognized the insufficiency of empiricism and accept the necessity of integrating such an inference with scientificity. The concept of interpretation adds a special meaning that is not included in the ideas of deduction or inference. Just like the latter, psychoanalytic interpretation makes it possible to articulate the concrete manifestations and the processes underlying their origin, which are not accessible directly but only represented by such manifest productions. But it differs from these logical methods by the recognition that scientific elaborations conceal unconscious wishes linked to denials of reality.

"The interpretation of dreams is the royal road to a knowledge of the unconscious activities of the mind," wrote Freud (1900, p. 608). This quotation is often thought of as a simplified overdetermination. The manifest productions are then supposed to interpret – as with the musician and the score or the actor and the script – the elements of the unconscious represented in a hidden way in the manifest productions and sublimations. Actually, interpretation reveals. The function of translation often attributed to interpretation underlies a very simplified idea of the unconscious. The unconscious is then a particular form of repressed positivity expressed through substitutes. The unconscious and the manifest result are conceived of as being close or similar in nature, following the analogy of two different languages, but this is something that Freud always opposed, even in his first conception of the unconscious that seeks to become conscious. The unconscious of infantile contents is the tip of an iceberg consisting of instinctual drive impulses that belong to the primal repressed and contain a powerful negative attraction. Further, the idea of an extinctive attraction as an elementary quality of the drives shatters once and for all any notion of consubstantiality between the unconscious and language. There is a fundamental heterogeneity here that gives psychoanalytic interpretation its specificity. It constitutes a leap between two fields that are totally foreign to each other.

Freud had already drawn attention to this leap in his studies on hysteria, where he referred to the mysterious leap from the somatic to the psychic sphere through bodily conversion. In fact, all mental expressions and productions that are presented to consciousness participate in this leap. They are two-sided, both drive representatives and forms of language. It is this path that made Lacan say that "the unconscious is structured like a language" (Lacan, 1973, p. 149). He gave priority to the aspect of psychic formations linked to language at the expense of their other function of being ideational representatives of the drives. At the end of chapter 2 of *Studies on Hysteria* (Freud, 1895, pp. 179–180), Freud speaks of a patient, Frau Cäcilie M, who enabled him to discover that conversions are linked to language. From this point of view, they are symbolizations, regressive expressions of language-based formulations. This aspect can also be found in *The Interpretation of Dreams* (Freud, 1900). Through formal regression, dream contents are language riddles. Their other, drive-related side, is expressed through wish-fulfilment.

Psychoanalytical interpretation follows a regressive, backward path, the reverse of that which promotes manifest substitutes. Starting from the manifest product, it verbalizes the unconscious wish that is accomplished in a hallucinatory way, and thus expresses the language formula that is put into abeyance. This two-sided interpretation substitutes language statements for psychic formations. It articulates drive and language. It enunciates the unconscious element concealed within the manifest product that is the result of a psychic work of *distortion*. The interpretation thus produces a new manifest language content. This *substitutive* interpretation is completed by a *resolvent* interpretation and pertains to the excluded contents.

This method in no way reduces the negative essence of the unconscious. It is opposed to the negative attraction, which is forever active. Through the registration of a new content, it generates a contribution of libido that has the economic value of a hypercathexis. This is the psychic function that Freud recognized in language, a specifically psychic function that is different from those recognized by linguists. Hence, the fundamental rule and its requirement to put things into words. The resolvent interpretation interprets the substitutive interpretation. Each of them implies operations of renunciation, first, the renunciation of drive extinction and, second, the fulfilment of unconscious wishes. It should be emphasized that the negative tendencies can only be formulated by materials falling within the positive category of registrations, which is therefore heterogeneous with them. Thus, the formulation of an interpretation contains a denial of the reality of these tendencies. The enunciation amounts to a negation. Culture as a whole participates in such a collective denial. Extinction is a reality that does not only concern the mind. The 21st century has been caught up by this reality that has been denied since the end of the 19th century by the era of progress.

The regressive attraction of the drives and the imperative of mentalization

This *generalized theory of interpretation* is thus more complex than the theory of becoming conscious envisaged at the time of *The Interpretation of Dreams*. The negativity of the id is no longer a portion of repressed positivity that seeks to find a path of access to consciousness. It is an irreducible negative regressive attraction that requires psychic work in two stages and bears successive names: regressive attraction of the traumatic nucleus, negative attraction of the primary repressed, and extinctive attraction of the regressive tendency to return to a previous state, even as far as an inorganic and inanimate state. This regressive attraction to the point of extinction calls in counterpoint for a psychic work of restraint and registration using operations and psychic processes opposing this drive negativity. Restraint and registration are the hallmarks of this work of renunciation. The counter-appeal has a value of *thirdness* governed by an imperative to accomplish this work of renunciation and to promote increased awareness and a bonus of desire open to the world of objects.

The work required takes place according to the operation of après-coup, in two stages and in two directions, along the regressive and the progressive path. Its ideal aim is the promotion of a bonus of desire that can become available and find its place depending on various vicissitudes in the mind and in the world.

The operations and processes involved in this diphasic work are themselves permeated by a negativity that tends to reverse their work.

Henceforth, the term *unconscious* designates a quality that concerns both the instinctual drive tendency towards extinction and the portion of processuality that does not participate in psychic work. There is an unconscious of instinctual drive impulses and an unconscious of the superego.

A psychopathological picture can therefore be defined and interpreted positively in terms of the processes involved in the accomplishment of a drive modality and negatively in terms of the excluded unconscious processes. Psychoanalytic nosography takes these two aspects into account. It is processual. For example, the transference neuroses are the result of the fulfilment of repressed infantile wishes, while the process of mourning desires for Oedipal objects is lacking because it has been eliminated.

Interpretation focuses on these two aspects, on what was eliminated and on the material summoned in order to respond to this elimination. This is what in the Oedipus complex is called murder of the father and incest. The phenomenon called the return of the repressed is therefore not spontaneous. Its function is to respond to regressive attraction by supporting the assumption of desire.

Integration of novelty and dreams

Any novelty introduces difference and brings with it the effects of lack and truth. A lack of representation of novelty, and a failure to represent inherent in difference itself, are combined. Only the first effect is reducible; the second cannot be reduced.

A particular constraint weighs on any apprehension of a new portion of reality, whether internal or external to the mind, because of the traumatic awakening that accompanies every novelty as a difference. Once represented, the novelty will no longer be part of the strict category of perception. It will belong to what is perceived-represented. But the effect of difference will be maintained, in an attenuated fashion, it is true, where the elements belonging to the category of what is perceived-represented are concerned, but it will retain all its vivacity owing to the difference between what is perceived and represented and what is perceived and unrepresentable. The latter falls strictly within the category of perception.

The perception of the difference between the known and the unknown requires further work that has already been carried out. When this work does not occur, the novelty remains an unknown with its traumatic charge. The anxiety is thus "generated anew" (Freud, 1933a, p. 94).

The effect of difference is based on the endowed-unendowed pair, and it is typically operative in the difference between the sexes. Ultimately, for the mind, it is the lack inherent in all difference that constitutes perception proper.

Any novelty summons the transference of unconscious desires that are supposed to fill any lack, the lost object, the object of the drive and the object of the ideal (the search for the Holy Grail), hence, a sense of exaltation and truth-effect. And it is also linked, because of the experiences of lack, with the extinction of instinctual drive tendencies, hence, the awakening of traumatic experiences. The rejection of novelty follows from it. The perception of lack through that of difference challenges the reality and threat of extinction, the *seen* and the *heard* of the castration complex, embedded with the other difference of the sexes, the masculine and the feminine. Anxiety is a sign of ambivalence towards the imperative to carry out the psychic operations capable of using this extinctive tendency in favour of the registration of the drives in psychic life. This work requires two stages and is the object of all kinds of resistance during the sessions, hence, anxiety. It is at the origin of all the theories that are supposed to explain the traumatic dimension and to limit its scope, after the immediate immobilization and containment due to the initial "shock" (*coup*). The psyche is theorizing. It is why the act of thinking called interpretation is an irreducible and inevitable truth, even if the content of the interpretation may be wrong.

The novelty emanating from representable perceptions must first be dreamed in order to construct the corresponding thing-presentation before it is able to gain access to a conscious appropriation. This regressive path makes it possible to mutate the regressive economy awakened by the novelty and to orient it towards consciousness by means of a new manifest content. A very new reality must first follow the path of dream-work before it can become conscious, while acquiring the capacity to participate in regressive psychic activities.

This is how any new scientific theory is necessarily mixed with a theorization that is necessary for the mission of psychic life to process the traumatic dimension that belongs to drive reality and that is connected with the sensory perception of differences. All knowledge is a deferred effect, that is, the culmination of psychic work accomplished according to the two stages of the operation of après-coup subject to this regressive traumatic attraction.

No product of the mind escapes the extraordinary capacities of the human psyche to impose, as in dreams, its wishes and denials by means of its hallucinatory realizations. The psyche creates perceptual identities that can be brought together under a category, "perceptual activity" (*le perceptif*) (i.e., what is perceived, representable and reproducible through hallucinatory activity as perceptual identity), which has to be differentiated from *perception*. Both awaken a subjective feeling of concrete reality. These categories must take account of the difference recognized above, between what is perceived and represented, what is perceived and unrepresentable and what is hallucinated as perceptual identity. It is here that reality-testing and judgement take place, requiring successive operations of comparison and mentalization that are spread over time in a nonlinear way and involve successive renunciations. The reality-test and its avatars and stumbling blocks take place in the usual way during each awakening.

Emergence and intensity

All discoveries are presented in an atmosphere of exaltation and intensity that diminishes over time, without calling into question the discovery itself. The truth-effect contained in the exaltation thus only concerns to a small extent the content of the discovery. Subsequently, it is always much less. Freud (1937) refers to J. Nestroy: "Every step forward is only half as big as it looks at first" (p. 228). As a result, truth and knowledge cannot be superimposed.

Lacan emphasized this truth-effect with a succinct phrase whose secret he held: according to him, the truth is what is lacking in knowledge. That is to say, unconscious psychic truth as opposed to knowledge of reality. Thus, if knowledge always contains an error to be rectified, truth will always escape knowledge. It is this truth-value granted to discovery, and the hope that it will resolve the question of lack, that is responsible for this intensification and the dramatization of discoveries in myths. In fact, many discoveries are quickly ignored or forgotten after being accepted with a greater or lesser degree of excitement, and they are recognized at their fair value only at a second stage.

Emergence and renunciation

Any recognition of a portion of reality requires a renunciation of its utilization at the levels of hallucination and phantasy. Prior to this, the capacity to achieve hallucinatory fulfillment must be fully developed. So another renunciation precedes that which initiates the transition from the pleasure principle to the reality principle, namely, the renunciation of extinction. The establishment of the pleasure principle depends on it. The capacity for oscillating between the materials of renunciation and those of infantile illusion is essential for psychic life. The psyche can realize such renunciations only over several stages involving this oscillation. The superego respects these oscillations, allowing the realization of the operation of après-coup and the generation of a bonus of desire. Thus psychic contents are regularly subject to a series of subsequent revisions while, at the same time, these revisions bring with them new contents. Like the choice and destiny of words, the course of contents is subject to hazards that give it an order that is neither linear nor chronological, and which escapes human willing.

No new reality is accepted at a single moment, except to covertly satisfy an unconscious human desire. The history of thought offers many examples of this conflict between two sorts of conceptions, those that go in the direction of human desires and those that plague them.

Here is one example from the history of science, among many others. What was called the first law of thermodynamics (Joule's first law) was discovered well after that which became the second law of thermodynamics (Carnot's second law), which had been stated more than 40 years earlier. Carnot's law was forgotten for a while because it contains the recognition of a loss, whereas Joule's law was in keeping with the theories of equivalences without loss, such as Lavoisier's law

(Nothing is lost, nothing is created, everything is transformed), which he himself took from the Greek philosopher Anaxagoras (Nothing is born or perishes, but already existing things combine, then separate again). The theories of equivalences, even when false, obtain immediate success, sometimes even popularity.

Overdetermination of thought and desire

Psychoanalysis is the science of unconscious psychic processes and operations and of the necessities, constraints and imperatives that animate them. The various and more or less accomplished expressions and achievements that constitute human thought are thus overdetermined by negative and positive attractors. At the therapeutic level, it is the science of the historical overdeterminations, individual and collective, that guide all psychic formations from the simple acts and forms of behaviour of waking life to the most rebellious clinical pictures of psychopathology.

This overdetermination is very much involved in all human productions. In a general way, it allows one to approach, within any realization, the element of reminiscence in the situational history of a subject. Reminiscence is a kind of memory without memories. It refers to the identificatory history insofar as this plays a part in the establishment of thought-processes. In order to become operational, the laws of these thought-processes, albeit generic, require a transposition onto the psychic processes of "fellow human beings" (*Nebenmenschen*) (Freud, (1950 [1895]); and then an identification with them. The expression of psychic laws is therefore dependent on random factors.

All psychic productions, whether driven by the generativity of the psyche or, on the contrary, marked by reductive and soothing tendencies, are the result of a universal processual memory and a situational historical memory, both individual and collective. Psychoanalysis works on conjunctural history with the hope of obtaining liberating effects for processual memory. The bonus of desire of awakening is a fragment of impersonal universality with ephemeral duration.

This unconscious processual memory is found when there is a lack of mentalization, as a memory of tendencies and not of traces. The effects of the extinctive tendencies of the drives and the reductions in the efficiency of psychic processes are reminiscences of this double negativity that inhabits us.

Freud (1910) gives us a perfect illustration of these combinations of overdetermination in his work on Leonardo da Vinci. Following Oskar Pfister, he recognizes in the folds of Mary's robe, concealed at the heart of the famous immortal work, *The Virgin and Child with Saint Anne*, and intertwined with the extraordinary gifts of Leonardo, the deferred effect of the unconscious childhood phantasy of little Leonardo's kite, and the synthesis of his entire childhood history.

The negative tendencies active in the regressive attraction of repression can be inferred from the incompleteness of the painting, thought to be deliberate by certain art critics. An incompleteness can be conceived as the pictorial representation of an idealization that is by definition beyond representation. By this incompleteness Leonardo wanted to express impersonal generative desire. Such an interpretation requires a theory that serves as a referent, according to which all the productions of the psyche are instinctual drive vicissitudes.

Emergence and libidinal sympathetic excitation

Created by Freud at the turn of the 20th century at the heart of a Europe in full cultural effervescence, psychoanalysis may be seen not only as a product of a fertile breeding ground of which Vienna was then the main focus, but also as a major step in a long elaboration of human thought pursued for millennia, an emergence emanating from innumerable potentialities that had never seen the light of day and had remained on hold, awaiting revelation (to put it in the very terms of Leonardo da Vinci, a genius of that other period of intense generativity that was the Renaissance), a potentiality of nature revealed in an atmosphere of intense creativity in response to intense disarray.

Freud showed an interest on various occasions in this question of intensity, especially in dreams. He recognized Medusa's head (Freud, 1922) as its perfect illustration. The numerical and quantitative registers permit a plastic transposition of this intensity. Freud offered an interpretation based on the apotropaic function resulting from an exacerbated representation, thus on a saturation of consciousness. It is a matter of concealing a lack by resorting to such an exacerbation, and thus of expressing in a hidden way the terror of the extinctive attraction elicited by the perception of a lack. A first response to this regressive attraction is an act of immobilization and restraint resulting in the repression of a portion of drive activity that is not yet represented. This repressed material serves as a force of restraint. It associates that which is unrepresentable – the extinctive regressive attraction – with that which is not yet represented, an unelaborated drive. The first anti-cathexis is thus created. It brings together the traumatic experience of the regressive attraction, the painful tension of restraint, and the potentiality of an emerging drive. Without describing it in detail, Freud caught a glimpse of the existence of this elementary process generating libido, underpinning psychic drive functioning. He called it *libidinal sympathetic excitation* and likened it to primary erotogenic masochism.

Masochism of renunciation

From this temporary period of intensity pervading Vienna at the end of the 19th century it is possible to guess the presence of intense feelings of lack and helplessness. Beyond these, negative powers can be inferred that had begun to emerge due to the decline of the illusions hitherto sustained by the Enlightenment and then by Romanticism. They soon manifested themselves through a whole series of collapses: of the empires, political regimes, religious beliefs, economies and values upon which Europe was based. The myth of technical progress attempted to recapture the disappointed hopes placed in the former values; but the catastrophic atmosphere in which these collapses took place continued with the exponential atrocities of the two world wars, with the large-scale deployment and methodical fury that characterized the second. These horrors put an end to the final illusions. The glorious 1930s were their swansong before extinction. Since then, the West seems to have been engaged in a resigned and operative pragmatism, with niches of idealization turned towards the search for factual realities supposed to bring calm. This ideal of calm aims to destroy all sources of excitement. This hatred and rage can also be turned against the instinctual and libidinal sources. They are expressed through surgical interventions on the body, that of the subject himself but also of children, operations often legitimized and trivialized by some collective discourse and group theory. This hope of being the genitor of one's own drive sources comes into conflict with a basic renunciation that has the value of mutating the primal scene into a generative scene. Through the destructive attacks aimed either at external objects, the subject himself, the body of the other or one's own body, it is the libidinal source of these experiences that is the target.

Psychoanalysis developed in this context, between hope and disappointment. This is what makes it a *deferred effect* of the extinguishing tendencies inherent in psychic matter, tendencies taken up here in the light of civilization, of the collective asset that is culture. These tendencies require a foundational work of civilization for the sake of humanity.

Psychoanalysis presented itself as a new way of thinking about and dealing with terror. By revealing the existence of several modalities of renunciation involved in the restraint towards the negative regressive attractions of the id, psychoanalysis sought to mutate terror into a play of oscillations of affects – between hope and disappointment – of psychic work – between day and night – of objectives – between cultural ideality, sensual emotion and dreamlike regression.

This elementary restraint grounds thought and desire on a platform of pain, a masochism of functioning, a masochism of restraint, which is part of the superstructure of the *masochism of renunciation* concealed by the realizations of thought. Every desire, every act of thinking is indexed by pain that is generally concealed by the emergence of a bonus of desire.

If in its early years psychoanalysis offered some group illusions, these were gradually destroyed by disappointment; this explains why it is currently the object of strong accusations of deception, or neglected with scorn and disdain for other methods that know better how to maintain collective illusions. These typical affects are those experienced by all children faced with adult psychic life. In every case, the *primal scene* effect linked to being excluded from the desire of the other, but also the exclusion of one's own drive source, causes hatred, destructive movements and a denial of reality.

As a deferred effect within civilization, psychoanalysis attempted to realize an act of emergence in the form of a new mode of thought and the function of resolving the traumatic dimension specific to the negative regressive attractions haunting civilization and the subjects who participate in it.

Emergence and unconscious guilt

Freud, the founder of psychoanalysis, devoted himself to the realization of this operation of après-coup, not only for himself, but also for humanity as a whole. He made his own destiny a cause for humanity. His investigation and theorization of human thought became his first and last causes. He carried within himself this traumatic dimension, both individual and collective; but he also felt the duty to deal with it and to resolve it through the production of an *oeuvre*, a new way of thinking about the world, the human being and himself. Genius could be defined as offering humanity a generative operation of après-coup, a collective solution for the traumatic dimension that haunts every human being. As it develops, civilization cultivates significant unconscious group guilt that offers, in turn, a hold on the destructive and negative tendencies. If all men are equal from the point of view of the basic necessities imposed on them, and only differentiated by their achievements, the latter pave the way for unconscious guilt, which, in turn, reactivates the basic necessities. This is probably the origin of the discomfort felt in reading the last lines of the famous letter that crowns the exchange between Einstein and Freud (Freud, 1933b). Freud demonstrated that the international tribunal that would be necessary for resolving conflicts between nations in ways other than war could not guarantee its prevention since it would be a human-led product of men. Then he expressed the view that cultural development on the scale of humanity remains uncertain or could even lead to the extinction of the human species because it is detrimental to the sexual function. Freud ends his letter by asserting that "whatever fosters the growth of civilization works at the same time against war" (ibid., p. 215). How is it that he disregards the fact that fostering the growth of civilization cannot fail to secrete unconscious guilt that threatens in an underhand manner to overthrow at any time the fine mission so prized by the ego-ideal? His reflections on the impairment suffered by the sexual function are much more realistic, and they suggest that cultural activities should be regularly put into abeyance for the benefit of erotic activities. Without being a guarantee, this oscillation contributes to the attenuation of unconscious guilt. If such an oscillation exists on the individual level, what is the situation at the level of civilizations?

References

Freud, S. with Breuer (1895). *Studies on Hysteria. S.E. 2*. London: Hogarth.
Freud, S. (1900). *The Interpretation of Dreams. S.E. 4 and 5*. London: Hogarth, pp. 1–621.
Freud, S. (1910). Leonardo da Vinci and a Memory of His Childhood. *S.E. 11*. London: Hogarth, pp. 51–137.
Freud, S. (1920). *Beyond the Pleasure Principle. S.E. 18*. London: Hogarth, pp. 1–64.
Freud, S. (1922). Medusa's Head. *S.E. 18*. London: Hogarth, pp. 273–274.
Freud, S. (1933a). *New Introductory Lectures on Psycho-Analysis. S.E. 22*. London: Hogarth, pp. 1–182.
Freud, S. (1933b). "Why War?" *S.E. 22*. London: Hogarth, pp. 195–215.

Freud, S. (1937). *Analysis Terminable and Interminable*. *S.E. 23*. London: Hogarth, pp. 209–253.
Freud, S. (1950 [1895]). *Project for a Scientific Psychology*. *S.E.* 1. London: Hogarth, pp. 281–397.
Lacan, J. (1973). *The Four Fundamental Concepts of Psychoanalysis*, trans. Alan Sheridan. London: Routledge, 1977.

Chapter 2

Semantic and semiological vicissitudes of the term *Nachträglichkeit*

This chapter is didactic. It deals with the definitions and meanings of *après-coup* in psychoanalysis. It follows the course of the use of the term in Freud's work and in that of post-Freudian authors, as well as various translations in a number of languages. As William Shakespeare wrote in *Hamlet*, "Words without thoughts never to heaven go."

Nachträglich and its derivatives in Freud's work

The term *nachträglich* is common in the German language. This term and its derivatives appear about 160 times in Freud's work (Guttman et al., 1995); six for the noun *Nachträglichkeit,* the others for the adverb and the conjugated forms of the adjective. To these six instances must be added five utilizations of the noun in the letter to Fliess dated 14.11.1897, and another in the letter dated 9.06.1898 (see Masson, 1985, pp. 278–282, 315–316). The letter dated 14.11.1897 refers to the "Project" (Freud, 1950 [1895]) and particularly to the case of Emma, in connection with which the operation of après-coup is described with great precision without the concept of *Nachträglichkeit* appearing; only *nachträglich* was used at the time by Freud.

It is worth noting here that the terms *nachträglich and Nachträglichkeit* are both absent from the key words of the *Werkkonkordanz* (Meyer-Palmedo & Fichtner, 1989), just as the term *après-coup* was absent for a long time from French dictionaries.

The noun created by Freud, *Nachträglichkeit,* is comprised of *Nach* (after) and *Tragen* (carry, bear). Its semiotic meaning is therefore *carry towards an after*, carry forwards. The suffix *-keit* gives the noun a feminine gender.

In Freud's writings *nachträglich* denotes the diachronic ordering of a phenomenon *in two stages* and the link of causality and determinism existing between two manifest, but also mental events. This phenomenology characterized by "a biphasic process" had already been described by Charcot in the context of his theory of traumatic shock. But the attention Freud paid to the *interval* between the two stages led him to forge the noun *Nachträglichkeit* in order to account for a psychic operation whose complexity remains to a large extent imperceptible and takes place latently.

The noun *Nachträglichkeit* therefore denotes the *unconscious psychic operation*, while the adjective and adverb *nachträglich* denote the *dynamic* and the phenomenonological *results,* the determinism and the diachrony of this operation.

Other terms with an equivalent meaning were also used by Freud, even before he abandoned the use of the noun *Nachträglichkeit,* such as after-effect, subsequent to, *ex post facto* (a Latin expression meaning "starting from what comes after"), placed alongside the adverb after the event, as, for example, in "Contributions on a Discussion on Masturbation": "For we are in the habit of forming our opinion of individual dispositions *ex post facto;* we attribute this or that disposition to people after the event, when they have already fallen ill" (Freud, 1912, p. 253). He also used many adverbial expressions, such as subsequent abreaction, subsequent understanding, subsequent elaboration, subsequent compulsion, subsequent guilt, subsequent compliance, subsequent action, subsequent effect and so on.

By insisting on the idea of carrying towards an after, thus, forwards, all these terms give priority to the progressive path and suspend the theoretical logic of inference required by the course taken by psychic work along the regressive path towards what comes "before," denoting the past, combined with what moves "forwards" and points, on the contrary, towards the *after* of the future, towards the progressive result to come, which is the manifest product of the operation of après-coup. The regressive "before" of the past assumes the successive forms of reunions, then of the return to the state of primary narcissism, and finally of a return towards the earlier state of things, even back to the "inanimate state" (Freud, 1920, p. 38).

The temporal adverb *nachträglich* immediately finds its place in Freud's aetiological line of questioning and fits into the *genetic point of view*. The notion of return introduces a discontinuity within this temporal dynamic that, above all, follows the progressive path. The concept of après-coup is often thought of in terms of a succession of returns. Nevertheless, an oscillation between the progressive and regressive paths is already included in this conception according to which the operation of après-coup is a series of re-registrations. Freud's attempt in the case of the "Wolf Man" (Freud, 1918) at dating was the peak moment of the priority given to the progressive aim, which can also be found in the importance Freud accorded to the notion of *periods.* Gradually, the function of the regressive path would become more and more essential in the psychic and economic economy. The disappearance in Freud's writings of the use of the term *Nachträglichkeit,* even though he continued to refer to the two stages of this operation, may be interpreted in terms of the increasing importance accorded to the regressive work along the regressive path.

It is worth emphasizing here the gap that exists between the use that Freud makes of the terms formed from *nachträglich* and his much more frequent reference to the phenomena and operations denoted by these terms. Shakespeare reminds us that if the smell of roses had another name, it would not prevent us from being delighted, even if with other associative concatenations.

Thus in the "Project" (Freud, 1950 [1895], pp. 353–356), only the adverb is used. In the case of Emma Freud discusses the links among memory traces, repression, infantile trauma, sexuality and the appearance of symptoms. He stresses the *precocious sexual unbinding* and its subsequent consequences. Then, in "Heredity and Aetiology of the Neuroses" (Freud, 1896), he once again describes the phenomenon of après-coup when referring to the *posthumous action of an infantile trauma*. Likewise, in "Little Hans" (Freud, 1909), his interpretations and the intelligibility of the case follow the logics of the phenomenon of après-coup even though it is not named; once again, in "Some Psychical Consequences of the Anatomical Distinction between the Sexes" (Freud, 1925), when Freud links up the *things seen and heard* of the castration complex with the denial of the reality of the perceivable absence via sensory paths, he uses neither *nachträglich* nor *Nachträglichkeit,* even though he is referring to a dynamic unfolding in two stages.

This may also be explained by the fact that in this text, he gives priority to the view that the traumatic excitation requiring the work of après-coup is of external origin, even if he attempts to posit a certain internalization by appealing to phylogenesis, castration-anxiety being a reminiscence of the past of humanity. In so doing he neglects the role of transposition that exists between the tendencies and effects of extinctive regressivity and what has been heard in the messages of castration as well as what has been seen of the absence of a penis on a girl's lower abdomen. However, he maintains his intuition that castration-anxiety has an endogenous origin that is responsible for the organization of psychic life in two stages. Though he attempts, by appealing to phylogenesis, to reinternalize the reason for terror, originally external, he does not confuse anxiety and fear. Castration-anxiety is thus a failure of the work of après-coup, a failure regarding the internal traumatic elements, hence the production of subsequent symptomatic effects.

The term *nachträglich*, as an adverb of temporality, finds its place quite logically therefore in Freud's early lines of questioning with regard to aetiology and the *genetic point of view*. While its manifest reference to the progressive path lends support to such a linear genetic point of view, the notion of *return* already introduces a discontinuous temporal dynamic. Freud's preoccupation with dating in the case of the "Wolf Man" (Freud, 1918) is linked to the importance that he accorded to the notion of cycles of time. This meticulous dating is an effect of the traumatic factor reintroduced by discontinuity, a counter-effect of restraint. The meticulous dating of passing time has the same origins here.

An important remark is necessary at this juncture and provides us with food for thought: this gradual reduction in the use of the term *nachträglich* in Freud's work is noteworthy, and even more astonishing is the disappearance from 1917 onwards of the term *Nachträglichkeit* in all his writings. I have pointed out that this can be explained by the fact that the word *progressive* was gradually completed by a term that ascribed a major role to regressive longings. I am referring to Freud's elaboration in 1920 of what, in 1895, was called an attraction by the pathogenic nucleus, then in 1915, the negative attraction emanating from the primary repressed, then in 1920, the regressive tendency back towards an earlier inanimate state of things, and finally in 1926, the regressive attraction of primal repressions. This makes it possible to consider *extinctive* regressivity as the essential quality of the drives, a quality that seems to have been decisive in this disappearance of the noun.

The notion of *return,* hitherto attached to a hypothetical spontaneous tendency to become conscious, and then to instinctual drive thrust (Freud, 1915a), needs to be revised. The so-called returns, in fact, respond to this regressivity, which they limit as a formal and libidinal regression by opposing and offering it perceptual traces. These traces are then differentiated as thing-presentations, allowing for a mutation of the regressive economy and its direction along the progressive path until it reaches its destiny as a *bonus of desire*, of free cathexis. Hence, a new reflection on the so-called shock (*coup*), on the specific work demanded by this drive regressivity, work that has the value of a *counter-shock* and is realized thanks to the intervention of an imperative of constraint, of psychic registration and cathexis. This appeal to such an imperative is often referred to the "father" to the paternal function, to the category of the Symbolic. Under its aegis the first anti-extinctive act of restraint, the various registrations of the drive impulses and the progressive orientation of cathexes are realized for the benefit of the mind.

The elaboration of metapsychological notions, such as drive regressivity, the *processual imperative* as a reference to the paternal function (third) and the *biphasic nature* of psychic work is a legacy of the abandonment by Freud of the use of his concept of *Nachträglichkeit,* a renunciation that gives the impression that the term *Nachträglichkeit* is a concept waiting to be given greater complexity and to be theorized. This theorization must combine the two pairs of death drive/life drive and drive regressivity/superego. Consequently, the fundamental ambivalence of which Freud speaks in *Civilization and Its Discontents* (Freud, 1930) cannot simply be defined by a conflict between the tendencies pertaining to drive duality. It concerns the relationship to the processual imperative and to the work of renunciation that is involved in all psychic operations. The Oedipus complex is the locus of such ambivalence. In the case where the Oedipus complex dominates, there occurs a "murder of the father" (Freud, 1900a), that is to say, the imperative of renunciation is eliminated. By contrast, in the case where the Oedipus complex is dissolved (Freud, 1924), a process of renunciation occurs that bears on drive regressivity and has the significance of a *foundational murder*. The *biphasic* character of the operation of après-coup bears witness to this conflict of ambivalence concerning the realization of the psychic operations denoted by the word *murder*. The two paths, regressive and progressive, are the locus of psychic work, which itself will be the object of this ambivalence between an eliminating murder and a foundational murder.

The translations and stand-ins for *nachträglich* and *Nachträglichkeit*

In French

By opting for the expression *après coup,* the first translators of Freud in French were applying the method of translation recommended by Goethe in the "Notes and dissertations" of his volume the *West-Eastern Divan* (Goethe, 1819). Goethe proposes as an ideal reference for every translation the combination of *literalness* and *meaningfulness*. The term chosen, he writes, "must not simply give the idea of the original but stand in for it," it must not "replace" the original but "have value in its place." Lacan, who was sensitive to this formula, introduced the notion of *in lieu of* and imposed the same nominalization on the adverb *après coup* that Freud forged from *nachträglich*.

Translation is a procedure that is reminiscent of the operation of après-coup itself. The difference between them, however, lies in the aim of *attributing new meaning* in the operation of après-coup, which implies a work of distortion (*Enstellung*) and a modification of the regressive economy. It also lies in the role of the unconscious in each of the procedures.

In fact the method of translation recommended above seeks not only to pass from one language to another, but to use a third reference, in our case, *metapsychological language*, which may be considered as a foreign language with regard both to the target language and to the original language.

Thus, the word *Graben* suggests the idea of carrying and supporting, hence masochism. *Coup* expresses the idea of sadomasochism, but also that of what is traumatic. Likewise *nach* and *après* both denote the future. They introduce the optative and hallucinatory wish-fulfilment. The notion of *après-coup* thus suggests two theories that attempted to turn what is traumatic into its contrary, theories required for the purpose of dealing with this traumatic quality. These theories attempt to explain a lack by a painful event or shock (*coup*), which may not have taken place, and they affirm that a painful event or shock took place in the past at the point where there is a lack, though the pain may nonetheless signify that there is no lack. Hence, the two theories: the lack of a penis as a consequence of the act of castration following a transgression; pain as the experience of an unaccomplished lack. The effect of attenuation becomes a subterfuge, and even an artful dodge, when the lack is denied by a theory of a painful shock that becomes satisfying through pain. Consequently, where there is a shock, there is pain; and where there is pain, there is no lack (it hurts, so it exists). The words chosen carry within themselves theories that deny the thing denoted.

In addition, it is to be noted that the term *après-coup* only appeared in the index of French translations at a late stage, with the *OCF.P* (*Oeuvres completes de Freud (psychanalyse)*). Thus in *L'interprétation des rêves* (Freud, 1900b) translated from the German by Meyerson in 1926 and revised by Denise Berger in 1967, these terms are present, and even with inverted commas when the term *après-coup* is used as a noun, on one single occasion (p. 182). But it is not in the index. On the other hand, it is listed in the index of the *Écrits* (Lacan, 2006) and in the *Language of Psychoanalysis* (Laplanche & Pontalis, 1973).

It is further to be noted that the apparent dilettantism of the first translators was based on the flexibility and variations of Freud himself, the creator of the neologism *Nachträglichkeit*. Lacan exacerbated this handling of German and French terms in his own way, according to the taste of the prince. He uses and abuses neologisms, for example by nominalizing the German adverb in his own way. He writes "the *Nachträglich*." But since his insistence on the notion, all the translators have followed his approach of conceptually enhancing the term *après-coup*, and they have sought to stabilize and better differentiate, in the image of Freud, the uses of this term as an adjective and adverb and those as a noun.

In *Traduire Freud* (Bourguignon et al., 1989), the translation teams and the commission of terminology involved in the *OCF.P* suggested using the expression *après-coup* with a hyphen for the adjective and adverb, and introducing the expression *l'effet de après-coup,* with a hyphen, for the noun *Nachträglichkeit*. These initial choices were based, in part, on the English *Standard Edition* translation, for which Strachey had opted for the expressions *deferred action* and *deferred effect,* each with the same spelling.

But very soon after, in successive volumes of the *OCF.P,* they differentiated between the translation of the noun *Nachträglichkeit* and that of the adverb *nachträglich*. They chose to translate the noun *après-coup* with a hyphen, as in the expression "le facteur de l'après-coup" (*SE.* "the factor of deferred action [1900a, p. 205]). And for the adjective and adverb, they used the term *après coup* without a hyphen, closer to ordinary French.

This usage follows Freud's approach of nominalizing an ordinary term, referenced since 1650 in French dictionaries in its unhyphenated form as an adverb of time, and of hyphenating it when it is being used as a metapsychological concept. This is the usage I follow in this book.

Other remarks could be made here, in particular those bearing on the variants that would appear in Freud's work and in translations of it. They insist, in general, on the temporal and deferred aspect given pride of place by foreign translations.

Finally, let us note that we come across a variety of expressions in Freud's work that stand in for the term "deferred action," such as *the effect of deferred action and the path of deferred action* (1950 [1895]), *the factor of deferred action* (1900a), the *period of time* during which the effects are deferred (1918, p. 58).

Other languages

The translation of Freud's work into English in the *Standard Edition* (1950–1974) would dominate the choices of all the other Latin languages. Whether in Italian, Spanish or Portuguese, the translations all accorded priority to the adverbial dimension of temporality, and they use expressions of varying length.

The root *post* is generally preferred for the adverb, the adjective and the noun, except in Italian where the noun is translated directly from the *S.E.* as *azione differita.*

In English, in the *S.E.*, we find a large number of expressions echoing the absence of a noun. They are all derived from the transitive verb "to defer," used to denote the phenomenon of après-coup, in particular *deferred:* deferred understanding, deferred revision, deferred operation, deferred use, deferred fashion and so on.

The English expressions *deferred, deferred effect, deferred action* account, in fact, only for aspects of causality and progressive temporality, thus of the temporalized determination proper to the result of the operation of après-coup.

That is why English authors subsequently introduced the notions of *retrogression* and *retroactive attribution* in order to complete the progressive orientation imposed by the regressive orientation. The aspects of retroaction are thus perfectly well understood on the other side of the Channel. Confirmation of this can be found from reading the debates organized with English colleagues at the Paris Psychoanalytic Society in 1997 in the *Revue française de Psychanalyse* (Cournut, Neyraut, Sodré et al.) and in the *International Journal of Psychoanalysis* in 2005 (Faimberg, 2005a; Sodré, 2005).

But the common identity that unites the various successive stages named deferred effects, namely, of being actualizations of a regressive unconscious conflict presented by a manifest substitute, remains ousted by these terms: for instance, the primordial economic function of the regressive work of the operation of après-coup and its connection with masochism; and also the ambivalence with regard to realizing psychic work, ambivalence concerning the fate of the operation "murder." It is this retroactive economic mutation realized by regressive work that implies recourse to both timelessness and a retrograde process along the regressive path that itself requires psychic work.

All the above-mentioned terminological choices tell us about the implicit aspect of conceptions of mental functioning and the therapeutic method of those who employ them. However, a demarcation between the various psychoanalytic schools based on semiotic criteria alone is worth thinking about.

These differences concern the issues related to, and the definitions of, the operation of après-coup, the conceptions of mental functioning and the therapeutic method much more than a demarcation between schools or a geographical line such as the Channel. This merely emphasizes the fact that this operation is both the object of a *tendency towards conflict* (Freud, 1937) and the very locus of this ambivalent inclination.

Psychopathology of everyday translation

The terminological differences discussed above account for the fact that this operation is the object of an *inclination towards conflict* and the very locus of a *fundamental ambivalence*. These are actualized by a semiology of translation and by slips of the pen affecting the term *après-coup*.

When Goethe describes three possible methods of translation, he stresses that the French often give priority, even in translating poetry, to what he calls the *parodistic* tendency: "Just as the French adapt foreign words to their pronunciation, so they treat feelings, thoughts and even objects; for every foreign fruit they demand a counterfeit grown on their own soil" (Goethe, 1819, Lefevere's translation, 1977, p. 36).

Freud was very reserved with regard to this propensity to orient metapsychology towards a *psychoanalysis French-style*.

But, as Proust suggested to Marie Nordlinger, an English lady, is there not a tendency in every translator to impose his mother tongue? He wrote:

> Not only do you write French better than a French woman, but like a French woman. But when you translate English all the original characteristics reappear; the words revert to their own kind, their affinities, their meanings, their native rules. And whatever charm there may be in this English disguise of French words, or rather in this apparition of English forms and faces breaking through their French accoutrements and masks, all this life will have to be cooled down, gallicized, distanced from the original, and the originality extinguished.
>
> (Proust, Letter to Marie Nordlinger, Spring 1904, cited in Gamble, 2002, p. 107)

Another more specific remark is called for: the translation correlations for the term *après-coup* are marked by a great deal of looseness: Thus, for 160 instances found in the German text of the *Gesammelte Werke* (Guttmann et al., 1995) only 46 are listed in the *Standard Edition*. And it was not until the *Oeuvres complètes* were published (Bourguignon & Cotet, 2004) that there was a concern for stabilization in French, without overlooking the difference between the various volumes and with the volume titled *Traduire Freud* (Bourguignon et al., 1989).

The most significant of all these remarks remains the existence of slips of the pen concerning the concept of après-coup. In *Problématiques VI*, Jean Laplanche (2006) is himself astonished by the misprint that had found its way surreptitiously into the *Vocabulaire de psychanalyse*. In it, the English translation officially announced for *nachträglich* is *differed*. In fact, the English word is *deferred*, from *to defer*, a transitive verb meaning *différer* in the sense of *ajourner* (to adjourn), while *differed* comes from *to differ*, a transitive verb from which *different* and *difference* are derived, meaning *différer* in the sense of being different, and also *différend* in the sense of not being in agreement. Admittedly, for a French person, but for the word stress (di'fɜː and 'difə), the pronunciation of the two terms is similar and the French term *différer* undoubtedly lends itself to slips of the tongue and pen. But in *Traduire Freud*, we find once again another symptom that persists through the creation of a neologism based on spelling: *deferred*. The devil is in the detail!

These slips of the pen mingle the temporal gap, difference and conflictuality. In one sense, they insist on the raison d'être of the concept of après-coup. *Deferring*, by means of temporality and discontinuity, introduces a difference and awakens traumatic experience, with the updating of the heterogeneity that exists between *extinctive regressivity* and the *imperative of registration*.

These slips and the substitutive formations espouse the inclination towards conflict characteristic of the operation of après-coup between the repetition of the shock, shock after shock and the *biphasic process*. We may also take into account the conflict between the two economic modalities involved, which create the gradient of the après-coup, that of the pleasure principle and that of what is beyond the pleasure principle. This brings us back to the conflict of ambivalence discussed above, namely, whether or not to realize the work of economic mutation making it possible to pass from one modality to the other. It is the difference between the tendency towards extinction and the imperative of psychic registration that calls for the work of counter-shock with the ambivalence in realizing it that accompanies this appeal, thus the ambivalence between the two murders, one eliminating and the other foundational. This inclination towards conflict finds its extension in polemics over the notion of après-coup, over the tendency to turn the après-coup into a *missing concept* implied in the "Controversies" (Faimberg, 2005; Perelberg, 2006), and by its status as a latent concept, a shibboleth of recognition and exclusion, a marker justifying anathema.

On two occasions in his work Freud uses a cruel and macabre allegory recounted by Victor Hugo in order to show the impossibility of finding such a shibboleth that makes it possible to judge the chances of success of psychoanalysis and psychoanalytic training (Freud, 1912, p. 253; 1933, p. 155). He called it the Scottish king's test for identifying witches: "This king declared that he was in possession of an infallible method of recognizing a witch. He had the women stewed in a cauldron of boiling water and then tasted the broth. Afterwards he was able to say: 'That was a witch,' or 'No, that was not one.'"

He says that this test can be used only after the event. But this scene indicates the limits of the après-coup from the moment that the *initial event* is irreversible. Time is then the object of a murder. This is not a tortured time as is the case when a subject is hounded into a corner and faced with a race against time in order to prevent any regressive psychic work of latency and dreaming. In this scene, it is a matter of a murder of time with a derision of the operation of après-coup, since it is the author of the initial murderous act who accomplishes the operation himself.

Semiology of theorization and conceptualization

Within the metapsychological corpus, compared with other concepts, that of après-coup follows a very specific destiny. In fact, the path of the conceptualization of metapsychology can be followed according to what Freud himself calls the "three *steps*" of his theory of the drives (Freud, 1920, p. 59). The concept that prototypically illustrates this evolution in three stages is that of *working-through*. It is used by Freud on only three occasions, in 1895, 1914 and 1926, which correspond, respectively, to each of these three *steps*: in succession, infantile sexuality (1895–1905), narcissism (1910–1915) and the regressive tendency to return to an earlier state of things and even back to the inanimate state (1919–1923). The term *working-through* initially denoted the regressive work taking place at the level of the infantile *associative stratification*, subject to the negative attraction of the pathogenic traumatic nucleus, and then the work establishing narcissistic anti-cathexes on the basis of remembering and thanks to repetition, and finally, the work on the resistances of the id, on the extinctive regressivity of the drive impulses thanks to the requirement of a processual imperative of registration. This evolution is, in fact, noticeable for many other concepts, for instance, libidinal sympathetic excitation, but in a less schematic way.

As further examples, we could follow the arrival of other concepts that gained access to their full metapsychological significance through successive corrective stages, like those of projection and fetishism.

In the case of projection, this concept was applied in a premature and fixed manner to the clinical picture of paranoia, but according to the model of repression pertaining, in this case, to homosexuality. This prevented Freud from producing, as he had announced, an article on projection in 1915, and obliged him to contradict his own elaborations in an article called "A Case of Paranoia Running Counter to the Psychoanalytic Theory of the Disease" (Freud, 1915b). Finally, in his differentiation of three kinds of jealousy (Freud, 1922), normal, projective and delusional, he restricted the role played by projection to one form of it. Henceforth, it was possible to distinguish projection from other much more general mechanisms, such as displacement and transposition, the first being involved in phobias and the second in animism. The concept of projection could then be reserved for the distorted utilizations of transposition linked to the mechanism of denial. What is projected corresponds to what comes back from the outside after being denied/foreclosed inside.

These conceptual elaborations of Freud in successive stages, according to the three steps of the drive theory, would give rise to different definitions of this or that concept within theories built around one of these stages.

The concept of après-coup also followed such peregrinations. We have followed them. After being discovered by Freud in 1897, then named by him with a neologism based on a nominalization, he used it in his work on six occasions until 1917. Then he abandoned it totally as a term in favour of the metapsychology of the operation that it was supposed to denote. In this way he brought about its demise. Its resurgence would be exalted by Lacan more than 35 years later.

The term *après-coup* has thus gone through successive stages, which enact its very operation. The adverb of time, which was used very early on in a diachronic conception of the genesis of symptoms, was changed into a noun referring to the operation of mentalization that takes into account the biphasic nature of this operation and the interval of the regressive work of latency, that is, the psychic activity of passivity that separates the traumatic moment and the manifest production of a new cathexis. Subsequently this noun was abandoned in favour of the metapsychology of the tendencies, operations, functions and processes of which the operation is comprised in favour of the recognition of the discontinuity, timelessness and unpredictability that characterize it, but also of the tendency to conflict that inhabits it. At the same time as it was enacted in the theorization, it gradually became the very model of psychic functioning, the theoretical ideal reference for every psychic operation, while their subsequent results reflect and present their multiple clinical vagaries.

References

Bourguignon, A. et al. (1989). *Traduire Freud*. Paris: Presses Universitaires de France.
Bourguignon, A. & Cotet, P. (Eds.) (2004). *Sigmund Freud Œuvres Complètes (Psychanalyse)*. Paris: Presses Universitaires de France.
Faimberg, H. (2005). Après-coup: psychoanalytic controversies. *International Journal of Psycho-Analysis*, 86 (1): 1–6; 11–13.
Freud, S. ([1950]1895). *A Project for a Scientific Psychology. S.E., 1*. London: Hogarth, pp. 281–397.
Freud, S. (1896). Heredity and Aetiology of the Neuroses. *S.E. 3*. London: Hogarth, pp. 143–156.
Freud, S. (1900a). *The Interpretation of Dreams. S.E. 4–5*. London: Hogarth.
Freud, S. (1900b). *L'interprétation des rêves*, trans. Meyerson. Paris: Presses Universitaires de France, 1926; revised by Denise Berger, 1967.
Freud, S. (1909). Analysis of a Phobia in a Five-Year-Old Boy. *S.E. 10*. London: Hogarth, pp. 5–149.
Freud, S. (1912). Contributions to a Discussion on Masturbation. *S.E. 12*. London: Hogarth, pp. 243–254.
Freud, S. (1915a). *Instincts and Their Vicissitudes. S.E. 14*. London: Hogarth, pp. 109–140.
Freud, S. (1915b). A Case of Paranoia Running Counter to the Psychoanalytic Theory of the Disease. *S.E. 14*. London: Hogarth.
Freud, S. (1918 [1914]). From the History of an Infantile Neurosis. *S.E. 17*. London: Hogarth, pp. 7–122.
Freud, S. (1920). *Beyond the Pleasure Principle. S.E.* 18. London: Hogarth, pp. 1–64.
Freud, S. (1922). Some Neurotic Mechanisms in Jealousy, Paranoia and Homosexuality. *S.E. 18*. London: Hogarth, pp. 223–232.
Freud, S. (1924). *The Economic Problem of Masochism. S.E. 19*. London: Hogarth, pp. 159–170.
Freud, S. (1925). Some Psychical Consequences of the Anatomical Distinction between the Sexes. *S.E. 19*. London: Hogarth, pp. 248–258.
Freud, S. (1930). *Civilization and Its Discontents. S.E. 21*. London: Hogarth, pp. 57–146.
Freud, S. (1933). *New Introductory Lectures on Psycho-Analysis. S.E. 22*. London: Hogarth, pp. 1–182.
Freud. (1937). *Constructions in Analysis SE 23*. London: Hogarth, pp. 257–269.
Freud, S. (1950–1974). *Standard Edition (S.E.)* of the *Complete Psychological Works of Sigmund Freud*. London: Hogarth Press.
Goethe, J.W. von (1819). *West-Eastern Divan*. Northampton, MA: Gehenna Press, 1970.
Guttmann, S., Parrish, S., Ruffing, J. (1995). *Konkordanz zu den Gesammelten Werken*. Waterloo, ON: North Waterloo Acad. Press.
Lacan, J. (2006/1966). *Écrits*, trans. Bruce Fink. New York: Norton, 2006.
Laplanche, J. (2006). *Problématiques VI*. Paris : Presses Universitaires de France.
Laplanche, J. & Pontalis, J.-B. (1973/1967). *The Language of Psychoanalysis*, trans. D. Nicholson-Smith. New York: Norton.

Masson J.M., editor (1985). *The Complete Letters of Sigmund Freud to Wilhelm Fliess, 1887–1904*. Cambridge, MA: Belknap.
Meyer-Palmedo, I. and Fichtner, G. (1989). *Freud Bibliographie mit Werkkonkordanz*. Frankfurt: Fischer.
Perelberg, R.J. (2006). Les controverses et l'après-coup. *Revue française de Psychanalyse*, 70 (3): 647–670.
Sodré, I. (2005). "As I was walking down the stair, I saw a concept which wasn't there...": Or, après-coup: A missing concept? *International Journal of Psycho-Analysis*, 86 (1): 7–10.

Chapter 3

The work of Freud and his followers as a clinical illustration of the operation of après-coup

In order to help the reader grasp the power of realization of the operation of après-coup, this chapter explores several clinical situations offered by Freud, including the cases of Emma, Little Hans and the Wolf Man. This chapter follows Goethe's famous advice: "What you have inherited from your father must first be earned before it is yours" (Goethe, *Faust* I, ll. 682–3). This reading of Freud and his followers also makes it possible to recognize the implications for the operation of après-coup in the process of theorizing.

Neither Freud nor his patients are there to oppose the inevitable need for additional work, a process of reality-testing involving the addition of associative material revealing the lack specific to every construction developed from stabilized and non-evolving materials. The clinical elements that Freud offered posterity are free from this constraint of the lack and left to the work of exegetes. In the name of the truth of the Shakespearian precept that "There are more things in heaven and earth, Horatio, than are dreamt of in your philosophy" (*Hamlet*, Act I, Scene 5, 166–167), each one of us can therefore apply to them other theorizations and attribute to them infinite meanings.

Without being tested by the patient's associations and the interpretations with which life provides all of us, our own "posthumous" interpretations have first to do with the satisfaction of recognizing in them the desired meaning and of using them to illustrate and demonstrate our own theoretical developments.

Thus, making the past speak without any possible backlash, fulfilling the narcissistic wish "to have the last word" on such infinitely flexible material, since it is finished and non-evolving, on a *dead* text, just as we speak of a *dead language*, is a source of embarrassment. Fortunately, there will never be a last commentary because, when dealing with Freud's clinical cases, over-interpretation never ceases.

In our clinical experience, neither patient nor analyst, and even less the commentator who offers his own interpretative reading, has the last word. The operation of après-coup remains open. The embarrassment seems to stem more from the hope of doing better than from the father of psychoanalysis, of going further than him in a conflict involving another pole, piety towards him. We are reminded here of Freud's very fine letter to Romain Rolland in which Freud, instead of interpreting Romain Roland's oceanic feeling, offered him an interpretation of his

DOI: 10.4324/9780429198953-3

own disturbance of memory on the Acropolis (Freud, 1936). Freud sets out his method of thinking. He speaks of the conflict between the wish to go further than the father – "too good to be true" – and the subsequent sense of guilt that leads to elevating him once again. Hence, the temptation to breathe new life into ancient texts and to turn them into cult objects.

It is when a theoretical elaboration is in progress that the use of such stabilized materials is sensed, whether they are literary works, myths, historical works, biographies or famous clinical cases already published and closed. Freud used this method of transposition and drew on the support of such closed material on many occasions; thus Fliess's periodical theory, Sophocles' *Oedipus, Totem and Taboo*, Leonardo da Vinci's dreams, Michelangelo's sculpture of Moses, President Schreber's *Memoirs*, Jensen's *Gradiva*, Hoffman's *Tales*, the Medusa's head, the 17th-century demonological neurosis and much scientific knowledge, etc.

He was often reproached for applying his theories in this way. In fact, such a transposition on to immobilized material is an essential detour in the theorization of thought-processes that requires abstraction. The transposition allows for an animistic metaphorization of a theory in the making by drawing on the support of immobile tangible material. This first step must be followed by a second, that of the differentiation of the thought-processes and the object that served as a support for the transposition. In order to gain access to a metapsychological status, the theorizing must free itself from the material initially used. It can therefore be confronted with living material.

The psyche approaches reality along the two complementary paths of representation and putting psychic processes to work. A tangible reality that is encountered repeatedly requires the path of representation, whereas moving reality confronts the psyche with differences and lack, hence, the obligation to think. While each element involved in the perception of differences can be represented when taken separately, the difference itself is not. It introduces the relationship to lack through the pair endowed/unendowed. While representable perceptions of tangible reality lose their primary traumatic quality, the perceptions of the reality of lack that are not representable retain their traumatic quality and are a source of feelings of lack. They constitute perception proper. Hence, the temptation to concentrate on representable materials offers a minimum of possible differences. This gap is one that exists between a case study and direct confrontation with a patient. It is also what happens during supervisions.

All perception of moving materials is apprehended by means of the representation of the materials themselves and by a dynamic of thought induced by the perception of the lack inherent in any difference. Two categories can be distinguished that are intertwined with all perception: perception with representation and perception without representation. The traumatic quality of the perception of a lack requires a dynamic of thought, which, to realize itself, utilizes adjacent perceivable materials, "details relating to" the contents that can be represented (Freud, 1937b, p. 266). The unrepresentable hole of the molar is depicted by the image of the molar before the hole, and then by its edges.

By revisiting the clinical cases that Freud published from the point of view of the phenomenon of après-coup, I am going to give priority to what strictly concerns the operation of après-coup in order to show how clinical thinking follows the dynamic of this operation.

The truth of the following approach lies in the fact that the writing of the clinical experience as well as the "readings" of it, even in the case of stabilized clinical material, are all motivated by the presence, in them, of the traumatic dimension. It is the latter that induces a new operation of après-coup.

This phenomenon will become more complex in the next chapter, when I will discuss the clinical material collected from patients in session.

The letter to Fliess dated 14.1.1897 and the retroactive reference to the "Project"

It was in a letter to Fliess that, for the first time, Freud used on three occasions in the space of a few lines, the noun *Nachträglichkeit* (*S.E.* "deferred action"). In this letter, he forged the noun *Nachträglichkeit* (Masson, 1985, pp. 279–280), and referred to "A Project for a Scientific Psychology" (Freud, 1950 [1895]). One of the sections of this pre-analytic work, titled *The Hysterical Proton Pseudos* (Part II, Section 4 [false premise], ibid., p. 352) is devoted to a patient called Emma. Freud describes the phenomenon of après-coup in detail and uses the term *nachträglich* (*S.E.* "by deferred action"). He never speaks again about Emma.

He thus took up Charcot's theory, which he had already set out in the *Studies on Hysteria* (Freud, 1895) with the diachronic formation of symptoms in two stages. This theory of trauma conceives the genesis of the symptom in two stages. Stage 1 is defined by the event described as traumatic, the *shock*, and stage 2 by the appearance of a psychic production, the *symptom*. With great intuition, Charcot called the interval between them the period of *incubation* or *psychical working-out* (ibid., p. 134), which would become in Freud's theorization the *period of latency*. The doyen of the Salpêtrière hospital did not develop what he was referring to by these terms. His intuition even led him not to name stage 3, the interval period, recognising implicitly the nature of the difference that exists between stage 1 (official shock) and stage 2 (manifest production) and this interval period dominated by an invisible latent work in contact with what has been repressed.

Preoccupied by his aetiological quest, thus by the notion of *shock*, influenced by Breuer's notion of retrogressive memory, Freud followed the *backward path* of cathartic remembering as it unfolds in the session, in search for the objective shock, and he turned his interest to the interval period that had remained mysterious in Charcot's theory.

So he described a series of stages, in particular those of the backward path of associative remembering, and inverted the course of time. He broke stage 1 of the shock down into several scenes of a different nature with regard to their relation to the unconscious. The first belongs to the latent unconscious, that is, the preconscious, whereas the second belongs to the repressed unconscious, the *Ucs*.

proper. He later introduced the unconscious of the primary repressed whose force of negative attraction was the origin of a new term, the id. Regarding stage 1, the official shock suffered by Emma that was repressed, he called scene I: "The memory of the laughing shop-assistants when Emma entered a shop at the age of 12"; and scene II: "Emma's repressed memory of being touched sexually in another shop when she was 8." The symptomatic stage 2 was her manifest *agoraphobia* in connection with entering shops alone.

The chronological reconstitution of the history of the symptom resulted in envisaging a stage 1 broken down into an early scene II and a later scene I, followed by a stage 2 defined by the appearance of the manifest symptom, the two stages being separated by a period of latency that is defined by the work that takes place during it. The interval period is thus the work of latency. It was Freud's interest in this psychic work that had remained mysterious in Charcot's theory, that of the period of latency, that would be at the origin of the theory of dreams and of *The Interpretation of Dreams* (Freud, 1900). Dreams are the typical daily products of the operation of après-coup. They are also the work of latency between two successive days.

The regressive logic of temporal regression, the recent scene I – the earlier scene II, involves associative remembering and is part of the general regressive operation of formal regression and of associative concatenation. It differs from Breuer's *retrogression*, which had a cathartic purpose through the repetition and liberation of "strangulated" affects. This cathartic method consisted in returning to a traumatic point of the patient's history, in taking up the history from this point in the past, in repeating it by following a diachronic course of events and in creating a new history. It was a matter, then, of constructing a neo-reality, of concluding that what was reported to have taken place did not happen or can be reconstructed differently or repaired. For Freud, only the manifest expression of the symptom follows the progressive path.

Emma shows that remembering links adolescence to childhood, starting from adolescence. It is the sexual precociousness of the *traumatic shock* proper, that of scene II of stage 1, which is reactualized in scene I of stage 1 on the awakening of drive activity in puberty. The common sexual element between II and I appears clearly and is expressed by the signifier "shop," which serves as a junction point and means of concealment. Attention is then directed towards the operation of remembering, towards the psychic work in the interval period, towards the drive analogy between the two scenes I and II and towards the concealment of the result, the dream or the symptom. Freud was greatly interested in the psychic work of the interval period, and the *work of distortion,* to the point of calling chapter 4 of *The Interpretation of Dreams*, "Distortion in Dreams" (Freud, 1900, p. 134).

The Interpretation of Dreams arose, then, from this interest in the underlying regressive operations specific to the interval period. On the other hand, the nature of the *traumatic shock* was no clearer than before, other than being linked to a sexual thought and occurring too early (the theory of seduction and the *neurotica*).

The backward path of remembering was first conceived as being spontaneous, as Breuer had thought, but gradually it became clear that it had to be supported, as in hypnosis, by an imperative of remembering. The prescription, however, was not renewed by the therapist. Each session and the treatment as a whole was placed under the influence and prescription of a *fundamental rule* that was supposed to oppose the attraction of the "pathogenic nucleus" (Freud, 1895, p. 289) awakened by the conditions of analysis. The fundamental role thus has a twofold role: it awakens the traumatic quality by its requirement to say "everything" and it counters it by its imperative of "speaking."

What was called "deferred action" and "shock" varied according to the theories, those of Charcot, Breuer and Freud. According to the logic of the shock, it is the appearance of the symptom that is the deferred effect. According to the logic of cathartic retrogression, it is the successive memories that, starting from the symptom, are deferred effects; and according to psychoanalytic logic *each remembering is a deferred effect of an unconscious memory that has acquired, subsequent to its repression, the force of a traumatic* shock. As Freud (1895) writes, "We invariably find that a memory is repressed which has only become a trauma by *deferred action*" (p. 356).

The notion of *shock* changes radically from one model to another. In the first, the *shock* is linked to a traumatic event, or even to a chance event recalling a first traumatic event; in the second, to the "barred" affect of the memory; and in the third to the transference on to the analysis of the regressive attraction and of the verbal imperative of verbalization. The analyst thus finds himself identified with both the pathogenic nucleus and the imperative of remembering of the fundamental rule, thus an imperative of elaboration under the sway of the superego, more precisely an imperative of restraint, of registration and resolution.

Freud's work and *Nachträglichkeit*

Freud used the noun *Nachträglichkeit* [*S.E.* deferred action; Fr. *après-coup*] only on six occasions in his work extending from 1898 to 1917. Afterwards, the term disappeared.

Sexuality in the aetiology of the neuroses (Freud, 1898)

The text in which the two first instances of the term *Nachträglichkeit* can be found was still dominated by his aetiological concerns. He places the phenomenon of après-coup at the top of a list of the "chief factors on which the theory of the psychoneuroses is based" before what he calls the "infantile state of the sexual apparatus and of the mental instrument" (Freud, 1898a, p. 281).

The operation of après-coup is presented as a means of the therapeutic method of the psychoneuroses by which unconscious traces can be exhumed. Consequently, the therapeutic operation of après-coup uses the same operation as that which is involved in the formation of symptoms. The psychoanalytic method takes it over in its own name in order to accomplish it completely. This operation is clearly identified with a determining link and announces a theory of causality.

Freud underlines very clearly its role from the therapeutic point of view: "Since the manifestations of the psychoneuroses arise from the deferred action of unconscious psychical traces, they are accessible to psychotherapy" (ibid., p. 281).

The Interpretation of Dreams (Freud, 1900)

Freud used the term *Nachträglichkeit* on only one occasion in *The Interpretation of Dreams,* in connection with a humoristic anecdote: "A young man who was a great admirer of feminine beauty was talking once – so the story went – of the good-looking wet-nurse who had suckled him when he was a baby: 'I'm sorry, he remarked, 'that I didn't make better use of my opportunity'" (Freud, 1900, p. 204). Freud treated it as a *prototypical reference* of his conception of the phenomenon of après-coup: "I was in the habit," he wrote, "of quoting this anecdote to explain the factor of 'deferred action' in the mechanism of the psychoneuroses" (ibid., pp. 204–205).

Henceforth, the phenomenon of après-coup became a non-specific modality of thought of the psychoneuroses and of psychopathology, but it was also a feature of our normal everyday way of thinking, and even of its most fruitful aspect, the possibility of being employed in humour and jokes.

In fact, this anecdote, just like the famous joke about the criminal who was being led to the gallows on Monday morning and remarked, "Well, the week's beginning nicely!" (Freud, 1905a, p. 229) involves a combination of the denial and recognition of the reality of castration. What is expressed is a wish to deny this reality and the illusion that the denial could be successful thanks to the creation of a neo-reality supporting this illusion. In the case of the nostalgic anecdote, the illusion consists in considering that infantile sexuality and adult sexuality have the same characteristics, are consistent with each other, and that the relation to castration has not been encompassed in the discontinuity between the two.

To grasp the significance of this anecdote with regard to the theory of après-coup, it needs to be recontextualized. Freud reports it in chapter 5, "The Material and Sources of Dreams, sub-section (B) 'Infantile material as a source of dreams'" (Freud, 1900, p.189ff). In this chapter, it is the material that participates in the dream-work as a source of dreams that is being studied: in sub-section (A) recent and indifferent material in dreams; in (C) the somatic sources of dreams; and finally, in (D) Freud introduces *typical dreams,* that is, the processual sources intervening at the heart of the dream-work and governing it.

It is in sub-section (B) "The infantile material as a source of dreams" that Freud illustrates, in the same way that he did in the first chapter, through four examples of dreams, the role played by childhood memories in the dream-work. At the end of this second sub-section, having studied four dreams, he goes on to study two further dreams of his own. He places particular emphasis on the combined and congruent role of the two first sources of dreams, showing how their respective and complementary contributions are combined in the dream material.

Through the activities of condensation and displacement the recent past and the distant past are intertwined. Their respective economies are mutually transferred. Childhood memories are vehicles of the infantile unconscious wishes characteristic of *primary* regressive functioning. They transfer their intensity on to daytime wishes. This transference combines a negative attraction and an elaborative yearning.

The anecdote appears in Freud's writings as an association to one of his dreams: the "Three Fates" (*Knödel*) (pp. 204–208, 233). He even presents it as an incidental thought that occurred to him in the course of his associations.

The study of his dream follows the dream of a patient whose infantile reminiscence was one of always feeling *rushed*. She rushed to go out and do the shopping. She rushed to the Graben, a famous avenue in Vienna where she *fell* down on her knees. This dynamic was as much a part of her life as it was of her dreams. She associated this behaviour with games and romping about when she was a child.

Freud does not link this fall to the meaning of the word *Graben,* the root of which, *Grab*, means "tomb." He leaves to one side the fact that the event takes place in the dream on the Graben, a fine avenue in Vienna where there is a mixture as usual, he says, of elegance and prostitution, without, however, pointing out the link between this fall and the sense of *Graben/Gräber* in German.

But shortly after, what also comes to him "quite unexpectedly," as an incidental thought in the dream of the "Three Fates" (*Knödel*), is a genuine return of the *Gräber*.

This incidental idea concerns the first novel that he read at the age of thirteen about a young monk who went mad and kept calling out the names of the three women who had brought the greatest happiness and sorrow into his life (Freud, 1900, p. 204) One of these three names, Freud recalled was *Pélagie*. And he continues:

> I still had no notion what this recollection was going to lead to in the analysis. In connection with the three women I thought of the three Fates who spin the destiny of man, and I knew that one of the three women – the inn-hostess in the dream – was the mother who gives life, and furthermore, as in my own case, gives the living creature its first nourishment.
>
> (ibid.)

In fact, one of these three women is called Pélagie; another, Greek, Hypatia; and the third, Jewish, Myriam. They are not the women of the three Fates but those of the theme of the "Three Caskets."

His incidental thought leads him, then, to the funereal destiny of man. He does not name the three Fates, Clotho ("the spinner"), Lachesis ("the allotter") and Atropos ("the unturnable"), the first of whom weaves the thread of life, while the second measures it and the third cuts it. And he only refers to a woman who gives life, who nourishes. He thus mixes the three fates with the three women of the theme of the three caskets in which the three ages of woman are present, one of which corresponds to the mother.

The result of this is a theory of conception in which the child is born of the earth and returns to it. The nourishing mother conceals the poisoning seductress, and life is a source of guilt and debt. Freud took up this theme of debt again in 1915 in connection with war and death (Freud, 1915a): "To anyone who listened to us we were of course prepared to maintain that death was the necessary outcome of life, that everyone owes nature a death and must expect to pay the debt – in short, that death was natural, undeniable and unavoidable" (p. 289), and then pursued the theme again in 1936 with the sense of piety (Freud, 1936).

This debt is an association of the dream of the "Three Fates" (*Knödel*) and follows Freud's memory of his mother's demonstration that men are made of earth:

> When I was six years old and was given my first lessons by my mother, I was expected to believe that we were all made of earth and must therefore return to earth. This did not suit me and I expressed doubts of the doctrine. My mother thereupon rubbed the palms of her hands together – just as she did in making dumplings – except that there was no dough between them and showed me the blackish scales of epidermis produced by the friction as proof that we were made of earth. My astonishment at this ocular demonstration knew no bounds and I acquiesced in the belief which I was later to hear in the words: "*Du bist de nature einen Tod schuldig.*"["Thou owest Nature a Death."].
>
> (1900, p. 205)

It was just after these incidental associations, this series of incidental deferred effects in connection with the novel, then the three Fates, and then his confusion with the three women of the three ages of life, and before drawing our attention to these memories, that Freud placed the anecdote of "deferred action" of the young man who regretted that he had not made better use of his wet-nurse. In reading the text, the anecdote itself appears incidentally. It is caught in the dynamic of *incidental thinking* specific to the session discourse and associations based on a dream extending the "deferred action" that led to the production of the dream.

The return of the *Gräber* is thus particularly clear in the associative series of the *Knödel*, a dumpling of earth, the first infantile sexual theory supported by Freud's mother, a theory applied to everything that is separable, including life itself of course. This associative series is permeated by guilt fomenting this return to earth, clearly linked to incestuous wishes.

We recognize the unconscious guilt in which incestuous wishes (seeing the mother naked) and the desexualization underlying narcissism are amalgamated: here the establishment by the little Sigismund of his maternal function, experienced by him as a murder of his mother, hence the debt and the guilty return as offerings to Mother-Earth. Freud's reply, "Thou owest Nature a Death" is an adaptation from Shakespeare permitting Freud to envisage his mother's guilt, whereas in Shakespeare's *Henry IV*, Prince Henry expresses this guilt towards God the Father: "But you owe God a death" (Act III, Sc. II).

The castration complex takes over the guilt secreted by desexualization and promotes religious and expiatory mindsets towards a parent who is believed to be wounded and in need of reparation (Freud, 1928). The weight of the alienating unconscious demands of each parent can also be surmised. For Freud, his *beloved mother*, of whom he was the eldest son; moreover, he was concerned not to leave her *without* him, by dying before her; and his father to whom he addresses feelings of piety. These remarks outline the Oedipal tragedy supported by the counter-Oedipal displays of the parents (Pasche, 1988). A wish for unconscious identity is expressed that involves being part of the maternal matter that is separable from it, being what the mother is lacking and which can therefore restore her as Mother, that is, a non-woman.

A line is thus traced starting from the Graben, of the lady who rushed to go there, then from the *Knödel* and the Fates, towards death, the tomb, via castration as a punishment for incestuous wishes, but also as an expiation and reversal of the construction of the child envisaged as putting a parent to death. The weight of the castration complex can be surmised here, which is apt to follow a transvaluation of its value in promoting renunciations, and to take over the unconscious guilt secreted by the desexualization at the origin of narcissism. Religious mindsets, feelings of piety and devotion, the expiatory mindsets toward a parent who is thought to be wounded and thus repaired, are thus promoted (Freud, 1928).

In the dream of the "Three Fates" material appears that corroborates this logic of guilt. The question of transgression arises in connection with trying on another person's garment, an overcoat that was too big and embroidered with a Turkish design. In addition to the Oedipal wish to take the place of another person, the word *Turkish* features three times. Freud says nothing about it. But a deferred effect in the theorization, the forgetting of the name Signorelli, involves his guilt about the death of a former Turkish patient who committed suicide a few years after his treatment with Freud on learning that he was suffering from an irreversible illness depriving him of his sexuality. The tragedy is related to the sexuality and *irreversibility* of certain realities. Castration makes present and embodies the category of what is irreversible.

The logic of guilt and the wish to exonerate oneself are constant in all Freud's interpretations of his dreams of this period in the name of his *responsibility*: "the blame lies with" (see the dream of Irma's injection, the dream of the uncle with the yellow beard, the dream of the Three Fates, and so on).

His insistence on linking his guilt and his responsibility as a doctor is presented in very secondarized terms and suggests the risk of sexualizing the medical function through infantile wishes associated with guilt. This guiltiness can be surmised further, against the background of humour, in the regret regarding the wet-nurse, albeit concealed by the pain of passing time. The anecdote fulfils the wish to be young, which is a way of venting guilt for having had so many experiences of mourning and committed so many murders.

This reading of the material gives us a glimpse into another aspect of the theory of après-coup, namely, its link with unconscious guilt, with the body and with castration as recognized on the body itself. It is a good illustration of this intimate connection with the body, particularly with a woman's body and thus with the difference between the sexes. According to this point of view, all this material reveals a transference of precipitation of incestuous desires and a fear of castration (Chervet, 2004).

The guilt that Freud insists on in this material appears to be more generic than singular, even if it uses singularity to express itself. It concerns the relationship to castration and, in particular, to the castration of the sisters, absent from his associations, and to that of the mother. Each child is, in fact, caught up in this double source of guilt for what he (the child) has done to her (the mother), and also for what he has not done. Unconscious guilt turns out to be the motor of the oscillatory activity of mental life, as described by Denise Braunschweig (Braunschweig & Fain, 1975) and in the biphasic nature of many psychic operations. It is thus one of the determinants of the operation of après-coup.

This lengthy elaboration concerns the context in which the humorous anecdote in *The Interpretation of Dreams* about the regret concerning the wet-nurse appears, as an association to a dream and as a link in an associative network. The economic value of humour here concerns guilt that is already recognized. The interplay of denial and recognition helps to avoid submitting to it.

It is therefore possible to credit me with the wish to produce a deferred effect, through infinite over-interpretation, by replacing this written and non-evolving material at the heart of Freud's scientific productions, written during the same period, by linking them up according to the determinations and logics of the operation of après-coup. Although this effect presents plausible criteria, it certainly has its limits inasmuch as it is only the product of my constructions. But this provides an opportunity to discover the disposition of thought to unfold according to the operation of après-coup.

Indeed, one of the aspects emphasized in this book is the generativity of human thought, its unlimited and infinite character. Thought can also retain its qualities when it is dealing with the questions of castration, of limits and what is irreversible, where the operation of après-coup plays a role in terms of style.

Freud's biographers could certainly propose other reconstructions, for example, by linking this guilt to the death of his brother Julius, to his younger sisters, and also to many other memories from his childhood. The above construction follows my *interior paths* (Chabert, 1999) and is only of interest in showing how the operation of après-coup can appear manifestly in a clinical and theoretic text, while being acted upon by the disposition of the elements of the text and also by the reconstruction of the reader.

The probability of my construction should not lead us to overlook Freud's remark to Wittels in 1923, in response to the tendentious biography that Wittels was about to publish on Freud, "What seems true is not always the truth" (Freud, 1924a, p. 287, note 1). If the operation of après-coup is always present, active and recognizable in a text by its effects, it does not necessarily yield a specific truth of the author. It is an essential method in literature and art, where its *mise en abyme* become a style.

Starting from the history of an infantile neurosis (Freud, 1918)

The term *Nachträglichkeit* reappears later on, in 1914, in the "Wolf Man" and then in a note of 1917 (Freud, 1918, p. 45, note 1, and p. 58).

In this text Freud takes a very particular approach. Indeed, a compulsion for numbering and dating appears that is applied to temporality. One way of holding back time, since it cannot be represented by thing-presentations, is to refer to numbers and their measurement. Unlike spatiality, temporality is expressed by several systems of calculation, thereby revealing all the more that it eludes us.

Like a Master of time, Freud tries to note with clock-like precision the chronology of the recollected psychic events, each of which is considered as a result of an operation of après-coup, as an attempt of the Wolf Man to deal with the state of disarray, combining fright and distress, experienced on perceiving the primal scene.

Just like his patient, Freud also tries to establish an anti-cathexis against this attraction and seduction of the primal scene. He has recourse to a sketch, thing- and word-presentations, but above all to an act of numbering and dating. Caught up in his identity as an archaeologist, he tries to situate these stages with extreme clarity, with a chronological precision worthy of carbon-14.

The operation of après-coup turns out to be serial, fractal in its form, plural in its substrata and elusive owing to the leap between extinctive drive regressivity and the imperative of registration of a psychic product. Hence the attempt to *calculate* an "amount" (Freud, 1918, pp. 42–44).

The recourse to numbering shows the extent to which the category of thing-presentations does not completely correspond to the attraction of the primal scene. In fact, the jouissance of the protagonists eludes any possibility of representation. It can only give rise to a sensory conversion and to motor acts (defecation) and to the employment of abstract signs (numbers). A close link among the primal scene, primal phantasies, affect and mathematics is revealed here: "Mathematics is the poetry of science," says Léopold Sédar Senghor. What Freud tries to approach in this text, then, is the establishment of the primary anti-cathexis by the primal phantasies acted out through sensoriality, an anti-cathexis of distress and, underlying this, of the attraction of extinction, while at the same time maintaining an objectalization of the formulas seeking to preserve the function of the primal phantasies and their links with the characters who are their supports.

What dominates in this dating is the importance of what are called *trauma* and *castration* in psychoanalysis. This attraction/seduction affords a glimpse of the crucial issue of the subject's disappearance, of his topographical disorganization, of his dilution in the scene of the ecstatic enjoyment of the other, of this other couple; hence, the appeal to measurement (Guedj, 2000) and to time-keeping (Chervet, 1995). A new conception of *shock* (*coup*) emerges that is more internalized and related to infantile distress, traumatic regression and the operations known as primal phantasies that are aroused. These are all linked by their common function of establishing anti-cathexis. They reflect the necessity of establishing the foundational identifications of the narcissisms arising from both the cathexes of bodies and of objects. They express the dynamic of psychic work and the issues that are operative at the junction of fright and traumatic anguish.

It is worth noting the disequilibrium emerging between the three phantasies. The first two express the attraction by the object of the drive, represented in this case by the Beast with two backs but open to something beyond representations owing to its ecstatic enjoyment. On the other hand, the third appeals directly, by virtue of its very formulation, to the consequences of this negative attraction, thus to the fright of castration and to a theory that castration is the work of the father. In fact, it is an *appeal to the father*, and therefore a limitation of the disappearance and an attempt to save the whole by focalizing the loss on a part. The anti-cathecting function of this appeal is then brought to the forefront. By depicting the links between the agencies, the representations of motor actions (Perron-Borelli and Perron, 1995) provide an anti-cathexis to this attraction via the extinctive trend of the drives.

The organization in two stages of the operation of après-coup is thus a consequence of this function in which they participate. A regressive period taking into account the regressive drive attractions proves necessary for the reestablishment of anti-cathexes, both primary bodily anti-cathexes and secondary object-related anti-cathexes.

Freud draws attention in this text to the fact that the different manifestations presented by the Wolf Man, namely, the dream, the phobia of wasps, the various recollections and the session transference are all instances of deferred action. They perform the function of screen-memories against experiences of distress and traumatic extinction.

Concerning the transference in the session, Freud writes: "This is simply another instance of *deferred action*" (Freud, 1918, p. 45). It is thus the dimension of actualization through transference repetition, of transference "*Agieren*" (acting out) that dominates; at the same time, the elaborative aspect by stages, by working-through is affirmed. The *old* unconscious material, the *recent* recollected material and the *present* repeated material are linked.

Having rectified several temporal disparities, Freud introduced the notion of "the amount of après-coup" when he wrote: "The period of time during which the effects were deferred is very greatly diminished; it now covers only a few months of the child's fourth year and does not stretch back at all into the first dark years of childhood" (ibid., pp. 58–59). He thus turns his attention to the value of this operation from the point of view of the intensity expressing the regressive economy, to the differences of potential between the two scenes and to the important consequence of taking into consideration the role in the regressive economy of the intermediate links and various screen registrations. It is this retrograde role of the regressive work, specific to the operation of après-coup, on the regressive economy and on the production of regressive registrations that is reflected in the term *retrospective phantasies* (ibid., p. 59, addition of 1917–1918). Thus temporal quantification restrains the traumatic regression and circumscribes the disparities of the libidinal economies between the various psychic spaces as temporal disparities. By expressing a temporal disparity, the *amount* of après-coup reflects economic disparities and the various states in which the libidinal cathexes find themselves.

The operation of après-coup creates links of temporal causality with the function of anti-cathecting binding. This is an economic function, a response to the disparity of the regressive economy existing between the two events belonging to the shock (stage 1), between the economy of scene II (the old and earliest scene) and the economy of scene I (the recent scene, the infantile element). The dating restrains the traumatic regression and circumscribes the *tensions* of the libidinal economies between the various psychic spaces. Formulated as a temporal *disparity*, the *amount* of après-coup reflects an economic disparity revealed by intensity.

A case of paranoia running counter to the psychoanalytic theory of the disease (Freud, 1915b)

The sixth instance in which Freud uses the term *Nachträglichkeit* can be found in this text of 1915. In it he presents a female patient struggling with the failures of her erotogenic cathexes, which she tries to compensate for by means of the palliative construction of a delusional neo-reality.

When examining the delusion of the patient who had consulted him, Freud concluded that what was involved was precisely the operation of après-coup. This young woman found means of protecting herself against the disorganization that occurred during the erotic scene with her lover, when she was frightened by a suspicious "noise." So she began to search for rational explanations and reassurances that might anti-cathect and stop the noise of her disorganization and create a self-reorganization (Faure-Pragier & Pragier, 1990).

Her lover proposed to her the simplest infantile transposition on the model of a phobic solution. He said that the *noise,* the *shock,* probably came from the ticking of a clock on the desk in the room. In so doing he offered her a substitution and a displacement on to a conscious idea supported by a possible actual perception. Such a transposition could have helped her to change her anxiety into fear of a danger by drawing on the support of a tangible and perceivable object, and thereby to avoid the danger (Neyraut, 2002). The designation of this object and its avoidance are the defensive means used by every phobia from childhood on.

But this solution did not suit her. She continued her search for explanations, speculating that the small, covered box she had seen a man carrying on the staircase as she was leaving might have been a camera that had been used to photograph, to *capture* her naked body, her sexuality. She was convinced that a camera had been hidden behind the curtains in the bedroom, and that she had been *taken,* in the sense that her erogeneity had been robbed: a spoliation-capture-castration. This belief replaced the penetration and sexual satisfaction thereby avoided. Thus, her genital sensations, in particular clitoral sensations, Freud notes, were transformed into a delusional and paranoiac construction explaining her lack. On the basis of found/created indications, she created a *false* causal connection and a theory, which, in spite of everything, expressed part of her truth, the dramatic failure of her genital sensoriality and her feeling that she had been deprived of it.

This sense of reality reflected the failures of registration and appropriation of her bodily erotogenic cathexes that had been mortgaged historically and had since remained topographically outside her body-ego (in the staircase).

There was no question for her of making do with an anti-cathecting idea. She had to provide herself with a perceptual scenario of capture by drawing on the indications of reality in connection with her own truth of which she herself was unaware, namely, of having been deprived/divested of her genital erogenous zone. The beats of her clitoris, as well as her longings to capture the penis in her vagina, awakened in her what had remained topographically outside her ego (in the staircase), and which was still caught, captured, held outside of herself by another person. This other person was an old lady of whom the lover and the young men in the staircase were merely the agents. The noise of the extinction of her drive beats could not be transposed ordinarily on to the ticking of the clock. Her transposition did not occur therefore according to the animistic logic of the primary processes; she needed an external scene giving substance to the subtraction. The noise is that of the subtraction; hence, a new conception of the *shock*: what is lacking is denoted as *shock*. This shock is akin to the traumatic origin.

She reconstructs the cause of what she is lacking within outside herself, in the same way as the failure of the genital bodily cathexis, of which she is the vehicle, returns to her from the outside and not in the form of anxiety accompanied by the subjective feeling of an internal origin. This return from the outside means that that ordinary transposition becomes a projection. For her it is a matter of imagining an external origin of this deprivation. She needs an external scene. No internal origin can be recognized, unlike the phobic subject who is never sufficiently certain of the link that he makes with an external object and who, therefore, must regularly repeat his encounter with it in order to strengthen the defensive value of his false connection.

What she is deprived of is the sexual cathexis of her erogenous zone; consequently, it is no longer an erogenous zone. Her genital zone is barred from this sexual cathexis. The whole representative field of feminine vaginal desire for a man's penis is *barred* at the same time.

A new concept of *shock* emerges: what is lacking is denoted as *shock*. She reconstructs outside herself the cause of what she is lacking within. The failure of her genital cathexes returns to her from the outside and not in the form of signal anxiety transmitting the internal origin. Ordinary phobic transposition makes way for a projection with a return of the outside. The operation of après-coup creates neo-realities that are no longer concerned with the most regressive economy on account of a more recent scene that is less coloured by the traumatic quality. Its mission is to produce a material, a theory, a connection that has the function of making up for this failure of primary cathexis of the sexual body, thus the lack of primary narcissism arising from erotogenic sexual cathexes reflected by sensations of organic disorder (Freud, 1914) and sensual impressions (Freud, 1915c): Freud writes: "This deferred use of impressions and this displacement of recollections often occur precisely in paranoia and are characteristic of it" (ibid., p. 270).

This defensive function reflects the state of primary narcissism of this patient, narcissism originating in erotogenic sexual cathexes. The results of the operation of après-coup not only convey the fundamental trends involved in psychic work but also its failures, along with the excluded regressive and extinctive drive longings, as well as the need to deploy defences against such longings for extinction and against tendencies to disorganize everything that has hitherto been elaborated by the mind.

This occurrence of the construction of paranoiac neo-realities invites a few remarks on the unconscious logics specific to *Beyond the Pleasure Principle* (1920), a subject Freud was to return to between 1936 and 1938 in *Moses and Monotheism* (1939) in connection with *pre-verbal traumatic impressions* that cannot give rise to direct recollections, but only ones that can be inferred from psychic formations such as dreams or delusional beliefs. In fact, such impressions have their origin in processual activity that does not result in a memory of contents or identifications but rather an amnesic memory without content, a processual memory of psychic activity accounting for the history of the establishment of psychic processes and of the various systems and vicissitudes of their functioning. *Processual memory* is made up of such *endogenous impressions.*

Revisiting the case of Schreber will make it possible to clarify these defensive logics. Freud describes four modes of *opposition* to the direct drive formulation: "*I (*a man*), love him* (a man)" (Freud, 1911, p. 63ff), formulations that all use a negation and a negativization. To achieve this resistance, the first three transform respectively the verb, the object and the subject of the positive formulation; hence, the persecutory solutions: "I do not *love* him! – I hate him! Because *he persecutes me*"; or erotomanic: "I do not love *him* – I love *her* because *she* loves me; or on account of jealousy: "It's not *I* who loves the man; *she* loves him." To these three solutions must be added that of absolute negativization: "I do not love at all – I do not love anyone – I only love myself."

The contribution of 1920 allows us to determine what these logics of transformation oppose and to understand why the statement "I love him" is irreconcilable and cannot be elaborated. The reason is that it signifies a total transformation of the primary process experienced as a *metamorphosis* of the body achieved by means of castration, a longing for psychic and physical transformation, *beyond,* as formulated by Schreber. "I love him" means, in fact, for the latter that "it must be beautiful to be a woman submitting to the act of intercourse" (1911b, p. 234).

Hence the obligation to radically oppose the wish to be transformed into a woman, to come like a woman when she is castrated by the act of intercourse.

These logics of the beyond articulate the *denial* and *transvaluation* of castration, which becomes the path permitting access to the object of the drive under cover of the object of the ideal. Every child is faced with such longings and will have to respond to them by elaborating his infantile sexual theories of castration. In paranoiacs, they appear to be no more than attempts at self-healing.

Castration makes it possible to meet up with God/the parental couple and, under such a benediction, to satisfy the drive once and for all; that is, to be the absolute jouissance of the instinctual drive couple of the primal scene.

This study of the occasions when Freud explicitly uses the term *Nachträglichkeit* in no way exhausts the use by Freud of the dynamic of the operation of après-coup in other very famous texts. The presentation of the case of Dora, and even more so the treatment of the phobia of Little Hans, show the part played by the operation of après-coup both in the clinical account and in the therapeutic process, even if the terms *Nachträglichkeit* and *nachträglich* are not used by Freud. This is what would happen permanently after 1917. All of Freud's texts, between 1923 and 1925, that were supposed to complete the *Three Essays on the Theory of Sexuality* (Freud, 1905b) exalt the role of the operation of après-coup in the advent of human sexuality and in its concretization throughout life without ever using the term.

Another clinical example: Freud's process of theorization

Signorelli and writing in two stages

Earlier, when examining the humorous anecdote that served Freud as a reference point for generalizing the operation of après-coup to thought as a whole, I pointed out that he left one aspect out of the picture in his analysis of his dream, the "Three Fates" (*dumplings-Knödel*). In this dream, the second overcoat "had a long strip with a Turkish design let into it" and these Turkish embroidery designs are mentioned on three occasions in the account of the dream. He word *Turkish* appears three times. Freud offers no associations. Yet this content forms a remarkable link between two articles that he wrote during this same period concerning a commonplace forgetting of a proper name, *Signorelli*: one, "The Psychical Mechanism of Forgetfulness" (Freud, 1898b), and the other, "The Forgetting of Proper Names," in *The Psychopathology of Everyday Life* (Freud, 1901a, pp. 1–7).

In the first, he gives free rein to his associativity and to the formal regression made possible by putting into latency thoughts concerning a traumatic reality connected with drive regressivity. This long associative concatenation serves, precisely, to counter this appeal of regressivity. In the second text, thus later on, Freud clearly identifies the recent traumatic event, the death of a former Turkish patient, as a result of which this regressivity was actualized by keeping in a state of latency the thoughts concerning this patient and by suppressing the painful affects. Freud wrote in 1901 that he was still in a state of *shock* from this news that had diverted his attention from thinking about this painful event, under whose *influence* he had been when he writing the article of 1898. His former patient of Turkish origin had taken his own life when he understood that his sexual impotency was incurable and therefore irreversible (Freud, 1901, p. 3).

Freud enacted the operation of après-coup in his theoretical elaboration in two stages. He enacted a dynamic in two stages by writing these two articles that complete each other in the theorization of forgetfulness. This operation in two stages becomes the ordinary manifest form of every process of theorization. Two elements are thus linked up in two stages: an initial *denial,* under the umbrella of which the long associative concatenation of the first article unfolds; and then the subsequent lifting of this denial, followed by recognition of the *traumatic impression* that was initially denied, through the expedient of moral pain.

The denial belongs to the first stage. Insofar as it is reversible, it makes the regressive work, associative and preconscious, nocturnal and unconscious, possible. It liberates the regressive psychic activities of passivity and the regressive freedom, reacquired momentarily, of libidinal cathexis. This work accomplishes a reestablishment, a restoration of narcissistic anti-cathexes. A *bonus of desire* is the ideal outcome that is reflected by the unpredictable results of dreaming. Freedom, diversity and unpredictability are the major qualities of the libido. The work of interpretation really ends only in the second phase, with the final rupture of this inaugural denial.

It can be seen here that such a process in two stages, regressive then progressive, has an essential function that cannot be replaced by some sort of intellectual, immediate, direct and premature understanding operating as a negation.

The period of denial allows for work on what is repressed and regressive, work that makes the second phase possible from the rupture of the denial until the recognition through pain of the existence of the traumatic dimension within the drive.

Abandoning the denial completes the regressive process and only occurs in a second, terminal phase that completes the regressive work and is made possible by this work.

Here, at the level of the work of interpretation in the session, we can see what was to become fundamental in the theory of dreams after 1920. The dream acquired its third identity of being a *normal psychosis* producing *a perceptual activity* that is supposed to saturate consciousness from the inside and thereby supplant all sensory perception of the reality of *castration,* but also any sensual feelings of lack (Chervet, 2017).

A crucial issue is thus the mechanism of denial and the possibility, by virtue of it, of opening moments of regression favourable for libidinal regeneration. To this end the denial must be reversible and intermittent. Two forms of denial must therefore be distinguished: reversible and temporary denial, which is psychically creative, and chronic denial, which, on the contrary, is damaging for regressive mentalization because it impedes the dynamic in two stages. The difference between the two lies in the existence and utilization of a concomitant period of latency. Only the pair reversible denial/putting into latency is favourable for regressive psychic activities of passivity and for their progressive consequences.

Furthermore, it is worth noting that the operative factor in both these articles of 1898 and 1901on the forgetting of the name *Signorelli* is guilt, a sense of being *guilty* for not having been able to repair the castration of someone who was likely to inflict it on himself in the form of suicide (*sui caedere*: cutting oneself).

I have already emphasized that Freud's recurrent insistence on linking his guilt to his responsibility as a doctor, found in the "forgetting the word *Signorelli*" in "Irma's injection" and in the dream of the "Uncle with a yellow beard," presents a version of things that is much too rational. He himself taught us that this way of giving priority to the facts of adult life conceals other, older and more regressive sources and thus amounts to a negation of the infantile past. This does not, however, detract from its value.

Responsibility for these events containing a traumatic quality is integrated within theories that were probably built in order to respond mentally to the perceived disappearances or erasures and to the extinctive drive attraction of intra-drive origin connected with these erasures.

The Acropolis, the ruins and the oceanic feeling

Other moments in Freud's theoretical elaboration could lead to the recognition of a dynamic that reveals that the operation of après-coup is in progress. This is the case for the *disturbance of memory on the Acropolis*, already mentioned above.

The very fact that the event reported in "A Disturbance of Memory on the Acropolis" took place in 1905, while the letter to Romain Roland was written in 1936, already gives a manifest temporality that endorses this idea. But more important still than this manifest two-stage process is the echo that exists between the feeling of piety that Freud refers to by way of interpreting his disturbance, a feeling expressed by the famous words *too good to be true,* and the situation in which the disturbance was felt by Freud: standing in front of the ruins. The immortality of the Greek Pantheon was not able to guarantee timelessness and prevent decay and dilapidation.

The two events, the disturbance of memory and the writing of the letter, are both deferred effects of the echoes that took place between the *impression* awakened by the perception of the ruins, grief in connection with his father and mother and the extinctive quality of the elementary drives.

Hence his interpretation of the oceanic feeling, of religious feeling and of all the group and private beliefs that human beings adopt as anti-traumatic solutions: direct solutions through denial and indirect solutions by turning them round into their opposite.

The Beyond, clinical scenarios of conviction and the superego

As soon as *Beyond the Pleasure Principle* (1920) had been written and drive regressivity, even to the inorganic and inanimate state, had been recognized, anti-traumatic clinical situations, both collective and individual, became central to Freud's theorizations. This was the reason that led him to write *Group Psychology and the Analysis of the Ego* (1921), but also for his interest in the compulsions of destiny (destiny neuroses), *collusions* relating to thought-transmission and telepathy (1941; 1922) or adhesion to a *Weltanschauung* (1933a) such as the demonological religious worldview of the painter Haizmann. These different solutions have the function of "deferred obedience" at the heart of the father complex. They come into conflict with the superego, the uncertainty and fragility of which they reveal, and they function as stand-ins for the superego. The superego acquired its place as an agency in the metapsychology of 1923 after the study of these situations in which it was replaced by various modalities that turned to the quantitative and to massification, then to inhibition, calm, and psychic and somatic degradation.

The defensive solutions utilizing narcissism (1914), such as the withdrawal of libidinal cathexes back upon the ego – "Concentrated is his soul in his molar's narrow hole" (Wilhelm Busch, cited by Freud, ibid., p. 82) – are employed with increasing frequency and resort to mass elimination and destruction.

In 1921, it was around an object chosen in place of an individual superego, an object conveying an *ideal without mourning*, that entire battalions massed. It was no longer a matter of concentrating narcissism around a *hole,* but of denying feelings of lack and of replacing them with a longing for an ideal. The role of the cultural sphere and of the denial conveyed by culture itself made its entry into the understanding of the recourse to the masses and to mass destruction.

"The Economic Problem of Masochism" (Freud, 1924b) helps to take these reflections further. The imperative of restraint establishes a masochism of mental functioning and a pain of restraint, in fact, a *masochism of renunciation.* The cathexes that arise from this restraint are converted in the body and form the basis of erogeneity. The basis of all desire is a pain of restraint masked by the pleasure of experiencing desire. Denial circumvents this pain of mental functioning. The imperative of restraint resists the attractions that strive to regress beyond the masochistic nucleus and to disorganize it. The operation of restraint is thus concerned with such a "tendency to conflict" (Freud, 1937a, p. 244). This tendency amounts to recognition of the reality of the extinctive trend felt through feelings of lack.

When the masochistic nucleus is under threat, it is necessary to establish urgently, and at whatever price, equivalents of restraint in response to the extinctive regressivity that strives to turn a "hole" into an abyss, an ideal into passion and elation. It is then that there is recourse to the mass and mass destruction, a prelude to the risk of suicide.

Freud's preoccupation with collective beliefs as anti-traumatic expedients runs through the rest of his work until *Civilization and its Discontents* (1930), including *The Future of an Illusion* (1927a). We can see the emergence of *clinical scenarios of conviction* that may co-exist with other modes of psychic functioning. Indeed, in ego-splitting two modes of functioning co-exist: one governed by the *imperative of renunciation* and another by conviction and conformism. The ideal ego may then serve as a means to escape mourning. The sense of being misled by such a ruse and ploy of falsification led Freud (1920) to describe this clinical material as "hypocritical" (p. 165).

Freud also turned his attention to clinical scenarios involving private anti-traumatic convictions, the strictly personal ones that men form. The key example of this is provided by fetishism, the model of which has its extension in delusional neo-constructions. Here individual beliefs are upheld whose aim is not to be shared, and theories are supported whose function is to saturate consciousness and reinforce the repression of feelings and perceptions of lack, as well as the denial of castration. At this point an important differentiating clinical point needs to be made: personal delusional beliefs do not have the same degree of contagiousness and do not require the participation of others, as mass delusions do. The latter question the function of culture, which imperceptibly unites individuals as a mass. When this function is challenged, masses are created openly with their convictions and their mass destructive acts.

Telepathy, divination and the occult

The texts on telepathy (Freud, 1941, 1922, 1925a, 1933b) are a fine example of deferred effects with an anti-traumatic aim, without entailing any modification of the pathogenic regressive economy. Immediately after 1920, Freud considered the idea that, under particular conditions, thoughts can circulate between different people, independently of any concrete perceptual substratum and any tangible indication. The wish-fulfillment that people who are distanced from one another and separated physically will remain close and united through their affects and their thoughts is clear to see. This belief is opposed to de-objectalization and asserts that there are links beyond separations. This is what all occult sciences do that disregard the capacities of reconstruction of the operation of après-coup in the name of such a wish.

1. Such constructions in two stages can also be found in canonizations. Many examples present themselves here. One of them was in Palermo. In 1159, the legend goes, a young fifteen-year-old girl, Rosalia, withdrew for reasons of piety to live as a hermit in a cave on Mount Pellegrino, where she died many years later, forgotten by everyone. In 1624, at a time when the town was ravaged by the plague, someone in the city saw in a dream the exact spot where Rosalia's remains lay. On awakening, he was persuaded that a procession of her remains could save the town and managed to convince the authorities of this. Some human remains were found, said to be those of Rosalia, gathered together and carried in procession through the town. It was declared that Rosalia had saved Palermo and she was venerated as its patron saint (Durell, 1979). The conjuratory need to ensure an anti-traumatic and magic predictability rests on a private trauma, bestows it with the significance of an occult message and offers it to the community. We live with horoscopes, lotteries and weather forecasts.

All the examples cited above, arising from Freud's work of theorization, show that the dynamic of his theorization follows the two stages of the operation of après-coup. He himself declared that the process of theorization is determined by a precise order: "If psychoanalysis," he writes, "has not hitherto shown its appreciation of certain things, this has never been because it overlooked their achievement or sought to deny their importance, but because it followed a particular path which had not yet led so far" (Freud, 1923, p. 12). This predetermination is nonetheless the source of a conflict concerning the appreciation and rejection of the traumatic quality of the drive impulses that can facilitate or oppose the work of elaboration.

The trajectory traced above is far from being exhaustive. It would also have been possible to follow the disparity between the article of 1908 on fetishism, presented in the Minutes of the Wednesday Psychological Society but never published, and the article published in 1927 (Freud, 1927b). In the first, Freud envisages the creation of the fetish on the model of the work of substitution active in the formation of symptoms. In the second, he introduces the role of denial; hence, the identity of the fetish as a neo-reality that serves to deny lack. The two functions of denial and substitution are involved in the operation of après-coup that links them. For example, in the case of Emma, her shop agoraphobia unites scene I of the shop assistants, which is a substitute for scene II of the shopkeeper, and scene II which was denied to repress the dreadful anxiety. Together, scenes I and II are opposed to the extinctive drive tendency that is the real traumatic factor. In order to realize the psychic work that reduces this traumatic attraction, a denial of the sensory perceptions of lack must be made regularly and temporarily. This is what happens each night.

I have already mentioned the repercussions of the phenomenon of après-coup for the organization of human thought according to a highly determined biphasic, bidirectional and discontinuous dynamic whose result remains unforeseeable. The unfolding of this operation is subject to the randomness of the second, searched for/found *shock*, namely, the attenuation and fulfilment of the work of distortion, both of which are responsible for the production of all sorts of vicissitudes and stumbling blocks.

Theorization itself is influenced by extinctive regressivity and by the psychic operation that takes account of it, and, at the same time, one of the specific and obligatory means for dealing with it. That is why the phenomenon of après-coup is always an enacted theory. It gives the process of theorization its very form.

While Freud immediately followed up his recognition of this traumatic regressivity with an appeal to collective beliefs and private neo-productions, it also obliged him to reconsider the psychic topography as a whole and to establish in it a pole, an agency, that opposes this traumatic regressivity and is responsible for the development of the mind and mentalization, namely, an imperative of psychic registration. This is not the case for the majority of the anti-traumatic solutions built around beliefs based on a stable denial.

The traumatic extinctive attraction thus requires the establishment in the metapsychology of a processual pole, of an imperative of restraint, renunciation and registration at the basis of psychic functioning, an imperative that is called upon to become the processual imperative of the superego.

The power of regressivity led Freud (1923) to call the article in which he elaborates this imperative pole *The Ego and the Id* rather than *The Ego, the Id and the Superego,* thereby leaving this last term in abeyance, even though the aim of this article was to establish the superego at the heart of the theory. This text is thus isomorphic with the very establishment of this agency at the heart of the psyche, an agency that is involved at the heart of the operation of après-coup since it watches over its accomplishment.

The superego is both the heir of the Oedipus complex and the promoter of the Oedipal resolution on which its own establishment depends. It has its origin in an already-there, a potentiality that is already operative. The superego is the outcome of inchoative imperatives that prepare its advent and are subsumed under its superstructure.

Freud's conceptions of the operation of après-coup

The effective reality of the operation of après-coup is thus easily identifiable at the heart of Freud's theorizing and conception of thought, which is fundamentally bivalent and bidirectional. He enacted it throughout the elaboration of his work. The movement in two stages of all psychic work that ideally eventuates in a rich progressive production of an authentic detour via the regressive path is recognizable at each stage. This process in two stages thus has the function, through the work of the interval period between the stages, of modifying the regressive economies, of drawing libidinal resources from them and of involving them in the final production of a bonus of desire.

Although Freud seems to direct his attention more particularly to regressive psychic work (formal regression and representability) and to the work permitting transferences and economic mutations (operations of displacement and condensation), his work itself enacts the importance that he accords to progressive productivity. The latter is not merely a secondary elaboration. There is a real promotion of a new regenerative economy of the mind turned towards the libidinal cathexis of objects.

Freud's conceptions of the operation of après-coup and of the *shock* are dependent on the evolution of his views about *regression.* He initially conceived the regressive movement of thought in terms of a triple stratification (Freud & Breuer, 1895), and then in terms of various intersecting regressions. He attributed the regressive attraction successively to the pathogenic nucleus (ibid.), to the negative attraction of the unconscious (Freud, 1915c), to the tendency to return to an earlier state of things (Freud, 1920), and to the attraction of the prototypes of the id (Freud, 1926). Regression was envisaged in 1900 as culminating in sensory discoveries; in 1914, its horizon was the return to the bosom of foetal primary narcissism; then, in 1920, it opened out on to the abysses of a beyond with the inorganic, inanimate state as a consequence.

It was this regressive dynamic that Freud was referring to in 1920 when he spoke of his three "steps" (1920, p. 59) in the theory of the drives, thereby outlining, as Lacan well understood when he spoke of Freud I, II and III, the three periods of theorization of the processual steps at the basis of human desire, that is to say, from the most elaborate to the most regressive, respectively, infantile sexuality, narcissism and the extinctive regressive quality of the drives.

The ideal operation of après-coup is thus formed of several moments, the three essential features of which are the work of formal regression, the work of economic mutation and the work of progression. More precisely, we can describe the moments specific to the interval period: formal regression – regressive representability – economic mutation – drive representation – progressive production – presentation to consciousness. These moments are inaugurated by a state of latency and a temporary denial of materials in connection with the traumatic regressive economy, and then completed by the production of manifest material that conceals the first material in latency and the entire work of distortion in the interval period.

Freud's process of theorization is also characterized by these three principal moments. It follows a regressive, backward path. In this way, it elaborates regressive constellations studied according to a predetermined order and is followed by a presentation of new conceptions that has an effect of retroactive reverberation on earlier conceptions. All this unfolds under the aegis of an imperative to elaborate, an imperative governing the unfolding of the process of theorization as a whole, its initiation and its accomplishment until its completion.

This evolution was to have an influence on all Freudian concepts. Henceforth, they could no longer be thought about without this reference to the three processual moments elaborated by Freud. His theorization unfolded according to the operation of après-coup which became the model of theorization of the mind, characterized by the processual moments described above.

To define the *shock*, he establishes a theoretical demarcation beginning with the traumatic events of external seduction constitutive of the pathogenic nucleus and leading up to endogenous extinctive drive regressivity. Between the two, he denotes the misuses of sexuality in the present, the *neurotica* and its shocking transgressions, infantile sexuality, infantile amnesia, the posthumous effect of unconscious phantasy, the mutual interferences and articulations of the agencies reflected in terms of primal phantasies, the effectiveness of alienating inclusions, the shadows of narcissistic identifications, defective identifications and their consequent flaws, unconscious guilt and its need for punishment and illness, the denial of reality, in particular concerning the difference between the sexes and femininity, the biological bedrock and the question of the reality of castration.

Gradually, it was the pair extinctive regressivity/processual imperative of registration that defined the shock best. This term offers a double meaning in French: that of the libidinal coexcitation that links painful restraint and the *masochism of renunciation*, an operation that is auspicious for growth; and that of a solution that may be described as perverse (sado-masochism) in which the sexualizations of hate prevail shamelessly (Janin, 2007) over the work of desexualization. Freud (1919a) studies this deviation in "A Child is Being Beaten." He sees how hate can be sexualized instead of being used to promote desexualized and foundational identifications. Following which he recognizes the traumatic regressivity of the drive and then the necessity for an agency to oppose this trend, the superego. Freud's approach to the operation of après-coup thus involves two intersecting conceptions: one, restrictive, the other, extensive.

His restrictive conception reserves the term après-coup for productions with precise qualities, in fact for the symptoms of transference neuroses with the use of a substitute. It was only in 1925 that Freud made explicit reference to the two aspects, positive and negative, of every neurotic symptom, the substitute concealing the negative aspect. Since the discovery of traumatic neuroses he had been faced with clinical pictures in which the negative aspect was no longer concealed and had become manifest. The act of forgetting is paradoxical due to the apparent absence of a substitute. In fact the *hole* of memory serves as a substitute fulfilling the function of anti-cathecting the hole of mentalization. Freud enlarged his conception to include psychopathology as a whole as soon as he thought that all the clinical pictures could be conceived from the point of view of reminiscence (Freud, 1937b).

The term *après-coup* thus initially concerned substitutive expressions for a latent content at the level of which there is a conflict between an unconscious wish and the hypercathexis of the preconscious content. The result of the conflict is then a compromise borne by the substitutive material. This restrictive conception was developed by Freud between 1895 and 1900, a period during which the term *après-coup* appears most frequently. Four of the six instances belong to this period. And they all concern psychopathology.

Freud thus gives us an idea of the operation of après-coup in stages. His process of theorization reflects this operation. At the end of his work, his conception includes the whole field of psychopathology. The operation of après-coup was no longer reserved for either of the three great nosographical categories (1924b) as he had grouped them in 1923, the neuro-psychoses of defence (1894, 1896), the narcissistic psychoneuroses (1914) and the psychoses (1924c). In his *Overview of the Transference Neuroses* (1987), each of them is already considered as a deferred effect, but of phylogenesis. In *Thalassa*, Ferenczi (1924) extends this proposition to sexual life.

The importance attributed by Freud (1918) in *From the History of an Infantile Neurosis*, but above all in "A Case of Paranoia Running Counter to the Psychoanalytic Theory of the Disease" (Freud, 1915b), already heralded a broader conception subsuming the restricted view pertaining to content. His attention was taken up with the conflict concerning psychic work itself, which could henceforth be conceived as an operation independent of any content.

It is worth recalling that the anecdote provided in *The Interpretation of Dreams* had already broadened the use and the conception of the phenomenon of après-coup to thought regardless of the type of mental functioning. It often appears, however, in partial or distorted forms. Freud's remark that human thought is, in reality, radically foreign to conventional wisdom is not unrelated to the operation of après-coup. While the accomplished result of the latter makes us aware of feelings of continuity, successiveness, causality and rationality, the slightest vicissitude reveals experiences of timelessness, discontinuity, repetition and irrationality, and allows us to infer and sense the fractures, oddities, losses and other amputations and losses of reality.

This gives me the opportunity of pointing out that the phenomenon of après-coup appears both in accomplished as well as in partial and distorted forms. It can be elaborative, regressive, repetitive and even defective. It is involved in all semiologies and is not specific to any of them. Its operation is realized in stages. The biphasic model is thus schematic and phenomenological. The operation of après-coup is, in fact, much more serial, gradual, fractal and random with respect to its temporal course and its unpredictable result. It includes leaps and heterogeneities, which makes it difficult to think about it in terms of a model.

Concretely, psychoanalysis is dealing an umpteenth time with transference actualization. The operation of après-coup, its vicissitudes and its stumbling blocks, unfold during it as much through incidental thoughts, associative material and dreams as through the transference. It is the model of reference of analytic listening.

The extensive conception considers that every psychic production, whatever it may be, is the result of such an operation in which the fundamental universal trends, denoted by the terms *death drive* and *Eros*, are involved – the reductive tendency of the death drive and the extensive tendency of Eros towards the infinite. The primordial conflict of ambivalence thus lies between this double extinctive regressivity and a principle of renunciation that opposes, from the beginning of life, the first by means of restraint that can be exercised by all *measures of protection* and defence. This conflict requires and explains the organization of psychic work in two stages, as well as its bivalence.

Freud thus allows us to envisage the operation of après-coup as being inherent to his definition of thought described as bivalent and bidirectional, regressive and progressive, extending well beyond its contents and representations. Thought also integrates affects and feelings, the qualitative indications of the psychic work accomplished; but also impressions, sensual sensations of internal origin, which are the vicissitudes through physical conversion of the libidinal production realized by the underlying psychic work. The operation of après-coup becomes the model for psychic functioning, a model that can unfold in a more or less ideal way but also produce all the semiologies.

The place Freud gives to the dynamic of this operation of après-coup is thus fundamental, irrespective of the period in which he discusses it. He considers it as a central quality of psychic functioning and sees the diphasism of human sexuality (Freud, 1925b, p. 37) as its principal domain of impact and even as proof of it. He thus regards it as a universal characteristic of all mental life. This generic aspect certainly contributed to his renunciation of the term in general. But it was probably the lack of certainty that henceforth hung over its realization that led him to suspend this usage of a term that contains in itself the denial of the imperceptible regressive work of the interval period and of the threats and defections realized. All the terms employed – in German, in French and in English – give a very imperfect account of the complexity of the operation of après-coup. They all insist on one aspect at the expense of others.

We understand better now the dynamic that consisted in initially attributing the term *après-coup* with a conceptual value represented by a noun inscribed in the pantheon of the monosemic concepts of the corpus of metapsychology. It was a matter of opposing the extinctive trend of the regressive economies, a concept affirming a psychically positive outcome.

In the discontinuous dynamic of après-coup there is a predominant conflict between taking this traumatic regressivity into consideration and rejecting it. The productive mission of this operation can be deduced from the multiple reeditions of the transference, from the conviction of paranoiacs, from the disseminated and sterile generativity of hypomanic patients, from hysterical symptoms and dream narratives, of course, and from session associativity via incidental thoughts. The effectiveness of the teleological imperative is, in fact, threatened and is very often reduced to a few substitutes like repetition, generativity, insistence, saturation, persuasion, pleading, cursing, etc.

The need to underline the significance of the dynamic of après-coup is certainly at the basis of this book, just as it is active in the contributions of our predecessors, whether those of Freud and Lacan, those on biphasism and diachrony of Michel Fain, those on temporality of André Green, as well as the more targeted studies of Claude Le Guen, Jean Cournut, Michel Neyraut and Ignês Sodré in the *Revue française de psychanalyse*, those of Haydée Faimberg and Ignês Sodré in the *International Journal of Psychoanalysis*, or the more recent ones of Rosine Perelberg and Jean-Luc Donnet.

In sum, the operation of après-coup is the model of reference for thought-processes, whatever the circumstances, day or night. Freud (1925b) recognized the evidence for this in the diphasism of human sexuality (p. 37). He treats it as a universal characteristic of mental life, determined by a *physiological factor* that can be expressed only by means of historicity. This generic aspect was one of the reasons why he ceased to use this term, especially as uncertainty hung over the realization of the operation itself, since the word contains the denial of the threats and defections related to it. Once it had been established in the theory, the imperative governing the operation of après-coup proved fragile and uncertain. By creating initially a noun containing the affirmation of a future, Freud was opposing negativizing regressivity. Subsequently, he was obliged to recognize it, as well as the uncertain nature of the agency that was supposed to guarantee the psychic work required, namely, the superego.

Other instances of the operation of après-coup

Lacan: As the deferred effect of Freud

Extracting the metapsychological conceptions from Lacan's work is a real challenge owing to his art of *disconcerting* his reader by his capacity for upholding two incompatible forms of logic at the same time. Through his style, first of all, of "half-saying" (*mi-dire*), he wants to make the reader feel that the truth is what knowledge is lacking, that all discourse is coupled with an attempted hallucinatory wish-fulfilment and that it is an operation of après-coup determined historically and at the level of the drives by the interplay of signifiers. For him, the latter are the representatives of the drives, a conception that distances him radically both from linguists and from Freud for whom the share of words functioning as a drive representative is minimal (Freud, 1923). In psychoanalysis, words are not representatives of the drive, but above all an exterior whose nature is at odds with that of the drives.

Lacan's "half-saying" has the function of transmitting the message that the jubilatory assumption of the ego in the One of a self-image is simply a lure into which the divided subject of the unconscious falls. He writes, in so many words, that the subject does not come into being because of its first division. This means that a signifier represents a subject only for another signifier that is originally repressed (Lacan, 1967) and that the subject can only be constructed due to the fact that the unconscious is structured like a language (Lacan, 1972).

The session discourse is constituted by its *ambiguities*. Because it is at once a scene narrative and a scene of the narrative, it is polysemic and has a double meaning, the locus of a transference that makes any conception of human relations in terms of intersubjectivity alone erroneous. These lures are realizations of an infantile longing to be an ideal ego, a Whole, His Majesty the Baby, the Phallus of another erected as Other. This identification with the totemized penis has a function: classically, with Priapus, that of being apotropaic; then with the Devil, a function of warding off evil; for psychoanalysis, one of supporting a denial of castration; and for a subject, that of excluding any affect of lack.

His style is thus supposed to reflect the division of the subject and preserve the subject from the mirage of being One. With it, Lacan makes himself the herald/hero of the Freudian message.

By employing this disconcerting style and resorting to hermetism, Lacan claims that he avoids being caught up in his own lures, contrary to his interlocutors whose *absurdity,* that is to say, castration, he exhibits. Lacan's derision is in full swing.

In so doing, he states truths about the operation of après-coup that he embodies. The operation of après-coup has to "commence over and over again" (Lacan, 1972) "all discourse is always forced to return again to the same place, as *nachträglich*, après coup." By means of this ruse, he tries to take possession of the operation of après-coup himself.

To understand the impact of his style, it is necessary to add to his *half-saying* his barbed sarcasm with which he enacts beyond the divided subject, the split subject.

The dilemma of the subject is thus located between neurotic entanglement through which he gets tied up in knots in imaginary substitutes, while taking account silently of the existence of castration to which he is subject owing to his complex, and a mode of functioning involving denial, which is apparently liberating but based on feet of clay, with the risk of a colossal breakdown due to the incapacity to keep up such a denial completely. His solution for escaping this dilemma is a continual *extension* in the name of the ego ideal, thus a refusal of all regression, even formal. The ideal ego proposes itself on the horizon of the ego ideal, attaching the latter to narcissism.

This was the paradox in which Lacan's conception would be caught. He extracted better than anyone else all the Freudian findings concerning the phenomenon of après-coup and, in the same flourish, he stigmatized it with the interplay of the signifiers alone, thereby escaping its economic implications with regard to the reality of what is traumatic. He wrote: "*Nachträglickeit* (remember that I was the first to extract it from Freud's texts), or deferred action (*après-coup*) by which trauma becomes involved in symptoms, reveals a temporal structure of a higher order" [than retroaction] (Lacan, 2006/1966, p. 713).

Lacan's famous statement that the unconscious is structured like a language is entirely acceptable when the dynamic unconscious of thing-presentations, the latent preconscious of picture-puzzles (or rebus) and the manifest conscious of word-presentations are linked together in an act of speech functioning as a derivative, a return of the repressed thereby registered, transcribed and concealed. Lacan draws on Freud's article of 1898 in which he follows the verbal concatenation linked to his forgetting of the name Signorelli, leading him to the substitutes Botticelli and Boltraffio. But Lacan does not link this text up with the one of 1901 in which Freud recognizes that his act of forgetting and the formation of the substitutes came about against a background of denial, the denial of the death of a former patient who had committed suicide. This exclusion of one of the two elaborative moments and the priority given to the other one reveals the *mission* that Lacan entrusted himself with and which conferred on him the neo-identity of being *the deferred effect of Freud*, the return of the Freud of 1898.

More than anyone else, Lacan was sensitive to the fact that every theoretical conception tends to dress itself up as knowledge, which, in turn, may pall and get lost if it is not, like every psychic registration, regularly revisited and reinvigorated libidinally. Lacan unearths these negativizing tendencies and makes fun of others who are vehicles and victims of them. He presents himself as the spokesman of the Freudian spirit, assumes the identity of a subject who is able to extract the pith and marrow of Freud's thought, enhance the power of truth of Freudian notions that have been reduced to vile knowledge or that have fallen into oblivion, while escaping their laws. It is Lacan's sarcasm that makes it necessary to think about the relations between his theoretical elaborations and denial.

He rips to pieces part of Freudian *knowledge* in the name of revealing and restoring its power of truth, the sexual part of all discourse. He displays fidelity to Freudian terminology, reads Freud in the original and upholds the German word against all translations/betrayals/reductions of the Freudian spirit. At the same time, he personalizes as he pleases the usage of German terms. Thus, he only uses *nachträglich* and makes a noun out of it, *le "nachträglich"* (see also Lacan, 2006, p. 713) in place of *Nachträglichkeit*.

Let us take just one citation, among many others. It contains in itself everything that I have just been saying. It is taken from a paper given in 1967 in Lyon, shortly after the publication by Laplanche and Pontalis (1973/1967) of their book *The Language of Psychoanalysis*: He writes:

> I want to end with living things, as they say. So here is a little example. "If I'd known," said one of my patients, "I'd have wet the bed more than twice a week." I'll spare you what led up to him coming out with that. It came after a whole series of considerations about various privations and after he had cleared some of the debts he felt he was burdened with. He felt quite at ease and rather oddly regretted the fact that he had not done so earlier. So, you see, one thing in particular strikes me: the psychoanalyst does not realize the decisive position he holds by articulating *"nachträglich"*, as Freud puts it, a deferred action that establishes the truth of what came earlier. As he doesn't really know what he is doing in doing that. "Retroactively" [*après-coup*], you can find in the first pages of a certain *Vocabulaire* that came out not so long ago. I needn't tell you that no one would ever have included this "deferred action" in a Freudian vocabulary if I hadn't brought it out in my teaching. No one before me had ever noticed the importance of this *"nachträglich"*, even though it is there on every page of Freud. And yet it is very important to detach the 'retroactively' in this case. No psychoanalyst had thought of this, I mean ever written this, even though it is directly in line with what he does as a psychoanalyst. When someone tells us "God in heaven, why did I not wet my bed more than twice a week", if you know how to listen, it means that the fact of only wetting the bed twice a week has to be taken into consideration, and we have to take into account that figure 2 is introduced in correlation with the enuretic symptom.
>
> (Lacan, 2005, pp. 46–47)

His *return to Freud* also claims, through his voice, to be a *return of Freud,* whom he refers to as the "master." He presents himself as a return of the repressed, or a return of the outside, thus of what is denied, for the whole analytic community. With regard to Freud as the big Other, he becomes the fertilizing deferred effect, the Word fertilizing the analytic community.

He makes this mission his destiny by attributing himself with the unconscious identity of being *the deferred effect of Freud*. As a signifier for another signifier, the five letters of Lacan's name for the five letters of Freud's name, he can make a return to Freud, according to the model of the dream. In the latter, a verbal thought put into latency makes a return to the sources of the drives along a backward path. Formal regression makes it pass over from verbal thought to a pictogram/rebus, then to an image/figure capable of entering into contact with memories of the infantile past and through these with the sources of the drives. These are the transformed into drive thing-presentations and promoted along the progressive path as images capable of giving a secondarized narrative that can be presented to consciousness, and even to other conscious minds via the enunciation of a narrative. This is the Freudian metaphor of the architect and of the promoter in the production of this overdetermined phenomenon of après-coup that is the dream, in which latent thoughts, daytime residues, memories of infantile amnesia, the drive impulses of the id and an imperative to realize the discontinuous processuality described above are all involved.

This return to Freud, as an attractive drive source, requires the regression of the word into picture-puzzles organized according to a logic of encoding.

But the *return of the drives* couples this logic with the representative function of the drive impulses, which are outside language. Hallucinatory wish-fulfilment results from this double identity of code and impulse outside language. All speech is marked by this heterogeneity. The signifier alone, extended to the various forms of psychic representation, cannot account for it. The code is opposed by extinction, registration by erasure and castration.

By enhancing the term *nachträglich*, Lacan denounced the facelift that psychoanalysis underwent in the postwar years, marked as it was during this period by a psychologizing geneticism, by a developmental, linear, continuous and progressive theory of temporality, thus by an eviction of the topographical point of view in favour of a genetic point of view, of an apology of strengthening the ego, of the "liberation of the ego" as the aim of the treatment obtained by a "dissolution" of the transference, all expressions that, at the very least, are caught in double meanings centred on an act of murder of psychoanalysis itself.

It was the spirit of psychoanalysis that was renewed. Lacan obliged psychoanalysts to read Freud's text again attentively, to return to the sources of Freud's inspiration, albeit without sharing his mission. If French psychoanalysis has developed so much over the last quarter of a century, it owes this to a large extent to the prodding of Lacan and to the work that analysts carried out at his instigation. Lacan opened analysis up again, asserting that "its foundations must be laid open to criticism, without which it will degenerate into effects of collective subornation" (Lacan, 2006, p. 300). He sought to ensure that contact with the unconscious remained open, having understood that all knowledge about the unconscious amounts to *closing it again*.

It was in the name of *what is said* during the session that he insisted on recalling Freud's discovery in the *Studies on Hysteria* of the distinction between cathartic speech and speech inducing an effect of meaning in which the Symbolic is expressed. Lacan contrasted the risk of confusing the chatter of becoming conscious by means of infinite substitution and awareness including a judgement of meaning, an interpretant in waiting.

Lacan noticed this facelift in the reduction of the notion of après-coup to its form as a simple time adverb and to the linear determination between two events. This flattening is, in fact, itself a return of the work of another mentor, Charcot, a return of the theory of trauma/shock and of the consequent hysterical symptom.

Freud had anticipated this reorientation of his metapsychology by French authors towards a psychoanalysis French-style.

He himself had drawn on the conceptions of Charcot. But he developed them and reorganized the aetiological foundations to the point of proposing quite a different conception of the hysterical phenomenon. In particular, he enriched the temporal and causal effects of the operation of après-coup with his theory of the work of latency as it takes place during sleep, which governs the production of dreams.

Drawing on the role of the operation of après-coup in the genesis of hysterical symptoms, Lacan sought to associate psychoanalysis with Charcot and the French psychiatric tradition. He replaced Charcot's terms and those of Freud with expressions giving priority, as Charcot did, to temporal logic alone. Charcot had described the genesis of symptoms in three stages. Lacan rebaptized them as *the instant of the glance, the time for comprehending and the moment of concluding* (Lacan, 1945, p. 167). Here we find again the association between what is traumatic and *things seen,* coinciding with the importance accorded by Freud to the perception of the difference between the sexes. The *time for comprehending* replaces Freud's period of latency, but pulls the operation of après-coup towards the secondary process. The *moment of concluding* corresponds to the productions of symptoms, of dreams, of all discourse.

Lacan reminds us of the theory of symptoms as reminiscence, as deferred effects containing various memories, and, in particular, processual memory, as involved in the accomplishment of the operation of après-coup: "The nature of the construction of symptoms," he writes, "is to be deferred (*nachträglich*)" (Lacan, 1956, p. 324). The operation of après-coup is presented as a *restructuring* of past events, a *resubjectivization* of an unconscious past that is transcribed, in fact reactualized, in a formation of the unconscious that conceals repressed drive activity and the unconscious work realized. By using the term *le nachträglich,* Lacan was re-presenting the whole theory of dreams and symptoms, the whole period of Freud between 1895 and 1902. To do this, he of course revisited the clinical cases of Freud, in particular Dora, the Wolf Man and the texts on paranoia.

With his personal language, he points out, as I have already said, that "*Nachträglickeit* ... or deferred action (*après-coup*) by which trauma becomes involved in symptoms, reveals a temporal structure of a higher order" [than retroaction] (Lacan, 2006, p. 713). Referring to the two stages and the latency period, he writes: "The after was kept waiting [*faisait antichambre*] so that the before could assume its own place [*pût prendre rang*]" (Lacan, 1945, p. 197). But he does not follow the significance of the latency period and of the regressive work with regard to the traumatic economy. He insists on only one aspect, the overdetermination involved in the verbal chain "by the deferred action [après-coup] of its sequence" (Lacan, 1958, p. 446). Here, at the heart of Lacanian causality, we find that primacy is accorded to progressive temporality.

Although I have already emphasized the decisive involvement of latent thought, of repressed memories, of unconscious drive impulses and of the negative attraction of drive regressivity, Lacan obliges us to revisit a determination on which Freud had placed particular emphasis, namely, that linked to the hypercathexis carried by the language of free associations and of the analyst's interpretations. From the outset psychoanalytic treatment was a talking cure through words. A hypercathexis is sustained by the word-presentations enunciated. It is constrained by the fundamental rule. The processual imperative is transmitted by word-presentations. Authority and post-Oedipal tenderness are sustained by the voice. In this way, starting from the overdetermination of language involved in the operation of après-coup, Lacan reintroduced the most specific particularities of psychoanalysis, its theory of causality and its theory of temporality. But he left to one side the difference of nature between the drives and language.

The theory of causality is inherent to the notion of the repressed. It includes an attraction of the repressed that captures certain present thoughts. These will then be infiltrated by drive impulses and transformed into ideational representatives. Manifest productions are compromises between these two movements, between a negative attraction seeking to eliminate every registration for the benefit of an extinction of the economy and a processual imperative supporting restraint and a production of registrations. This imperative is sustained by the principle of encoding of language and by that of renunciation. This is where the full complexity of the operation of après-coup can be seen because what is forgotten and buried has a disorganizing potential, while at the same time links are maintained with a potential for becoming conscious through language and finally with a new awareness signifying the establishment of a completed topography. These various stages are governed by the principle of renunciation.

At the heart of causality we find the temporal dynamic already noticed by Charcot, to which Freud subsequently gave much more complexity, first of all by breaking its linearity and successivity. By calling the period of incubation and elaboration a period of latency, by emphasizing, therefore, the unconscious regressive mental work that takes place during it, Freud introduced *timelessness* into thinking. But, in addition, he inverted the course of time.

His conception took on greater complexity still when he suggested that the recent scene I has a retroactive effect on the earlier Scene II, such that the latter becomes involved in the symptom. By an effect of "symbolic" resonance (Freud, 1924c, p. 187), the recent scene reactivates the earlier one, which itself is searching for a recent scene. This, in turn, allows for a modification of the earlier scene from an economic point of view. It is important, therefore, to be just as attentive to the fact that the earlier scene II seeks, and even induces and creates the existence of a recent scene I in order to successfully bring this elaboration in suspense to completion. The aspect of constructive transposition of the transference can be recognized here. The theory of dreams enacts a cooptation of a present towards a past; this is necessary so that the past can be elaborated and not only be immobilized and repeated. If we coordinate this cooptation of a present towards the past and the transposition of the past on to the present, we find ourselves back at the heart of animism and faced with a machine for creating metaphors.

This bidirectional work realized during the period of latency and culminating in the production of a new manifest material, that of the symptomatic stage 2, brings about a modification of the material of Stage 1, in fact of the traumatic regressive economy of scene II. This specific psychic work concerns drive regressivity, an economy described as beyond the pleasure principle that dominates the scene II of the *shock*. This work of economic mutation is carried out in two stages, thanks to the two scenes that make up stage 1. The earliest scene proves to be most subject to the traumatic economy of drive regressivity. This economy, which is also present in the recent scene, albeit in an attenuated way in the form of the infantile, unites the two scenes. The second scene is, in fact, linked much more strongly to the elaborative imperative and is dominated by the pleasure principle. This is what permits the realization of this retroactive work on the material of the earliest scene whose regressive economy is described as beyond the pleasure principle. The mutation of this economy takes places thanks to the contribution of a hypercathexis linking the earliest scene, through the recent scene, to the imperative of registration. This contribution of a libidinal hypercathexis occurs with the aid of the material of the second, most recent scene. This hypercathexis involves a specific form of libido characteristic of the imperative of renunciation and registration, thus a processual libido. This difference of economic quality explains the fact that the recent memory gives rise to quite easy remembering, whereas the earliest memory is actualized as reminiscence. There is no symmetry between the two scenes. Freud noticed that they appear during therapeutic work on the backward, regressive path, inverted in relation to the chronology of stages 1 and 2. I have already said that scene I, the most recent, is the one that gives rise first to a memory; scene II, the earlier one, is recalled only secondarily. This is explained by the degrees and gradients of intensity characteristic of each of the scenes, of the regressive attraction by the pathogenic nucleus. These developments make it possible to recognize the operative force in II – the earliest scene – of a yearning for elaborative mutation. There exists, therefore, at the level of II, an expectation, or a search for a scene I, with the aim of realizing this economic elaboration, which can only be accomplished if such a scene I is found/created. Winnicott's found/created has its place within this dynamic of the operation of après-coup. The movements of transposition and cooptation articulate scenes I and II and produce the material of stage 2, the stage of symptomatization and actualization in the transference neurosis.

Lacan was sensitive to all these parameters. He describes the psychic causality of the operation of après-coup as "circular and nonreciprocal," clearly perceiving the dissymmetry that exists between scene II and scene I, just as it exists in the session between the two protagonists. He takes over from Freud the presence of this operation at the level of the session discourse. He anchors himself from the outset to associative speech, whereas Freud's starting-point was hysterical symptoms and physical conversion. This speech is inhabited by the operation of après-coup constitutive of the transference. But Freud was much closer to a conception of analysis consisting of a series of deferred effects (the

Wolf Man) in which the conflictual aspects of the transferences on to the body, on to language, on to the other and on to the object are combined at the very heart of the act of speaking.

Lacan preferred to extend the language code structure to all the levels of the mind. This aspect contains an element of truth. Processuality is involved in the three constitutive steps of the drive. Language is its principal mediator as a support for the principles of encoding and renunciation. A similarity exists between what may be called processuality, that is, the operations of the work carried out by psychic processes under the aegis of the stimulus barrier, censorship and the superego, and Lacan's symbolic order (Lacan, 1975). Freud thought that prototypes of the id existed, suggesting that the latter was also concerned with very specific processes.

There is no better way of approaching psychic functioning than by means of spoken language, and psychoanalysis is a therapy that uses speech to reach all the levels of processuality. These knots of processuality are not language. Moreover, Lacan speaks of structure and says: "structured like a language." But all unconscious processes involve a principle of encoding whose most elaborate expression is language. This helps us to understand their resistance to sexualization. Word-presentations do not originate in a desexualization of the drives, and therefore have no propensity for becoming resexualized. The processual as an agent of reduction, of desexualization and of mourning, cannot have its origin in a reversible desexualization. It cannot be inverted by resexualization. But it can be excluded, eliminated and reversed by murder. This murder corresponds to the *murder of the father* of the Oedipus complex. Lacan regards the Oedipus complex, in keeping with his conception of the signifier, as an articulation of the signifiers father/mother/infant. In order to introduce irreversibility, he was obliged to introduce a fourth element at the heart of this fluctuating ternary structure, namely, death. "And without going into the fruitful exercises of modern game theory, much less into the highly suggestive formalizations of set theory, the analyst will find sufficient material upon which to base his practice by simply learning to correctly count to four (that is, to integrate the function of death into the ternary Oedipal relationship)" (Lacan, 1955, pp. 299–300). In other words, the renunciation that can be depicted by the position of the deceased.

Lacan thus proposes a structural topology of the subject in which we can recognize a depiction of the operation of après-coup, the image of the torus (*tore*). The session discourse becomes the culmination of a series of *turns of saying* (*tours de dire*) made possible by the presence in this torus of a cut, a rift, the division of the subject. These *turns of saying* allow this torus to become a Moebius strip, that is to say, for Lacan, a message that can be stated.

The *symbolic* subject is depicted by such a *torus* and by such *turns of saying*. On the other hand, when the symbolic is absent, the *hole* at the centre of the torus sucks the subject in, in particular parts of the symbolic. Lacan provides us with *a topology of our practice of saying,* the operation of après-coup and its stumbling blocks being depicted by contortions, reversals and inversions of these *turns of saying*.

These late propositions amplify his earlier optical definition of speech, as a message that comes back to the subject in an inverted form. "In language," he writes, "our message comes to us from the Other, in an inverted form" (Lacan, 2006, pp. 3–4). The notions of toruses, loops and knots constitute a formal representation of the operation of après-coup, and in this topology the term *après-coup* becomes a "knot whose trajectory closes on the basis of its inverted redoubling" (ibid., p. 6). This imagery unquestionably echoes the dynamic conception of Freud's après-coup, in other words, the pairs continuity/discontinuity, regression/progression.

The role of the *hole of the torus*, when there is a failure of the symbolic and of regression to the imaginary, has the significance of *return* within Lacan's theorization. He himself conceptualizes it in terms of primal repression. What appears most excluded from his theory of the signifier, the role of the traumatic and the economic function of the operation of après-coup, make their return here. He places this *hole* at the beginning. In 1967, instead of the famous line, "In the beginning was the Deed" (Freud, 1912–1913, p. 161), Lacan states: "In the beginning was the 'hole.'" Freud had taken up Goethe's attempt to translate, via Faust, the first verse of St. John's Gospel: "In the beginning was the Word" (in fact, we might say, "In the beginning was 'speech'"). Lacan both converges with and separates from Freud here, who opens the psychic towards the somatic by means of a *regression to the inorganic state,* but recognizes the equally primal presence of an imperative of economic mutation of somatic sexual excitation into psychic sexual excitation thanks to a foundational act of the mind linked to language. The regressive end wall or limit of the somatic body and the risk of the latter becoming disorganized, as well as the risk of the somatic being misused, are articulated by Freud at the level of erotogenic primary masochism, but this aspect is excluded from Lacan's conception. Moral pain as the basis of all the other affects is not present in his theorization. The body does not articulate the soma, the psychic signifier and the object.

In keeping with his conception of the signifier, Lacan asserts that *there is no sexual relationship* insofar as jouissance cannot be registered at the level of language. Jouissance is a barrier "against the advent of the sexual relationship in the discourse," he writes (Lacan, 1993, p. 14). Following this logic, he writes, "ultimately language only connotes the impossibility of symbolizing the sexual relationship for the beings who inhabit it" (ibid.). In affirming this, Lacan reintroduces the heterogeneity between the signifier conveying processuality and the signifier as a drive representative. It is not possible to make love with words. Words are involved only in foreplay activities. This double meaning of language is reminiscent of the impossibility of accomplishing definitively a denial of castration and of extinctive regressivity. If this were the case, we would be faced with the inanity of the operation of après-coup, which would amount to a real pact, not with the signifier Devil but with its beyond, the *hole.* Such a pact would reverse the signifier as Word into a state of unbeing.

Kleinian and post-Kleinian authors

Melanie Klein was interested very early on in psychotic and non-neurotic patients suffering from acute anxiety, for whom anti-traumatic solutions and narcissistic splitting or fragmentation were the sole means of defence. The emerging topography is *fragmented* and primary repression weakened, or even partly destroyed or incomplete. The clinical picture is dominated by logics of intra-narcissistic conflict, which are transformed into struggles and battles in an external world that is itself split into *good* and *bad* objects depending on their defensive value. The contents are those of destruction, persecution and the danger of paranoia. They conceal feelings of annihilation and call for solutions of reparation. The fear of being destroyed is the main sensation in response to this state of anxiety.

These contributions originated at the crossroads of fright and distress relived during the session in the form of reminiscence. The Kleinian postulate affirms that this is the basic position of every baby. Klein's interpretations show that she considers that even with a young child the contents that explain his anxiety are already there. While for André Green the archaic is constructed after the event (Green, 1982), for Klein it is already there. Both conceptions are interrelated when one considers that what is already there is a potential that is in search of contents that make it possible retroactively to transform the potential into realization.

Seen from the angle of Freud's work, this postulate prioritizes the situation in which distress is unable to oppose what created it and attempts to conceal it, a conflict that is expressed for Freud by fright, for post-Kleinians by anxiety of fragmentation, a fear of breakdown, nameless dread, or by the idea that a breakdown or experience of primitive agony has already occurred. The Kleinian postulate argues that the operations capable of establishing a primary masochistic restraint do not exist as potential baggage in the baby (Diatkine, 2008). These operations must therefore be involved in a battle or come from the outside. They are thus provided from the outside by a helping person with reparative capacities. Freud's "fellow human being" (*Nebenmensch*), the support of identification, becomes a repairer. These operations can, for example, be carried out by a thought-process of the mother, maternal reverie (Bion, 1967). What dominates here, then, is the model of substitution based on feeding or that of commensalism (Bion, 1962) at the expense of the model of anaclisis that initiates the process of identification.

The transformation of primitive anxiety through the elaboration of unconscious material, elaboration that includes regressive work on the model of the dream-work, is not part of Kleinian theory, which gives priority to supporting development, growth and progressive generativity. It is a matter of struggling, thanks to such generativity, against a basic traumatic experience that is irreducible because it is linked to the struggle between the battalions whose commander in chiefs are called Thanatos and Eros.

This primary struggle is at the centre of Klein's theory in the form of a symmetrical, direct and noisy conflict between the life drives and death drives. Admittedly, her successors hold slightly different positions concerning this primordial conflict. As I have already pointed out, they give priority to the idea that this distress opens out on to a conflict in which primary destructivity is said to be involved. Important studies on primary destructivity emerged from this.

We can consider that these authors are all referring more or less to a clinical situation close to that of the elementary traumatic neurosis as described by Freud from 1917 onwards in connection with extreme and external situations of war (Freud, 1919b), then in 1920 (Freud, 1920) as a consequence of a disorganizing endogenous negative attraction stemming from a drive quality called beyond the pleasure principle, the tendency to return to an earlier state of things, even to the inanimate state. In traumatic neurosis, the dynamic in two stages of the operation of après-coup is reduced to a repetitive dynamic giving the impression of an inefficient and exhausting struggle involving *shocks in quick succession.* But Freud states that such a neurosis is reserved not only for an external context and that ordinary repression is the common consequence: "After all, we have a perfect right to describe repression, which lies at the basis of every neurosis, as a reaction to a trauma, as an elementary traumatic neurosis" (1919b, p. 210).

This crossroads of distress, when it is devoid of alarm signal anxiety and thus of hate appealing to the subject's psychic means of preservative restraint, means that are supported by identification with the psychic processes of the people around him, is the very locus of automatic anxiety (Freud, 1926), which Freud described as anxiety constructed afresh (1933a, p. 94). Related to it are the actual neuroses (1916–17), traumatic neuroses (1919b) and all sorts of disorganizations, breakdowns and agonies. Freud's terms *inorganic* and *inanimate,* which are not to be confused with death, resonate with these vicissitudes as well as with somatic illnesses, the stages of disorganization-reorganization and regression-fixation discussed by Marty (1979; 1980).

Unlike Klein, Winnicott and Bion follow closely on the heels of a much older postulate belonging to the English philosophical tradition, according to which thought develops against a background of sensory experience, which is not an acquisition of the subject's processual history but rather a basic fact, namely, the category of preconceptions from which thought develops. There is a very clear difference here with Freud, who thought that this primary hysteria of sensuality has a history, that of the identifications governing its establishment.

These authors have a theory of anxiety that differs from Freud's for whom the primary state of anxiety reflects unconscious contents whose regressive economy is potentially disorganizing. For Freud, such anxiety can be diminished and resolved by the specific contribution of interpretation. In fact, interpretation also operates in two stages. It contributes verbal material that has the value of an *attenuated shock,* of a moderated scene I on the basis of which a formal regression and a modification of the regressive economy specific to the repressed scenes, the scenes II, can unfold. In so doing, interpretation is destined initially to be forgotten. It thereby facilitates the production of regressive registrations and its rediscovery will occur only at a later stage in a new form that will be felt and considered by the subject as his own creation. Its efficacy depends, therefore on the analyst renouncing gratification as its author.

For Winnicott and Bion, and for post-Kleinians, interpretation must oppose the power of deterioration that the primordial conflict contains and support the growth of the mind, its generativity. This priority accorded to *accomplishment* is conducive to the role of the operation of après-coup of producing regenerated cathexes. And due to the importance accorded to the generative, productive and progressive mission of the operation of après-coup, attention is turned towards what opposes it, for them, anti-narcissistic forms of destructivity. French psychoanalysts prefer to emphasize another moment of the operation of après-coup, namely, the counter-cathecting construction and function of the regressive path.

These differences of approach evoke a Shakespearian truth: "What's in a name? That which we call a rose by any other name would smell as sweet" (*Romeo and Juliet*, II, ii, 1–2).

We can recognize the Squiggle technique (Winnicott, 1971) as a means for supporting such productivity. Winnicott uses these shared squiggles to approach the history of his little patients and, like Klein (1961), to take account of the links of overdetermination. Likewise, when Bion envisages the optimal conditions of psychic growth, of this *Language of Achievement* (Bion, 1970, p. 125) of the session, he includes the analyst's *experience,* the state of patience and security, the regressive point "O" (ibid., p. 31) "without memory, desire or understanding" (ibid., p. 129). He takes up the words of John Keats who considered that the necessary quality for the training of a *Man of Achievement* was "Negative capability, that is, when a man is capable of being in uncertainties, mysteries, doubts, without any irritable reaching after fact and reason" (ibid., p. 125).

Bion says nothing about the analysand's formal regression, but he emphasizes the value of the analyst's formal regression. For him, this regression is characterized by a negativity of all content in the sense of being latent. It is a question of an absolute ideal, without content, apothatic (Pasche, 1988), close to the *oceanic feeling,* but not extinctive, thus without anxiety. It is a response to the patient's distress of breakdown and to his regression to dependence. This session tuning, this *analytic après-coup* can be understood as a search for the processual platform conducive to the *reduction* of drive regressivity, a search for libidinal sympathetic excitation that requires congruent tuning between the stimulus barrier and psychic processes in order to establish restraint and to open it to a destiny of registration leading to libidinal object-cathexes. The process of sympathetic excitation realizes the mutation of the extinctive regressive economy into an economy of cathexis.

All these authors, both English and French, share a common interest in the modalities of breakdown, both psychic and somatic, which all express a failure of the processes of *reducing* drive regressivity (the *taming* of the drive), a stumbling block in the process of libidinal sympathetic excitation and a lack of congruence in the pair stimulus barrier/ psychic process of restraint, thus a failure of the masochism of renunciation. These are aspects that Freud discussed in 1924, admittedly without developing them, in "The Economic Problem of Masochism" (Freud, 1924b). The outlines of a masochism of restraint are sketched, which, through its conversion in the body, becomes erotogenic masochism. The foundations of sensuality were thus established.

Kleinian theories do not exploit the solutions proposed by Freud concerning the primary masochistic nucleus, with its value of being the result of two poles, namely, extinctive drive regressivity and the imperative of renunciation opposing the regressive attraction of the first.

In "The economic problem of masochism" Freud outlined a theorization of this moment of psychic work that ensures this mutative and generative function. He calls it libidinal sympathetic excitation. It is supposed to promote libidinal cathexes towards the body, objects and language. Kleinian theories approach this relationship to the *pain of masochistic restraint*, to the *lost object* and to the process of sympathetic excitation from the angle of regression to dependence on another person.

The subject of Kleinian theory, when he is grappling with *extinctive regressivity back to the inorganic state,* is deprived of the process that functions as a guardian of life as described by Freud (1924b), and then developed by Benno Rosenberg (1991), except for a struggle that requires the support and participation of another person who serves as a stimulus barrier and as a palliative thought-process.

Primary masochism has been explored with regard to the genesis of psychic life by French authors, both at the Paris Psychoanalytic Society (SPP) and at the Paris Institute of Psychosomatics (IPSO) (Asséo, 2004; Fain and Dejours, 1984; Aisenstein, 2020). It is activated during the operation of après-coup by the restraint that founds the drive source, the economic mutation producing psychic libido (Braunschweig & Fain, 1981), and psychic autoeroticisms.

Kleinian approaches are attentive to the failures of congruence between the potential of the child and the responses and contributions of an environment favouring more or less the emergence of this potential by serving as a palliative rather than as a support.

Attention is then turned to the analytic après-coup, which is involved in the analytic relationship. Bion attributes the processes of transformation to the alpha function and to *maternal reverie,* thus in an *outside* that serves as *an intermediary*. The notions of assistance, helping object, commensality, positive and negative projective identifications find their meanings and coherence here.

Implicit presences

The dynamic of such analytic après-coup including the two protagonists has been the subject of many studies. I am referring in particular to Winnicott's (1953) *transitional space and object,* de M'Uzan's (1978) *chimera,* Green's (1975) *analytic* object, Ogden's (2004) *analytic third.* It is this object that is also the focus of studies on transitionality and play (Roussillon, 1995), on "shared animism" (Janin, 1990) and "working as a double" (Botella & Botella, 2005). The operation of après-coup unfolds in each of the protagonists and also has effects on both protagonists through a distribution involving the delegation of its functional poles.

Referring to this configuration of the analytic après-coup, Donnet (2006) insists on the random nature of the effectuation of the operation of après-coup. This aspect is in conflict with the determinism that hangs over this operation, leading the subject to find/create the perceptions this effectuation needs in order to be realized.

Haydée Faimberg has made considerable efforts to forge pertinent links between French and Anglo-Saxon theories around the concept of après-coup. She invites analysts to be particularly attentive to how the patient has heard the analyst's interpretation. She advocates *listening to listening* (Faimberg, 2005a) and has made a method of it. It involves the analyst listening to the way in which the patient himself listens to the analyst's interventions. She has also made links between the Freudian concept of après-coup and Winnicott's concept of the fear of breakdown.

The emergence of a quarrel between analysts on the two sides of the English Channel as to whether the concept of après-coup represents a psychic operation is based on the tendency to a conflict inherent to the operation of après-coup itself, transposed on to schools, and even on to geography and history.

The difference of economic tension that the operation of après-coup has the task of reducing and transforming tends to be actualized in polemics between schools. While it is the process of latency for the French school, it seems to be absent, or put into latency, in the English school. Some English authors, or authors linked to the English school, have sought to rediscover it under different names in the contributions of English authors. At the level of exchanges between analytic schools, they have described it as the *missing concept* (Sodré, 2005), for example, in the Controversies (Perelberg, 2006), as the missing link in the production of concepts such as the fear of breakdown (Winnicott) or primitive agony. They therefore interpret the official absence of the concept of après-coup with reference to these substitutes.

According to this logic of absence, the concept of après-coup can also be identified with a Shibboleth of recognition and exclusion justifying and promoting anathemas, and explaining quarrels. It is then used to fight what requires it.

I would like to refer here once again to a cruel allegory in one of Victor Hugo's novels, recounted by Freud (1912), that shows the limits of the use of the concept of après-coup. A Scottish king "boasted of an infallible method of recognizing witchcraft: he had the accused woman stewed in boiling water and then tasted the broth. He then judged according to the taste: 'Yes, that was a witch' or 'No, that was not one'" (p. 253).

Let us not forget the citation from Shakespeare made above and the fact that Freud generalized the use of the operation of après-coup in his theorization while ceasing to use the term *Nachträglichkeit* itself.

If the concept of après-coup was chosen as a support for a "tendency to a conflict" (Freud, 1937a, p. 244), it was because it was particularly suited to the task given that this tendency is inherent in the fact that it seeks to articulate a heterogeneity between extinctive drive regressivity and the imperative of renunciation, earning it its characteristics, its biphasism, its bidirectionality and its discontinuity.

Such a tendency to conflict has already been actualized regarding the concept of après-coup in France itself, between the psychoanalytic community of the 1950s and Jacques Lacan. We have looked above at the importance of the enhancement of this concept by Lacan in contrast with the French psychoanalytic community of the period, which had effected a reduction of the metapsychology. The concept of après-coup had been reduced to its simple form as a time adverb and to a summary linear determination between two events.

Fortunately, numerous exchanges (Cournut, 1997; Guillaumin, 1982; Neyraut, 1997; Sodré, 1997), debates (Faimberg, 2005b; Sodré, 2005), and studies (Chervet, 2006a; Donnet, 2006; Faimberg, 2007; Fain, 1981; Fain, 1982) took place and were published, showing that a constructive exchange between psychoanalytic schools is possible and that the incompatibility is an effect of simplification. Furthermore, the term *après-coup* is frequently used by analysts in its current meaning of a temporal displacement and of anterograde reflexivity that does not imply the attractions of the unconscious to the same degree as the psychoanalytic concept.

All psychoanalytic contributions can be considered as deferred effects of what motivated Freud's own work. By following in his footsteps, they develop, refine and give new meaning to his propositions. By tackling certain elements that remained imprisoned in the regressivity at the very heart of his work, they enrich and rectify them. A return to the source is necessary so that a new aspect of reality can be elaborated.

They could be approached in the best of cases along these two paths: the elaboration of a new aspect of what is regressive and a resignification through a new production that represents a theoretical advance.

A typical example of resignification is the presentation by Kohut (1979) of the two analyses of Mr Z. It gives a perfect account of the work of the interval period. The modifications of the drive source and of psychic functioning are unfortunately not explained. They are suggested by the author, who clearly considers the second to be much better than the first.

Likewise, the resolvent path can be illustrated by the work presented in *L'enfant de ça* (Donnet & Green, 1973). The two authors, André Green and Jean-Luc Donnet, rehearse the setting used by Freud and Breuer for Anna O, which was to become the model of supervision. The challenge for each of them is to modify a specific point in this clinical configuration by means of a theoretical elaboration. Donnet extracts from it a deeper exploration of the *method,* in particular, of the enacted transference (*l'Agieren*) and Green draws new aspects of psychic functioning from it, in particular, the "blank" of thought arising from the *negative* and not only from repression.

Of course, many other contributions could be discussed from these two angles.

References

Aisenstein, M. (2020). *Désir, douleur, pensée: masochisme originaire et théorie psychanalytique*. Paris: Presses Universitaires de France.

Asséo R. (2004). Que pouvons-nous apprendre sur l'inconscient à partir de l'expérience avec les patients psychosomatiques? *Bulletin de la Fédération Européenne de Psychanalyse*, 58: 109–120.

Bion, W.R. (1962). *Learning from Experience*. London: Heinemann.

Bion, W.R. (1967). *Second Thoughts: Selected Papers on Psychoanalysis*. London: Heinemann.

Bion, W.R. (1970). *Attention and Interpretation*. London: Tavistock.

Bion, W.R. (1998) Notes on memory and desire. In: E. B. Spillius (Ed.) *Melanie Klein Today. Vol. 2 Mainly Practice*. London. Routledge, pp. 17–21.

Botella, C.S. and (2005/2001). *The Work of Psychic Figurability: Mental States without Representation*, trans. A. Weller, with M. Zerbib. London: Routledge, 2005.

Braunschweig, D. & Fain, M. (1975). *La nuit, le jour. Essai psychanalytique sur le fonctionnement mental*. Paris: Presses Universitaires de France.

Chabert, C. (1999). Les voies intérieures. *Revue Française de Psychanalyse*, 63 (5): 1445–1488.

Chervet, B. (1995). Tempus fugile-Carpe Diem: du temps, de ses tempo et de sa mesure; réflexions psychanalytiques. *Bulletin de la Société Psychanalytiques de Paris*, 38: 110–122.

Chervet, B. (2004). *L'interprétation du transfert: débats de psychanalyse, monographie*. Paris: Presses Universitaires de France.

Chervet, B. (2006a). L'après-coup, prolégomènes. *Revue Française de Psychanalyse*, 70 (3): 671–700.

Chervet, B. (2017). La saturation de la conscience dans les rêves, les séances, les sciences. *Revue Française de Psychanalyse*, 81 (4): 1177–1194.

Cournut, J. (1997). Le sens de l'après-coup. *Revue Française de Psychanalyse*, 61 (4): 1239–1246.

Diatkine, G. (2008). La disparition de la sexualité infantile dans la psychanalyse contemporaine. *Revue Française de Psychanalyse*, 72 (3): 671–685.

Donnet, J-L. (2006). L'après-coup au carré. *Revue Française de Psychanalyse*, 70 (3): 715–725.

Donnet, J.-L. & Green, A. (1973). *L'enfant de ça*. Paris: Minuit.

Durrell L. (1979). *Le carrousel sicilien*. Paris: Gallimard.

Faimberg, H. (2005a/1981). *The Telescoping of Generations*. London: Routledge.

Faimberg, H. (2005b). Après-coup: psychoanalytic controversies. *International Journal of Psycho-Analysis*, 86 (1): 1–6; 11–13.

Faimberg, H. (2007). A plea for a broader concept of *Nachträglichkeit*. *Psychoanalytic Quarterly*, 76 (4): 1221–1240.

Fain, M. (1981). Diachronie, structure, conflit œdipien: quelques réflexions. *Revue Française de Psychanalyse*, 45 (4): 985–998.

Fain, M. (1982). Biphasisme et après-coup. In: Guillaumin J. (Ed.) *Quinze études psychanalytiques sur le temps: traumatisme et après-coup* (pp. 103–124). Toulouse: Privat.

Fain, M. & Dejours, J. (1984). *Corps malade et corps érotique*. Paris: Masson.

Faure Pragier, S. & Pragier, G. (1990). Un siècle après l'"Esquisse": nouvelles métaphores?: métaphores du nouveau, CPLF, *Revue Française de Psychanalyse*, 54 (6): 1395–1500.

Ferenczi, S. (1924). *Thalassa: A Theory of Genitality*, trans. H.A. Bunker. New York: Psych. Quarterly, 1938.
Freud, S. ([1950]1895). *A Project for a Scientific Psychology. S.E. 1*. London: Hogarth, pp. 281–397.
Freud, S. (1894). The Neuro-psychoses of Defence. *S.E. 3*. London: Hogarth, pp. 45–68.
Freud, S. (with Breuer, J) (1895). *Studies on Hysteria. S.E. 2*. London: Hogarth.
Freud, S. (1896). Heredity and Aetiology of the Neuroses. *S.E. 3*. London: Hogarth, pp. 143–156.
Freud, S. (1898a). Sexuality in the Aetiology of the Neuroses. *S.E. 3*. London: Hogarth, pp. 263–285.
Freud, S. (1898b). The Psychical Mechanism of Forgetfulness. *S.E. 3*. London: Hogarth, pp. 287–297.
Freud, S. (1900). *The Interpretation of Dreams. S.E. 4–5*. London: Hogarth.
Freud, S. (1901). *The Psychopathology of Everyday Life. S.E. 6*. London: Hogarth.
Freud, S. (1905a). *Jokes and their Relation to the Unconscious. S.E. 8*. London: Hogarth, pp. 9–236.
Freud, S. (1905b). *Three Essays on the Theory of Sexuality. S.E. 7*. London: Hogarth, pp. 123–243.
Freud, S. (1911). Psychoanalytic Notes on an Autobiographical Account of a Case of Paranoia. *S.E. 12*. London: Hogarth, pp. 1–82.
Freud, S. (1912). Contributions to a Discussion on Masturbation. *S.E. 12*. London: Hogarth, pp. 243–254.
Freud, S. (1912–1913). *Totem and Taboo. S.E. 13*. London: Hogarth, pp. 1–161.
Freud, S. (1914). On Narcissism: An Introduction *S.E. 14*. London: Hogarth, pp. 69–102.
Freud, S. (1915a). Thoughts for the Times on War and Death. *S.E. 14*. London: Hogarth, pp. 273–300.
Freud, S. (1915b). A Case of Paranoia Running Counter to the Psychoanalytic Theory of the Disease. *S.E. 14*. London: Hogarth, pp. 263–272.
Freud, S. (1915c). The Unconscious. *S.E. 14*. London: Hogarth, pp. 166–215.
Freud, S. (1916–17). *Introductory Lectures on Psychoanalysis. S.E. 22*. London: Hogarth, pp. 1–182.
Freud, S. (1918 [1914]). *From the History of an Infantile Neurosis. S.E. 17*. London: Hogarth, pp. 7–122.
Freud, S. (1919a). A Child Is Being Beaten. *S.E. 17*. London: Hogarth, pp. 177–204.
Freud, S. (1919b). Introduction to Psychoanalysis and the War Neuroses. *S.E. 17*. London: Hogarth.
Freud, S. (1920). *Beyond the Pleasure Principle. S.E. 18*. London: Hogarth, pp. 1–64.
Freud, S. (1921). *Group Psychology and the Analysis of the Ego. S.E. 21*. London: Hogarth, pp.
Freud, S. (1922). Dreams and Telepathy. *S.E. 18*. London: Hogarth. pp. 197–220.
Freud, S. (1923). *The Ego and the Id. S.E. 19*. London: Hogarth, pp. 3–66.
Freud, S. (1924a). Letter to Fritz Wittels. *S.E. 19*. London: Hogarth, pp. 286–288.
Freud, S. (1924b). The Economic Problem of Masochism. *S.E. 19*. London: Hogarth, pp. 159–170.
Freud, S. (1924c). Neurosis and Psychosis. *S.E. 19*. London: Hogarth, pp. 149–153.
Freud, S. (1925a). *Some Additional Notes on Dream-interpretation as a Whole (See Section C "The Occult Significance of Dreams" pp.135–138). S.E. 19*. London: Hogarth, pp. 127–138.

Freud, S. (1925b). *An Autobiographical Study*. *S.E.* 20. London: Hogarth, pp. 7–74.
Freud, S. (1926). *Inhibitions, Symptoms and Anxiety*. *S.E.* 20. London: Hogarth, pp. 75–174
Freud S. (1927a). *The Future of an Illusion*. *S.E.* 2. London: Hogarth, pp. 1–56.
Freud, S. (1927b). Fetishism. *S.E. 21*. London: Hogarth, pp. 152–157.
Freud, S. (1928). A Religious Experience. *S.E 21*. London: Hogarth, pp. 169–172.
Freud, S. (1930). *Civilization and its Discontents*. *S.E.* 21. London: Hogarth, pp. 57–146.
Freud, S. (1933a). *New Introductory Lectures on Psycho-Analysis*. *S.E.* 22. London: Hogarth, pp. 1–182.
Freud, S. (1933b). Dreams and occultism. In: *New Introductory Lectures on Psychoanalysis*. *S.E.* 22. London: Hogarth, pp. 31–56.
Freud, S. (1936). A Disturbance of Memory on the Acropolis. *S.E.* 22. London: Hogarth, pp. 239–250.
Freud, S. (1937a). *Analysis Terminable and Interminable*. *S.E.* 23. London: Hogarth: 209-253.
Freud, S. (1937b). *Constructions in Analysis*. *S.E.* 1. London: Hogarth, pp. 257–269.
Freud, S. (1939). *Moses and Monotheism*. *S.E.* 23. London: Hogarth, pp. 1–138.
Freud, S. (1941). Psychoanalysis and Telepathy. *S.E. 18*. London: Hogarth, pp. 177–193.
Freud, S. (1987). *A Phylogenetic Fantasy: Overview of the Transference Neuroses*. Cambridge, MA: Harvard University Press, 1987.
Green, A. (1975). La psychanalyse, son objet, son avenir. *Revue Française de Psychanalyse*, 39 (1–2): 103–134.
Green, A. (1982). Après coup, l'archaïque. *Nouvelle Revue de Psychanalyse*, 26 « L'archaïque »: 195–216.
Guedj, D. (2000). *Le Mètre du monde*. Paris: Seuil.
Guillaumin, J. (Ed.) (1982) (and Preface). *Quinze études psychanalytiques sur le temps: traumatisme et après-coup*. Toulouse: Privat.
Janin, C. (1990). Les souvenirs appropriés. *Revue Française de Psychanalyse*, 54(4): 973–986.
Janin, C. (2007). *La honte, ses figures et ses destins*. Paris: Presses Universitaires de France.
Klein, M. (1961). *Narrative of a Child Analysis*. In: *The Collected Works of Melanie Klein, Vol 4*. London: Hogarth Press.
Kohut, H. (1979). The two analyses of Mr Z. *International Journal of Psychoanalysis*, 60 (1): 3–27.
Lacan, J. (1945). Logical time and the assertion of anticipated certainty. In: *Écrits* (pp. 161–175), trans. Bruce Fink. New York: Norton, 2006.
Lacan, J. (1955). Variations on the standard treatment. In: *Écrits* (pp. 269–302), trans. Bruce Fink. New York: Norton, 2006.
Lacan, J. (1956). Intervention on Monsieur Hesnard's paper: "Réflexions sur le 'Wo es war, soll Ich werden'" de Freud à la Société française de Psychanalyse, 6 Nov, published in *La psychanalyse*, 1957, 3: 323–324.
Lacan, J. (1958). On a question prior to any possible treatment of psychosis. In: *Écrits* (pp. 445–448), trans. Bruce Fink. New York: Norton, 2006.
Lacan, J. (1967). Place, origine et fin de mon enseignement, Transcription (J.-P. Chartier) d'une conférence prononcée à Lyon en automne 1967, à l'invitation de psychiatres en formation. https://ecole-lacanienne.net/wp-content/uploads/2016/04/1967-00-00.pdf
Lacan, J. (1975). Séminaire XXII, R.S.I. *Ornicar*, 5, (hiver 75/76): 37–46.
Lacan, J. (2001/1972). L'étourdit. In: *Autres écrits* (pp. 449–495). Paris: Éd. du Seuil.

Lacan, J. (1993[1971]). *Untitled text published in the Bulletin de l'Association freudienne*, 54, pp. 13–21. http://www.lutecium.org/fr/1971/06/jacques-lacan-bulletin-de-l-association-freudienne-no-54/1514

Lacan, J. (2005). *My Teaching*, trans. D. Macey. London: Verso, 2008.

Lacan, J. (2006/1966). *Écrits*, trans. Bruce Fink. New York: Norton, 2006.

Laplanche, J. & Pontalis, J.-B. (1973/1967). *The Language of Psychoanalysis*, trans. D. Nicholson-Smith. New York: Norton.

M'Uzan, M. de (1978). La chimère et la bouche de l'inconscient. In: F. Duparc (Ed.) *L'art du psychanalyste: autour de Michel de M'Uzan* (pp. 235–242). Lausanne: Delachaux et Niestlé, 1998.

Marty, P. (1979). *Les mouvements individuels de vie et de mort, 1*. Paris: Payot.

Marty, P. (1980). *Les mouvements individuels de vie et de mort, 2*. Paris: Payot.

Masson J.M., editor (1985). *The Complete Letters of Sigmund Freud to Wilhelm Fliess, 1887–1904*. Cambridge, MA: Belknap.

Neyraut, M. (1997). *Les raisons de l'irrationnel*. Paris: Presses Universitaires de France.

Neyraut, M. (2002). Essai sur le danger. In: C. Botella (Ed.) *Penser les limites; écrits en l'honneur d'André Green*. Neuchâtel: Delachaux et Niestlé, pp. 315–318.

Ogden, Th. (2004). The analytic third: implications for psychoanalytic theory and technique. *Psychoanalytic Quarterly*, 73 (1): 167–195.

Pasche, F. (1988). *Le sens de la psychanalyse*. Paris: Presses Universitaires de France.

Perelberg, R.J. (2006). Les controverses et l'après-coup. *Revue Française de Psychanalyse*, 70 (3): 647–670.

Perron-Borelli, M. & Perron, R. (1995). Autour des représentations d'actions, *Revue Française de Psychanalyse*, 59 (spécial): 1791–1997.

Rosenberg, B. (1991). *Masochisme mortifère et masochisme gardien de la vie*. Paris: Presses Universitaires de France.

Roussillon R. (1995). La métapsychologie des processus et la transitionnalité. *Revue Française de Psychanalyse*, 59 (special volume): 1375–1519.

Sodré, I. (1997). Le sens de l'après-coup. *Revue Française de Psychanalyse*, 61 (4): 1255–1262.

Sodré, I. (2005). "As I was walking down the stair, I saw a concept which wasn't there…": or, après-coup: a missing concept? *International Journal of Psycho-Analysis*, 86 (1): 7–10.

Winnicott, D.W. (1953). Transitional objects and transitional phenomena. *International Journal of Psycho-Analysis*, 34: 89–97.

Winnicott, D.W. (1971). *Therapeutic Consultations in Child Psychiatry*. New York: Basic Books.

Chapter 4

Evolving clinical situations

Insistence and persistence in clinical sessions

As "there are more things in heaven and earth, Horatio, than are dreamt of in your philosophy" (Shakespeare, *Hamlet*), this chapter will present some personal clinical situations to illustrate the presence and functions of the operation of après-coup in both the patient's and the analyst's mental functioning, and as an organizer of analysis itself and interpretation, both of which are carried out in two stages. Thus, analytic treatment unfolds according to this biphasic process, and it promotes the advent of this biphasic functioning at the heart of the patient's psychic life.

The previous chapter concerned clinical situations that had been written up definitively, with a stable content that was unlikely to be modified by the contribution of new elements from the patient or new thoughts from the analyst. In the clinical situations studied, neither of them were in a position to reconsider, complete or interpret the thoughts previously committed to paper. It was therefore an exegetic reading.

Another scenario, shattering any form of exegesis, occurs in the session when material has been excluded without either the patient or the analyst realizing it, in such a way that this ordinary and commonplace knowledge is then the object of a denial. This occurrence is different from the situation in which each of them knows that repressed material will come to light in the course of the sessions and is felt to be missing for the moment. In the case mentioned above, this latent knowledge is denied concerning this or that repressed or suppressed material. When these new elements come to light, the analyst then has an uncanny sense of having participated in this joint denial unwittingly. This unexpected contribution is equivalent to a lifting of denial and a wild interpretation. A traumatic countertransference is then activated. In these cases, the temptation is great to do what Albert Einstein humorously formulated: "If the facts don't correspond to the theory, change the facts."

This aspect is often concealed by a symptom that presents itself in the form of acting out in the session. The return of repressed material then serves as a cover to mask such a denial. This was the case, previously mentioned, of the forgetting

DOI: 10.4324/9780429198953-4

of the name Signorelli, an act of forgetting centred in Freud's associations on the last judgement and guilt, but which concealed Freud's denial of the suicide of one of his former patients on learning that he was suffering from an incurable somatic illness.

This logic concerns the analyst's forgetting, which pertains in general to material particularly concerned with the tendency towards traumatic extinction. Sometimes, the analyst had been aware of these contents; he had heard them and then forgotten them.

This disturbance of the analyst connected with such an act of forgetting is all the stronger in that the material concerned has resonances with his own personal psychic life. But forgetting is part of the psychic dynamic that is indispensable for processing the traumatic quality transferred during the session. It is situated between a radical immobilization and a temporary putting into abeyance.

A typical sequence of a traumatic experience may be described as follows: a first traumatic stage 1 occurs, that of the shock, which may be linked to an external or internal event of the mind; then there is a denial of this event in order to immobilize the extinctive drive yearnings; then we have one or several second stage 1's that are again more or less traumatic, stages that follow the logic of that which is sought-found-created with a transposition on to an external tangible and sensory reality perceived as seductive and frightening; then unpleasant thoughts linked to what had been denied are put into abeyance; hence, there is a co-optation of the materials that had been sought-found-created and their transformation into representations. This process of putting into abeyance makes it possible to diminish denial and to carry out a work of regressive psychic elaboration, such as the dream-work, thereby subsequently permitting the orientation of psychic cathexes along the progressive path. Finally, stage 2 can occur with the production of substitutive thoughts, dreams or symptoms or a bonus of free libido that can be cathected in external objects. A work of interpretation and construction is sometimes necessary to complete this trajectory of the operation of après-coup.

This sequence offers a good description of the ideal prototypical series of the work of dreams, sessions and symptoms, but also of the successful series that produces a bonus of desire that is available on waking up.

In the previous chapter we studied *dead* clinical narratives, in the sense of dead languages, which are consequently highly malleable for the purposes of exegesis. They have shown us the operation of après-coup in the guise of an operation that is realized through a series of psychic actions or operations that can be inferred from their results. These are themselves deferred effects, productions of the operation of après-coup. A large part of this operation belongs to the regressive psychic activities of passivity that elude the ego and require, on the contrary, the ego to be put into abeyance momentarily. Dreaming allows the ego to rest, while furnishing the dream-work with materials to accomplish its task of libidinal regeneration.

In this chapter, we will look at the polymorphism of the manifest results of the operation of après-coup, as it imposes itself upon the analyst's listening during the sessions. As we proceed, we will make a few forays into the theory of technique.

Presenting a variety of clinical situations sometimes requires one to be schematic. This inclination constitutes my *basic countertransference*, that which precedes all transference (Neyraut, 1974). Depending on the analyst, the basic countertransference may give priority to theorization, representability or emotional experience. In general, these three vertexes are interwoven in the listening of each analyst with individual variations that are also in resonance with the patient's mental state.

In fact, transference and countertransference are inextricable, as are offer and demand. The primacy of one over the other remains undecidable. The parable of the hen and the egg raises the question of the impact of the rooster, of the paternal imperative on the emergence of thought.

When the dream fails to result in a bonus of desire, the dreamer turns to an interpreter, to an oneiromancer, to whom he gives the task of finalizing his dreamwork. But the interpreter is himself a dreamer who has had this experience and who knows that such an appeal to an interpreter will occur. He therefore proposes his services in advance in order to respond to the dreamer's future demand. Dreams and the interpreter go together, just like night and day.

Another reason that calls for a certain degree of schematism concerns the duty of confidentiality, and beyond that the psychoanalyst's ethics; that is to say, the obligation to turn the psychic life of patients into internal objects that are capable of evolving depending on the elements brought by the patient and by the analyst's thinking.

These two aspects, confidentiality and the internal object of analytic thinking, are included in the part of the fundamental rule addressed to the analyst, namely, "strict discretion" (Freud, 1940, p. 174). The announced schematism thus implies theory and discretion.

It may further be noted that all day-to-day clinical situations could find their place in this chapter. This presents a dilemma. The most pertinent would be those where the operation of après-coup has unfolded without eliciting attention, those that have passed unnoticed and thus have simply been forgotten. There then are those where, on the contrary, attention, or even speech and writing, have proved necessary, thus where the countertransference has been involved in a more manifest manner. These situations are ones where the operation of après-coup has found itself in difficulty. We can recognize here the same disparity between the successful dream, which leaves the awaking dreamer with a sense of well-being and a bonus of desire, and one that is registered as a memory on awakening and is in search of interpretation.

The operation and its clinical productions

The clinical material of sessions gives us a glimpse of the role played by the operation of après-coup in the construction of multiple connections between more or less distant temporal moments, apparently independent events and heteroclite psychic elements. These connections will have to be undone by analysis for the benefit of the work of libidinal regeneration.

A point of complexity emerges here. Recognition of the unfolding of the operation of après-coup can only occur after the event. It is always a matter of a secondary reconstruction. It is easy, therefore, to oppose this theorization of the mind by employing the argument that it involves a theoretical application or an a priori that invalidates the existence of the operation that it is supposed to identify and reveal. No argument can be mustered to counter this opposition. The intelligibility provided by the light shed by the operation of après-coup can foster confidence in this approach to understanding clinical material; but we cannot forget that probability is not always the truth. Reality-testing can itself only be a deferred effect. Freud reminded us of this at the end of his life in referring to Nestroy: "It will all become clear in the course of future developments" (1937b, p. 265). The introduction of temporality is essential in the theorization of reality-testing, which is always a deferred effect of what was at the origin of the psychic production to be evaluated, a deferred effect liable to be revised. This raises the question as to whether this operation can furnish a finite content or whether it is destined to continue infinitely; unless, that is, both completion and lack are combined within it. The completed operation of après-coup offers certainty that is affected by an experience of lack, which is very different from a doubt. The experience of lack has a double origin. It is due to the recognition of incompleteness, since certainty can be rectified by taking new parameters into consideration, and also to the renunciation that is involved in completion, a renunciation that generates the affect of lack.

The operation of après-coup organizes the manifest content of associations, the style of the associative discourse, for instance when it refers openly to a biphasic process.

This was the case of a man who, at the beginning of his analysis, constantly referred all the contents of his dreams, all his thoughts in the session, to this or that aspect of his conscious childhood history.

This conscious organization must not be confused with the operation of après-coup. A true operation of après-coup can be inferred between this manifest discourse, which has the biphasic nature of the deferred effect as a conscious content, and an unconscious reminiscence conveying the traumatic dimension.

The converse is also very frequent and appears in every analysis, sometimes more insistently. It is then a matter of establishing continuity between the sessions.

Another patient, for instance, tried at the beginning of each session to pick up his associations where he had left them at the end of the last session, thereby seeking to suppress the interval between the sessions and the work of latency.

In both cases, the attempt to control the dynamic of the operation of après-coup is obvious, whether by means of an artificial or forced construction, or by his manifest undoing of temporal discontinuity.

These styles, as associative materials, are reminiscences, and they belong to the operation of après-coup itself, which escapes any form of control. They reveal the influence of a *neo-rule* in place of the fundamental rule announced by the analyst, such as *making links between the past and the present, following a thread, being coherent, doing work*, rules reminiscent of the education of secondary processes underpinned by the school and educational system or by the collective discourse concerning the psychoanalytic method.

A phenomenology thus appears of the relations of determinism, causality, temporality and memory, but also of representation, resignification and translation, substitution, concealment, falsification, interpretation, transvaluation and, in a general way, theorization.

By means of these connections, the operation of après-coup realizes the most essential function that defines it, namely, that of opposing the extinctive regressivity at the origin of discontinuity. It is this function that gives it its full significance. This is the reason for its participation in all the categories of productions, in all psychic emergences, those of the infantile register, those of the symptoms of hallucinatory satisfaction, those of narcissism and its character traits, and finally those of the very qualities of the libidinal source.

As I have already shown, the operation of après-coup is involved in all the forms of psychic work involved in human thought and its multiple forms of expression. It is the model of all psychic work. We also find it in the dream-work, in the session work and, thus, in the analysand's incidental speech and in the listening of the analyst's evenly suspended attention, but also in the particular product peculiar to the sessions and to the analytic couple, namely, the analytic après-coup that is established in the session. And it is also from this process that the therapeutic and healing effect of analytic treatments emanates. The close connection between the operation of après-coup and the superego appears clearly insofar as the latter watches over the unfolding of each of the stages of this operation. Just as the superego must already be there to bring about the Oedipal resolution of which it is the heir, the operation of après-coup must be a potentiality that is already there in order to realize the efficient unfolding of the psychic operations that constitute it.

It thus plays a part just as much in the clinical field of the infantile register, which takes into account the traumatic regressive economy, as in that of the denial of the traumatic quality. By virtue of the work of *distortion* in dreams, it integrates extinctive regressivity with the mind and permits the institution of the pleasure principle and of the infantile register. In parallel, the denial of extinctive regressivity opens up the fields of conviction and beliefs, of interpretative constructions and ideological theories. The articulation of these two logics is essential. Denial is inherent to the process of falling asleep, which permits regression to the pleasure principle. And then the dream-work permits the dissolution of denial and libidinal regeneration beckons the moment of awakening.

We can infer from this that the operation of après-coup plays a role in the resolution of conflicts taking place within psychic processes, such as those of the Oedipal conflict, and promotes the emergence of a bonus of desire that is free and open to the world.

Its particular involvement in the process of theorization has already been emphasized and will be commented on further. The operation of après-coup is the matrix of all theories. It is an enacted theorization. Its realization can be translated retroactively by theories. Primal phantasies are the finest illustration of this. It thus makes it possible to overcome the Manichaeism between denial and recognition in favour of a commensalism between denial and regressive psychic activities.

Einstein's statement, which was apparently a joke, was enacted when, faced with the test of the Hubble telescope, he preferred to distort his equations than call into question his theorization. He fell into deep silence for seven years when the findings of the telescope contradicted his conviction and prevented him from saturating his own consciousness and that of the physicists of the time with his conception of a static universe. His silence amounted to an infantile sulk combining a desire to appropriate matter and a refusal to admit his helplessness faced with the independence of desire and matter. At stake was a need to maintain denial and impose theoretical constructions that supported their author's need for conviction. Freud renounced this approach, and this renunciation plays a part in both the admiration and the hatred of which he is sometimes the object.

Perceptual activity and perception

This chapter is concerned with the insistence of facts in face of the attempt to impose a perception created from the inside, a perceptual identity through hallucinatory functioning and secondary theorization. Perception and perceptual activity can thus be distinguished. The latter unites two categories of intertwined perceptions: *sensory perceptions* that do not give rise to traces and representations destined to remain perceptions proper and *endogenous perceptions* in the form of perceptual identity created from representations. These are hallucinatory productions projected on to the internal surface of the screen of consciousness whose function is to saturate the latter and to deny perceptions without traces.

A form of complexity already mentioned appears again that takes account of the difference between sensory perceptions that give rise to traces and representations and those that do not. What is involved here is the perception not only of lack, of disappearance, of erasure, but also, more abstractly, of the perception of differences. The perception of difference as well as its effects accompany every sensory perception of two representable elements. Their difference is not representable and results in an experience of lack as well as theories explaining this lack. The prototype is the difference of the sexes. The genitals of boys and girls are representable but their difference as such is not. This difference is conceived in terms of lack combining invisibility and subtraction; hence, infantile sexual theories allying the invisible, the hidden and loss, castration.

The difference between the sexes is thus a combination of two differences: the masculine-feminine tangible couple with its representations and the pair endowed-unendowed, one of whose terms is intangible and without representation. The pair masculine-feminine includes the tangible pair, visible-invisible, making it possible to represent invisibility and its sensitivity (vaginal impulses) by representations of what is visible and sensitive (penile impulses).

The absence of representation of what is missing brings with it a hallucinatory hypercathexis of the endowed, a perceptual identity in place of what is missing.

Sensory perceptions without trace remain of perception proper. With hallucinations in the form of perceptual identity, they constitute "*perceptual activity*." All perceptions with representations belong to the category of the representational.

Sensory perception is a passive phenomenon to which the human being is subject, and against which he can employ the mechanism of denial, which is differentiated from the original stimulus barrier. The denial can be temporary and reversible or, on the contrary, stable and chronic. The first is a functional denial with an attendant regression of cathexes towards regressive psychic activities that saturate consciousness momentarily with formations in the form of perceptual identity. *Decathexis with regression* corresponds ideally to sleeping and dreaming and to free association in the session. *Decathexis without regression* is the specific logic of the chronic denial involved in psychopathology. The attendant constructions attempt to saturate nocturnal and diurnal consciousness with a stable and continuous conviction, which, although derived from the hallucinatory system of perceptual identities, requires its persistence without regression. Convictions obtained through construction are non-regressive formations. Temporary and reversible denial is favourable to the regressive psychic activities of passivity. Chronic denial requires a continuous reinforcement of progressive saturation. To this end, it has to replace regressive formations by private convictions or beliefs and collective ideologies. This is the breeding ground for every *Weltanschauung* (Freud, 1933).

An important distinction concerns the use of denial with regard to sensory perceptions that give rise to traces and with regard to those without attendant traces. The first are open to the formal regressions that produce regressive registrations. The second bring into play more directly mental operations acting on the regressive economy, which are reflected by the impressions, endogenous sensations and feelings that form the basis of sensuality. They do not give rise to registrations that are specific to them but, in order to facilitate the psychic work that they require, utilize those derived from sensory perceptions with traces. The first concern the tangible realities of the world, both visible and invisible, and the second the intangible reality of the elements of lack attendant upon the perception of all differences.

In psychoanalysis, this reality of lack is approached through expressions such as the perception of castration (what is seen) and the sensation of the threat of castration (what is heard) associated with the difference between the sexes and a theory that explains this difference, that of castration.

Generally speaking, perceptions with representations are used to produce the contents of thought; those without representation, the qualities of thought.

The differences presented above make it easier to distinguish negative hallucination and denial. The first belongs to regressive psychic activities and participates in fulfilling unconscious wishes through representations such as invisibility, disappearance and erasure. These are productions of the mind, endogenous perceptions affirming the wish that what is not perceivable exists invisibly or has been subtracted, a desire to become an object of invisibility. On the contrary, denial without regression does not fulfil wishes hallucinatorily; it imposes a progressive perceptual mode of functioning in the guise of a neo-reality. Consequently, the operation of après-coup becomes distorted on the structural level and makes room for manifest *monophasic* productions. These only retain certain characteristics of the operation of après-coup, such as determinism, the utilization of the past, the relation between cause and effect, temporal succession and the principle of repetition, explaining the fact that they are approached as deferred effects, but the regressive economy is not changed. This throws light on the very disparate clinical use of the noun *après-coup*, which includes under its auspices both the results of an accomplished process and those arising from its vicissitudes, stumbling blocks and avatars.

The role of denial in the oscillation between night and day

The sleep-dream system shows how denial is involved in an ordinary and customary process. It is useful, necessary and even indispensable and psychically rich, on the condition that it is temporary and reversible. In this form, it belongs to the conditions of dreaming and is required by the need to sleep and dream. When it occurs in waking life, in the best of cases it occurs sporadically in order to let periods of latency occur and participate in the process of falling asleep. In this way it makes possible the crucial psychic activity of the dream-work. In return, the dream-work supports the inaugural denial during the night thanks to its saturating endogenous productions, until libidinal regeneration calls for the progressive orientation towards the objects of the world via the body.

The discovery of this third property of the dream-work, consisting in promoting and presenting (Kahn, 2001) an endogenous saturation to consciousness is a direct consequence of the third "step" made by Freud in his theory of the drives, namely, his recognition of the regressive quality of the drive. Having noted on several occasions the similarity between dreams and psychosis, he asserted: "the dream is a psychosis" (Freud, 1940, p. 172). Consequently, the dream has three functions: it seeks *to fulfil a wish hallucinatorily*; it is the *guardian of sleep*; and it *forms a saturating endogenous perception*. Together they work towards the success of the most essential dream function, which consists in reducing traumatic extinctive regressivity and in regenerating the psyche with libido. This genesis of libido is based on an operation of *reduction*, which is related to a principle of *renunciation* that is also at the basis of the operations of desexualization and mourning, with mutations of a portion of the sexual libido into narcissistic libido and object-libido. This operation of renunciation, at the basis of all psychic operations, implies the intervention of a specific libido, namely, *processual libido*, which Freud denoted by the term hypercathexis and linked in particular to language, which is its vehicle, either directly or through symptoms.

The awakening call proves that an internal reality, which was subject to periods of latency accompanying denial, seeks to find its place again thanks to a new openness to perceptions and a return to libidinal object-cathexes. In contrast to unconscious guilt, which drives the subject to renounce his secondarized and object-related cathexes, *unconscious shame* is produced by maintaining the regression of sleep. It prompts awakening, which itself will be once again replaced by the *unconscious guilt* produced by the work of diurnal desexualization. The oscillation, discussed by Freud only in the context of guilt in *Totem and Taboo*, is, in fact, that between night and day (Braunschweig & Fain, 1975). It may be conceived as a swing driven by these two typical affects of processual functioning, unconscious shame and unconscious guilt (Chervet, 2003). To understand them completely they must be linked up with the conflict concerning *unconscious pain*, the pain linked to renunciation, the pain of restraint, registration and mourning. Through the shameful quest (incest) concerning the *object of the drive* and through the guilty elimination (murder) of the imperative promoting *the lost object*, it is the *pain of renunciation* that is avoided. These unconscious affects are thus the products of the operation of après-coup. They are the qualitative markers of its dynamic.

It is starting from this situation of elimination that denial sometimes continues in waking life by trying chronically to maintain the dream function of saturation and to impose a neo-world that is purely libidinal in essence, eluding the various stages of renunciation.

The associative discourse, analytic listening and the tempo of the operation of après-coup

The most ordinary occurrence of the operation of après-coup that the analyst can observe in his day-to-day practice is his patient's *free association*; but it also includes his own thought-processes during the session as he is listening with *evenly suspended attention*, as well as the *analytic après-coup* that emerges from the combination of the thoughts of the two protagonists.

Free association in the session is, in fact, a production of incidental thoughts, thoughts that *come to mind* (*Einfallen*, lit. "fall or drop into" one's mind; "*tombent*" in French) and create the effect of surprise on the screen of the two conscious minds of the analyst and analysand. It is a particular way of *thinking* manifested in the session discourse, which may be described as an *incidental discourse*. *Incidental speech* is specific to sessions. Rather than associativity, it is incidental speech that constitutes the *regressive psychic activity of the passivity* characteristic of sessions. The classical French expression describing the patient's discourse as the *coq-à-l'âne* (skipping from one thing to another) emphasizes the sexualization of language by appealing to significant members of the bestiary. But a restraint on this sexualization is supported by the constraint to maintain the cathexis of language. This imperative is inscribed on the frontispiece of analysis by the *fundamental rule*. There is thus a formal regression of the patient to incidental speech and a delegation to the analyst of the processual pole called *evenly suspended attention*. Just as sleep is necessary for dreaming, so this delegation is necessary for incidental regression. A system, that of shared animism, will seek to establish itself during the sessions, in conflict and in complementarity with the individual modes of functioning of each protagonist, consisting in a distribution of two processual poles, the incidental regressive pole and the accomplished pole of the judgement of meaning.

The fundamental rule outlines scenes that are adjacent to that of the session. It opposes their respective attraction by requiring them to be objects of verbalization. This is the case for sensual regression outside language and the formal regression of dreams; but also for paradoxical forms of regression that use language in connection with desexualization, as in idealization and sublimation.

The session is thus bordered by other scenes, sexual, oneiric, social, sublimatory, militant, ideological and so forth. Each of them is present in the scene of the session in the form of a discourse concerning it; this discourse contains a conflictual attraction that seeks transgressively to take the place of that of the sessions.

The clinical situation of the session is thus constituted on the analysand's side of the pair dream narrative-free association, a pair that enacts the transference. Two deferred effects are intertwined in it, the dream narrative and the session discourse, accounting, respectively, for primary and secondary narcissisms. It is of course through its recital that the dream is recognized in the session as a deferred effect. The dream itself, that is to say the dream-work, as a prototypical regressive psychic activity, must be located in this period of psychic elaboration represented by the *hyphen* in the term *après-coup*, the interval period. And it is also from the dream narrative that free association was born, well before psychoanalysis, as a variation of the dream-work; hence, the tendency of the dream to finish in daytime by using an accommodating ear and a subsidiary interpretativity in the service of repression and the amnesia of waking up. The psyche is at the origin of the institutionalization of forms of oneiromancy and of the keys to dreams; psychoanalysis is their heir.

From this proximity with *dream thought*, free association turns out to be *incidental thought*. Associative work promotes the incidental nature of speech and listening (Clerc & Maugendre, 2007). This proves to be the me/not-me object of the session par excellence (Winnicott, 1953), in the twofold sense of this expression, as mixed blood of the unconscious and as material of the session belonging to the analysand and analyst alike.

This distribution of functions within the analytic situation will affect not only the production of the discourse of each session, but also the unfolding of an analysis as a whole, for both the analysand and the analyst. As examples of deferred effects we could thus take any session, in isolation, or several organized as a sequence, or even a period of analysis over several years or an entire analysis. The insistent presence of the deferred effect can be identified in all the occurrences.

The clinical examples below include these different possibilities. The operation of après-coup appears in them at different tempos and various speeds of realization. The fact that it is extremely rapid in some cases but hesitant, and even soothing in others, suggests that yet other parameters, historical and economic, are involved in this diversity.

Biphasism and repetition

As soon as a psychoanalytic treatment lasts for a certain time, analyst and analysand are caught up in repetition, and compulsions of repetition and reduction. One way of avoiding them is to reduce the length of treatments and sessions, but also to introduce some sort of enactment such as scansion or a change in the protocol. All analyses enact a manifest two-step course when the patient is in difficulty with the unfolding biphasism of the dynamic of the operation of après-coup. Sometimes, the temptation is to put into action outside what is lacking inside.

While this biphasic operation is at the basis of the regular repetition of the sessions, such enactments impose a *before* and an *after* artificially in the hope that they will serve as a support for the creative process of the past, a process that belongs to the very essence of the superego because it is the very illustration of it. As Freud (1940) writes: "In the establishment of the superego we have before us, as it were, an example of the way in which the present is changed into the past" (p. 207).

The technical handling of such acts is particular tricky. It is open to arbitrariness and theoretical justifications. But above all, acting in this way is to reject a significant aspect of clinical experience, which concerns, precisely, the patient's repetition and his acting out in analysis. Indeed "successive" analyses show that their sequential tempo is the patient's way of trying to register the dynamic of the operation of après-coup and to accomplish its economic function; at the same time, it reveals resistance.

This shortening of a treatment deliberately consists in not allowing psychic processes the time needed to establish themselves thanks to their main tool, repetition, that Freud identified as operating positively in the play of children. The theory of the session refers just as much to the theory of dreams, due to the production of incidents, as to the theory of play, with the place of repetition, which differentiates the work of association from the dream-work. Play is not embedded in sleep and uses language as a support for repetition, which is in the service of the setting-up of psychic operations, even when it repeats their vicissitudes. From both these points of view, free association is the equivalent of children's play and language takes the place in it of the wooden-reel of the *Fort-Da* (Freud, 1920a).

This solution of precipitating a voluntary interruption of the analysis had been prescribed by Freud in the case of the "Wolf-Man." In view of his analytic history it is possible retrospectively to imagine that Freud had anticipated unwittingly the long sequential journey of this famous patient. Indeed, he was probably one of the first to confront analysts with the clinical practice of "successive analyses," a practice that includes not only interruptions of analysis and new phases with the same analyst or another analyst, but also all the clinical situations of *lateral* ruptures in the course of analysis. I have already pointed out that this clinical situation is completed by its opposite, that of continuities.

The enactment of "successive analyses"

Mrs A. was living in a homosexual couple. After several years of analysis, she began to use her analysis to allow her heterosexual interests to emerge. Her whole psychic organization and its consequences for her object-choices were disturbed. She very soon broke off her treatment pretexting a promotion at work that required her to move abroad. She also broke off with her partner and her friends. A few years later, I learnt from a colleague working in the country where this former patient was now living, that she was in analysis with her. She was living with a man with whom she had had a child. I learnt nothing more. Did she use the geographical move to reestablish a split that had become fragile for the benefit of her heterosexuality and/or maternity? Or did she act out a two-step sequence in order to set up a renunciation in two stages in favour of new drive vicissitudes? I do not know, but her decisive enactment may be thought of as a hitherto unsuspected reminiscence that belonged henceforth to her manifest analytical clinical material.

Overdetermination and fragmented topographies

As long as the clinical situation remains open and evolving, as long as it has the last word and presents itself as the shingle on which all theoretical schematisms run aground, it presents itself to listening as plural and *fragmented*. Semiology expresses the various registers that make up the infantile aspects of psychic functioning with the hallucinatory satisfactions obtained in the spheres of sexuality (autoerotisms), of narcissism (His Majesty the Baby) and of generativity (the horn of plenty), to which it is necessary to add all the distortions that make them an amalgam of inextricable complications. Interpretation and metapsychology are also plural and fragmented. The work of the psychoanalyst consists in taking into account the global context of the singular history of the analysis and of this plural and fragmented semiology.

The dream of the dropped baby

Mrs B. dreamt that she had dropped a baby. She woke up feeling anxious.

By virtue of its quality as a short dream, this dream gives almost immediate access to the three processual registers on which the polymorphism of interpretation are based. One can make out in concealed form the infantile desire to have a baby from her father (getting pregnant), the narcissistic wish to be His Majesty the Baby (never being dropped or let down), and the idealizing aspiration to remain young (escaping the grave). No choice of interpretation can arise from *such an approach, which turns out to be strictly theoretical. If, on the other hand, I take into account the fact that this patient had a younger brother whose life was in danger for many months after his birth, to the point of leading their mother to transform herself into a nurse and to require her little girl to do the same, the dream appears under other auspices. It reflects the attempt by this woman to gain access finally, supported by the analysis, to the three registers envisaged earlier. By taking her personal history into account, her "dropping" the baby expresses her desire to be rid of this burden and to free her Oedipal desires from this burial in an auxiliary medical identity, thereby burdening all her future potentialities. Her desire to free herself from this alienating role can be expressed by the expression "dropping."*

The expression *fragmented topographies* accounts for the various condensations linked to overdetermination, but also the complications and amalgams resulting from incompatible modes of functioning.

In 1895, in exploring the case of Emma, Freud followed the implications of the overdetermination of fixations to infantile modes of satisfaction and repressed wishes. Then, in 1914, he supplemented this with the alienating narcissistic inclusions haunting a subject. Finally, in 1920, he enriched this further by taking into account the regressive dimension of the drives and the counter-response of the processual imperative. Overdetermination combines the three registers of the drives within which conflicts occur at the level of the superego and of hypercathexis, between denial and recognition of the reality of castration. These conflicts concern the processing of instinctual drive regressivity by a specific form of psychic work, which makes it possible to reduce the tendency towards extinction by utilizing it to produce representations. This reduction is the first renunciation, a renunciation of extinction. The restraint thus created gives rise to the masochism of renunciation and forms the basis of instinctual drive sources. All desire is therefore linked to a nucleus of masochism of renunciation. Consequently, the prefix *Über* in *Überbestimmung* (overdetermination) does not only signify *multi,* but also denotes the involvement of the specific hypercathexis of the superego imperative in overdetermination.

This allowed Freud to elaborate fetishism as a prototype of the constructions of neo-realities and psychoses. Closer to clinical reality, he described the mechanism of ego-splitting, with the possible coexistence, without any mutual awareness, of incompatible modes of functioning. Concretely, this entails amalgams of modes of functioning based, in some cases, on denial and in other cases on recognition, but all concealing ego-splitting.

Clinical situations are constantly becoming more complex, as is our listening. An Oedipal dynamic may be concealed by an apparently different manifest picture or, on the contrary, it can be brought to light with the aim of concealing modes of functioning based on an elimination of Oedipal logic. This represents a challenge for analysts whose interpretations are always capable of being pertinent from the point of view of one approach and in the service of repression from the point of view of another approach, and thus bound up with a denial of reality.

Determinism and reminiscence

All nosography can be envisaged from the angle of distortions of the operation of après-coup. All clinical pictures belong to the category of reminiscence (Freud, 1937b). A counter-appeal, opposing extinctive tendencies, is made to mnemic materials offering an anti-traumatic materiality, thus to perceptual traces. Returns occur, not as Freud had long believed prior to 1920 owing to a spontaneous propensity for joining up again with consciousness, but rather due to the necessity of having to respond to extinctive regressivity. Resurgences and emergences occur in the name of this anti-traumatic necessity. Traces are differentiated in order to respond to this need for materials; likewise psychic operations are activated that had hitherto remained in abeyance. The passionate arena of the transference is the untempered principle of this.

The elementary and universal reminiscence is that of regressivity and of all the means that a psyche has at its disposal to respond to it. In this sense, there exists a *processual memory,* without content, which Freud describes as phylogenetic, a memory of the operations of thought and of the conditions and uncertainties of their emergence. This processual memory includes the repetition involved in the establishment and efficiency of all psychic processuality, as it has already unfolded in infancy and through the play and phobias of childhood. Processual reminiscence is thus an actualization of repetitions of the operations involved in psychic work.

The reminiscence of a psychic operation in abeyance: A severe school phobia

C. was a little 7-year-old when his mother asked me for a consultation. I saw him with his mother and his stepfather. He had not been going to school for about six months following panic attacks that occurred each Sunday afternoon and each evening before returning to class. Even when accompanied, his anxiety did not abate. He was now doing his schooling via correspondence classes.

I learnt that he had lost his father in an accident when he was five. His mother was living once again with a man who had his own children. C. was his mother's only child.

I let them speak spontaneously for a while and then turned the parents' attention towards the bereavements that they had suffered, hoping that C. would hear how they each related to their moral pain.

The scale of C.'s paralyzing anxiety, the announced involvement of a tangible trauma, C's transference disposition that was noticeable in the very first interview, the concern of the parents and my sensitivity to the transference of this little boy led me to think that there was a strong potential for a resumption of growth in C. I proposed to see him once a week.

He entered immediately into an associative and narrative discourse. For more than a year and a half, perhaps two, he talked to me freely about very repetitive themes which I could do nothing with: video games, providers, mobile telephones, mobile packages, operators, as well as trains, locomotives. He was a subscriber to the magazine "La vie du rail"! He took the TGV, alone or accompanied, to visit his grandfather's family, which was one of the only places where he felt well, he said. There he met up with uncles, aunts and cousins. But he never talked about his difficulties at school or about his father's accident, of which I knew nothing. More than a year went by like this during which I hoped, without any certainty, that he would give me the keys to think about the material that he was bringing that resonated with the centres of interest of children of his age but seemed cathected by him in a more unusual way. From time to time, I invited him to speak about his difficulties or to give me more details about his centres of interest, or drew attention to his silence concerning his friends, his schooling, his school memories, his nights and his fears. He seemed to pay hardly any attention to my remarks. They seemed to slip like water off a duck's back. However, he let me know now and again that he would have to speak to me one day, thereby warning me that I needed to put my curiosity on hold and my urge to think about the manifest aspects of what he was bringing.

In one session, he told me about his schoolwork by correspondence, said he was missing the time when he used to go to class with friends, and associated immediately to his mother who was always worried about what was to become of him. I noticed his feelings of guilt and fear towards her. In the context set out above of his refusal to allow any contents conveying a traumatic quality to manifest themselves regressively, and becoming tired of all this repetition, I said to him: "If you go back to school and get down to work, you are afraid you are going to do to you mother what you have already done to your father." He froze and almost immediately rebelled. He told me with an angry gesture that he couldn't understand a word of what I was saying, that therapists talked a lot of rubbish and were completely crazy; that he had really understood nothing at all, that I should explain what I meant and he tried to repeat what I had said without success. He continued, angrily, telling me that I must be completely mad to say such things, completely crazy, etc.

For several sessions, he took up his repetitive themes again but his wrath appeared regularly, indicating very clearly his mistrust of anything I might say. He referred several times to the session in which I had said things that he didn't understand. Feeling shaken once again, he watched me, fearing and waiting for a new intervention on my part.

He said he had spoken about it to his mother and that she had told him that I had certainly been speaking about what he was thinking, about what was going on in his mind. But he was still furious and asked himself if he was going to continue coming here if it was to hear such crazy things.

Then, for many months, I heard no more of this. He returned to his repetitive themes and I grew tired of them again. I understood, in passing, that he was in the process of being reintegrated within the school system on a part-time basis and that it was planned that he would return to school full-time the following year.

At the same time, he was attending several times a week a small structure for psychological care where he saw intermittently a psychiatrist, a psychologist and educators with whom he could talk, he said.

It was then that he began to tell me, here and there, about his former panic attacks. He still had anxiety attacks, sometimes waking up in the night, and said, "but it's O.K. and when I'm at school, I'm happy."

From time to time, he would look at me with contempt, saying: "Well, I hope you're not going to start talking rot again, like the last time, those are things therapists say ... but where on earth do you get such ideas?"

From time to time, he added: "One day I'll have to speak to you."

One day, after we'd been seeing each other for more than three years, he sat down and said to me: "Well, I have to speak to you." He then described his father's death to me in detail, the moment he was called away from school, his grandmother who had come to fetch him, the announcement of the accident, the telephone, his mother's calls, his absent mother, the trips back and forth to the hospital for three days, his father in a coma, and so on.

Then the accident as he had reconstructed it: his father had borrowed a "big motorbike" from his mother's brother; he had tried out the bike; 200km/hr; then the precise spot, in the middle of the town, where the accident happened; the edge of the pavement, a yellow 2CV, multiple fractures, his father at the hospital, the coma, and finally the morgue.

He then trotted out all the repetitive elements of the session: telephone, changes of location, video games involving racing, planes, lorries, and above all trains; high speeds, accidents. All of them were involved in the scene when he learnt about his father's death. The fixation to the trauma was obvious. During several sessions, he described to me all the medical details that his mother had allegedly told him about; but above all the accident itself, the burial, the candles, the lady in the yellow coat (like the 2CV), the people behind the church who were having fun, the cemetery, etc.

In a confident tone, he added: "I have never been able to go back there, even with my mother." His phobia of the cemetery, his school phobia.

Later, he explained to me by insisting that after his father's death, he had been frightened of his mother; he couldn't stand her approaching or touching him.

A few weeks later he recalled a dream that he had repeatedly for a while after his father's death: "I was on a piece of terrain, a building site, with machines everywhere. My mother tried to catch me; she ran after me; I ran away, I ran and ran and ran. I came to a bend, there was a wall, I slipped and crashed into the wall." Without any prompting, he spontaneously associated the wall with the 2CV and with the pavement which his father had crashed against.

Six months later, he returned to his class and his schooling. His sensitivity to the demands of schoolwork is a reminder that the desexualization implied in work has unconscious resonances with murder.

The progression of the associative diluting of his phobic fixation was particularly noteworthy. It took time for it to appear in the sessions as well. The operation *of murder could be put in the service of remembering, verbalization and mentalization rather than in the service of the repression on which his phobia was based.*

Faced with my silence and certain lapses of my attention as a result of distraction or thinking, he would jump and ask me why I was looking at him like that, who I was looking at, and turn round quickly to check that there was no one behind his chair. Then he transformed his concerns into play. This re-dynamization of his persecutory impulses embedded in his phobia allowed him much more latitude than before. He was able to go to school without anxiety, and also visit his father's family and experience, there too, phobic impulses without splitting spaces.

Here is a moment in a session after more than four years of therapy: playing in the arenas in the town where his paternal family lived, he and his cousins were accosted by some rascals looking for a fight. He felt extremely anxious when faced with this provocation to get into a fight. "I was afraid of their vengeance," he told me quite irrationally, evoking a vengeful return of his father and of his guilt.

His dream activity gradually followed the path of his associations. He told me many dreams involving murders and accidents; dreams in which he fell and told himself that he was dead, and that that was what being dead was. In one of them, a father asked him to kill his child. He reenacted this dream in the session, while he was telling it, in an almost hallucinatory manner, by imitating the gesture of grabbing the child by his neck. Although he had been wearing a helmet, his father had fractured his cervical vertebrae. He then told me, in the form of a denial: "Don't tell me, now, that it's about my father." I pointed out to him that it was now possible for him to think about it, and I interpreted his dream: "So it is necessary to kill the child who is beginning to think about his father's death." He was attentive and replied: "I'm trying to understand how you think." Then: "When I told my mother that I would like to know where these dreams could lead me, she told me to tell you about them." On the doorstep, as he was leaving, he said: "It was really a good thing that I came today! Well, we'll continue next week."

These sessions are deferred effects of the interpretation given more than a year before, an interpretation that had reintroduced the repressed traumatic quality. Even if this interpretation came after years of benevolent listening and tender attention, it contained a certain degree of violence. His reactions of hate were inhabited by the reactualization of murderous impulses towards his father that had been paralyzed since his death. His first transference reaction, full of hate and criminal impulses, initially prevented any appropriation of the operation of "murder" and maintained a logic of retaliation originating in his feelings of persecution. The arenas offered a killing place that was particularly suited to the transposition of this operation and to the substitutive activity of displacements and condensations. A fight could take place there without involving murder. Sadism and masochism belong to life.

The biphasic process thus permitted the liberation of this operation of "murder" and its integration in the service of psychic processes. The function of interpretation emerges clearly. It had the significance of a second "shock" in the aftermath of the first really traumatic "shock." By its violence, the interpretation thus shattered the amalgam murder-extinctive regressivity that had set in since his father's death, while liberating the psychic operations necessary for processing this regressivity, in this instance, being able to think about murder. Thinking is an act of restraint.

A long period of abeyance was necessary before he could turn another event evoking the question of murder into an internal "other scene," also felt to be traumatic but much less so than the first. The double connection between the two scenes is obvious: the more recent scene of the arena awakened the earlier scene of the accident. But the earlier scene had found and co-opted the recent one in order to pursue its elaboration that had been in abeyance for years and to mutate the extinctive regressive economy that dominated it into a psychic sexual economy. It is this function that best defines the operation of après-coup.

Before, the deferred effects of the session were reduced to the state of reminiscences without any therapeutic effect. After the shock produced by the interpretation, recollections appeared in detail as in a process of mourning. This made it possible for anti-traumatic solutions concocted after the accident – in particular, his phobia of his mother based on the theory that she was responsible, via her brother, for his father's death – to be represented during the sessions in the form of memories, hallucinations and acts: a yellow 2CV, a motorbike, a sister – this was the sequence depicting the cause of the father's death. For him, his mother's female sexuality and her craving for high speed was fatal for her father. She might, therefore, be fatal for him too.

It was still unclear at what point the creating-finding of the event capable of being used occurred, and what the favourable conditions for the double transference were, through the transposition of the old on to the new, and through the co-optation of the new towards the old. Unquestionably, the transference scene had awakened unconscious homosexual impulses and activated, in turn, the operations necessary for an elaboration of them. The unfolding of these operations involves the repetition of old solutions and recourse to other more recently established defences, finally bringing about a murder "in presentia" of drive regressivity in order to reduce it in favour of psychic life and the act of thinking. Through the interpretation, the analyst's involvement as an identificatory support for the operation of "murder" is obvious. The analyst is thus involved in the resumption of the dynamic of the operation of après-coup. But the transposition of this operation of "murder" on to the anaclitic object supporting the transference depends, ultimately, on the patient. The analyst proposes, the patient disposes.

An important point needs to be underlined here because it is at the origin of psychoanalytic theories that put the object in the foreground. This transposition creates a false connection between the murder and the object. The operation is then envisaged as bearing on the object and not on the extinctive quality of the drive. Of course, ambivalence about carrying out this foundational operation on the drive is at the origin of this preference for the murder-object connection. It is a question, then, of limiting guilt by making sure that the object is still alive. The Oedipal dynamic is thus realized by means of a murder of the imperative to subject the drive to renunciation and of the consequent abandonment of the drives to their regressive vicissitudes.

The vicissitudes of the evolution of this little patient were, of course, far from over. Many detours, interruptions and resumptions of his treatment were necessary before he was able to take interest in his father's personality, in his "hotheaded" and "daredevil" aspects, and get beyond the event of the accident, give up his screen and take interest in the events of his mentalization. He was still unable to go to the cemetery. His object-choices of a young man remained hesitant, marked by his attempt to maintain a relationship that could keep his father alive.

Sensory reminiscence and holidays: A dream of ecstatic enjoyment

Mrs B.: *"I dreamt ... well, no ... when I woke up ... I was very happy about what I had just experienced and felt in my dream. In fact, it was just a sensation; there were no other memories or images."*

It was the day before the holidays. The interpretation thus spontaneously gravitated towards keeping and retaining the missing object, towards feeling its presence in herself. The mystical solution of the dream empty of content was therefore not foreign to her. Moreover, anonymity realized the wish to have all the objects of the world at her disposal, against the background of the object missing forever; and, in a more realistic way, that of taking advantage of her holidays to meet a man.

The woman who had this dream of nocturnal sexual pleasure is abstinent on account of unconscious guilt. She has a younger sister who is severely disabled by a major form of epilepsy. Her dream is thus a compromise. It allows her to keep the presence of the object that is going away and to remain present for the object that she is leaving. To do this, she has recourse to a sensual regression and to its bodily conversion in the guise of restraint and satisfaction. Sensual sensation stands in for epileptic object.

While the dream-work ordinarily ensures that sensual regression is restrained by maintaining, thanks to the representations in images, a relationship to object-cathexis, in this case, we are in the presence of a sensual deferred effect within sleep. It has the interest of showing us that the operation of après-coup can do without representative contents and use sensuality, that it is involved in the setting-up of a libidinal economy converted into bodily erogeneity.

A palliative acoustic reminiscence

Another occurrence may appear, where language is neither decathected nor maintained under the sole aegis of the secondary process; nor is it open to the double meaning of primitive words through the formal regression of incidental speech, but rather is the object of a sensual regression.

Language becomes, then, in the dream or the session, an acoustic hallucination. The sensory field of sound is opposed to the internal noise. This use of the voice echoes the ordinary anti-traumatic phenomenon of "talking to oneself," which consists in speaking to oneself out loud. Auto-sensoriality conceals the noise of drive activity. It is the latter that is involved in the auditory hallucinations of the mental automatism typical of chronic hallucinatory psychosis. This important dimension in the session often goes unnoticed. It creates an anti-traumatic saturation by acoustic means.

Mr P. was born three weeks before his father's death in a transit camp. Of Ashkenazi origin, the latter had been arrested in a round-up on coming out of the metro 6 months earlier. So he had no memories of his father. His mother, an Ashkenazi from Poland nourished the legend of a father who had died in war as a hero. Mr P. was hidden as a small baby in a foster home, and his elder brother, 3 years his senior, was placed in another family. He returned to live with his mother at the age of 13. Neither his mother nor his brother spoke to him about his father. During his schooling he had to hide his name, i.e., his father's name, and use another as a replacement. After returning to his mother, his subsequent educational achievements were brilliant and he obtained many diplomas. Then he worked in a very large company without obtaining any of the promotions that seemed to be on offer to him, but they never amounted to more than promises. His doctoral thesis received unanimous commendations and augured a brilliant professional career.

It was later, as an adult, that he gained access thanks to his brother to some documents concerning his father: the father's ID card and a piece of paper with his father's handwriting on it, in the transit camp, asking for a blanket because he was cold. My patient's active interest in writing had an affective dimension to it inasmuch as a written request had not been heard. He had the same conviction about his own writings and their circulation, namely, that they were not being heard, understood and listened to, an aspect that was easily identifiable in the analysis of course.

Three years after his mother's death, when he was over the age of 45, he began an analysis complaining about a general sense of ill-being, an impression of having remained on the outside of life, about a total absence of affectivity after his mother's death, which never ceased to surprise him. His mother had worked to pay for the board and studies of her sons. During her days off she would go and sit on a bench by the cemetery that was closest to her, even though, to the best of her knowledge, she personally knew of no one who was buried there. Her primal scene was melancholic.

After a few years of psychoanalysis, he undertook studies in psychology, and then negotiated, in a very determined showdown with his employer, early retirement with a salary in the form of an annuity: the economic situation at the time made this quite feasible, even if this arrangement was dominated by the procedural or, at least, conflictual aspects of it.

At the same time, he began to write, publish and edit and also wanted to distribute his books, but in a dispersed, autonomous and megalomaniac way. His approach and his grievance were reminiscent of unknown inventors; they were condemned to failure.

In the sessions he talked in a high-pitched voice, struggling against the vanity and sterility of his grievances. He exhausted himself in an endless quest. He wanted to be read, to be received; he wanted his books to be accepted in libraries, archived on the shelves, registered. This painful and insistent quest gave his remarks a pathetic tone of acute distress covered over by the powerful sound of his voice. He spoke of receiving very negative reactions, very disparaging judgements, movements of rejection and disdain reinforced by his insistence. He stubbornly invested in this mission to "get people to read" (by "being read himself") the missive of his father, to have the latter's written word heard, this cry of alarm that he had addressed to his own sister, a very rich woman with a lot of social skills, albeit prudent. She had not gone to put her name on the list of Jews and had tried to dissuade her brother and sister-in-law from doing so, but in vain. So she could not intervene on her brother's behalf without denouncing herself. The legend was enriched by a suspicion. My patient's father was allegedly given some medication by "mistake," or during clinical trials, or with the deliberate aim of precipitating his end.

During his analysis he decided to go to Poland with the aim of following on the tracks of his father and mother; she was so silent that he knew nothing about her history. One evening, he returned to his hotel by car and did not wait till the tilting garage door was completely open, with the result that he damaged the roof of his car. He himself was unhurt, but stunned!

His father's message could gradually be read as an element of perceivable reality signifying the cachexia of his dying father, but also serving as a screen against his mother's melancholia.

These clinical elements may be conceived of as various deferred effects, some symptomatic, others elaborative. They help to draw attention to the importance of the deferred effect of sound in the session. The difficulty in accomplishing psychic registrations can be heard in the saturation of sound and in the quest sustained by writing and its circulation. The compulsion to write is sometimes concealed by sublimation and aestheticization, but these are usually largely superseded by defective historical identifications.

The above examples show that the reminiscence that subsumes all clinical work is indeed of a processual nature. What is involved is a memory of the psychic operations and processes involved in the elaboration of these diverse clinical pictures, a memory without recollection, a *processual memory* that uses traces and representations and the body itself to realize itself. This memory can be made explicit only by means of metaphors of theoretical value, such as the assertions of the Oedipus complex, the formulations expressing primal phantasies, the concept of the murder of the father and so forth.

The depiction of the operation of après-coup by a sequential dream

Mr F. This patient had a dream in which the operation of après-coup was enacted within his dream by the means of three scenes with three intermediate ruptures. It finished almost as a nightmare.

First scene of the dream: *I was with my wife, the one I'm divorcing. We were arguing; she took up everything I said with an ironic smile and transformed it in such a way as to make me feel guilty and to show me that I had never done what was necessary. It was to do with the children's departure on holiday, their clothes weren't ready, the bags were not ready; the whole aim of my ex is to show me that I am a bad father. She takes up everything I say in order to turn it to my disadvantage and to her advantage. Things were getting increasingly tense. Her smile became absolutely ironic and sadistic. At a certain moment, I threw myself at her and took her by her shoulders, pinned her on the ground and started shouting, "But can't you see that I'm going to kill you?" At that moment, I felt someone's hand behind me grabbing me by the neck, by my collar and my clothes and pulling me backwards. A voice said to me: "Come over here," and he pulled me backwards. It was your voice. I was pulled by this hand that took me on a long trip backwards, and I could see my life unwinding before me as I was going back in time, pulled by this hand. And so I found myself at the age when my brother was twelve and a half years old."* This was the age at which he had lost his father.

Second scene of the dream: *I was in a courtyard, one that I know, though without being able to locate it, because I have already dreamt about it in other dreams. I was with my brother. Some of his friends were also there. In fact, it was friends that he had when he was older, one of whom had caught AIDS and been very ill. I went to see him at the hospital, but my brother always refused to go and visit him. This friend has been dead for a long time now. It made me think about homosexuality."* At that moment, I woke up in the dream and I said to myself in my waking state in the dream: "Oh! That's very important, I must tell Chervet about it."

Third scene of the dream: *I was in a city; like the courtyard before, it was a town that I know without really knowing it. In fact, it was Budapest. A city that is like Lyon. In fact, it was Lyon; I was at certain places in the city, which resembles Budapest with part of the city on a hill separated from the other part by a river, like Buda and Pest. I met up with a whole group of friends that I knew well. We decided to go for a walk; I was with my two children, holding them by the hand, one on each side of me, and I felt great affection for them, great pleasure. We were talking with our friends and we decided to go for a walk in the park (he called the park by its Budapest name). He then said that it was a bit as if he had come to Grange Blanche (an area of Lyon). Then we decided to catch the bus. At that moment, my mobile phone rang; I tried to take it out of my pocket, did so successfully, and answered. It was someone at work who was asking me for an article of about 1200 words. I replied that I had promised to do this article for the 15 September, and that there was no question of doing it before, but that it would be ready for the 15 September. This friend insisted, and I responded firmly. I ended the call and noticed that my friends had all gone. I caught sight of them in the distance, in certain alleys. At that moment, I noticed that my children were neither with my friends nor with me. The bus had passed and they had taken the bus; they had got in and I had stayed on the pavement. I was distraught, began to cry and felt extremely anxious. At that moment, my tears began to turn into laughter; then I had a huge fit of sarcastic laughter and went completely crazy. I woke up with tears in my eyes and feeling intensely anxious.* End of dream.

Each part takes up the previous situation after a shift of place and time. The representation of the analyst is used to depict someone who facilitates forward spurts and surges in fits and starts. The analyst is the support of the function that stops the precipitation along the regressive path. In the transference he is the support of the counter-shock in response to the regressive yearnings of the drives. The three counter-shocks are thus depicted directly by the visual, but also the sonorous presence of the analyst, which allows the dream to end on a note of compromise: he finds himself in the position of a stray father who has lost his children, who are themselves lost, in a big city.

This man lost his father at the age of 5. The beginning of his treatment was concerned with intense homosexual assertions that could only result in the compromise of what had been lost. And it was just before the summer holidays that he had brought this "magnificent dream, a real dissertation," he said.

The analyst's role as the author of the counter-shock is depicted explicitly. Hence, the possibility of inferring the fragility of the processual imperative. The analyst's direct presence in the dream, as well as the fact of referring to him directly in the dream within the dream, leads us in the same direction. This increased restraint conceals the desire to get rid of the analyst and to keep the father intact both instinctually and ideally.

Après-coup, signification and advent of meaning

It is now widely accepted that the operation of après-coup makes it possible to process old, but also recent traumas. The correlation between the two is generally recognizable. The fact that a recent trauma can be sought after, then found or even constructed in order to respond to and modify an earlier trauma is taken into consideration less often, as is the notion that an endogenous traumatic dimension may still be active independently of external events.

We have thus already added greater complexity to the notion of trauma and noted that its processing by the mind includes the mechanism of transposition on to sensory perceptions and sensations and the mechanism of co-opting recent events. The latter are often minor for an outside observer, but traumatic for a subject due to the fact that such a correlation between the two events, in fact between two stages, has been established. These correlations, transpositions and co-optations are in the service of the economic function of the operation of après-coup and its aim of producing a bonus of desire turned towards the world of objects.

This schema is rendered even more complex by clinical experience. For example, the processing of a trauma thanks to the deferred effects of dreams and the session discourse may seem so self-evident that it is nothing more than the lure and concealment of another deferred effect that has remained in abeyance. According to this logic, Freud (1920b) described the dreams of the young homosexual woman as *lying and hypocritical.*

Mrs D. *The patient was a young woman who had sought therapy on account of strong inhibitions. During the therapy, she learnt that her pregnant elder sister was going to undergo an amniocentesis due to a suspected Down syndrome congenital malformation. In the sessions, she associated frenetically to her sister and no displacement was possible. The examination took place, Down's syndrome was confirmed and a therapeutic abortion was planned. Three weeks passed during which time the analyst heard no more about it. Privately, he was astonished, but was also aware of the need for a period of abeyance.*

Then she had a dream: "I was with three men and I killed two of them; after a moment of hesitation, I killed the third." End of dream.

For the analyst who asked himself which internal path the traumatic charge of these sad events was following, the dream provided an answer: three men, trisomy; two, then one, 21, Trisomy 21.

Of course, the correlation with the three sessions also permitted this triple murder to depict the silence observed during the sessions with regard to the shock of the recent events and their correlation with past and current murderous impulses.

The operation of "murder" is the basic mechanism of all mentalization. It is carried out on the extinctive tendency first, and then on the sexual impulses of the id in order to desexualize a portion of the sexual libido into narcissistic libido. It is repeated a third time on oedipal objects. The oedipal resolution combines these three foundational murders, which have the status of renunciations. The dramatization in this dream proves that mentalization emerges from a conflict between integrating the frightening traumatic news within an activity of representation and denying it. This dream is the sign of a resumption of mental activity, in particular of associativity concerning the relations, ambivalent to say the least, between the two sisters; the unconscious fratricidal dimension can be deployed.

I simply underlined the link between three men and trisomy, hoping thereby to strengthen this link with the aim of preparing for the possibility of taking up with her again the traumatic attraction trisomy/empty belly. In so doing, I succumbed to an animistic conception of the dream-work, according to which the latter is completely concerned with resolving the effects of event-related traumas.

Admittedly, this dream invites such a theorization in that it seems to accord priority to external reality and to conceal this in the dream-work. Such a conception links up with Charcot's pre-Freudian theory of trauma/shock, with a silent period of incubation situated between the traumatic event and the appearance of the dream.

Three weeks went by once again. The young woman, in the course of her associations, indicated that she had been pregnant for more than two months. She had not spoken about it before. The dream and the whole foregoing discussion therefore have to be reconsidered from the point of view of her thoughts about her pregnancy kept in abeyance in the course of the sessions.

The main event concerned her desire for a child and her being pregnant. She chose and co-opted her sister's trisomy and abortion in order to transpose and depict unrepresented internal threats linked to her desire for a child as a way of countering these threats. It was this mixture of a desire for a child and internal threats that was actualized in this woman's inhibitions. The analyst thus participated unwittingly in this animistic transvaluation of external reality. The traumatic quality of the latter was, in fact, coupled with another reality, internal, which was much more significant and therefore concealed, to which the murder and the hesitation about killing the third man, the 2+1, was addressed. Her own desire for a child, via the male genitors, almost suffered the same fate as her sister's pregnancy, and her analyst was also almost satisfied with the first deferred effect. The concealment could then have followed its path under the cover of a shared denial.

This dream helps us to see how the operation of après coup articulates the significance of its formations and the meaning of the operation. It produces significance and can conceal meaning.

The first interpretation seems to be in the order of meaning but turns out to be one of the significations of the dream as soon as the element left out of the picture – the situation of a pregnant woman – is taken into account. Thus, the production by the operation of après-coup of significance pursues its first mission, that of placing regressive contents under the regime of the pleasure principle. As for meaning, it includes consideration given to the internal origin of the traumatic reality. It is the consequence of fully recognizing the reality of this extinctive drive regressivity. It depends on the test of the judgement of existence. This situation is reminiscent of the one to which Freud ascribed a favourable therapeutic prognosis. In fact, this prognosis was based on a conception of trauma and après-coup centred on external reality, a theory guaranteeing the supremacy of the pleasure principle.

The twofold movement of the operation of après-coup is revealed here: its accession to consciousness and its concealment, which also serves as a link with consciousness. Thus, the operation of après-coup operates between significance and meaning.

The countertransference, a definition

Let us take an example of countertransference that proves to be a deferred effect of the analytic situation. A few years ago, I had to present an analysis unfolding over several years. I had the history of this analysis quite clearly in my mind. So I gathered together my notes concerning it and re-read them. How surprised I was! The history that I had in my memory was a reconstruction with an intimate conviction that was very different from the one that I rediscovered in my notes. This important difference caught my attention.

Just after the joint decision to begin her analysis, with a waiting period of several months, my patient had decided to see another analyst of a different persuasion, who agreed to see her immediately for several short sessions a week. Then she broke off her sessions with him to begin her analysis with me at the planned date. She had thus created a *stand-by* analysis.

During the first summer vacation of her analysis with me, she had joined a club for meeting people and had taken a lover for the summer; a *holiday* and *stand-by lover*.

In my reconstruction, I had displaced this last sequence to the beginning of her analysis. So in my memory, she had taken a lover during the waiting period. I had substituted the holiday lover for the stand-by analyst to the point of creating a stand-by lover and a holiday analyst. Why had I excluded the stand-by analyst?

My patient had asked for an analysis within a particular context. She had been in analysis with a colleague whom I knew. One morning, she arrived at her analyst's for her session; she entered and went into the waiting room, where she found her analyst lying on the floor. She called the emergency services and saved her analyst, who had had a heart attack. A few months later, by common agreement, they took the decision to stop the analysis and to continue it with another, younger analyst.

What I had put aside, albeit without forgetting it, was therefore the incident: an analyst is dying and is saved by his patient. The amusing scene: "an analyst is saved by his patient" had enabled me to conceal the sad reality of the mortal analyst, a concealment reinforced by my forgetting of the stand-by analyst in favour of an analyst/lover who was very much alive.

A lesson can be drawn from this little scene. I had carried out, quite unwittingly, a psychic work of displacement and condensation culminating in a reconstruction of the history of this treatment in order to diminish the traumatic impact of the identification with the "dead analyst," which was itself concealed by the series of enactments of this patient.

In this case the psychic deferred effect of the analyst was completed, while the patient's was not. One definition of the countertransference can be inferred from this. The countertransference is not only an identification with the psychic functioning of the patient; it is also an identification with the psychic processes that the patient is lacking. The analyst therefore completes the patient, just as a mother does with her newborn baby.

These two forms of countertransference are entangled in every analysis: one arises from contamination through hysterical identification (Braunschweig & Fain, 1975) with the regressive hallucinatory fulfilments of patients and the other from the loan by the analyst of psychic elements that the patient is lacking. These two paths also play a role in the patient's choice of analyst by virtue of a transference that is already there.

The forms of countertransference that seek to provide the patient with what he is lacking are particularly stimulated by the associativity arising from the amalgam of several incompatible modes of psychic functioning, an amalgam of clinical situations of denial with those in which castration is taken into account. Clinical pictures dominated by distress, disarray, deprivation and disorganization play particularly on the analyst's wish to come to the rescue and to lend the processuality of his own psychic apparatus in order to make up for this lack. Likewise, patients who present severe disorganizations devoid of regression to infantile levels of functioning elicit in the analyst's countertransference listening the presence of the missing instinctual drive functioning.

In a more general and theoretical way, the countertransference is measured by the gap that exists between the functioning of the analyst imposed in the session by the patient's associativity and the analyst's ideal and theoretical functioning of reference, permitting his evenly suspended attention. The "sum" of the countertransference is measured by the yardstick of this gap.

This ideal situation, which is accessible at certain moments in sessions, links up two processes at the heart of the analyst's thinking: mourning and the regressive infantile sphere. It is the tension between the two that makes possible the strategic choice of interpreting either the regressive materials of the infantile pole or the mourned material of the pole of completion. At the same time this conflictual tension has a function in relation to the extinctive tendency opposed by the imperative of psychic registration, which finds the solution of conflict to fulfil its aim. This is what makes the *tendency to conflict* of which Freud (1937a, p. 244) speaks intelligible. It is the result of another more elementary conflict, the *fundamental ambivalence* of which Freud (1930) speaks between the extinctive tendency of the drives and the imperative to register them in the form of impulses within the id. It is also possible here to catch a glimpse of the two poles constitutive of the unconscious: the unconscious of regressive wishes and the unconscious of wishes born of renunciation.

Neo-identities and perceptual saturation as deferred effects

I have already drawn attention to the existence of unconscious neo-identities that are apt to reveal themselves in the course of analyses. I have recognized their value as deferred effects due to the fact that regressivity is highly present in the transference, stimulated by all the frustrations and impressions of lack that these neo-identities are supposed to counter and suppress. They are potential identities that have remained latent for years, generally buried in some kind of idealized professional or other activity. They become manifest under the pressure of the transference, which exacerbates regressivity and makes the appeal to unconscious resources unthinkable. They are called upon, emerge and reveal themselves as responses to the extinctive urgency. What had hitherto remained latent emerges from the shadows.

Mrs A. sought analysis on account of a barely definable impression, a vague feeling, of "not having her feet on the ground." Although it was fairly easy, when presenting this analysis years later, to recognize what this expression implied, a great deal of work had been necessary before these inaugural words assumed a density of latent identity, before the neo-identity involved in this feeling could be constructed in her sessions; and yet more years before this process of becoming conscious could mutate into new awareness following a renunciation of this idealization with the therapeutic consequences that followed from it.

Mrs A. was born one year after the death of a sister who had died when she was just a few days old. When she died, my patient's maternal grandmother allegedly declared that this child had been taken by the hand of God, that her daughter had been chosen by God to accomplish this sacrifice and that she should be delighted by this election. So she did not visit her daughter.

The grandmother's family was known throughout the region. Several of its members had had very vivid visions. They had been "visited." The value of these visions as messages through direct contact with divine powers was shared by the local group. Furthermore, with each new generation, several members of the family joined religious orders. One of her sisters lived in seclusion. One of her brothers had been to a seminary.

As for the patient's father, he found dignity by living in modesty and self-effacement. He worshipped some lady in blue of his dreams. He gave his daughter, my patient, a first name recalling the redeemer, but which was also the first name of a young girl whom he had known during his captivity as a prisoner of war. She played the violin. My patient made her daughter learn this instrument with great determination. As a counterpoint, the father's nights were haunted by horrible nightmares about the war and his bedside table was occupied by a life of Christian martyrs.

The neo-identity that she had built was a compromise between becoming a subject and supporting the denial of her parents. This woman had identified with a hallucination of her parents, in fact with what could give constancy to the hallucination that they needed to maintain in order to assure themselves that their dead daughter was still alive. The permanence of their hallucinatory fulfilment supported the commandment of their religious system, enjoining them to exclude all work of mourning in their psychic life.

My patient thus had to live in order to ensure that her sister was well and truly alive, and not show herself to be too alive because this would have reminded her parents of how she was different from her sister. "Not having her feet on the ground" was thus a compromise between these two positions, terrestrial and celestial. She offered her parents a perception that had the value for them of continuous perceptual activity. She embodied the perceptual activity of another, turning this perceptual activity into a perception for this other.

Mr X. Drawing on the life of George Bryan Brummell, I have studied another neo-identity, that of dandyism (Chervet, 1993), based on providing another person with a perception that has the function of suppressing the traumatic echo of nudity and the difference between the sexes. Thus, the dandy maintains a denial of nudity by saturating the consciousness of others with the sight of a fetishistic piece of clothing that is supposed to clothe the void of another (the knots in Beau Brummel's ties).

Such neo-identities appear in fact in all analyses. They are identities of denial. Their common point is that they provide an anti-traumatic palliative from the outside for the traumatic neurosis of another person that is active internally as an imago of identification (see Denis, 1996, 2002), an anti-traumatic palliative that this other person is unable to produce himself, a palliative for psychic processes that this other person is lacking.

The isolation of the two poles of the operation of après-coup

Mrs E. – This 45-year-old woman suffers from frigidity. She is sterile and describes herself as a "vomiter." She eats normally but makes herself vomit immediately afterwards in secret.

Here are two sequences of a dream:

1st sequence: "A man in black, with a black pullover; I saw him from behind; I recognized my father from the pullover; it was his ski pullover. He went away."

2nd sequence: I was in a house, a bit like yours and like my grandparents' house. There was a sort of animal, a camel; in fact, an animal with dust all over it. It had the body of a praying mantis and a camel's head. My cousins arrived; I have forgotten the rest."

The correlations between her associative affirmations and the contents of the dream and the regression to the double meanings of primitive words could be heard without difficulty in each of her sentences. She talked about her household tasks, about the fact that "he would just have to manage with his pullovers; that there was no question of doing any more than the strict minimum."

She continued on the subject of her gym teacher who had tried to get her to take part in a game, which she had refused to do. This ball game is called "La passe à 10,"[1] *"I do not like collective games. In any case, I will do as I please."*

*Then she associated to her work, to the errors made by others which obliged her to do everything again and to cover up what she had already done. She is an artist/sculptor. "Au moins une fois par mois, il faut que je mastique," she said, without hearing the double meaning (*mastiquer *means using putty, while* m'astiquer *means to clean oneself, and in slang to masturbate).*

She returned to the two animals in her dream. She pointed out that this animal seemed to be waking up, emerging from the dust. I intervened, prematurely: both these names could be applied to women.

She associated to herself and her mother; then she asked herself: "What could give me more pleasure than eating?" I said: "Devouring the male" She replied: "No, for me it's eating that is bad (mal)" (double meaning mal/mâle).

She went on to talk about a scene that her husband had told her about the evening before: a woman arrived and parked in the carpark in front of the company's offices; she got out of the car and paced up and down, smoking. Then she entered the lobby area, got undressed and lay down naked on the sofa.

My patient continued, grumbling about "those big male idiots" who all came to subdue her. Then she added that this woman was in fact on medication. Her brother had killed himself in a car accident a few days before. She could not get over it. An ambulance was called and she had been hospitalized.

It now became possible to offer an interpretation, provided that one took into account the fact that this patient had lost her father 1½ years earlier, and that her mourning was blocked by a fixation of feelings of hatred towards him. It was this unaccomplished mourning that she recognized in the co-opted story of the nympho-manic crisis. She made use of the story to transpose on to it that aspect of her which went well beyond the death of her father and concerned the construction of her psychic life and her desires as a woman towards men, that aspect of her drives that was still not available to her and could be expressed only by making an offering of her body.

The first sequence is oriented towards what, in her, is going away. The second is an enactment of female greed through animal imagery. Strictly drive-related interpretations concerning the devourer of men, the Passe à 10, masturbation, the praying mantis, the camel of the "che vuoi" (Lacan, taken from Jacques Cazotte (1772)), do not account totally for the compulsive greed as it appears in the scene of the young woman. This compulsion requires restraint through the reference in the dream to static mineral elements, the habitat, the dust, the pullover. The restraint realized by the dream-work is the image that dominates in the first sequence of the dream. In contrast, the second is much more impoverished and we are faced with dislocated psychic work. The instinctual drive pole and the processual pole, that which is responsible for the reduction of drive extinction, are isolated from each other in each of the parts of the dream and cannot produce a common content that corresponds to the two poles.

An interpretation of the impasse in which she has invested her drive impulses to the point of making an unconscious neo-identity out of it emerges: "being exciting enough to awaken the dead."

Via this identity, the dreamer is entirely occupied with holding back the drive regressivity that is unfolding in her. It is with this aim that she uses representations arising from various realms of organic and inorganic matter, mineral, vegetable, animal, human, inert, moving, living, etc., in order to depict and register the various qualitative states of her emerging drive impulses in an identity of denial.

The various operations underlying psychic animism can be recognized here. First, the transposition of the unconscious elements of the psyche on to concrete and perceivable material elements; then, the election and choice of these elements in terms of whether their qualities are more or less suitable for serving as a support for the transposition of drive qualities such as the extinctive tendency, narcissistic tonicity and infantile versatility; then the creation of representations of these external elements of perception in order to be able to make use of them and co-opt them in dreams, myths, tales and stories. These operations permit an interplay of reciprocal identifications of internal and external elements. Double meanings and metaphorization are the results, while a confusion between them is maintained by means of amalgam and substitution.

Waking animism, however, does not have the combinatory facilities of the displacements and condensations of dreams. Perception insists and resists. The difference between perception and representation produces a traumatic effect that is amplified by the existence of another difference already discussed above, with a much more powerful traumatic impact, between perceptions with traces and perceptions without traces. This is the case of the perceptions of lack and of all differences that give rise to affects of fright and terror, as well as of explanatory and causal theories, of which the central one in psychoanalysis is the theory of castration. The primal phantasy of castration by the father corresponds to this traumatic effect of all difference. The most important effect is linked to the so-called difference between the sexes; the least important is due to small differences, between perceptions and representations and between representations. Hence, the need to combine perception with a hallucinatory mode of perceptual activity providing a perceptual identity; and, to this end, to add to the operations of dreams other waking mechanisms fulfilling roles similar to those of sleeping and dreaming. Such is the role of the denial of the reality of perceptions without representation and of the animistic transvaluation of the value of perceptions by theories that conceive of them as hallucinatory representations. The study of reality-testing must take account of all these differences between the diverse realities that present themselves on awakening on the two sides of the screen of consciousness, the external side of the sense-organs and the internal side of endogenous productions. The reality of sensory perception, the reality of hallucinatory perceptual identity, the reality of perceptions with representation, the reality of drive representatives, the reality of perceptions without representation and the reality of the extinctive drive tendency can therefore be distinguished, confused and concealed.

This is where the connecting link between the animism of dreams and that of the session lies. Both bestow psychic values on representations and perceptions of reality and present to consciousness a perceptual reality that is exempt from what is experienced as traumatic by a subject and that is at the origin of the correlation between the extinctive tendency of the drives and perceptions without trace.

To reach this aim of concealment and then utilization of the extinctive quality of the drives, the dream-work and that of session animism will have recourse to a saturation of consciousness by productions in perceptual identity, along the internal path for dreams and along the internal and external paths during the session (the voice of enunciation). The more internal traumatic reality is experienced compulsively, the more the scenarios presented draw on memories of traumatic events. Hallucinatory perceptual identity cannot be continuous. Language therefore reinforces the need for theories and conceptions that interpret the world according to beliefs and ideologies, private or group-related, in the service of denial of the correlation between the extinctive tendency and perception without traces.

Dreams, animism and session discourse have the use of interpretation in common. These productions of the psyche can be differentiated in terms of the aim of the interpretation. For dreams and session animism, it is a matter of modifying the value of the realities perceived by bestowing on them a perceptual value, whereas the therapeutic aim is based on the recognition of unconscious psychic realities concealed in the manifest representations of reality. The confusion is thereby removed. The reality of extinctive tendencies is taken into account and perceptions without traces are recognized. Access to the difference between the sexes is reached by taking this long trajectory with all the hurdles that I have described.

Mrs Da. – "I have had two dreams: the first was just after the last session, and then there was the weekend; I had the second at the end of the weekend."

The first dream: *I saw a spider, and then lots of spiders that that were coming out of my bed, out of the walls; they were everywhere, on the ground, on the ceiling and perhaps they were even coming out of me. I could see their very furry paws. But, strangely enough, I was not anxious in the dream; it was not a nightmare.*

Such a dream makes use of a precise mode of defence, namely multiplication as an anti-traumatic response, as it appears in the image of the Medusa's head. The increase in number is a response to the perception of a lack. The compulsion to represent appears where an absence requires a psychic process that cannot make do with representations alone. But in the case of this dream the absence of anxiety is striking. It suggests that family complicities are involved in the difficulty in bringing about transformations of drive impulses, transformations that have the significance of murder.

Through her associations, this woman evoked childhood spots, mosquito bites, and then spider bites with a childhood fantasy/theory mixing puss, swelling, bites, infection and inoculation; thus, a childhood theory according to which spiders lay their eggs under the skin and may multiply there. I could not fail to notice the importance ascribed to the skin, a skin characterized by itching and generativity.

The second dream: "*I was in my house and realized that my neighbour had enhanced his house, that he had redone the roof and that he had taken advantage of this to add an additional floor to his house with large bay windows which overlooked the porch of my kitchen. I was furious about having this situation imposed on me.*"

The wish fulfilled under cover of her anger is obvious: "I am so interesting, so beautiful, so irresistible, that he is prepared to climb up high to see me." Certainly, in the course of the session and transferentially, I was the one who was "on the balcony." I had noticed, moreover, that this woman never wore even the suggestion of a neckline.

She then brought associations to her house, her father, his relationship to the work on his house and the wooden structure. Then she talked about a phone call from her father at the weekend; about the way he would impose himself when speaking about the work on his house; she recalled her childhood solution of letting him go on talking while she went off into daydreaming. Here we can easily recognize the neighbour who imposed himself.

She then talked about her profession and about supervision, a supervision that she had done a few years back with a famous child analyst. One day, she had had the impression that the analyst was saying to her: "Child psychotherapy is not for you." This had upset her so much that, after continuing her supervision for a while, she then stopped it.

I commented out loud on the importance of "seeing" in her associations to the second dream: the bay windows – the super-vision – the name of the supervisor that contained a syllable connected with sight; and she added: in the first dream, it was a question of skin.

She heard immediately my allusion to the separation of the members of a couple, in analogy with the separation of the two dreams and of the sensory paths, touch and sight. She went on to say that her supervisor's husband had written on the theme of skin; then she burst into tears and continued crying for a long time. I then learnt that at the age of three, she had burned herself seriously and had been hospitalized for fifteen days. She then told me about a scar she had on her shoulder. She hesitated and no longer knew which one. For years, she hadn't "given a damn" about it, but now she was unable to wear a neckline, and didn't feel well in a swimsuit. The words attributed to the supervisor turned out to have masked another statement: "Necklines are not made for you." Then she went on with some sort of bizarre logic. She explained to me that her son made a slight hissing sound when pronouncing certain syllables and that the child's father had insisted on his doing speech therapy; she, however, knew where it came from because she had realized that when pronouncing certain syllables her son twisted his mouth slightly and that this reminded her of the time when he was at the breast. She thought that it was linked to the period of breastfeeding and that her son had probably screwed up his face when he was put to the breast on the side where she had a scar. She linked this to something an uncle had said to her when she was a young girl to the effect that she would have one breast that would not "be good"; "which is not true," she added animatedly.

I understood, then, that the most important symptom for this woman, namely, her belief that a man could not stay with her for very long, a belief that was acted out in the reality of her love life – her successive relationships all broke up after a few years – was based on this bodily trace, this reality of castration that, gave her an identity of being banished, reversed into feelings of being irresistible.

The dislocation of the processes involved in creating the deferred effect makes each of them perceivable, respectively, in each of the dreams. The first stage of anti-traumatic immobilization is replaced by a compulsion of counter-shocks depicted by the multitude of spiders connected with bodily sensations linked to the burn and to the constant tingling sensations of the regenerating skin. The second stage producing a content arising from a psychic work of distortion and regeneration shows a greater concealment of the traumatic dimension and distancing from it. This is clearly taken up again in the pair exhibitionism/voyeurism, but it is limited to the neighbour. The persecutory tone persists. The regressive attraction is therefore still dominant. At the end of the session, I told her that the bay windows were an allusion to those of the hospital and that the neighbour was trying to see her wound and the scene that had taken place.

This intervention took into account the fact that during the session, she told me absolutely nothing about the scene and the circumstances of the accident, thus leaving it buried within a primal scene by means of a causal theory treating the scar as evidence of her passage through the primal scene.

The deferred effects of defective identifications

The following sequence of analysis is dominated by defective logic, such as we are familiar with in melancholia and the negative therapeutic reaction. The deferred effects of these clinical pictures may be described as defective and apprehended as reminiscences of defective identifications that have been imposed, that have "fallen on" the ego.

Mrs G. – The distribution of the sexual cathexes of this woman had already been remarked upon during the sessions but remained as such. In her associations and in her life, two separate worlds could be identified. This woman had a rich erotic and affective life. She had a friend, the father of one of her children, and some quite joyful adventures satisfying her desires for novelty, but adventures that could be abandoned without much difficulty in the name of her partnership. In parallel, she expressed strong feelings of suffering and a deep sense of affliction in connection with her ex-husband. According to her, he had a morally sadistic attitude towards her that involved privations and frustrations. He never replied either to her letters or to her phone calls concerning the children, which left her in great disarray. For her, a divorce ought to result in a reasonably friendly relationship, as the function of the divorce was to eliminate all hatred. To speak to her ex-husband she had to go through lawyers, which drove her to despair. Entire sessions could be taken up with her grievances against this sadistic "ex" who made her suffer. Her sadomasochism was thus isolated and unintegrated with her overall erotic life. For her, this drive quality should not exist, either in the form of arguments or domestic fights. If she was speaking about it, it was not because it existed in her, but solely because of her ex. She did not understood arguments and domestic fights at all and, while what she said came across as apparently mature, it was in fact devoid of any possibility of regression to sadomasochistic dynamics.

When a former friend/lover, who had been so much in love with her that he had had to move away from her geographically when they broke up in order to get over his lovesickness, got in touch with her again, she sank in the space of a few sessions into a state of "erotic melancholia" (Ferrand, 1610). She became silent, languished and was dying; she could no longer swallow anything, lost weight and had an acute sense of the vanity of all things.

My encouragements to associate and explore what was happening to her, what had made her lose her taste for living completely, my cautious interpretations concerning her way of escaping sadomasochistic conflict by subjecting herself to more and more suffering, to seek satisfactions bypassing suffering, had no effect.

Nevertheless, she continued her sessions. Sometimes her friend or her parents accompanied her. She raised the possibility with me of being hospitalized. After taking time to consider whether this request belonged to the associative material, I replied that only she could know if hospitalization was absolutely necessary. I added that if she was hospitalized, we would try to maintain the sessions, for only her psychic state could improve her condition.

After leaving a session during which she had clearly been very desperate, she went missing. Her friend telephoned me. I had no arguments to alleviate his concerns, apart from my confidence in her mental resources. It was her ex-lover who found her, huddled up in her car, lost and immobilized, waiting perhaps.

In the next session she told me I had really been "pushing things" ("*j'ai été vraiment limite*") to let her leave like that; which was true. By using the word "*limite*," she was stressing that she was at the limits of her possibilities of maintaining her anti-cathexes by drawing on her masochism. She continued, in quite an unexpected way, with several dreams. She pointed out how intense they were. Several hours after dreaming them, they continued to impose themselves on her with a real sense of reality impeding any authentic awakening.

"I asked my friend if it was true or not, because I was so doubtful."

A dream: "France found itself excluded from Europe. It was under the domination of Cyprus. For me, it was a reality, an intense conviction in my dream; an immense feeling of oppression, of being under foreign domination." She associated to the fact that she had voted "yes" at the last referendum on Europe. Then she added that she had had another dream: "I was with my former husband; I noticed that I had several teeth that were falling apart; I lost them; they were my molars, the teeth at the back, they fell out in small pieces." I said: "When you say yes, you find yourself under the domination of your impulses again and your teeth fall apart."

She went on immediately to talk about her mother, about her mother's silence and lively and hostile reactions towards her. "I asked her to do me a favour; she did not respond and when she learnt that I had asked someone else, she got grumpy." I said to her: "She feels you are asking too much." She then went on to speak about a conflict of avidity that had existed for a very long time between them; ever since she was a little girl, she had been unable to express her desires or ask for anything at all. Her mother would impose silence on her. I said: "When you say yes to your desires, you are confronted with your mother's silence." And I formulated what had been happening over the last months: "Recently, you said yes on several occasions: you asked more of your ex-husband; you said yes to your desire for your lover; and since then you have been faced with your mother's silence. For you, this means that ever since you were little you have felt that you must renounce your needs and your desires."

This was how the repression of her infantile and Oedipal desires occurred in her, giving the impression that her Oedipal desires had been resolved even before they had been expressed. She had renounced her desires themselves instead of renouncing their satisfaction. By means of this apparent ego prematurity, she suppressed her desires for her father and ensured the protection of her mother. A mother/daughter complicity thus set in instead of an identification with the maternal function. Nevertheless, in the case of this patient, her suppression enabled her to keep her father secretly hidden within herself. The ultimate path of suppression, suicide, turned out to be limited by this secret cathexis. In her dream she depicted her extreme avidity in an image that signified devouring to the point of exhausting the means used, in this case, her teeth.

A few sessions later, just when she was gradually able to snatch short periods of sleep and rediscover a bit of appetite, and when her sessions were taken up with the elaboration of her avidity and the consequences of the negative impositions prescribed by her mother, she had another dream: "I was with my mother; she was standing silently." Then another woman arrived, an actress (perhaps Bonnaire,[2] an actress that I don't like at all, a tall skinny woman); she was naked in my dream; she lay down and I examined her body very slowly, as if with an apparatus; her skin was very soft, without any creases, smooth, beautiful, very beautiful. Not a touch of cellulitis, I was impressed." She associated: "Cellulitis, I don't like that at all, how awful!" After a few more associations, I said: "Silence is golden, like this lean and smooth body. Cellulitis is money, like speech and the urge to bite."

She continued: "I was thinking about your silence, like my mother's." Then she added: "A few days ago, I was with her for quite some time and I was surprised because she started talking and told me a lot of things."

In this situation what dominated was an identificatory imposition not to utilize foundational murderous operations. The object is born in hate, and the subject too. This woman had to be exempt of hate of any form of murderous identity. The prevailing risk was of a negative therapeutic reaction as a defective deferred effect. The operation of après-coup integrates this demand imposed by means of identifications. It is a reminiscence of these historical exigencies. The defectiveness presented itself in the form of an absence of dreams and was interrupted thanks to dreams that took over in a salutary manner this imposition to exhaust the drive by representing it through the degradation of her teeth.

Overdetermination therefore includes such identifications as a result of which the subject is unable to develop himself. The failure of the function of sadomasochism in the psychic life of this woman also determined her object-choice. She needed a man whom she felt was sadistic, thereby exciting her masochism. The law of mental life according to which what is lacking inside is sought/found outside (or returns from the outside) can be clearly seen. In this patient, sadomasochism is found extraterritorially through her object-choice and her divorce. The operation of après-coup is then reduced to a succession of "effects" that are successive shocks.

Mrs L. – This woman was suffering from bouts of insomnia. She was going through a manic period following several months of depressive stagnation, of abulia rather than really sad depression.

Her insomnia was associated with long-standing and totally inappropriate drowsiness and with the ensuing consequences, in particular, at the wheel of her car, but also, of course, in her sessions. She suddenly decided to have a few days of holiday, which amounted to real acting out with regard to her treatment. She went abroad to visit her friends' family.

When she came back to her sessions, she was once again very angry with her father and her mother, and with her former husband. During this holiday period, she had had a lot of nightmares of which she had no precise memories – just a very strong sense of having had nightmares. She also spent a lot of money, which she justified by saying she had got "good deals." She added that she made such purchases in a very particular state of mind, in a timeless daze. After buying without counting, she noticed that several hours had gone by and that she had totally forgotten everything that she been thinking about during this time. Both the timelessness and the loss of the notion of temporality are present here and are also accompanied by an absence of all restraint. In fact, spending was a means of resisting the pull of the void that was absorbing her, the experience of being emptied that she was going through.

"In such moments, I resemble my mother, and that frightens me," she said. Her mother had in fact been suffering for many years from powerful manic-depressive swings during which she made impulsive trips and spent immoderate sums of money, directly linked to her manic states. On top of this, her father also had to spend considerable sums to extricate her from the tricky situations into which she had got herself.

Mrs L. pursued her associations by moaning about her father who sometimes called her by a first name consisting of the three first names of her three brothers, as he could no longer remember hers: "to assert my individuality and express my freedom," she said, "I had to achieve very high grades in the Baccalaureate exam, higher than those of my brothers."

She continued to express her angry feelings towards her father by recalling that he had often told her that her mother had been very well before her birth and that everything had changed after she was born.

One of her three brothers is considered to be schizophrenic. In a moment of great anger towards his father, he had set all the family paintings on fire, portraits of the father's forebears, in a fit of euphoria associating dance, nudity and mutilations.

Throughout her childhood, she had witnessed or participated in a multitude of scenes involving her mother, generally at night. The latter would burst into her bedroom in order to wake her up or impede her from sleeping; she was a mother who disrupted her sleep. Her father took refuge in an office he had built in the attic, where he would shut himself in with a key. And there were other scenes too, such as those of her mother in the kitchen preventing any family meals from taking place.

Between her father's tormented complaints and her mother's scenes, she still could not find her place and was shaking with anger; she felt she was in an impasse.

After this long period of anger in the session, she felt a huge sense of void, which may be understood as a lack of internal objects linked to her parents' own lack of construction; these lacks entered into close correlation with her own guilt about constructing herself, about appropriating objects narcissistically; hence, her difficulties of anality.

These deferred effects remained centred on her narcissistic identifications and their defective qualities, which explains the fragility of her sleep, the importance of the compulsion to repeat in her associations and her recourse to bodily retention and inefficient anger.

The analytic situation instrumentalized as a palliative operation of après-coup

Mrs X. – In order to throw light on this possibility of a palliative identity that the operation of après-coup can itself assume, based on the analytic situation reduced to the sole function of anaclisis, I am now going to evoke the situation of a young woman who had been in psychoanalysis for a few years as a result of infertility. She supposed this was psychic in origin since she had been pregnant a few years earlier and this infertility had set in since the occurrence of a very precise event.

She had arrived at an age that reminded her that the biological clock could soon ring for the last time. Hence, her solid manifest motivation for beginning such a treatment. In the background there were antecedents of anorexia with a few current extensions reflected by eating disorders dominated by minor precautions and ritualizations concerning the quality of food.

For the last few years she had suffered from amenhorrea following a romantic breakup imposed by her father when she was already adult. The patient was able to talk easily about her father's intervention and her submission to his prohibition, but not her father's reasons. What was striking in the course of the treatment was the close link that existed between the mother and her daughters, all unmarried, without children, who never brought men to their parents' home. This last point was officially attributed to the risk of displeasing her father. Thus, a paternal *anti-Oedipal* configuration seemed very evident at first sight with the idea that the father wanted to *keep his daughters for himself,* who were stand-ins for his childhood incestuous object, his own mother. But the existence of maternal anti-narcissism appeared very quickly, whose role was far from insignificant, consisting of the mother's utilization of her daughters in the service of her narcissistic defences. My patient's sisters had all organized their lives in such a way that they were sexless and that the only mother of the family was their mother. Their lives as women living with a boyfriend were to be kept in silence, even though everyone knew about them, and there could be no question of their becoming mothers themselves. They thus provided their mother with the anti-depressive context that she needed. Thanks to her daughters, she could be "His Majesty the Mother," echoing the probable deficiency of "His Majesty the Baby." She strived to convince her daughters that men were all abominations and that her own life with their father was just one example among others. However, my patient was different from her sisters: she had the feeling that she was a rebel against the maternal system alienating them. Many memories corroborated for her the different place that she had with her father, as well as her mother's reproaches concerning her closeness to her father, and even reproaches concerning her physical resemblance with the paternal family. She was thus her father's daughter. While being the youngest of the daughters, she had been the first and the only one to present a man to her parents, and this was when she was already an adult. The young couple was more or less tolerated. Under the cover of their respective jobs, each of them was supposed to have the same place of residence as their own parents. The father's demands towards his daughters was thus in the service of the narcissistic needs of his wife. The father's accidental discovery of a particularity concerning the racial origins of the young man meant that he demanded that she break up with him definitively. She complied. The amenhorrea set in soon afterwards.

A few years later, she met another man and managed to leave her parents' home. However, the couple had legitimacy only in the context of their respective jobs; all my patient's free time was expected to be devoted to her mother. She experienced intense anxiogenic conflicts and a strong feeling of guilt every time she had another project than that of being at her mother's side with her sisters.

Gradually, the question of having a child became increasingly urgent, while at the same time she continued to suffer from amenhorrea. On the advice of her doctors, she decided to do an analysis.

In her sessions, her dreams very soon led her back systematically to the old boyfriend with whom she had broken up. Through them, her relationship with her father could be broached immediately, only too clearly. Indeed, her attempt not to move away from her mother by getting involved with this ex-boyfriend appeared progressively to be the obligation dominating her dreams, while concealing the wish to move away and to de-alienate herself. Her repeated mentions of her father helped to prevent her from being buried in a homosexual relationship with her mother.

In this context, the patient had very little desire for a child. Her project was presented in a rational, and even "operational or mechanical" (*opératoire*) mode. She decided to consult a psychoanalyst for reasons that gradually proved to have little to do with a need for psychic support but were more a matter of having recourse to an "operational" outside world. In fact, she sought in medicine the tutelage necessary for what may be considered as a parallel transference, an "operational" transference on to medical professionals, and she saw her psychoanalysis within the medical protocol as the prescription of a medical act to which she had to conform, just as she had complied with the prescription of her father. She told me, very discretely, that she was pregnant.

She transferred on to the analysis the capacity to intervene in her somatic functions on the model of other medical treatments that she had followed. The hysterical conversion, that is to say, neither her desire for a child as a little girl or as a woman, nor her transference on to the medical profession of her wish to appropriate the narcissistic functions of her body, to recover what was mortgaged in her alienation with her mother, was experienced by her in any way as a psychic process. Nevertheless, I could see that the reappropriation of her fertility depended on precise psychic conditions established by her, which suggested the existence in her of an unconscious intuition alongside her apparent ignorance.

Her transference on to such a medical organization of her treatment, including psychoanalysis, became more and more noticeable for me as her pregnancy advanced. This instrumental protocol certainly had the function of excluding her father's anti-Oedipus and her mother's anti-narcissism, but also of relieving her of her responsibility for her project of becoming a mother. Her pregnancy was not supposed to be evidence of her identity as a woman or of her desire for a child.

During one of her sessions, she told me that since the last session she had been waking up systematically in the middle of the night, always at the same time, and this had been going on since she had told certain friends/colleagues that she was pregnant. Her associations led her to suppose that one of her colleagues, who was also having difficulties in getting pregnant, might be overwhelmed by insufferable envy, and particular towards her. She also thought that another woman who had recommended rest and time off was simply trying to get rid of her in order to profit from her absence to take her place with their hierarchical boss, imagining that she was his favourite. The session was taken up with suspicion, Machiavellian machinations and vengeful envy, all expressed in a tone of accusation, defiance, exclusion and persecution. As a matter of fact, she excluded herself from her work and her sessions by taking a week of holidays alone with her sisters, without their partners, by way of a compromise. Her feelings had their origin in maternal domination, in her mother's counter-movements to prevent her from making use of her instinctual drive impulses. Her mother's love was conditional. The phantasy of unconditional maternal love was unelaborated. The paralysis of her reproductive functions was testimony to this controlling maternal influence concerning her desire for a child.

This sequence made it possible to interpret the pleasure she derived from being a mother, her desire to experience the bodily sensations of being pregnant. Her early childhood memories, of doll games and others, led to an interpretation concerning her radically censored childhood wish to have a child with her father. Appropriating her representations of fertility was an act imbued with guilt, for it signified depossessing her mother of her own fertility. Homosexual hatred made its appearance with difficulty. Before, it was fixed in the system of maternal ascendancy, thus mortgaging her possibility of becoming a mother by controlling these genital functions.

This sequence derived from her sessions confirms the role of the transposition of psychic functions that have remained unconscious on to the organization of a protocol of life and care. This transference delegation contained the potentiality of gaining access to the realization of her desires as an adult woman, but without having to furnish the psychic work involved in constructing these functions. In order to gain access to the status of being the subject of her desires as a woman, she first had to allow her infantile desires to emerge and then to mourn them. The protests and assertions present within her alienating identifications were formidable obstacles. This explains the fact that in her case the initial transposition on to the protocol was transformed more into projection. This only became noticeable when the repressing function played by the setting, offered by the protocol that she had organized, was in difficulty. It was nonetheless possible to infer the projective activity from the fact that her associations remained narrative-based and factual, devoid of infantile and phantasy-related sources. Phantasies and infantile theories were excluded from it. Projection became less necessary as a result of the support she had sought-found in the treatment. It proved insufficient as soon as its repressing function was less assured. Due to the demand made on her for psychic work, the negative transference and impulses of hatred could emerge. What had been abolished on the inside by the demand of someone else in the past had to be restored from the outside by someone in the present. The disturbing return can occur only by means of what has been protective. It is commonly observed in the course of analyses that a parallel transference that occurs within a more general transference on to the frame and the protocol of the treatment provides external support for the resistance and, at the same time, sets in motion the beginnings of an elaboration within the psyche. In the best of cases, the parallel transference becomes the vector of the evolution of the analysis.

The analytic après-coup and the advent of interpretation in the session

A brief *clinical* vignette will illustrate how the associations and thoughts of the analysand and the analyst during the sessions are able to capture, utilize and co-opt materials emanating from sessions, in order to realize an "analytic après-coup," serving the advent of interpretation. The material of different patients can be interwoven into the work, which results in an interpretation intended for a specific patient. The operation of après-coup uses the sessions as an elaborative detour.

Miss A. was a young woman who had never consulted an analyst before. She was "tall, slim and blonde" with a certain naivety that increased the charm of her age. The analyst was able to write these remarks only after the session with Mr B., immediately following this consultation. It was this session that gave them their significance.

The consultation was dominated by a hystero-phobic colouring and a manifest discourse of resistance to the operation of après-coup. Miss A. had protected herself against the possible excess of her spontaneous returns by bringing with her several sheets of paper that she held onto during the consultation, even though she did not read them. For her, there was no question of revisiting her past; she had come to free herself from it. So what was the point of dwelling on it? She wanted to *move forwards* (*aller de l'avant*), without hearing the double meaning of the word *avant* (forewards and before)! Her uneasiness came from her irrational effort not to displease, in fact from her effort and from the belief that this effort would enable her to free herself from her history. What she wanted was to be loved in the present. The theory that anyone who arouses displeasure can only be rejected organized her remarks. She took care never to be that person.

This young woman, who had barely emerged from adolescence, felt alienated by her struggle in a way that went beyond her manifest remarks concerning her wish to acquire maturity. Listening to her, the analyst had no difficulty in recognizing a reminiscence and so was hoping for associative recollections against which she was struggling. But for her, there was no question of returning to her past.

As I listened to her, my thoughts turned towards the origins of such a resistance to temporal regression: she did not want to be caught by her identificatory characters, yet unwittingly enacted their prescriptions; she identified with the circumstantial discourse of young people who wanted to obtain a sense of well-being without having to make the detour via the determining causes of their malaise. A few years earlier, the wish to free herself from historical burdens would probably have taken a different form of resistance, a headlong flight into a systematic, not to say meticulous and unending remembering of the past to the point of foundering in it. In all cases, it is a matter of avoiding recognition of the passivity that is necessary for the potential accomplishment of an operation of après-coup.

I pointed out my astonishment about this silence concerning her past. She replied very logically that what mattered to her was to improve her current life and her future. Then she added that she felt that she had to adapt to the person she was speaking to. She then began to speak to me about her past. She tried to comply with a request that she had transposed on to me. The transference dynamic now became identifiable. By remaining silent, I was the one who was asking her not to refer to her past. By pointing this out, I became the one whom she was disappointing, so she tried to adapt to the expectations she assumed I had of her. Her manifest discourse of rejecting any possibility of deferred understanding was thus clearly her own deferred effect of conformity, her quest for love enacted here and now.

A few minutes after she had left, Mr B. arrived for his session. He was a married man and the father of several children and sought analysis because of his concerns about the irresistible nature of the young bodies of nubile girls, his perceptual clinging to Lolitas. Mature female forms were, by contrast, sources of abhorrence and disgust. His paedophilic tendencies were easy to understand from the angle of a phobic avoidance of perceiving castration on a woman's body, the young pubertal girl enacting through her emerging bodily changes the theory that what she is lacking can potentially still emerge.

He settled down on the couch: "Tall, slim, blonde, small breasts, young…"; "just as you like them," I said. "Indeed, just as I like them." He used my words to support his objectification, whereas from my point of view they were intended to prompt him to return to his internal world; however, they could also be understood as a participation in his defensive solution. He tried to stay with his doorstep perception, rejecting the value of his associations for remembering. He continued by saying that in future he would come in advance to see her going out. In so doing, he was fulfilling Miss A.'s wish to be loved in the present in order to avoid recalling feelings of not being loved in the past.

In the transference, does this mean that the analyst's patients/daughters have access to the analyst/mother who is in collusion with their unconscious wishes? For him, the mother/daughter couple is exempt from any renunciation. Going through the daughter gives him access to the mother.

"She's the woman you've always been waiting for," I said.

In the countertransference, I tried to reestablish the present/past doublet for Mr. B., but also for Miss A. who wanted to seduce a man (the analyst and the following patient) in order to satisfy in the present her mother's unconscious wishes and thereby to participate in being with her without renunciation.

He justified himself by saying that he had arrived in advance, by chance, and that he had no idea this patient would be there, that he had never seen her leaving my office and that, consequently, he could not have been waiting for her.

Given the work done over many years of analysis, I was able to point out to him one of his resistances: "You like what is rational." His rationalization had not, however, eliminated his feelings. He continued to talk about his expectations, his emotion, his disgust, etc. The interplay of temporalities had been reestablished.

My interpretation contained the implicit message that I had recognized in what he had said at the beginning of the session, namely, the transference of a perceptual activity that he had *created* from a perception found and chosen at the beginning of the session. His associations also enacted his attempt to transform his inaccessible traumatic past by taking hold of a current session event.

When Mr B. actualized in the session his "shopkeeper" traumatic past by involving me and using my patient, I took this up and used it as a "shop assistant" moment in order to deal with the regressive attraction of the "shopkeeper" transference scene. Interpretation then became possible. It was only after the interpretation that I was able to infer that I had previously been waiting myself for a "shop assistant" moment for this patient. But my thoughts also turned retroactively to the consultation session with Miss A. and to her capacity to seduce me.

It was thus *resistance to the operation of après-coup* that formed the link between Miss A., Mr B. and me. The connection between Miss A. and Mr B. was fortuitous, whereas the utilization of Miss A. by Mr B. was highly overdetermined, as was my own entanglement. The analyst was then obliged to make use of the associative object of Mr B., called Miss A., in order to reach her traumatic compulsion, and then to be able to elaborate Miss A.'s type of seduction that was active in my countertransference.

This sequence draws attention to psychoanalytic interpretation, to its substitutive and resolutive purposes that are accomplished according to the biphasic dynamic of the operation of après-coup. On the one hand, it supports the differentiation of thing-presentations and the deployment of substitutions that requires a temporary and reversible context of denial. On the other, it seeks to break this denial of extinctive regressivity in favour of an assumption of object-related desire thanks to a successful mourning of the pleasure principle. Between the two *the analytic après-coup* is deployed, the me/not me characteristic of the session, consisting of entangled reminiscences.

Notes

1 Translator's note: A classic ball game involving two teams of ten players; each team tries to pass the ball between themselves without being intercepted by a player of the other team.
2 Sandrine Bonnaire, French actress.

References

Braunschweig, D. & Fain, M. (1975). *La nuit, le jour. Essai psychanalytique sur le fonctionnement mental.* Paris: Presses Universitaires de France.
Chervet, B. (1993). Comment habiller un vide: Dandyisme et confection de fétiche. *Bulletin de la Société de Paris*, 28: 15–21.
Chervet, B. (2003). Les affects typiques: honte, douleur, culpabilité. *Bulletin de la Société de Paris*, 68: 63–71.
Clerc & Maugendre, D. (2007). L'écoute de la parole. *Revue Française de Psychanalyse*, 71 (5):1285–1340.
Denis, P. (1996). D'imagos en instances: Un aspect de la morphologie du changement. *Revue française de psychanalyse*, 60 (4): 1171–1185.
Denis, P. (2002). *Emprise et satisfaction: Les deux formants de la pulsion.* Paris: Presses Universitaires de France.
Ferrand, J. (1610). *A Treatise on Lovesickness*, trans. and ed. Donald Beecher and Massimo Clavolella. Syracuse, NY: Syracuse University Press, 1990 (translation of *Traité de l'essence et guérison de l'amour*).
Freud, S. (1920a). *Beyond the Pleasure Principle. S.E.* 18. London: Hogarth, pp. 1–64.
Freud, S. (1920b). The Psychogenesis of a Case of Female Homosexuality. *S.E. 18.* London: Hogarth, pp. 147–172.
Freud, S. (1930). *Civilization and Its Discontents. S.E.* 21. London: Hogarth, pp. 57–146.
Freud, S. (1933). *New Introductory Lectures on Psycho-Analysis. S.E.* 22. London: Hogarth, pp. 1–182.
Freud, S. (1937a). *Analysis Terminable and Interminable. S.E. 23.* London: Hogarth: 209–253.
Freud, S. (1937b). *Constructions in Analysis. S.E.* 1. London: Hogarth, pp. 257–269.
Freud, S. (1940). *An Outline of Psychoanalysis. S.E. 23.* London: Hogarth, pp. 139–207.
Kahn, L. (2001). L'action de la forme. *Revue Française de Psychanalyse*, 65 (4): 983–1056.
Neyraut, M. (1974). *Le transfert.* Paris. Presses Universitaires de France.
Winnicott, D.W. (1953). Transitional objects and transitional phenomena. *International Journal of Psycho-Analysis*, 34: 89–97.

Chapter 5
Metapsychological approach to the concept of après-coup

The operation of après-coup is involved in psychic functioning, in the session work and in the genesis of desire and human thought, to the point of merging with them. In order to study the concept of après-coup as an essential process of human thought, it is useful to present a metapsychological approach to it, in particular concerning psychic work and theory of drives.

After some *theoretical preliminaries*, I will go on to present the *work of the operation of après-coup* proper, its *moments*, its *stages 1* and *2*, its *scenes I* and *II*, its sequences and results, its stumbling blocks, its determinants and accomplishments and its raisons d'être.

What André Malraux (1967) wrote in *Anti Memoirs* illustrates perfectly this dynamic: "The forgotten gardener had had shrubs planted so that centuries later the unknown psalmody of the soil would make itself heard to humans" (V, 2, p. 475) (translated from the French for this edition).

This operation of après-coup is active in every analysis and in each session, in the thinking of the analysand and analyst alike. The analysand's *associative thought* and the analyst's *regressive listening* are part of this process. Each is already an individual après-coup that occurs under the aegis of the imperative of accomplishment with which this operation is concerned, an imperative underpinned by the fundamental rule as stated by Freud (1940a) in *An Outline of Psycho-Analysis*: "complete candour on one side and strict discretion on the other" (p. 174). The first French translations introduced the words "*contre*" (against) and "*absolue*" (absolute) that contain senses absent in Freud's sentence. The French *Œuvres Complètes* have adopted another formulation that removes the idealized reference to the absolute but keeps the idea of against (*contre*). Translations introduce different significations and induce variable paths of theorization.

The signifier après-coup and its signified

Two wishes are expressed by the term *après-coup*: first, that there will be an *after*, a future, and that the uncertainty disappears; and, second, that the future will be a reunion with the past, even through the paradoxical means of a return of an initial

DOI: 10.4324/9780429198953-5

traumatic shock (*coup*). The cancellation of the past through an actualization in the present of this event draws its resources from a nostalgia for lost time.

Beyond these generic wishes we can infer the quest for a dream event, an event that would condense in itself past and future as an idealistic present, a full saturation of consciousness: an event without an *after*.

This quest can be stated in terms of the nihilistic formula that served to rally a group of architects in the 1960s who wanted to break with the idea of utopian cities (Moncan, 2003) associated since 1516 with Thomas More. The slogan of counter-utopia announced the end of any *after*: "Owing to a total lack of interest, tomorrow is cancelled." This formula, which operates a subtraction by an affirmation and saturates consciousness in the present, imposes the wish of saving utopia from any disappointment tomorrow. The various libidinal qualities that, respectively, define the present, the past and the future transmit experiences of differences that remind us of what has been lost of the past and of hopeful expectations for the future (Chervet, 2014). The utopia is transferred to the *initial shock* in order to turn it into a dazzling dream *event*.

The quest is driven by the wish to save the *shock* and the *deffered effect* from any disappointment: the ideal *shock* and deferred effect that would reunite the traumatic power of the shock, beyond the pleasure principle, and the extemporaneous assumption of the libidinal principle involved in all desire. It is a matter of promoting the ideal registration, the advent of a "pure" libido. The initial shock and deferred effect would then become indistinguishable in instantaneity. The wish pertains to the absence of any work of latency. These would be then replaced by a dazzling and sublime après-coup, guaranteeing the saturation of consciousness by an eternal present, for ever and ever.

By introducing the pain of restraint and of what is deferred, the operation of après-coup denounces all mystical yearning. Through pain, the latter may nonetheless take the form of religious feeling. The lost then becomes a presence that takes the place of a substitute object for the lost object. Pain becomes presence. In this case, the pain of loss ensures nostalgia, which is close to the denial of loss.

Putting something into a state of latency allows for the advent of a *counter-shock* and the intervention of an imperative of registration that is opposed to traumatic extinction and that *tries to register what tends to disappear* due to latent and passive regressive psychic work.

The work of après-coup thus proves to be pulled between two extremes, the extinctive tendency and a requirement of registration opposing it. The result is a constraint on the accomplishment of regressive work and progressive realizations.

The work of après-coup is realized by regressive psychic activities of passivity of which the dream is the nocturnal prototype. Free-association and evenly suspended attention are those that are typical of sessions.

In the ordinary case of putting into latency and of the work of après-coup, the feeling of disappointment accompanies the acts of restraint and deferral. This feeling traces a path that will serve as a precursor for the moral pain of future mourning.

Theoretical preliminaries

The operation of après-coup condenses a great quantity of *theories in action*. It contains those of the temporality, causality, regression, repression (disappearance and returns), masochism of restraint, libidinal sympathetic excitation, libidinal regeneration, productivity and generativity that it enacts. As a foundational operation of human thought, it is truly a matrix of all human productions that attempt to apprehend the world and its genesis, mentalization and its advent, life and its extinction, whether artistic, moral or scientific.

It is driven by an imperative of registration that is involved in all human creative work. It is accompanied by other parameters, in particular talents and gifts. Freud's work on Leonardo da Vinci is one of the key illustrations of this, as well as all the discussions it has generated. The kite's tail recognized in the form of Mary's dress and the reminiscence of the unconscious phantasy of fellation are deferred effects concealed within a work whose aesthetic value cannot be reduced in any way to this personal overdetermination of this regressive return of the repressed. This unconscious content, which is registered without the artist knowing it and inferable from one of his personal recollections is correlated with the message of the painting, a message suggested "negatively" by its absence. By representing and insisting on the mother/daughter interaction and on the immaculate conception of the child Jesus, Leonardo sustains and transmits the essential place of god the father, insofar as he is the excluded third, and also excluded from the painting. God the father is the third element excluded from any represented form, the exclusion concerning both the father of Jesus and the father of Mary. The unfinished aspect of the painting is probably not a lack of completion, but the intuition of the painter that what could not be represented, could nonetheless be portrayed by this plastic means. The imperative of registration is an abstraction that is only representable visually by the productions it promotes, never directly. These productions are the figures of a principle of emergence situated beyond any form of representation, a principle conveyed by the imperative of registration. If the operation of après-coup is involved in all the great scientific and epistemological debates, it is owing to its essential function of having to mentalize the traumatic reality of extinction that is active at the heart of every psyche and of every creative act, experienced ordinarily as lack and realized, ultimately, by death.

These scientific ideas, even if they come within the field of the so-called exact sciences, have arisen from the transposition of unconscious psychic realities involved in the operation of après-coup on to perceptual realities, whether traceable and representable or not. Those that are traceable are chosen and co-opted in order to serve as materials of representation suitable for facilitating mentalization. They thus become vehicles of drives, ideational representatives of drive impulses and thing-presentations. The various forms of memory and modes of registration arise from such a need for psychic materials that can be used in the work of psychic processes, as is the case during the dream-work. It is possible to speculate that in the infant, the psychic work that has the task of modifying the regressive drive economy dominated by the extinctive function, is based, initially, solely on the economic processes on which libidinal regeneration is based. The utilization of traces and their differentiation as mnemic traces and thing-presentations facilitates the work of the psychic processes by offering a restraint through the containing materialization (the contained/container function) that facilitates the restraint based on processual operations, displacement, condensation, representability and secondary elaboration. It is thus possible to envisage that the infant dreams without images or memory, but that he dreams. The libidinal regeneration that is so obvious in very young children is evidence that dream processes are active even before they give rise to dream images and memories that can be verbalized.

The perceptual traces kept in reserve are destined to provide contents for the *returns* that will facilitate the processing of the endogenous traumatic reality, work that the psyche is obliged to carry out day and night. This function of returns calls into question Freud's over-simplified proposition of a spontaneous tendency that supposedly drives and pushes them to become conscious. Returns take place under the constraint of the imperative to promote a registration that is sought after, and even required, by the tendency that runs counter to extinction.

A *need for memory* emerges. These multiple memories, such as amnesic (Botella, 1985) memory, memories of sensual facilitations, registrations, identificatory functions and work processes, serve as a support for the tendencies that permeate and place constraints on the operation of après-coup. They are actualized as facts of memory.

Memory is a messenger of what obliges it to register, but also of what threatens it with erasure. It reveals itself as the memory of psychic operations, not only those that are already operative but also those that are impeded or that have remained potential. The operation of après-coup is a reminiscence of the operations and processes that constitute it and of the tendencies that constrain it and drive it. It is a *processual memory* without content, expressed by theoretical proposals (phylogenesis, the primal horde, the murder of the father, the murder of Moses the Egyptian, etc.). It is this processuality that is transferred as reminiscences during psychoanalytic treatments via remembering, repetition and construction.

The operation of après-coup is involved in processing the traumatic quality, while ensuring the denial of this reality. Its realization does not guarantee the complete integration of this quality, often denoted by the term reality, denied by the term truth (Freud, 1923a, 1923b; 1932). The stumbling blocks of the operation of après-coup give expression more to the truth of a subject than to consideration of the traumatic quality. The dynamics of disappearance and resurgence that are inherent in the operation of après-coup can apply to it in particularly traumatic circumstances. The disappearance of the term in the writings of Freud, as well as its *mise en abyme*, as in the *dream within the dream* (Chervet, 2006), constitutes the clinical dimension of this operation. The operation of après-coup reveals here its dual conflictual identity. It is subject to a double ambivalence to which I will return later: intra-drive (between life drive and death drive) and also with regard to the operation of restraint and registration at the basis of the mind, an operation that has the significance of a *foundational murder* for the mind.

I mentioned in the first chapter that the intra-drive traumatic reality recognizes itself and transposes itself on to the sensory-perceptions of everything that presents itself as *lack*, thus, in the perception of certain external realities such as acts of destruction, accidents, somatic illnesses, psychic symptoms, and much more generally in the perception of all the differences with which we are faced. The transposition on to perception of a lack cannot, by definition, be followed by the creation of ideas specific to it. The reality of the lack does not give rise either to traces or ideas but to feelings arising from the awakening of the tendencies to extinction and the operations that oppose it.

The difference between the sexes offers a prototypical reality to this transposition of the duality extinction/registration on to the perception of a lack by means of the noticeable difference between the lower abdomens of males and females. In fact, it contrasts two realities that can be perceived via the sensory path, on to which the two primordial tendencies involved in the foundation of psychic life, the regressive tendency to extinction and the imperative of registration, are transposed. The attraction to extinction can be recognized in the absence of a penis in the groin area of girls, while the realization of registration is backed up by the presence of the penis in the groin area of boys.

The perception of this *endowed/unendowed* pair is combined with another perception of differences between two tangible realities, masculine and feminine. The transposition reveals, in fact, a double difference between the sexes, the *masculine/feminine difference* of bisexuality and the *endowed/unendowed difference*, relating to the theory of castration in psychoanalysis.

Thus, all the differences resonate with the feelings of lack linked to the extinctive tendency called *beyond the pleasure principle,* but also with erotogenic feelings and causal theories. Lack is therefore the result of an act of castration, whereas desire is supposed to arise from lack. The theory links the extinctive tendency and the imperative of registration.

The qualitative variations and the rhythm of cathexes and of their regeneration, thus of the psychic work that promotes desire, are recognized much more indirectly, in particular via the acoustic rather than the visual path, which tends to reinforce theories according to which girls are also endowed with a penis but in a way that is not noticeable visually. It is true that both little girls and little boys frequently put their hand in their pants in order to check their integrity when they experience anxiety linked to the regressive tendency to extinction. Touching corresponds, then, to their need for tangibility. The visual lack of a penis is taken up in a theory based on the axiom of an equivalence between penis and desire. Touching demolishes this theory and promotes other theories in favour of what is invisible and what is heard, other ways of countering the lack of being unendowed.

The gravity of desire lies in the fact that it arises from work whose function is to respond to extinctive regressivity. Desire retains within it the knowledge of what underlies the history of its genesis, something it is also reminded of by its destiny. It is the first victim of neurotic conflict. In *The Indiscreet Jewels*, Diderot (1748) lets desire speak, just as Rabelais (1534) makes Pantagruel say that "giving words is what lovers do." Pantagruel's response to Panurge (in Rabelais's *Gargantua and Pantagruel, La Pléiade* Fourth Book, chapter 56, p. 670) can also be found in *The Adages of Erasmus* (Erasmus, 1536, I, 5, 49, *Dare verba*). "We saw gullet words – *gules* – and words *sinople*, words *azure*, words *or* and words *sable*, after they had been warmed up a little in our hands they melted like snow, and we actually heard them but did not understand them, for they were in some barbarous tongue … Panurge asked Pantagruel to give him some more. 'Giving words is what lovers do,' said Pantagruel. 'Sell me some, then,' said Panurge. 'Selling words is what lawyers do,' replied Pantagruel. 'I would rather sell you silence more dearly (as Demosthenes did with his money-quinsy).'"

The voice suggests the advent of desire and the work of the processes that govern its assumption. The extinctive aspirations will find a way of realizing themselves along the long path of eroticism, through an intensification of the libidinal cathexis that seeks to extend beyond any form of content and object and to become once again a regressive bonus of "pure" libido.

Eroticism is the typical scene of the conflict between registration and extinction. It manifests itself through this intensification and through an extension that are the basis of foreplay. The experience of satisfaction and the refractory period that follow inform the subject of the issues at stake in this conflict in which the two paths of extinction are involved, both leading to the "inanimate state," namely, reduction to the inorganic state and extension to the infinite.

An essential difference appears at the heart of psychic work between one aspect, which unfolds through transpositions from unconscious psychic realities on to sensory realities capable of giving rise to traces and ideational representatives, and another, which is inaugurated by a transposition of other unconscious realities on to the perception of lacks that cannot give rise to any traces. The first modality of transpositions concerns the unconscious cathexis, while the second concerns the extinctive tendency. This modality of psychic work will have to be accomplished by thought-processes alone, or by borrowing contents stemming from the first representable realities, designated by Freud (1937, p. 266) as adjacent *details relating* to unrepresentable traumatic reality.

This second modality of psychic work is at the origin of qualities of thought that are different from thought pertaining to ideational contents. It produces abstraction, affects, theorization and mysticism. They are initiated and exacerbated by the perception of the lacks characteristic of all differences, and they are experienced through the sense of lack.

The psyche is truly a *factory of operations of après-coup* in its function of mentalizing the traumatic quality, a factory that combines an anti-extinctive *function of restraint* and a *generative function* of registrations, a true matrix of returns consisting of contents, theories and experiences.

This psychic work that attempts to respond to the extinctive tendency of the drives is a condensation of enacted theories. Take, for instance, the theory of the father as the author of castration, called the third primal fantasy. Theorizing thought is enacted well before it is able to formulate the theories that it conceals.

The dream, the interpreter of drive impulses as wishes, is also a libidinal theory of the world, a theory of the denial of castration and an explanatory theory of castration based on the complex of castration. Except that the dream-work and its stumbling blocks prove that the extinctive tendencies remain active and require a work of distortion supporting a denial that remains unstable and fragile. The return of what has been denied thus comes from the outside, through the registration of ruptures, accidents and illnesses concretizing the denied reality of castration.

Waking psychic activity can also convey such a libidinal theoretical view of the world, even when it interprets the dream-work and integrates, by means of the castration complex, discontinuity, loss, erasure, the leap, the hiatus, extinction, etc. Within this line of thought, trauma, for example, is thought of as an external event, provoked or fortuitous. This way of thinking is *animistic*.

It is important to point out that it is necessary for psychic functioning that such regressive theories exist even if they are wrong. They are *libidinal* theories insofar as they try to establish the primacy of the libido, thus of desire. This aim of saturation explains the fact that they are also *theories of denial* of the traumatic experience called castration in psychoanalysis. A compromise attempts to establish itself between the hegemony of desire and the recognition of castration. Relations of causality are produced between the two providing a basis for the castration complex. These theories conceal the reality of castration. They take the place of the missing trace.

The function of distortion is absolutely necessary for processing all the awakenings of the traumatic extinctive tendency. Thus, the resolution of a situation of mourning can only be accomplished if regressive psychic activities are available. But these rely on the momentary capacity to deny the loss and to provide explanations that make the loss more or less reversible. Initially, the deceased must be *someone who disappeared* in a primal scene from which he might return; then, from being a *ghost*, he becomes a *lost object*.

The psychoanalyst's task is to make these two stages and their articulation possible. Although it attempts to deny death, it is important to establish the efficiency of this unconscious signification of death as disappearance in a primal scene. The unrepresentable nature of jouissance, the navel of the primal scene, is combined with the unrepresentable dimension of lack. The living, the human beings who are part of life, are therefore excluded from these two realities (primal scene and extinction), which continue, nonetheless, to question their place in life and require psychic work from them that regenerates a bonus of desire.

Denial has a psychically positive function on the condition that it is temporary and reversible. The duration of this temporary period is ideally that of a few nights, but it remains indeterminate. Such a denial makes possible the *regressive psychic activities of passivity* which come into contact with the repressed impulses and, via this detour, serve to promote libidinal regeneration. Subsequently, the denial must be abandoned until it is called for once again. The work of après-coup integrates these theories of denial, of the castration complex and of their resolution.

The above remarks help us to approach two characteristics of the operation of après-coup, its *complexity* and its *elusiveness*. Another characteristic reinforces the first two, its *uncertainty*, which, paradoxically, goes hand in hand with its *determinism*, hence, its multiple clinical vicissitudes.

Three inevitable stumbling blocks emerge in reaction to this *elusiveness*: the temptation to complicate, simplify and aestheticize the theorization of this operation. The fact of *complicating* the theory of this operation has its origins in the attempt to master it and in the refusal to accept that it eludes us, that we cannot master it or have control over it – a successful dream is a dream whose outcome is unforeseeable, just like the appearance of a symptom.

There is also a frequent temptation to *simplify* the operation of après-coup. In order to avoid recognizing what determines it, it is frequently approached from the angle of one of its components alone, particularly from that of temporality alone, the chronological succession of stages 1 and 2.

Its *aestheticization*, along with that of its formations, henceforth called creations, are themselves deferred effects whose function is to support the denial of the traumatic factor by a reversal into a bonus of pleasure of the unpleasure that accompanies it. The appeal to the aesthetic attempts to replace an unpleasure by a gain in pleasure.

Concretely, complexity and elusiveness are the reflection of the three "steps" of Freud constituting his theory of the drives, and particularly the third *step*. The first two are the *infantile register* and *narcissism,* and the third is *extinctive regressivity* recognized in 1920 (Freud, 1920).

Freud recognized that the drives are characterized by a very singular quality, their *conservative* character, which means in this case their *regressive quality, their tendency to restore an earlier state of things, and ultimately an inorganic, inanimate state* (ibid., p. 36). This extinctive regressive tendency can be called the *extinctive regressivity* of the drives.

The preservation involved is neither that which is guaranteed by the so-called drives of self-preservation nor that which is characteristic of narcissism. By means of this so-called conservative regressive character, this extinctive regressivity, Freud broke with the positivism that still dominated the first two *steps.* This is evidenced by the evolution of his conception of regression.

In 1900, regression included rediscovering early sensory experiences; in 1914, it nestled in the maternal breast; and in 1920, it fell into two extremes, the inert and the infinite. Clinical experience obliges us to take very seriously this third contribution of Freud to the theory of the drives. The frequently polemic reference that analysts make to the two topographies tends to marginalize this third "step." The new definition of the drives was the origin of a new topography owing to the introduction of a new parameter that was to acquire the value of an agency, a superego imperative. This third "step" recognized a new quality in the drives that gave intelligibility to the first two through a process of reverberation.

Freud's elaboration of the theory of the drives thus followed three levels of differentiation concerning processuality, all of which are involved in the work of mental activity, namely, the work of mourning in connection with the *infantile register*, the work of desexualisation in connection with *narcissism,* and the work of sympathetic excitation in connection with *extinctive regressivity.* This would have consequences for the way analysts think about clinical work in general. The establishment of infantile functioning makes the hallucinatory satisfaction of a wish possible; the establishment of narcissism leads to the montage of the three stages a-b-c, active, passive and self-reflexive of the drive (Freud, 1915a); libidinal sympathetic excitation keeps the drive impulses in the mind and registers them as psychic cathexes.

The establishment and unfolding of these three processual levels in analysis require a long period of working-though, which, like children's play, employs regression and repetition as tools. The extinctive attraction explains the difficulty of this work and its often lengthy duration. *Extinctive regressivity* has two poles, zero and the infinite: the *reduction to the inorganic state* of the death drive, Thanatos; and the *extension to the infinite* of the life drive, Eros.

Thus the operation of après-coup is overdetermined by regressive attractions, mnemic materials and the imperative of restraint and registration. These three realities are thus heterogeneous and without continuity. Taking extinctivity into consideration requires putting the imperative of registration into latency first and then counter-cathecting the regressive attraction. Owing to the leap between the two primordial extinctive tendencies, the work they require must be effected in two stages involving a period of latency and regressive work that ensures a function of counter-cathexis. This explains the discontinuity that is at the centre of the operation of après-coup. Furthermore, the latter is generally accomplished in stages and in a series of successive formations, for instance, a series of dreams that are elaborated in analysis by means of working-though. Interpretation is also part of this discontinuity. There is no continuity between the dream-thoughts and dream-contents. They can only be linked up by associations and interpretation, without erasing the solution of continuity that exists between them.

The work of après-coup is driven by an attempted accomplishment whose effectuation is always uncertain and outcome unpredictable due to the random nature of the links between the materials of memory that it uses and those conveying regressive attraction. How can continuity be created between the "shopkeeper," the "shop-assistants" and Emma's agoraphobia? (Freud, 1950 [1895], pp. 353–354). Only the signifier shop unites them, but the correlation between them is fortuitous and depends only on Emma's needs for elaboration. It is the work done by Emma, through her associations, and by Freud, through his interpretations, which is capable of finding the links of unconscious correlations and analogies that Emma has *created-found* between them.

The result of the work of après-coup is the object of variations expressing the vicissitudes and stumbling blocks of its operation. This results in *disconcertingly* fragmented clinical material, with significant consequences for the practice of psychoanalysis and its theorization, which are equally fragmented. Negative tendencies, in the form of reduction and idealization, historical uncertainties (as well as those of the day before), and the uncertainty of the superego and of its missions with regard to demanding and ensuring that these tendencies are used in the service of the registration of psychic destinies, are all responsible for this.

The *navel* at the heart of the work of après-coup is that this operation is permeated by tendencies that tend to make it disappear and at the same time marked by a singular dynamic of repeated *operations in two stages*. Hence its possible *mises en abymes* and the tendency to master this process deliberately by creating substitute operations of après-coup, for example, successive ruptures followed by new periods of psychoanalytic treatment or *successive* analyses. Here once again we come across a general law of work producing dreams and symptoms. When the processes are in danger, one solution consists in representing them oneself. Sometimes it is the dream characters that have served as a support for the efficiency of these processes that are employed; for example, the images of a father and mother appear in a dream at the moment when the maternal or paternal functions become uncertain. It is then a matter of guaranteeing the processes an existence or of warding off anxiety about not having time to accomplish their work. A feeling is then expressed that time is running short, with the accompanying fear that there is not enough time for the operation of après-coup to be accomplished, and that meaning is lacking. "It no longer has any meaning," were Freud's final words to Max Schur, his doctor. The expression *mise en abyme* was created by Gide [1869–1951] in 1893 in the context of his activities as a literary critic. It refers to a style that existed well before it became known by this term, which concerns all the arts. From the formal point of view, an analogy exists between this style and the fractals of physicians in which a reduplication of the same structure both at the macro- and microscopic level occurs, inducing the idea of similarity and repetition of the same. Concerning the operation of après-coup, a rupture, a leap of nature that has a power of regressive attraction exists at the heart of its structure. *Mise en abyme* refers in this case to a multiplication along the regressive path by means of a formal duplication in connection with an affect of distress and threat. The word *abyme* is not insignificant. Along the regressive path the *mise en abyme* is the equivalent of fractality along the progressive path. They are representations of the operations of restraint when these are in difficulty. Their principal examples are *the dream within a dream* (Freud, 1900, p. 338) and "Medusa's head" (Freud, 1940b [1922]).

Freud's abandonment of the noun *Nachträglichkeit* allowed other notions in his metapsychology to come to the fore. Thus, the notion of the biphasism of psychic functioning extended the biphasism already recognized for the phenomenology of human sexuality (childhood, adolescence). This notion was then given greater complexity by being linked up with the two phases of the castration complex, the *things seen* and *heard* of the first phase; hence, the significance of the messages of threat and feelings of lack of internal origin, transposed on to the perception of the two sexes. The notion of psychic work once again took centre stage, extending the nocturnal notion of dream-work. Attempts to succeed, threats of failure and the stumbling blocks of psychic work proved to be at the foundations of the psychoanalytic nosography. With regard to the success of psychic work, qualitative notions became predominant, such as unpredictability, variety, vitality, tonicity and intensity. This applied as much to nocturnal life and the qualities of dreams as to waking life with the variations of the bonus of desire, thus of erotic life and of erotogenicity.

The theory of après-coup integrates the oscillation between regression and progression, the bivalence of thought, the interplay of transposition/co-optation between the unconscious psychic elements and material reality, as well as the long path of working-through via serial stages involved in the process of becoming conscious and gaining increased awareness.

The unconscious identification of the unconscious psychic materials thus transposed, as well as the supports of this transposition, promote metaphors that maintain ignorance of the transposed materials. The associative discourse of the session follows this logic. Associations are the metaphorical reflections of unconscious functioning, and psyche does not know it. The test of differentiation can only occur later. Thus, feelings of threat are linked up with verbal messages, while those of lack are linked up with visual perceptions of differences. Recognition of the internal origin of these messages requires the intervention of a judgement that occurs progressively and subsequently as a second step; initially, the external elements perceived are thought to be responsible for these feelings of threat and lack. In the second phase the origin of these feelings is internalized leading to the recognition of psychic life itself. Psychology can then come into being.

At the heart of the operation of après-coup, the replacement of anti-traumatic causality by work that is realized along the regressive and progressive paths, promoting qualities, introduces a mechanism whose function is to reduce regressivity in a much more nuanced way. The *shock* (*coup*) of extinctivity calls for the *counter-shock* of the imperative, which changes into a chiasmus the *leap* existing between extinction and registration. This *reduction* through mutation uses latency and the regressive psychic activities of passivity to accomplish itself. It succeeds in producing continuity in a form that integrates discontinuity, biphasism. The reduction of this conflictuality constitutes the masochism of restraint that will become erotogenic through an operation of bodily registration, conversion. It allows a potentiality to be transformed into a reality, a *bonus of desire*. The notion of the *period of time* during which effects are deferred (*le montant de l'après-coup*) (Freud, 1918, p. 58) can be likened with those of *leap* and *shock*, which attest to the participation of the operation of après-coup from the economic point of view. They help us to see that the essential difference between scenes II and I lies in the economic gradient of regressivity of each. The transposition of the earlier-scene-II on to the recent-scene-I, and the intrapsychic co-optation of the latter, are basic operations that make it possible to reduce the regressivity beyond the pleasure principle of scene II and to open the drive economy to psychic vicissitudes.

Let us return now to the dimension of elusiveness. It is linked to this *attempt* that is itself subject to the conflict between extinctive regressivity and the imperative of registration, insofar as the extinctive aim cannot be transposed on to any traceable reality and escapes any kind of tracing, thus any specific thing-presentation. Lack in itself is outside thing-presentation; it can only be felt and named. The idea of what is missing is always grasped in relation to what exists adjacently or in relation to what is thought about in terms of remains according to a causal theory. What is supposed to remain can therefore be compared with what existed before the destruction, before the subtraction and before the erasure, or with what, in the name of such a theory, should be or should have been based on the wish for lack to be a consequence and not something in its own right. Every lack is thus interpreted as the result of a subtraction or impediment. With his metaphor of the *dream navel,* Freud was already thinking of this extinctive regressivity that escapes any form of representation and that can only forge links with a feeling, a sense of terror conceived of in terms of disappearance. The perception of the lack of the penis endorses this terror of traumatic extinction; it becomes terrifying. Theories of castration seek to introduce the hope of reversing it in the present, or a hypothetical situation that would have made it possible to avoid it in the past. The more the occurrence of what is traumatic is unforeseen, the more hallucinatory thought is concerned with rewriting history and supporting a causal theory whose aim is to attenuate the reality of lack.

Exctinctivity is consequently only represented indirectly, through its repercussions: on the one hand, through the constraint of using the perceptual traces emanating from traceable adjacent realities and of differentiating them as thing-presentations capable of opposing the extinctive tendency; and, on the other, through the qualities emanating from this work, the *experiences* of processuality at work, the pathways of affects and sensual experiences.

It thus requires the realization of psychic work, the establishment of the symbolic order and the involvement of the processual imperative of registration.

It is worth mentioning another particularity that has important clinical consequences, namely, the fact that the psyche may try to attenuate this elusiveness by replacing experiences of regressivity by words that have the value of a sign because they are not linked to thing-presentations, as these do not exist. This process of abstraction is the same that governed the polemics around the invention of zero in arithmetic in the third century B.C., and then for centuries thereafter. From a psychical standpoint this mathematization amounts to a negation. The intellectual path is liberated but accompanied by a privation of the sensual and affective qualities informing the subject about the state of the psychic work that is unfolding within him and about the object with which he is preoccupied, namely, the negative tendencies. This liberation is in fact an elimination. It is a matter of freeing oneself from the feelings of lack by suppressing them or preventing them from occurring. The sign is supposed to fulfil this function; it does not signify a substitute but a denial. By virtue of its abstract nature, its aim is to exempt the subject from the unpleasure linked to these feelings. It does not attain the status of a word-presentation insofar as it cannot be associated with a thing-presentation, since the latter does not exist. It cannot therefore follow the path of formal regression. This is the case of the word *castration* in psychoanalysis, like the word *zero* in mathematics. Both are linked to theories that stand in for a missing trace and a thing-presentation and that cannot fail to be missing.

The term *castration* cannot give rise to a thing-presentation insofar as it denotes the perception of a lack, the absence of a penis on the lower abdomen of girls on to which the extinctive regressivity of the drives that is unrepresentable has been transposed. It can only appeal to ideas or images arising from the imaginary theory according to which the perceived lack on the girl's lower abdomen is the consequence of an act of cutting, an impediment, retarded development, or a concealment. Thanks to these theories, it is possible to imagine what is thought to have been cut off, as well as the act of cutting, or the cause of the impediment. This takes us back again to the fantasy of being castrated by the father as well to theories about bodily mutilations, in particular, the bodies of women, and, of course, the custom of *bound feet* as practised in China from the 10th century to the beginning of the 20th century on girls and young women.

As for the complexity mentioned above, it is a consequence of the modalities of work that the psyche is compelled to accomplish in order to mentalize the extinctive drive tendencies. This work involves the conflict between the denial of this tendency and its recognition, as well as the natural heterogeneity that exists between the extinctive tendency and the imperative of registration that is too easily understood in terms of the duality between Thanatos and Eros. These differences, leaps and gaps explain the organization of this psychic work according to a two-stage procedure, that of the operation of après-coup, which proves to be the common referent of all psychic work. The dream-work, the work of mourning, the work of regeneration and the session work are all attempts to realize an operation of après-coup driven by the teleological aim of a link with consciousness, and through it with the object. The conflictual coexistence of extinctive tendencies and the processual imperative bestow on this work the stamp of biphasism. Thus all clinical work is an operation of après-coup that fails to be accomplished and that should be thought of in terms of this ideal model of which it is very often no more than an incomplete manifestation.

The clinical differentiation that permits the extension of the model of the operation of après-coup is not to be located between the productions that pertain to it and those that do not, but between those that pertain to this or that *moment* of this operation. This extension is present in Freud's clinical work. The distribution in terms of the moments of the operation of après-coup lies at the foundations of a psychoanalytic nosography (Chervet, 2011).

The operation of après-coup consists in two moments of work along the regressive and progressive paths, respectively, that are separated by a hiatus that is itself the locus of specific work. Thanks to the economic leap realized in these two stages, these three kinds of work play a role together in processing the traumatic dimension.

The third quality of the drive, extinctive regressivity, is the main source of the feelings of disarray, terror and unpleasure. The processual imperative is expressed through the impressions of complexity and elusiveness. Extinctive regressivity can henceforth be recognized as being responsible for the traumatic quality that was previously attributed to the various transgressive conflicts, first interpersonal, then intrapsychic. As a quality of the drives, traumatic experience may be conceived as a reality at the very heart of the drives and no longer as an effect of the drives. The fact that it is opposed to object-cathexes and narcissistic-cathexes alike throws light on their vicissitudes. This third quality is not of the same nature as the other two. Admittedly, it is responsible for the existence of an infantile aspect of objectality and a negative aspect of narcissism, but it does not have a regressive reverse side because it is the very principle of all regression. There is thus no linearity between this third step and the two others, a non-linearity that extends to the primal phantasies. The phantasy of being castrated by the father no longer belongs to the same register as the two others, namely, the seduction of the child by the adult and the primal scene. Regressivity strives towards extinction, narcissism has the task of conservation and infantile sexuality that of the assumption of desire. The third primal phantasy is an imaginary theory of causality whose aim is to attenuate, and even to deny, the extinctive tendency, whereas the two others announce realities of psychic functioning: regressive attraction in the case of the first, and the drive nature of the attracting pole though which the subject's psyche tends to disappear in the case of the second.

With this third step of drive theory, the traumatic quality is thus registered at the heart of the drives. It is no longer an effect of the drive on the already more or less organized psyche, but rather proves to be the primordial quality of the drives that is capable of burdening the very establishment of this future organization.

Complexity has as its corollary the fact that this extinctive tendency obliges us to think about another pole opposing it, a counter-constraint tasked with *registering psychically what tends to disappear*, even if only by the ultimate stylistic device of the *mise en abyme*. It is therefore necessary to introduce into the metapsychology an imperative of realizing psychic operations with the aim of registering drive functioning at the heart of the mind, a *processual imperative of registration*. This imperative had already been identified at the level of technique, without being theorized. The fundamental rule was accorded a fundamental role very early on by Freud in psychoanalytic treatment. Freud abandoned suggestion and influence in favour of this impersonalized constraint. The uncertainty of the operation of après-coup depends, then, on uncertainty about the response and efficiency of this imperative. This uncertainty is part of the definition of what is traumatic. The extinctive quality of the drive becomes traumatic when the imperative is lacking. What is traumatic is thus the result of the extinctive tendency and of the vacillation of the imperative of registration.

It is this pair *extinctive regressivity/imperative of registration* that form the basis of the operation of après-coup, that is, of the set of psychic operations and processes – in the sense of *Vorgang* – that accomplish the operation of après-coup, in the sense of *Prozeß*.

Certainly, it is henceforth easy to identify the initial *shock* as being the effect of extinctive regressivity, and the *counter-shock* as the response emanating from the processual imperative. From this viewpoint, the notion that there is something before the shock becomes meaningless, unless it is considered as a wish-fulfilment, the wish for something to exist prior to all existence, thereby resolving the enigma that all the sciences come up against, the passage from nothingness to being, the emergence of existence. The notion of an *avant-coup* seeks to guarantee a hegemony of what exists. It expresses a theory of denial. Nevertheless, my line of argument clearly leaves in the shadows the origin of the imperative of registration that is at the origin of existing.

The term *coup* is ambiguous, as I have already said. It refers to a sadomasochistic fate of hatred, with a possible transvaluation of the latter as it can be approached in "A Child is Being Beaten" (Freud, 1919). It was by undoing the amalgam sadomasochism/pain/hatred/traumatism, an amalgam that creates confusion, that Freud (1920) recognized the existence of the extinctive regressive quality characteristic of the drive. He later found he was obliged to think about another pole of a different nature with the function of opposing this tendency, the pole of the superego-based imperative.

The term *coup* introduces an implicit meaning that the notion of extinctive regressivity does not contain. It is an *appeal to masochism* when the subject is at grips with what is traumatic. It anticipates the first act of restraint that inaugurates the operation of après-coup, and it co-sexualizes the traumatic factor before this operation has taken place. It affirms an existence where inexistence is still the major issue at stake. Certain treatment techniques use this logic of the *coup* in order to provoke and initiate psychic operations or make up for their absence by employing a means of last resort.

The basic pair, extinctive regressivity/processual imperative, enacts a restraint that creates a tension and, thus, masochism, linked to the primary operations of mental functioning. This *masochistic functioning* may be called *masochism of restraint or functioning or renunciation*. It includes the operations of counter-shock and precedes sadism. It is involved in all psychic functioning in the form of reminiscence and concealment of what governed its advent, namely, the *shock* of the extinctive tendency and the *counter-shock* of the imperative of restraint.

It is through the masochism of restraint that the operation of après-coup is at the origin of the drive impulses constitutive of the id conceived as a large store of libido. Other operations will subsequently create the drive as described in 1915, with its source, its thrust, its aim and its object as well as infantile sexuality integrating with its different forms of autoerotism the erotogeneity of the organs and the object-presentations formed by following a formal regression starting from sensory traces.

The operation of après-coup is involved in each of these stages of drive theory. Subject to the constraint of yearnings to regress beyond the pleasure principle, it realizes operations characteristic of the regressive path and those that allow for the mutation of this traumatic mode of functioning into that of the pleasure principle. Oriented by the *principle of resolution* (the Oedipal attractor described by Michel Ody (1989), it works to establish principles of pleasure and reality that are both the result of renunciations.

Studied in piecemeal fashion by Freud, the concept of après-coup only becomes intelligible if we take into account this third drive quality. Indeed, it is this third quality that makes it possible to envisage the transformational and mutative economic function of psychic work. Its organization in two stages and its bipolarity are linked to the double constraint that inhabits it, the regressive constraint leading to extinction and the counter-constraint of the imperative to realize processual acts resulting in the registration of cathexes. One of the two poles is engaged in work oriented towards the tendency to disappear, a work of restraint and double mutative reversal; the second is engaged in a work of promoting cathexes and of a progressive orientation towards consciousness. This will be followed by secondary elaboration and presentation to consciousness leading to an even more complex stage, the moment of coming to awareness that introduces a value-judgement, an evaluation of the materials produced according to the point of view of the values of psychic life. In order to satisfy the specific characteristics of consciousness, secondary elaboration will put itself in the service of the tendency to think of the operation of après-coup in terms of a genetic, chronological logic and to render the result of this work coherent, thus to neglect the timeless work of regression and latency. Such is the effect of the imperative of registration that is expressed through the constraint to realize an encoding. There is a real difficulty in thinking about the various moments and movements of the operation of après-coup; especially as they all occur at the same time, hence, the impression of a confusion between different periods of time (Green, 2002).

The term *deferred effects* is often used to refer to the progressive results of this process alone, psychic formations as presented to consciousness. The operation that produces them is then neglected or simplified. This is the very meaning of the term *Nachträglichkeit,* ("carry forwards") but also of the term *après-coup.* Freud's abandonment in 1917 of the noun that he himself had created in 1897 can probably be explained by this intuition and by the value he accorded in 1920 to regressivity in this operation, a value that the term itself left to one side in favour of what is after and goes forwards. We will see that there are other reasons that may explain this abandonment, in particular the increasing complexity of the theory of causality. Determinism is not enough. The operation of après-coup teaches us that the first causes (extinctive regressivity) must be transformed under the influence of the last causes (the resolutive registration) in order to be put in the service of the mind; otherwise, they are psychically, and even somatically, harmful.

The double constraint and the biphasism that follows from it reveal a fundamental discontinuity. The hiatus is located between the constraint of extinction even back to the inorganic state and that of registration up to consciousness. Between the two all the intermediate materials of psychic reality are elaborated.

The fragmented heterogeneity of the topographical register, the entangled oscillations of the dynamic register, the dispersion of the qualities of economic register are the reflections of this hiatus. These three registers express, from three different points of view, differences that, in fact, have neither place, movement or energy, but which refer to the qualities of the registrations that together create articulations instead of a hiatus. The hiatus, as well as the intermittence of the psyche, remains inferable from the perception of the discontinuities of the cathexes at the origin of the notion of time. If psyche does not know it is extended, it does not know that it is intermittent either.

But where, then, does our sensation of continuity come from? It is one of the results of the work of the psyche and has two origins: the theories of denial and the secondary process. Secondary elaboration, as I have already mentioned, has a purpose of presenting to consciousness materials described as intermediate, thereby bringing the most regressive economies and modes of functioning into connection with it. At the same time, these materials fulfil a function of concealing the extinctive tendency. The dream-work succeeds in imposing an impression of continuity by realizing a dramatization and enactment uniting in one plausible story scattered, heterogeneous and incompatible elements. The dream-work makes them pass totally unnoticed through the "eye of a needle." They are subsequently revealed by free-association. At the moment of awakening, the transition to secondary processes occurs again in order to encode in language the thoughts contained in the dream images so that they can be verbalized. They can therefore also be interpreted. The dream-memory calls for an interpretation that is supposed to complete the dream, which, if it had reached its term, would have left no memory, only a bonus of desire. Every interpretation refers to a theory that brings into relationship the dream-contents and the code used to express them. Psychoanalysis increases the complexity of this correlation of the often-simplistic symbolisms proposed since the beginning of time by taking into account the work of distortion realized by the dream and the dreamer's associations.

Secondary elaboration creates syntax that imposes, by virtue of its very structure, succession and chronology. It is not possible to say everything at the same time or to express this simultaneity as it occurs. Secondary elaboration transmits a message of apparent continuity even when the reflection that it sustains takes discontinuity into account. The latter is thus denied at the level of its value but recognized at the level of language. This takes us back to the ambivalence enacted by negation (Freud, 1925).

Access to consciousness depends on this language encoding even when thinking is in images or sensual. Secondary elaboration may participate in the denial supported by the dream-work in yet another way, by using its capacity to give a name to what does not exist, to a lack, thereby enacting a negation of the lack. The resolutive aim of the secondary process is often accompanied or intensified by that of denial.

The polemic concerning continuity and discontinuity in living forms and their classifications, a polemic initiated between Linné and Buffon, bringing into confrontation the advocates of the continuity of all forms of life and those who accepted recognising the existence of leaps between them. The notion of "intermediate chain" (Freud, 1923a) was an attempt to reduce this gap, while placing the notion intermediate in an awkward position because it was sometimes used as evidence of continuity and sometimes also as a denial of discontinuity.

The transition to secondary processes supports the denial by attempting, via the code of language, to give the same status of existence to what is representable and to what pertains to lack. This takes us back to the invention of zero at the heart of the series of figures and the invention of castration insofar as this term refers to the reality of a lack, affirming that the latter is based on a causal theory. Hence, the ploy of the splitting that consists in speaking of castration with the aim of denying it all the better in so doing. This capacity is often associated with perversion, even though it is used in many clinical constellations and is a feature of language.

These considerations imply an isomorphy between encoding and the nature of consciousness. They also put forward the hypothesis of the existence of a network of relations among language code, consciousness and denial. This conception is also present in Freud's work when he bases the psychoanalytic treatment on the fundamental rule of speech, making psychoanalysis a "talking cure" with consciousness as its aim, consciousness being the very teleology of analysis. Initially, he considered that the enunciation of language guaranteed unfailingly such a process of becoming conscious. Then, in 1923, he called into question the trust he had hitherto placed in verbalization with regard to becoming conscious and he saw that words can also fulfil a function of saturation in keeping with that guaranteed in dreams by hallucinatory activity. He wrote: "When a hypercathexis of the process of thinking takes place, thoughts are *actually* perceived – as if they came from without – and are consequently held to be true" (Freud, 1923a, p. 23). His attempt to turn psychoanalysis into a science on the same model as the others took another blow. Reality-testing was no longer guaranteed by enunciation and interpretation, as language could be involved in supporting a denial.

This complexity of the operation of après-coup confers on psychoanalytic interpretation its subtlety and its uncertainty. Caught by its language-based nature in the guile of the psyche, it fulfils a double function of making conscious and of denying. Language is capable of freeing itself from the interplay of the double registration, thing-presentations/word-presentations, in order to name what is without thing-presentation. Interpretation can denote a reality and support the denial of its psychic value in one stroke. This bivalence is unavoidable, and psychoanalysis has no other path or method to accomplish its therapeutic purpose.

According to this line of thought, extinctive regressivity can be named at the heart of a theorization that integrates it, as in this book, without this naming ever abolishing its elusiveness! This reminds us of the difference between Mallarmé and Einstein.

The work of après-coup, its *moments*, stages 1 and 2, scenes I and II

The operation of après-coup underlies both the patient's *incidental speech* and the analyst's *interpreting thought*, which are the two typical ways of thinking in the session, whether or not they are announced. The session *discourse* is the analyst's only certainty. But the fact that they are the productions of processes that are accessible only by means of deduction obliges him to take into account the uncertainty and unpredictability of his own operations of après-coup, as well as the involvement of his subjectivity in evaluating the degree of their completion. Reality-testing for psychic productions is a mystery for psychoanalysis. The analyst must be able to recognize the existence of these formations of the unconscious, thus their reality, but the over-determination of their meaning and value requires another kind of testing than that of existence – an evaluation of their meanings that refers to a mode of psychic functioning considered as ideal and asymptote, which itself is related to the global clinical context of the patient and the analysis. This is quite a tall order! For the mind, it is not the judgement of existence that is most difficult; the classical tolerance advocated by the religions had prepared it for such an attitude. The judgement of value and meaning, that is, the comparison with an ideal psychic functioning of reference used to establish a means of reality-testing specific to the mind, remains a difficult issue. Freud came up against this difficulty on several occasions. For example, he had to abandon the first rudimentary version of his *neurotica,* which led him not to generalize the theory of seduction but rather to conceive of the existence of a "regressive attraction" (Freud, 1926, p. 154) emanating from primal repressions (ibid., p. 94). Likewise, in 1920, with the young homosexual woman, he had to give greater complexity to the famous formula he had used in 1900, according to which "dreams are froth" [*Traüme sind Shäume*] (1915b, p. 168) by the apparently redundant assertion that dreams could be "lying and hypocritical." Freud's judgement called into question completely his belief in dreams that would give direct access, through the pair of association/interpretation, to the repressed truths of the subject. The evaluation of a dream must, in fact, take into account the clinical context in which it takes place; in the case of the young woman, her homosexual object-choice. Thus the interpretation that she wanted to turn towards a heterosexual object is itself to be interpreted as a wish to elaborate the wishes she had as a little girl to have a child by her father. The clinical analysis of her attempted suicide after meeting her father, while she was in the company of a lady she loved, and of the furious look he cast at her, makes it possible to suggest that she had not formed such wishes during her childhood. Because heterosexual wishes were unavailable to her, the interpretation concerning them turned out to be "lying and hypocritical." The dream becomes lying and hypocritical in relation to wishes that were not developed during childhood and which do not have the "lying" status of the material actively repressed through the work of distortion. In this case, taking the path of homosexuality was an attempt to gain access to her heterosexuality that was in abeyance.

Post-Freudian studies allow us to think again about the classical *moments* of the operation of après-coup, stages 1 and 2, and scenes I and II. They are part of our common corpus. We came across them in a previous chapter, in the treatment of the little boy referred to as "C," not only in his *statements* and *acting out* during the session but also in the analyst's interpretations with their value of scansion and of dynamizing *moments* of après-coup.

The notion of *moment* is to be thought of as a period defined by an economic functioning and a precise dynamic that plays a role in an internal conflict in which several moments of different economic natures are involved. The *moments* form between themselves pairs or series in tension with each other, hence the rhythms of psychic life. *Moment* thus retains here its etymological origin of movement. The correlation with the notion of temporality is linked to the differences of potential existing between the economic modes of functioning, each moment consisting of a dynamic in two stages permitting the mutation of the most regressive economy into another more elaborate one. The aim of each of the moments of interpretation is thus different, depending on the modes of functioning they are addressing.

In the *Proton Pseudos* of the "Project for a Scientific Psychology" (Freud, 1950[1895]), with regard to Emma, Freud described, before naming it, the operation of après-coup and its moments. This young woman suffered from agoraphobia in relation to shops. Her symptom was related successively with two unconscious memories each connected with a scene: a-recent-scene I of the "shop assistants" and an earlier-scene-II of the "shopkeeper." Between the two was puberty. Freud replaced Charcot's event-based shock with a shocking event, a transgressive seduction by an adult who awakened prematurely the child's object-related sexuality.

Freud, who was concerned to free psychic disorders from the impasse of the theory of degeneration, took seriously the temporal markers proposed by Charcot. His key work, *The Interpretation of Dreams* arose from the interest he accorded to the work of latency with which the dream-work, its prototype, is concerned.

His *aetiological* preoccupation was isomorphic with the tendency to remember along a *backward* temporal path. He follows the path of *temporal regression* and added to it an obligation of verbalization. He put these two constraints, to regress and to bring to consciousness, in the service of the therapeutic aim and imposed them through the *protocol* (the couch/armchair asymmetry) and the *fundamental rule* ("complete candour on one side, strict discretion on the other").

As he was conceptualizing the aetiology of trauma, Freud extracted from the theory of *shock* a new conception oriented towards the *shocking*. There thus followed in succession the *neurotica*, the disorganizing role of unconscious phantasy, the resexualization of narcissism, which, ideally, guarantees the functions of conservation, and finally the negative attraction by an extinctive tendency called beyond the pleasure principle, revealed by traumatic terror. In the process, he proposed a series of contents suited to defining the *shock* ranging from the external traumatic events of the *pathogenic nucleus* to the strictly endogenic and intra-drive traumatic quality of the *extinctive regressivity* of the drives.

The first propositions constituted anticipatory theories with regard to that of drive regressivity. In the logic of childhood sexual theories and of those produced in the session, these theoretical moments express various forms of psychic work that are both active within the psyche and unconscious. They are not intended to be verbalized. Their participation in the anti-cathexis of the extinctive tendency is nonetheless essential. In general, their link with consciousness is ensured by their productions. They become conscious only when they do not succeed in fulfilling this function. This aspect is essential for interpretation, which expresses in language-based terms modes of psychic functioning that have never been thought about before, but which have had a more or less efficient psychic reality linked to consciousness. Interpretation reinforces this link by contributing the specific hypercathexis of the work of encoding.

The value of these theories lies in the causal links that they establish in the psyche. The operation of après-coup is at the basis of all the models of causality. To deal with the lacks felt and perceived, it explains the differences and links up discontinuity with continuity, heterogeneity with similitude and incompatibility with the amalgam. It participates in the production of symbols. It establishes the causal relation between first and last purposes, links the present to the past, the past to the future, fulfils wishes to revise the past and to predict the future. It produces perceptual and thought-identities and thus participates in the aim of the pleasure principle of imposing a psychically constructed *perceptual activity* in place of perception. Through dreams, the operation of après-coup creates perceptual identities, and through the hypercathexis of language-based thought, thought-identities.

Charcot had described the temporal organization of hysterical symptoms in terms of an operation *in two stages*, separated by an unperceivable third stage, which he himself described as a period of "psychic elaboration" or "psychic incubation," and which Freud renamed as a period of latency, situated between what comes *after*, the manifest symptom, and the initial traumatic event or shock (*coup*).

Remembering had been used within the context of hypnosis. Breuer's notion of spontaneous *retrogression* had made it possible to conceive the cathartic method. The constraint to sustain a link with consciousness, via the code of language, promoted the psychoanalytic treatment.

Thus recentred on the sessions, Freud divided stage 1, that of the traumatic event (*coup*) into two retrogressive scenes, a recent and recallable scene I, and an earlier-scene-II that is unconscious in the strict sense. He then opened up this schema to all the memories and returns of the repressed. The notion of *return* is a corollary of that of après-coup and both are required by the artificial state of the sessions. The transference/countertransference dynamic is part of the material thus revealed. Driven by the logic of registration, the progressive logic is also subject to the influence of an imperative of resolution that outlines an end to the operation of après-coup and limits its infinite repetition. At the same time the fundamental rule structures the regressive free-association as a network of statements linking multiple timeless scenes. The incidents of speaking and listening during the session that occur sporadically constitute the premises of the specific deferred effect of the analysis.

The analytic situation superimposes and interweaves the singular deferred effects of each protagonist and a neo-production, the *analytic après-coup*, the *me-not me* proper to the session, a neo-reality full of cross-reminiscences. Private and shared neo-identities that had hitherto remained latent and virtual will participate in this neo-reality. The invitation to put both psyches into a state of regressive tension reveals hitherto unsuspected materials.

The analytic après-coup is the lever of therapeutic effect. It has its place, in each session, at the heart of sequences and of the analysis as a whole. Each analyst's *countertransference of precession* is involved, depending on the diverse mixture of its emotional, figurative and theoretical modalities. One quality of the operation of après-coup is evident, namely, its fractality. Whether it concerns an intermittent aspect, a session, a sequence or the whole of an analysis, its processual unfolding is similar and can be found both in the occasional introduction of contents, the erotogenicity of a zone, and in the global establishment of thought and of eroticism. The various intermittent imperatives and the superego are linked up in it, while this latter superstructure is supposed to place all the imperatives under its aegis.

To enhance the notion of *two stages* and that of an *interval* between them, Freud coined the term *Nachträglichkeit*. Then he stopped using it when he saw that the notion of trauma was linked to a fundamental quality of the drive that requires significant regressive work, whereas the term *Nachträglichkeit* gives priority to the progressive result. The creation of the noun was related to the phenomenological approach to the dynamics of temporality; its abandonment coincided with the deeper metapsychological exploration of the operation.

The term *après-coup* refers to the temporal and manifest result of a latent and timeless psychic work and the very operation of this work. *The work of après-coup* pertains to the *regressive psychic activities of passivity*. It is driven by a *regressive impulse*, by an imperative to produce progressive material and by a reference to an ideal mental functioning of which it is the model when it is accomplished.

Later, in France, Lacan presented himself as the herald of the resurgence of this term. In fact, like Freud, the enactment of the operation of après-coup is identifiable in all psychoanalytic writings, whether or not they refer to it officially.

Freud's work draws faithfully on the contributions of his own teachers and predecessors, Charcot's theory of symptoms in two stages and Breuer's cathartic technique involving retrogression through remembering and associative elaboration.

Charcot described a phenomenology of the genesis of the symptom in two stages: stage 1(traumatic shock); stage 2 (appearance of the symptom); in-between (a period of incubation and psychic elaboration). Charcot's theory of trauma/shock links *stage 1*, the traumatic event, and *stage 2*, the appearance of the symptom. Charcot called this period of *psychic incubation, of psychic elaboration*, the interval.

Breuer showed the cathartic value of retrogression through remembering and associative elaboration. By *retrogression*, Breuer was referring to the fact of taking up one's history from a certain precise point in the past and repeating it with the aim of reconstructing it and freeing oneself from it.

Freud differentiated himself from Charcot and Breuer by his aetiological research, by the notion of regressive attraction of the pathogenic traumatic nucleus and by the content that he recognized in it, namely, a misuse of sexuality. He imposed a link with consciousness by means of the fundamental rule of verbalization. This led him to propose a new conception of symptoms and of the treatment. Henceforth, all remembering was a deferred effect of an unconscious memory that had acquired the value of a traumatic shock subsequent to its repression.

Freud paid particular attention to the temporality of *what the patient said* in the session. He added the path of remembering to the chronological path of the patient's history. He called scene I the memory Emma described as recent (that of the laughing shop assistants) and scene II the memory she described as earlier (the shopkeeper's hand on her dress at the level of her genitals).

To avoid any confusion between the numbering of stages and scenes, the *recent-scene-I* was called scene I ("the shop assistants"), and the *earlier-scene-II*, scene II (the shopkeeper).

A difficulty of identification arose from this interaction of crossed and inverted temporalities. One follows the associative chronology of the session and the other the chronology of the reconstruction of the history of the symptom, thus the biphasic theory of the symptom. The interaction of the scenes is much easier to differentiate because it refers to thing-presentations, the shopkeeper, his hand, the shop assistants, their laughter. The temporality requires numbered ordering.

The *recent-scene-I* is recalled and recounted first; the *earlier-scene-II* second. The memories occur chronologically in the associative discourse, thus in the reverse order to that of their content. These qualities of *recent* and *old* are associative descriptions of the patient who organizes her memories in two stages according to the more or less regressive quality of the cathexes to which they correspond.

Later, in the Wolf Man, Freud was to describe a series of recollected scenes in which dream, childhood phobias and screen memories were combined. He presents an exact chronology of these scenes to which he seeks to ascribe temporal certainty, whereas they could be approached according to the quality of the cathexes that they dramatize in scenes. The actualized scene of the transference becomes an umpteenth present scene.

The chronological unfolding of remembering thus constructs the regressive series of the memories/cathexes. Associativity constructs the regressive path. The regressive activity of the session thus follows at one and the same time two axes: a progressive axis (stage 1/shock, stage 2/symptom; and a regressive axis (recent-scene-I /earlier-scene-II).

Henceforth, three temporalities are superimposed: the chronological temporality of associative speech, the reverse chronology of the regression of the cathexes presented from memory and the chronology of the secondary reconstruction of a history of the illness.

Freud's essential contribution is his conception of the work of the interval period between two stages, based on the dream-work and on this double temporality in the session. The backward path of remembering is much more than a temporal inversion; it is a functional regression from the most elaborate to the most regressive level. If remembering espouses the traumatic charge of the shock, if the memory becomes the trauma, it is because regression opens out onto the traumatic mode of functioning. Remembering is the path of therapeutic effect because it permits elaboration of this pathogenic mode of functioning. The memory is, in fact, a reactualization of the shock of the extinctive tendency of stage 1 and, at the same time, a production that amounts to an incomplete elaboration in the form of a symptom, thus to stage 2.

The regressive attraction is accompanied in the session by sensations linked to the reactualization of the traumatic effect, via remembering, repetition and construction. The products of the operation of après-coup are *overdetermined* reminiscences indexed by the quality of work that is at their origin. The idea of *generalized reminiscence* (Freud, 1937) implies notions of historical reality, onto- and phylogenetic traces and, through the function of après-coup, historical truth. This function is to establish or reestablish the *pleasure principle,* but also the *reality* principle, to which the first is linked from the outset by the same imperative of registration based on renunciation. The pleasure principle has the task of utilizing *mnemic traces* in order to respond to the extinctive longings and thereby to deny all difference. It is in itself a reminiscence of the denial and of the object of the denial. It therefore contains the potentiality of recognizing the reality of the extinctive attraction. The latter is intrinsically bound up with renunciation, whereas the denial of this tendency points to the truth of the subject's unconscious wishes. This brings us back to the hiatus recognized above, but under the designations of reality and truth implying the conflict of recognition and denial.

Renunciation also takes place in two stages. The first stage uses denial and promotes the pleasure principle that conceals the renunciation of extinction, while the second accounts for the renunciation hallucinatory wish-fulfilment. In general, the term *mourning* is attributed to the second stage only, the first being that of dreaming and illusion, but, in fact, the process of mourning and disillusionment requires both stages.

What Freud presents is a conception of a psychical apparatus that is capable of *going back* in time (Fain, 1997) in the sense in which one winds one's watch, but via the detour of regression; in other words, that is capable, starting from an elaborate psychic mode of functioning, of allowing a *regressive psychic activity of passivity* dominated by a regressive economic mode of functioning to establish itself. The latter can then be modified thanks to this regression from the most elaborate to the most regressive level, and to a work of mutation that is carried out in a state of passivity leading to a libidinal regeneration of the psyche by using to its advantage the mechanism of denial. This process thus lets time take its course.

Between the two scenes, the recent one and the earlier one, there exists a *period of time* during which deferred effects are prepared, that is, a gradient of time expressing a *difference* between the libidinal economies of each of these moments. The interaction between them allows for the transition from a regressive principle characterized by the tendency to extinction to another called the pleasure principle that is associated with an imperative of registration. This mutation takes place under the aegis of the principle of renunciation, which requires various economic mutations until the resolution permitting access to libidinal object-cathexis, thus from that of the foundational restraint of the id to that which introduces the process of mourning, including the desexualisation characteristic of narcissism.

This differentiation of the session temporalities, insofar as they express qualitative variations of libidinal cathexes, allows us to add introduce further complexity. Freud's (1915c) article "A Case of Paranoia Running Counter to the Psychoanalytic Theory of the Disease," along with his studies on President Schreber and the Wolf Man, had already prompted us to pay attention to the temporal arrangement of what the patient says, to the precession of certain contents in relation to others, to their distribution over several successive sessions reflecting levels of regressive attraction. But it was above all studies after Freud that helped us to see that the *earlier-scene-II* can exist only from the moment that the *recent-scene-I* has been found-created by the patient. Consequently, the session becomes an attempt to seek, find and create a *recent-scene-I* that will give access to the regressive and pathogenic *earlier-scene-II*.

This *earlier-scene-II* becomes a repressed content only once the recent-scene-I has been found. Before that it is immobilized and denied by a stimulus barrier opposing the tendency to erasure, but it contains a potential evolution that is subject to extinctive regressivity. This *potential* is threatened with erasure even before it has officially become a trace and a content. The differentiation of the earlier scene II as a thing-presentation/shopkeeper that can be repressed is made possible by putting the idea of shop assistant into latency. The *earlier-scene-II* thus changes status. From the moment it is differentiated as a thing-presentation, its preservation is ensured by its repression. It gains access to timelessness.

In 1896, Freud spoke of an *imprint* to describe a trace that has not been differentiated as a thing-presentation. Hence, the possible hypothesis, based on the contributions of 1920, of an economy located at the level of the regressive and traumatic trace/shopkeeper, beyond the pleasure principle, threatened with extinction. Its repression requires a transformation. It is the task of the stimulus barrier to immobilize it and to deny everything that awakens the extinctive tendency, everything that may be connected with it. This process of immobilization, and then of reactualization through economic modification, is at the origin of what Freud calls *early impressions*.

The recent-scene-I serves, then, as a vehicle for a hypercathexis allowing the earlier-scene II to become a repressed thing-presentation and to be submitted to the pleasure principle, then to the principle of resolution by means of renunciation. The function of the latency period is to serve as a support for the consolidation of a link with consciousness through the production of a manifest substitute with a function of concealment. The formula according to which each psychic production turns out to be a deferred effect of an unconscious material that has acquired, in the aftermath of its repression, the significance of a traumatic event, is confirmed and made explicit.

The contributions of 1920 also help us to see that the *earlier-scene-II* is a stage in the processing of regressivity and in the production of drive impulses. Thus the trace/shopkeeper is already a first content of the transposition of extinctive regressivity on to a material capable of becoming an idea, a content/container offering a consistency that has the function of counter-cathecting the extinctive attraction, thus a *first* act of restraint opposing the latter. The *second* stage is the differentiation and repression of the thing-presentation/shopkeeper, thus the creation of the shopkeeper as a seductive object of the drive. It is accomplished thanks to the found/created memory of the "shop assistants"; the *third* is the advent of the shopkeeper as a lost object. The realization of these stages occurs under the aegis of the aim to be reached, the establishment of the lost object opening access to the libidinal cathexis of objects; hence, the importance of the concept of après-coup.

The existence, with respect to the *earlier-scene-II*, of a propensity for seeking-finding-creating a *recent-scene-I* that permits this transformation of the economic mode of functioning can thus be deduced. The operation of après-coup will elect, take possession of and co-opt certain external realities, *recent-scene-Is*, with the aim of permitting an opposition and a mutation through the restraint of the extinctive regressivity attached to the earlier-scene-II. This mutative quest will take place thanks to the operation of repetition, of the *fort-da* (disappearance-return). There exists, therefore, a preconception of the necessity of such a process in two stages.

An important differentiation follows between various modes of repetition. The repetition of the traumatic scene of the shopkeeper is driven by an extinction-compulsion. The operation of après-coup attempts to save the future potential of this traumatic scene. On the other hand, the repetition of the *recent-scene-I* marks, beyond the stumbling blocks along the path of accomplishment of the operation of après-coup, the impact of the imperative of registration, which, through successive stages of renunciation, seeks to find resolution through the advent of the quality of what is lost. Together, these two repetitions participate in the process of working-through until the completion of mourning. They are the motors of research in the sessions not only of the request to undergo psychoanalysis, but also of the future resistances in psychoanalysis.

To sum up, *what the patient says* unites four identities. It is a *return* bearing the traumatic dimension, thus a stage 1. It is a psychic *formation,* thus a stage 2. It is also a *recent-scene-I* giving access to an unconscious material and to an earlier-scene-II actualized as a quest for a *recent-scene-I*. The operation of après-coup is a reminiscence of all these processual identities.

No one will be surprised today to hear that the analyst is, in turn and at the same time, the seductive and shocking "shopkeeper," thus the one who awakens the traumatic moment, and the "shop assistant," that is, the fortuitous and intriguing seducer through whom the regressive economy can be modified.

By trying to subject the *statements* of the Wolf Man to the carbon-14 dating of chronology, Freud pushed his quest to its limits, while getting trapped by his own investigation. He was then able to free himself from it and see that the transference is a fresh attempt to take up again the operation of après-coup at the point where it was broken off. The request for analysis is made in the name of this hope. The rest of his work revealed retroactively the economic nature of this *quota* of deferred action of which the session was henceforth the locus of actualization. The function of the operation of après-coup is to reduce and articulate the differences between the various economic modes of functioning and thus to create time, the temporality of a long path.

Human time is a question of economy, its regeneration and the rhythm of its oscillations and qualitative variations, but above all its disappearance, that is, *the threat of losing a potentiality and its mutation into a "lost object" when it is transformed into effectiveness.* This mutation can only be established and sustained by the transposition of the unconscious processes on to the efficient processuality of another person, through a transference on to this *other of processuality*, the *Nebenmensch* or fellow-human being (1950 [1895], p. 331).

References

Botella, C. & Botella S. (1985). Pensée animique, conviction et mémoire. *Revue Française de Psychanalyse*, 49 (4): 991–1007.
Chervet, B. (2006). Le rêve dans le rêve. *Libres Cahiers Pour la Psychanalyse*, 14: 133–146.
Chervet, B. (2011). La démarche nosologique de Freud: Des topiques typiques aux topiques éclatées. In: *Nosographie psychanalytique: Monographies de Psychanalyse* (pp. 89–165). Paris: Presses Universitaires de France.
Chervet, B. (2014). Le présent, une qualité psychique: Éléments pour une métapsychologie de la conscience. *Revue française de psychanalyse*, 78 (4): 1078–1094.
Diderot, D. (1748). *The Indiscreet Jewels*, trans. Sophie Hawkes. New York: Marsilio Pub., 1993.
Erasmus, D. (1536). *The Adages of Erasmus*. Toronto: University of Toronto Press, 2001.
Fain, M. (1997). La machine à remonter le temps. *Revue française de psychanalyse*, 61 (5): 1685–1687.
Freud, S. (1900). *The Interpretation of Dreams. S.E. 4–5*. London: Hogarth.
Freud, S. (1915a). *Instincts and Their Vicissitudes. S.E. 14*. London: Hogarth, pp. 109–140.
Freud, S. (1915b). The Unconscious. *S.E. 14*. London: Hogarth, pp. 166–215.
Freud, S. (1915c). A Case of Paranoia Running Counter to the Psychoanalytic Theory of the Disease. *S.E. 14*. London: Hogarth, pp. 263–272.

Freud, S. (1918 [1914]). *From the History of an Infantile Neurosis. S.E. 17*. London: Hogarth, pp. 7–122.
Freud, S. (1919). A Child Is Being Beaten. *S.E. 17*. London: Hogarth, pp. 177–204.
Freud, S. (1920). *Beyond the Pleasure Principle. S.E. 18*. London: Hogarth, pp. 1–64.
Freud, S. (1923a). *The Ego and the Id. S.E. 19*. London: Hogarth, pp. 3–66.
Freud, S. (1923b). *Josef Popper-Lynkeus and the Theory of Dreams. S.E. 19*. London: Hogarth, pp. 261–263.
Freud, S. (1925). Negation. *S.E. 19*. London: Hogarth, pp. 233–239.
Freud, S. (1926). *Inhibitions, Symptoms and Anxiety. S.E.* 20. London: Hogarth, pp. 75–174
Freud, S. (1932). *My Contact with Josef Popper-Lynkeus. S.E. 22*. London: Hogarth, pp. 219–224.
Freud, S. (1937). *Constructions in Analysis. S.E.* 1. London: Hogarth, pp. 257–269.
Freud, S. (1940a). *An Outline of Psychoanalysis. S.E. 23*. London: Hogarth, pp. 139–207.
Freud, S. (1940b [1922]). Medusa's Head. *S.E. 18*. London: Hogarth, p. 273–274.
Freud, S. ([1950]1895). *A Project for a Scientific Psychology. S.E., 1*. London: Hogarth, pp. 281–397.
Green, A. (2002/2000). *Time in Psychoanalysis: Some Contradictory Aspects*, trans. Andrew Weller. London: Free Association Books.
Malraux, A. (1967). *Le miroir des limbes I Antimémoires*. Paris: Gallimard, 1972.
Moncan P. de (2003). *Villes utopiques, villes rêvées*. Paris: Mécène.
Ody, M. (1989). *Œdipe comme attracteur. Monographies de la Revue française de psychanalyse*. Paris: Presses Universitaires de France, pp. 211–219.
Rabelais, F. (1534). *Gargantua and Pantagruel*, trans. M.A. Screech, London: Penguin, 2006 (La Pléiade Fourth Book, Chapter 56, p. 670. Paris: Gallimard.)

Chapter 6

A theory of human thought

This exploration of the clinical aspect of the concept of après-coup, of its history and its presence in psychoanalytic literature, but above all its significance within Freud's theorizing process and our daily work with our patients, allows us to return to human thought and better understand the implications of the operation of après-coup for the theory of thought.

From a psychoanalytic point of view the definition of human thought includes all the modes of expression and registration involving the mind. Renaissance humanism had already employed such an approach by returning to Greek and Roman classics, while according a secular value to all the manifestations of the human mind. The expression *studia humanitatis* referred to the study of the *humanities*, that is to say everything that characterizes the human being. This had major consequences, ranging from the attention paid to the "alienated" and the gradual birth of a psychiatry that accorded dignity to the "degenerate" (Foucault, 1961) and to satirical works, which, on the contrary, described attempts to remain independent from the dominant group mentalities, supported by ideologies and imposed as a universal and eternal normality, as "follies" (Erasmus, 1509; Rabelais, 1534; Cervantes, 1607, etc).

Psychoanalysis, and science as a whole, directs its attention to unperceivable processes inferred more or less directly from observable manifest materials. The latter are considered to be the result of processes that are not apparent in themselves yet involved in the genesis, realization and accomplishment of all psychic formations, irrespective of their mediums of expression and the conditions of their appearance. The definition of science based on empiricism has long been insufficient. To deduction have been added inference, theorization, speculation and, with psychoanalysis, interpretation.

It is this enlarged conception of thought and science that Freud upheld throughout his work. We can sometimes find in his writings a more restricted definition of thought, more limited to language and representational contents. But even in *The Ego and the Id* (Freud, 1923), when he tries to better circumscribe how unconscious contents become conscious and, in this connection, differentiates ideational representatives from affects by taking into account the intermediate link of the preconscious involved only for ideas, whether affects present themselves

DOI: 10.4324/9780429198953-6

to consciousness directly or not, he brings together ideas, affects, feelings and experiences under the same heading of thought-processes.

Thus, in general, he offers a very broad conception of human thought. His work as a whole is a brilliant illustration of this. Admittedly, he never tackled head-on the question of thought-processes to the point of writing an article or book on them, even though he had discovered many of them, for which he proposed new conceptual terms. This is the case for *conversion, dream distortion, interpretation, repression, primary processes, narcissism, taming of the regressive tendency of the drives, negation, denial, splitting, construction* and so on.

He was specifically concerned with thought-processes from one end of his work to the other. As early as the "Project" (Freud, 1950 [1895]), it is possible to follow his interest in the *activity of thinking* in its different forms, verbal, visual, affective thinking, etc., and for the processes that produce these various forms of thinking. In this way, he participated in elaborating a theory of thinking.

After the "Project" came, of course, *The Interpretation of Dreams* (Freud, 1900) with its long passages on the thinking of the dreamer, thinking in images with its two aspects: formal regressive riddles with regard to verbal thinking and thing-presentations as representatives of instinctual drive impulses.

Then he opposed, differentiated and articulated still further the primary processes and secondary processes, particularly in "Formulations on the Two Principles of Mental Functioning" (Freud, 1911), that is to say the pleasure principle and the reality principle. In other, later texts, he pursued more specifically his study of the qualities of the primary process (Freud, 1915).

Later, he gave further complexity to this processual duality constitutive of thought by giving it a more fundamental function accomplished by tuning the two previous processes, a function of taming the extinctive regressive tendency. This operation of taming is at the origin of an *anti-extinctive restraint*, of a tension and pain of restraint, hence a *masochism of restraint*, in fact a *masochism of renunciation*. Freud recognized the essential issues at stake with regard to an instinctual drive economy that has a powerful traumatic potential owing to its extinctive regressive tendency. He situated this tendency "beyond the pleasure principle."

His entire work was thus an investigation and promotion of the knowledge of thought-processes and their function. In so doing, he himself enacted what he was describing. His work of thinking, theorizing and formulating fulfils the fundamental function of anti-extinctive restraint, of the creative registration of psychic drive functioning and of the elaboration of a bonus of desire available to be cathected in the world of objects.

Freud adopted on several occasions a Darwinian evolutionary point of view concerning the emergence of thought. He conceived it in terms of a theory that included the emergence of consciousness. Central to this view is the idea that both of them are the culmination of a long temporal process made up of successive stages forming part of the manifest field of the history of humanity, after that of the galaxy and that of organic life on earth. Freud writes:

The attributes of life were at some time evoked in inanimate matter by the action of a force of whose nature we can form no conception. It may perhaps have been a process similar in type to that which later caused the development of consciousness in a particular stratum of living matter. The tension which then arose in what had hitherto been an inanimate substance endeavoured to cancel itself out. In this way the first instinct came into being: the instinct to return to the inanimate state.

(Freud, 1920, p. 38)

The bidirectionality of thought

This macroscopic and progressive conception is Darwinian. It is progressive from the temporal point of view but discontinuous on account of the leaps of successive emergences.

Freud discovered in respect of thought that this progressive movement is accompanied by another logic that is not present in Darwin's theory of evolution, a retrogressive logic that is characteristic not only of dreams, but also of the analytic method and its process of exploration and theorization. This also follows a backward path, from the infantile object-cathexes of hysteria (Freud & Breuer 1895) to the traumatic dimension specific to drive regressivity (Freud, 1920), including the stumbling blocks in the establishment of narcissism (Freud, 1914). The same retrogressive path is taken by the psychic work at the origin of all unconscious formations, whether the dream-work or that which gives rise to the neurotic symptoms and ordinary symptoms of everyday life. It is also the path followed by daydreaming as well as by free association in the session. The regressive path is the theatre of the *regressive psychic activities of passivity*.

This regressive path turns out to be not only the path of refinding perceptual and mnemic traces outside time, but also the path along which the economy and regressive contents of thought itself are created and registered. Their elaboration as materials suitable for presentation to consciousness follows a series of differentiations guided by their links to linguistic codes.

Freud proposed this complex process as a doctrine of dreams. In so doing, he introduced a modification of Darwinism. The leaps and mutations of the progressive evolution can be separated and prepared by regressive work that is not perceivable. The successive stages are thus the result of regressive and unapparent stages of elaboration. They are deferred effects. The nominalization of adverbs and adjectives, *nachträglich* in German and *après coup* in French, as *Nachträglichkeit* and *après-coup*, respectively, became necessary once the various modes of thought had been recognized as the results of a precise psychic process linking the progressive and regressive paths. The operation of après-coup became an essential concept in the metapsychology.

The introduction of a dimension "beyond the pleasure principle" defined by its traumatic qualities gave greater complexity to the definition of the notion of après-coup by recognizing its function regarding this intra-drive traumatic dimension.

It turns out to be the psychic process by means of which the psychic apparatus attempts to resolve the traumatic regressive and extinctive attraction characteristic of the drives. The successive stages and results are thus deferred effects of the work made necessary by the regressive tendency to extinction and, ultimately, of this traumatic tendency. It could be speculated that this traumatic extinctive regressivity is a fundamental motor tendency of evolution as a whole, and not only one of human desire and thought. It is this extinctive tendency that induces or requires the intervention of processes producing various modes of existence, including consciousness, thought and desire.

Another aspect of thought now comes into view that differs from the progressive aspect that reaches consciousness. This is its regressive aspect, whose very particular nature can only be conceived by means of metapsychological speculation based on its various presentations to consciousness. This path utilizes the regressive materials created from the formal regression of language. It thus offers rebus shapes that can become regressive ideational representatives of the drive, which is shapeless. This differentiation pertains to quite another reality than that of language, namely, the regressive drive economy. This is captured by this regressive detour and oriented towards the future thanks to the imperative of registration, in the form of desire for the object. Thus, thought is bidirectional and doubly tensioned between a principle of registration sustained by language and the shapelessness of the drive.

Regressive thought has the twofold value of being a drive representative and a form of language. Every night it participates in the libidinal regeneration of the psyche, which has major consequences for somatic physiology. It is involved in the elaboration of the drives, in the primordial reversal of their extinctive tendency into an impulse that feeds the libidinal store of the id, and finally in the transformation of these impulses into psychic matter and erotic desire. It participates therefore in the "double reversal" underlying mentalization (i.e., a "reversal into its opposite" and a "turning round upon the subject's own self"). To facilitate their accomplishment, these transformations utilize perceptual traces as a concrete support. Regressive thought thus creates memory by transforming the traces into ideational representatives in order to respond to the need for restraint resisting the extinctive attraction and for the registration of drive impulses. Memory is thus both definite and indefinite. It has a double nature and its topography is two-sided. It is born of traces that are true imprints of mortification, transformed into pliable and unstable, living and uncertain, memory in contact with drive instability, with its elementary tendency to cause all memory forms, to disappear. The traces thus destabilized give rise to various forms of drive representatives, in particular thing-presentations, the mysterious substrate of which Freud had always recognized, but also the quotas of affect as well as all the experiences and impressions characteristic of sensuality, with its specific bodily facilitations overdetermined by the hands of maternal care and by the "onyx veins" of the somatic organs.

From the beginning of his theorization, Freud described the double registration of the representational contents of memory, as well as the oscillation that it allows between verbal thinking and thinking in images. The two registrations are not at all equivalent: one of them is in direct contact with the endeavour of the drives to make every form disappear, to the point of extinction, while the other is strongly linked to the imperatives of restraint and registration sustained by language. At a libidinal level, thing-presentations are marked by a regressive economy consisting of cathexes dominated by the extinctive tendency, whereas word-presentations are cathexes of quite a different nature; they are hypercathexes linked to the superego, which are put into abeyance during the various regressive psychic activities. In fact, it is the oscillation and alternation between memory and forgetting that guarantees the duration of registrations. Otherwise, they would be condemned to disappear – writing in water – or to mummification – engraving in marble. It is necessary to forget in order not to lose and to remember in order to keep memory alive.

The biphasism of thought

This path of differentiating one of the vertexes of thought by regressive psychic activities of passivity is realized thanks to a potentiality of accomplishment that is active from the beginning. The notion of beginning, in fact, seems elusive, if not twofold. The extinctive attraction seems to come first without being foundational, the founding processuality being a response at risk of extinction. If this response does not occur, no psychic life is generated. Thus, it can equally be affirmed that it is the processual operation that comes first because it is foundational. Nevertheless, it is only realized in response to what induces it, the extinctive tendency. The riddle of the Sphinx about the two sisters, one of whom gives birth to the other, who, in turn, gives birth to the first, becomes a metaphor for this questioning of the origins of the operation of après-coup. Each of the two sisters, day and night, is a deferred effect that participates in the function of the operation of après-coup, of processing the traumatic extinctive tendency by generating psychic cathexes.

Thus, regressive thought is a deferred effect that belongs to the whole of thought, the fulfilment of which is carried out under the aegis of a latent imperative. The complete fulfilment is a deferred effect of the contact with the traumatic quality made possible by the regressive detour. The aim to be reached is the locus of an active attraction, which constitutes the final cause involved in overdetermination. These two logics are perfectly illustrated by the riddle of the two sisters. But Freud breaks the simple circularity of the myth by bringing in a third point, their common function. The trivial aim of their circularity is to mutate the traumatic regressive economy into a libidinal economy oriented along the progressive path towards erotic desire and its multiple vicissitudes.

Freud developed a dynamic view of oscillating and bidirectional human thought, yet oriented by a purpose, the realization of the operation of après-coup until the production of a bonus of desire. This brings us back to the teleology of the foundational psychic processes. This aim requires the extinctive tendency of the drives to be recognized and taken into account.

The introduction of a regressive path gives greater complexity to the common evolutionary point of view. The so-called evolution in successive stages contains in a hidden way regressive intermediate stages and latent detours that are indispensable for promoting the evolutionary stages. Its major motive is the extinctive traumatic quality. The extension to the entire cosmos of what is true for desire and human thought is a speculation.

Such biphasism has the aim of processing the tendencies to return to an earlier regressive state. This law of a biphasic dynamic, consisting of two stages separated by a regressive intermediate stage, was discovered in relation to psychic life within which it is particularly operative. It is deduced from the genesis of symptoms, but also from the establishment of human sexuality, from the evolution of learning experiences in the child and the adult, and furthermore from the various alternations that constitute psychic functioning, those of daytime and night-time thought, those of thought in relation to work and eroticism. It deploys itself in analysis, which is a factory of deferred effects. The purpose of the cure is to restore this process so that those that have not been accomplished may be liberated and reach their completion.

This dynamic in two stages is realized concretely by this complex psychic process that unfolds partly in a latent way and which is only inferable from its manifest results. This is the operation of après-coup (Chervet, 2009). The fact of naming this functioning as the law of biphasism should not, however, lead us to overlook the fact that it is subject to fluctuations, vicissitudes, stumbling blocks and dysfunction, that it has no certainty of realization, that it is placed under the aegis of an imperative of efficiency over which a certain degree of uncertainty and distortion hangs. We illustrated these stumbling blocks in the previous chapters. They exist everywhere, in clinical work but also at the very heart of the theorization that is part of this clinical work.

This imperative applies to all thought-processes, to all the forms of work of the psychical apparatus. Its existence and function were discovered very early on by Freud. He accorded it a central place in his theory of dreams, through the active censorship in the work of *distortion*.

This imperative acquired much later on, in 1923, the value of an agency, the superego, thereby opening up a new way of thinking about clinical experience, and the perception of a new clinical field linked to the vacillations of this agency. It is the task of the latter to manage all the processes involved in psychic functioning, both in progressive and in regressive work.

The modes of thought are under the responsibility of the superego in the form of an imperative to carry out psychic work. The superego is the guarantee of reality-testing that integrates the recognition of the traumatic quality with the ideal aim of producing a bonus of desire. It makes it possible to evaluate feelings of lack. This work is achieved by links with consciousness sustained by the specific cathexis of language, the hypercathexis. In fact, imperative and consciousness together compose teleology of the mind, as approached by Freud (1900) at the end of *The Interpretation of Dreams* and maintained implicitly throughout his work.

The double nature of thought

Freud's anchorage point for understanding thought-processes, remained consciousness and manifest contents, from which he inferred a world of underlying unconscious processes. This unconscious realm was described first from a phenomenological and descriptive point of view, and then from a dynamic standpoint. Then it became a topographical reality designated by a noun, or a sign – the unconscious (*Ucs.*). Freud finally conceived of it as a psychic quality. The topographical distribution of the libidinal qualities is a metaphor that he considered as a convenient but misleading way of thinking based on the topology of the cerebral regions. Freud was a neurologist by training. The recourse to the visual sphere likens this metaphor to the functions of saturation guaranteed by dreams, with the denial resulting from feelings of lack arising from the extinctive attraction. The theory then becomes positivist.

So, throughout the development of his theorization, Freud constantly defended the existence of a specific nature called the *Ucs.*, quite different from that of consciousness, which was accessible by means of various regressions and required a particular act of thought, namely, interpretation. He asserted very early on that thought is above all unconscious, while considering that the unconscious processes that constitute it are driven by an aim whose final outcome is consciousness. Human thought is thus apprehended as bidirectional and two-sided, animated by a double dynamic and constituted by a double nature.

I have already pointed out that thought results from a tension between two incompatible natures. That is why thought cannot be reduced to verbal contents or to a single category of manifest contents. It certainly consists of words and images, but also of unconscious "contents" that cannot be grasped as such; they can only be deduced and included within a theory of human thought. This is the case with *thing-presentations*, the ideational representatives constitutive of the drive, whose instability separates them radically from images, which are, in fact, economic cathexes. These can also be conceived as economic drive charges and psychic qualities (Freud, 1940), Freud's ultimate attempt to apprehend thought as a concrete reality while limiting as far as possible the risk of positivist reification. This risk also entails reducing the usable paths of language to verbal language alone, an inevitable tendency because the privileged place of verbal language within the field of language and codes. With the fundamental rule, psychoanalysis does not do away with the other paths; on the contrary, it consolidates them by supporting their links with language. One of the early discoveries of Freud was the "symbolic" connection of hysterical conversions with their verbal expressions, which remain latent.

The *Studies on Hysteria* (Freud & Breuer, 1895) are filled with such demonstrations; in particular, the case of Frau Caecilie with the intense pain in her heel that prevented her from walking. The conversion was the translation of unaccomplished Oedipal mourning and used in a concealed way a verbal formula that was supposed to express a feeling linked to a traumatic experience accompanied by latent thoughts: "This news gave me a shock"; "My life is not going anywhere"; "It's my Achilles tendon."

In so doing, Freud introduced a new point of theory. The conversion of an unconscious wish is possible only thanks to such a connection with a latent verbal formulation. This discovery would later be exploited in the theory of dreams. From the point of view of language, the dream is a rebus, while from the point of view of unconscious drive impulses it is a representational vehicle of desire and of the extinctive tendencies that are at the origin of the latter.

One of the aspects of thought is closely linked to a principle of encoding that subsumes all languages. The contents of the latter may be of a wide variety: verb, image, drawing, rebus, affect, sensation, flight of birds, shadows, fleeting reflections, material impressions, diverse signs, astral bodies or imaginary superstitions, etc. In fact, all types of support can be used provided that they are attributed with a value as a sign. They must be recognized as bearing messages, according to a consensus or an arbitrary choice.

The other aspect of thought, that which is drive-related and radically separated from such a principle of encoding conveyed by all the messages, must not be neglected.

Thought eludes a strictly language-based definition, even though this is the only available means of expressing it and, of course, enunciating it. This twofold nature has its place in the two-sidedness and biphasism of general psychic functioning, already noted in relation to the operation of après-coup. It explains the primacy given by Freud to the notion of work involved in the various modes of thought; this work in two phases has the aim of linking up the two worlds whose nature is incompatible. Freud's favourite expression, thought-process, is thus related to that of work.

The notion of thought in Freud and the two sides of the screen of consciousness

The earliest intuition that Freud conserved throughout his work, well before he introduced differentiations and delimitations into *The Ego and the Id* (1923), was a very broad conception of thought. Thus in 1890, in the pre-analytic text "Psychical (or Mental) Treatment", he writes,

> all mental states, including those that we usually regard as 'processes of thought', are to some degree 'affective' and not one of them is without its physical manifestation or is incapable of modifying somatic processes. Even when a person is engaged in quietly thinking in a string of 'ideas,' there are a constant series of excitations, corresponding to the content of these ideas which are discharged into the smooth or striated muscles.
>
> (Freud, 1890, p. 288)

It will be recollected that it was through hysterical symptoms and Charcot's conception of their genesis in two stages that Freud approached human thought, perceiving, in particular, its ability to transpose itself into many substrates, including the physical (conversion). This capacity consists in expressing in manifest material two realities: a language-based content and an unconscious instinctual drive impulse.

In the case of hysteria, a content of verbal thought is regressively changed into physical expression. This allows for the hallucinatory fulfilment of a drive impulse whose nature is to be non-verbal, but which can be represented by means of such a formal regression converted into a bodily manifestation. Freud forged a term to refer to this substitutive mechanism that he had observed, translating and concealing the process of thought that affects both language and the drive impulse, that of *conversion*. That is how he introduced an enigma that would underpin all the other thought-processes, the link between the body and language, and then between the drives and language thanks to supports depending on perception, whether those arising from the body (sensual facilitations) or from the external world via the sensory path (perceptual traces). Other questions remain unanswered: that of "somatic compliance" (how is the choice of organ made?); that of the soma-psyche leap involving the nature of the drives as boundary entities, to be differentiated from the conversion of unconscious psychic material into the body; and that of the processual operations involved in this "leap" realizing a mutation of the economy of the regressive movement.

This question of the psychic mechanisms, processes and operations producing the various components of thought was to constitute the entire corpus of the metapsychology. This ever-growing complexity linked the various levels of the processes, the natures of the substrates and the psychic qualities with perceptual reality. It is amplified further if we consider the interplays of transposition and transference within the mind and on to the external world, which involve the soma, the drive, the body, the psychical realm, language and the object.

I have already pointed out that in 1923 Freud seemed to opt for a more restricted, representational definition of thought-processes. Having asserted that "all perceptions which are received from without (sense-perceptions) and from within – what we call sensations and feelings – are *Cs*. from the start," he asks: "But what about those internal processes which we may – roughly and inexactly – sum up under the name of thought-processes?" (Freud, 1923, p. 19). He asserts that these become conscious through a connection with the corresponding word-presentations, and he generalizes this function of language: "The part played by word-presentations now becomes perfectly clear. By their interposition, internal thought-processes are made into perceptions" (ibid., p. 23). Language turns out to be an external reality upon which unconscious thought-processes are transposed. It metaphorizes the latter and can be used to make them conscious, but also to express a hallucinatory truth: "When a hypercathexis of the process of thinking takes place, thoughts are *actually* perceived – as if they came from without – and are consequently held to be true" (ibid., p. 23). Verbal speech is now recognized as capable of supporting a hallucinatory conviction. It is no longer the guarantor of the act of becoming conscious.

However, Freud's preceding remarks account perfectly for the two-sided conception that I am developing. One side is linked to consciousness through language, through the preconscious mind and through representations from external perceptions. The other side is also linked to consciousness through language, but only insofar as this serves as an external perception of transposition on to unconscious elements that cannot find in external reality such transposition supports capable of providing representations. As Freud writes: "the real difference between an *Ucs*. and a *Pcs*. idea (thought) consists in this: that the former is carried out on some material which remains unknown, whereas the latter (the *Pcs*.) is in addition brought into connection with word-presentations" (ibid., p. 20). The difference introduced results in different uses of language. In one case it provides word-presentations for the preconscious, in the other case it becomes perception for the unconscious.

These developments allow certain deductions to be made concerning thought. There is a requirement to follow the regressive path and to constructing regressive contents that endeavour to escape any language-based structure, thereby entering into contact with instinctual drive impulses and with their tendency to extinction. This formal regression has a function of restraint, which offers a regressive limit to thought; a tension then appears that cannot be expressed in words. Words fail and give way to a sensation of extinction: sometimes feelings of terror when faced with the threat of erasure; sometimes a malaise linked to a lack of psychic registration; sometimes ecstatic enjoyment when the tension follows the path of conversion. Orgasm and death, a "little death" in the case of the first, are generic and extreme human experiences.

At the other pole, the imperative promoting the process of becoming conscious uses some sort of language-based code to realize itself. The connection between thought and consciousness is thus ensured, as is the connection between language and the object of perception. Thought exists only on the condition of the efficiency of this connection with language, a connection with a code that materializes the principle of registration by an act of encoding. But this principle concerns an ideal situated beyond the concreteness of all language, an ideal of full consciousness, thus outside language. It is a matter of being consciousness itself. The emergence of thought implies, then, an ideal devoid of all content, without any definite form, with an attractive power situating the ideal of thought beyond any material tangibility as proposed by language. It is on this ideal that mysticism is based: both the prohibition against giving any kind of form to the notion of God and the hope of an awakening to consciousness or of a full presence to a cosmic consciousness through silence. The tetragram offers a compromise between immutable letters and an enunciation that is inaccessible because it contains a vocal, affective and sensual regression. For the mystic, the attraction of this ideal is transcended in the form of an experience – the full consciousness of God – without representation, either verbal or pictorial. This extreme point of regression is part of Bion's glossary in the form of "O."

A quest combines the extinctive tendency and the principle of registration. The first of these appears in two forms, extinction in its version of the death drive through reduction and erasure, and extinction in its version of the life drive through extension towards an ideal independent of content. This quest runs after *absolute difference* and tries to capture *lack in itself*. God is the word that signifies this inaccessible in-itself uniting the extreme limits of negativity.

Thus, referred to an object of the ego-ideal, the desire promoted carries the tendencies of which this object is comprised towards a realm that lies beyond all matter. This aspect is deployed at the heart of analysis in the form of a quest for an object of the ego-ideal thanks to an objectless transference. It is thanks to this ideal that impersonalization can emerge along the paths of personification and incarnation.

More than sublimation, inspiration attests to this asymptote of thought, to this yearning for the creative act to surpass thinking itself, and to be itself the act of thinking.

Thus, thought is situated between two elusive elements: the extinctive regressive nature of the drives and the elation of desire in freeing itself from any material contingency.

The notion of process: *Vorgang* and *Prozeß*

This notion was introduced and used by Freud very early on. Its evolution is closely bound up with that of the theory of the drives, since the latter cannot be involved in the concrete phenomena of life without a processuality that first makes them a part of psychic life (Chervet, 2014).

The foundational forces of thought are therefore involved in the "three steps" (Freud, 1920) of the theory of the drives, that is to say, infantile sexuality, narcissism and the *extinctive regressivity* of all drives. Each of the three steps of instinctual drive cathexes corresponds to three forms of process involved, respectively, in each of the three foundational processes, mourning, desexualization and "taming." They are responsible, respectively, for the object cathexis, narcissistic cathexis and the sexual cathexes. Each of them is marked by ambivalence with respect to achieving the foundational work in which it is involved.

These processes are activated during analytic sessions by the fundamental rule. They must produce a work of thought along the regressive path and present its result along the progressive path through enunciation. Free association, or incidental speech, illustrates particularly well the construction of this regressive thought during sessions, while being subject at the same time to an imperative of progressive enunciation.

There is a difference, concealed by translation, between the meaning most often used by Freud and the immediate everyday meaning in French and English. The German language offers two terms, *Vorgang* and *Prozeß*, that are both translated by *processus*/process in French and English respectively. It was the first that was conceptualized by Freud. He put it at the heart of his metapsychology in an innovative way; hence, the difficulty of translation, with a risk of modifying the meaning linked to the respective definitions of the noun *Prozeß* (process in the sense of unfolding) and of the noun *Vorgang* (process in the sense of psychical operations and system of functioning).

When Freud uses the term *process* very early on, in his letters to Fliess and in the "Project" (1950 [1895]), he is referring to psychic work and to the functional systems that it comprises and by which it is animated, thus to thought-processes and to the two principles of mental functioning, to their specific qualities: unbinding, force and quantity, for the *primary process* ("no negation, no doubt, no degrees of certainty" (Freud, 1915, p. 186), binding, meaning and small quantities, for the *secondary process* (ibid.). Freud is therefore attentive to the tension inherent in the primary process/secondary process pair, consubstantial with the first topography and the dynamic unconscious, a tension from which thought can emerge in the place of the act of discharge. He thus uses the term *Vorgang* to refer to the actions involved in the realization of psychic work, actions that are subject to a constraint induced by a necessity, the *Ananke* of the traumatic extinctive quality of the drives. Process (*Vorgang*) does not refer to the unfolding of this work but to the operations and procedures that realize it. It is thus the process (*Vorgang*) that is first and foremost involved in his theory of thinking.

Just like *processus* in French, the German word *Prozeß* refers to an ordered sequence of events or phenomena, corresponding to a certain schema and culminating in something; or a continuous series of operations, of actions, constituting the way of doing or making something. This sense is faithful to the Latin etymology of process (*Prozeß*) (*pro, cedere*: go forwards, advance). This similarity of meanings between etymology and everyday usage does not hold for process (*Vorgang*), which refers very clearly to the operations, mechanisms and actions required and used for accomplishing a psychic work.

Much less frequently, Freud refers to the process of child development, of the mind, of a pathological sequence, of the treatment. When he follows this genetic and aetiological point of view, he uses the German term *Prozeß*, whose meaning is met with frequently in many other domains, referring to a process of unfolding, the result, certainly, of a series of actions and operations (*Vorgang*), but approached from the angle of a temporalized sequential logic with a more or less linear, and even discontinuous, orientation, albeit with a specific aim.

Thus, Freud did not privilege what he had known very well since Charcot, the genetic process behind the occurrence of a hysterical symptom, with stage 1 (the shock), stage 2 (the symptom) and the interval, the *period of incubation and psychic elaboration*. Likewise, he did not give much attention to Breuer's circular procedure, the *retrogression* specific to the cathartic method, with an initial timeless stage of retrograde remembering, then a second stage of psychic elaboration permitting, after the liberation of "strangled affects," the reintegration of memories and affects in the course of psychic events. From the process of *retrogression*, Freud retained the specific stage of the psychoanalytic method and of dreams, temporal, topographical, libidinal and formal regression; but, above all, he was interested in the operations occurring during each of the stages involved in regressive psychic work, such as remembering, formal regression, repetition, compulsion, etc. He turned his interest, in particular, towards the visual representation of verbal thought by thinking in images, and towards all the stumbling blocks that can occur along this regressive path.

Another of Freud's concerns that remained inexplicit is the operation of mutation that articulates these forms arising from language and unconscious wishes, the drive impulses, a mutation that occurs between a latent thought content and a manifest dream content. Likewise, he turns his attention towards the final operation that makes psychic formations suitable for presentation on the screen of consciousness. He then theorizes condensation, displacement, representability, dramatization and secondary elaboration, discovering a series of operations that had hitherto remained imprisoned in Kabbalistic books, books of symbols, the keys to dreams and animistic thought. The latter uses mechanisms such as transformation, metaphorization and analogy, which become major concepts in the theory of dreams. It is all these operations which together make up the work of the primary process and the regressive side of thought.

Thus, from the very beginning of Freud's work, a new category of process inherent to human thought emerged that is accessible solely by means of deduction from the stumbling blocks of psychic functioning and the regressive psychic activities of passivity, of which the dream is their habitual prototype and to which daydreaming, but above all the incidental speech and free association of sessions, as well as the analyst's regressive listening, also belong.

Analytic process and thought-processes

The difference between the two senses of the term *process* can easily lead to an inflection in the meanings transmitted by psychoanalytic texts translated into French and English from German, and consequently by those written in these languages. This parameter is not unrelated to the emergence of new schools of psychoanalysis with the risk of changing the object of reference proposed for metapsychological theorization.

Such a slippage generating mistranslations and developments based on a reduction of certain differentiations present in the original text, has manifested itself in the theory of practice by the difficulty of understanding the post-Freudian notion of frame associated with that of analytic process. This notion has been adopted with great success. It is very easy to use despite the confusion it maintains between the protocol of analytic treatments and the involvement of thought-processes (*Vorgang*) in the work of the session. The privilege accorded to process (unfolding) fulfils the wish to realize the work of mentalization, whereas the notion of the operations of psychic work recalls the traumatic quality. Marked by a risk of failure, the psychic work is accompanied by disillusionment with all idealization.

In this way a frame/process pair was established, in the sense of the unfolding of analytic treatment, and a theory of practice built on this pair. This theory plays a part in the repression of the notion of thought-process in the sense of the operations involved in the genesis of desire and thought.

These processes (operations) are subject to an imperative to carry out psychic work. The first reason to turn away from processes (operations) is a generic reluctance in the face of any constraint of work. But a second reason resides in the function vested in such work and in the denial of what requires it. It is rendered imperative by the extinctive and negativizing tendencies at the origin of feelings of unpleasure, and even of terror. The repression in the theory is thus underpinned by a denial of the traumatic extinctive quality of the drives and the hope of establishing the supremacy of the pleasure principle. The reality principle is defined by the recognition of the reality of extinctive tendencies. This aspect did not escape Bleger (2012/1967) who associated the ambiguity of the notion of frame with the clinical analysis of symbioses, the frame becoming what sets aside the differentiating constraints, thus thirdness (the paternal function, the symbolic or the imperative of mentalization).

The frequent and familiar articulation in our time of the notion of analytic process with that of the frame of analysis repeats the dialectical complementarity of sleep and dreams, along with the implicit narcissistic function of the pleasure principle characteristic of them, a function that requires the preliminary stage of falling asleep and of the denial that it sets up. The frame/process pair thus attempts to fulfil the wish that the analytic situation is more assured than it really is, that it is exempt from the effects of the traumatic extinctive tendency, as if sleep had fallen on the latter ("You are requested to close the eyes" (Freud, 1900, p. 317)).

The meaning of the notion of frame takes over the anti-cathecting function fulfilled by the "indifferent" characters of the first typical dream, "embarrassing dreams of being naked" (ibid., p. 241). In this dream, nakedness exalts and dramatizes the question of the naked/dressed difference by evoking the difference of the sexes. The anti-cathexis at work allows the dream to fulfil its attempted wish-fulfilment. Embarrassment about being naked succeeds in countering the attraction for *destitution* emanating from Oedipal cathexes. It contains the message of this concealed transgression, and of its consequences, the threat of castration.

The indifferent characters of this dream are opposed to any form of difference, in particular that of the sexes, revealed and evoked by inappropriate denuding. In the dream, this indifference is to be considered as the result of a work of thought sustaining a temporary denial opposed to destitution and portrayed by *denuding.*

The introduction of the notion of frame is related to the model of this typical dream. The classical recommendation, for the analyst at work, to present his patient with an impassive facial expression (Bouvet, 1967, p. 62) makes the analyst an "indifferent" figure, like those in the dream. Certainly, this attitude, inducing a *transference of authority*, is not sufficient in itself. It must endeavour to go beyond the level of behaviour, and to be the result of the analyst's mental work, thus the result of his thought-processes. It is this work of thought that is authoritative and not the relational authoritarianism imposing a conviction, such as hypnosis, suggestion and treatments that seek to influence the patient.

The psychoanalytic meaning of the notion of frame therefore has to be deduced. Speaking of the frame should, in fact, draw attention to the analyst's thought-processes, envisaged together with the protocol on which they are based. Thus, the frame of analysis is defined by the dynamics of thought-processes of the analyst and analysand at work. The slippage of the notion of thought-processes towards that of frame is a regression of the theorization of these thought-processes, which calls for reflection on the countertransference. The notion of frame contains through the ideas it signifies a message of immobilization, which seeks to keep at a distance the dynamics of the analyst's and analysand's thought alike. Symbiosis, as described by Bleger, is a form of shared denial based on the need to believe in certainty instead of a dynamic that is admittedly always fragile and random.

Freud clarified the elements of this frame/thought-process at work very early on, even before 1903 when he made explicit the frame-protocol of analysis (Freud, 1904). Thus, in the *Studies on Hysteria* (Freud, 1895) he theorizes the mode of speaking required of the patient, free association, and he announces clearly what he was later to call the fundamental rule. The latter was the heir of the injunctions imposed by hypnosis and the forcing of influence and suggestion enacted by the cathartic method. The impersonalization of thought-processes, the fact that they depend on only the identificatory history of the subject for their establishment and efficiency is regularly reaffirmed by Freud. There exists a constraint linked to psychic laws themselves and not only to the educational recommendations and messages emitted by the figures of childhood. In the "Project," he attributes the *Nebenmensch*, the "fellow human-being," the impersonal quality of being a helping *power*. In 1921, he added that this figure, this "other," was first and foremost a *model*. In fact, the child is in search of a model with which he can identify, a model of the functioning of psychic processes that can become operative only by means of such an identification realized thanks to a transposition of processual potentiality on to an operative processuality. Thought-processes arise from this *identifying transposition*. It is a generic process, but fragile and uncertain. Freud clearly emphasizes this impersonalization of thought-processes when he asserts that only dream-contents are influenced by waking life, and not the dream processes or the dream-work. In "The Acquisition and Control of Fire" (Freud, 1932), he calls this psychic processuality the "physiological factor" (p. 192), which is bound up in psychic functioning with the historical factor and the factor of symbolic phantasy.

In 1909, Freud completed his approach to the thought-processes involved in the session by the specific mode of thinking of the analyst induced by the fundamental rule; this gradually became the referential ideal by whose yardstick the countertransference can be recognized. I am referring to *evenly suspended attention*, which implies that value-judgement is suspended in favour of the judgement of existence, and then the judgement of meaning. In his very last technical articles, "Constructions in Analysis" (Freud, 1937), and then in the chapter in *An Outline of Psychoanalysis* (Freud, 1940) devoted to the technical dimension, Freud lays stress once again on the articulation in analysis between two scenes consisting of two forms of thought-process specific to each of the protagonists. To these would be added the reality of the combination of these two specific processes at the basis of an analytic après-coup and of transitional space (Winnicott, 1953), analytic space (Viderman, 1970), the chimera (de M'Uzan, 1978) the analytic third (Ogden, 2004), and the analytic object (Green, 1975).

This evolution might suggest a significant degree of confidence in the act of thinking. This was the case at the beginning of Freud's work. But the introduction of denial and instinctual drive extinctivity complicated the thinking of Freud and analysts. Thought-processes can themselves be used to maintain a denial of a part of mentalization, that imposed by this extinctivity and by the difference between the sexes in which it recognises itself.

Thus in 1923, Freud wrote: "When a hypercathexis of the process of thinking takes place, thoughts are *actually* perceived – as if they came from without – and are consequently held to be true" (1923, p. 23) (Freud's emphasis). This statement modified the conception of reality-testing. Previously, Freud had believed in speech as sustained in the session by the rule of complete candour and strict discretion. It inaugurated a new period of disillusionment on Freud's part that would enable him to grasp a new function of language arising from the function of saturation characteristic of dreams (Chervet, 2017). We find this function of saturation with the fetish at the heart of individual sexuality, with ideologies as the cement of social groups, and with productive delusions. Saturation, whether it occurs through words, images, feelings or any other substrate, concerns the message of lack conveyed by the extinctive regressivity of thought.

Freud's statement allows for other deductions. First, that this saturation of consciousness is one of the means of the dream to fulfil its function of hallucinatory wish-fulfilment. This notion is to be added to the theory of dreams. For the dreamer, what matters is the dream-thought, which I will develop in the next chapter.

This sensation of saturation also tends to impose itself in the session. It belongs to the regressive speech of the session and to the theory of the method using sound for enunciation. Thought, whether visual or verbal, can thus be used for the same purposes as those of the dream and thereby avoid the quality of deception and the process of renunciation.

This citation also reminds us that to become operative, unconscious processes must make a detour via an external perceivable support: "All knowledge has its origin in external perception" (1923, p. 23). The realization of this law requires a pathway and a particular mechanism, *transposition*, which is central in animistic thought: "only something which has once been a *Cs.* perception can become conscious, and anything arising from within (apart from feelings) that seeks to become conscious must try to transform itself into external perceptions" (ibid., p. 20). This sentence makes it possible to differentiate very clearly between thought-processes, internal process and supports in language, materials that can be perceptions of an external reality. Once again, we find the two-sided dimension of human thought and its bidirectionality, qualities that require a detour via the outside and a journey along the regressive path in favour of the construction of the regressive side of thought. Thus, through this stage of transposition into tangible and perceivable supports, thought passes through a period in which it is concrete and animistic before it can gain access to its share of abstraction, before it can account for relations, deductions, inferences and speculations. This first transformation into objects of external sensory perception allows unconscious processes to be deployed and metaphorized by the interplay of identifications, and then to attach themselves to internal ideas or images. It is only subsequently that thought will be able, at certain moments, to free itself from its initial dependence on its concrete supports and allow its operations to formulate themselves. Of course, a support of signs remains obligatory, whether it be the path of mathematics or that of abstract art, poetry or a scientific corpus.

The fragility of thought

The attention Freud paid to the notion of *regressive work*, a true cryptomnesia of Hegel's notion of the *work of the negative*, an expression Hegel used once in his work, and then his very original recognition of the reasons for such work and for its particular oscillating form, explain the fact that he never introduced a notion close to that of the frame. His metapsychology remained open to uncertainty. Even from 1914 to 1915, at a time when Freud was elaborating his theory of narcissism and he envisaged a form of regression whose aim was to return to the mother's womb, thereby guaranteeing complete narcissistic protection – a veritable metaphor of a sleep/dream system within which the guardian of sleep is totally guaranteed by an "other" – he maintained the notion of dream-work and its significant constraints on thought. In his "A Metapsychological Supplement to the Theory of Dreams" (Freud, 1917), he questioned anew the dual aspects of stability and security offered by this theory of a uterine setting, anticipating those of primary love, primordial fusion and primitive symbiosis, all notions that require the elimination of the dimension of thirdness inherent in Freudian thought. Owing to the importance Freud accorded to the notion of psychic work, he introduced a double attraction to which I have already drawn attention. The first, a negative attraction, arises from a regressive and disorganizing tendency beyond the pleasure principle, while the second is promoted by an imperative of elaboration that is opposed to the first. He envisages a primitive duality linked to a third principle and metaphorizes this model by the mother/baby pair linked to a father. The latter would later be called the categorical imperative, with reference to Kant, and eventually the superego. This is the excluded third that promotes oscillation between maternal narcissism and the erotic desires of the woman-as-lover, an oscillation that brings the excluded third into the position of a third excluding the child and partner of the sensual regression of the erotic couple (Chervet, 2013).

Freud was thus tempted during a very short period to stabilize a regressive system analogous to the everyday sense of the meaning of frame, instead of any constraint to realize a work of thought.

The existence of two terms for that of process probably helped Freud to open his theory of regression towards the navel of the unrepresentable, that of extinction. On the other hand, certain translations have facilitated the introduction of ambiguities of meaning between the two senses of the process of psychic work (unfolding and operations). The fact that the notion of frame conveys a significance of immobility was certainly an even stronger reason for Freud. This fixedness is, in fact, absent from the notion of psychic work or from the work of thinking, both when Freud refers to process in the sense of unfolding and to the foundational processual operations of psychic work. From this point of view, the notion of frame is in correlation with that of fixation, whereas the notion of resistance remains dynamic and double. Two points help to explain this appeal to the frame: the obligation to fulfil the anti-cathecting function of psychic work that is felt to be uncertain, and the instability of thought-processes. Hence, the reliance on the fixedness of the protocol in analysis, even to the point sometimes of favouring the confusion between frame and protocol and, consequently, between the dynamic thought-processes involved in psychic work and the metaphorical material supports capable of favouring the former but also of taking their place. All reflection on the analytic method is faced with such issues.

The real psychoanalytic "frame" is defined by the double work of thinking of both protagonists based on a protocol established in the name of the psychoanalytic method, which itself is more or less stable.

It is the instability of the analyst's thought-processes – the countertransference issues – that have the tendency to amalgamate psychic processes, analytic method and protocol. We all know that authentic analytic work can be achieved, every now and then, independently of any protocol. Ideally, and theoretically, this occurrence is thinkable, even if concretely the metaphorization by a minimal protocol proves indispensable in the long term.

This is why qualities that are usually attributed to the analyst, and that are sometimes taken metonymically for the method itself, are generally attributed to the notion of frame. Examples are: Freud's "strict discretion," Bouvet's "impassivity," Lacan's "dummy," Bion's "accomplished analyst ("without desire, memory or understanding"), etc. Each author thus tries to follow the vicissitudes of the analyst's desire, his way of offering himself as a processual object, as a support of the processuality of another person, as a springboard for rendering the patient's thought-processes operative, as a "seducer" of the identifications to be built by means of a transference of authority.

This double signification of the term *frame* as both protective and demanding, when it refers to the notion of psychic processes, is, in fact, in the service of the superego: it is protective because it provides the patient with thought-processes that are not sufficiently efficient in him, and demanding because it bears the message of an imperative to build such efficiency. Although the fixedness of the notion of frame is opposed to taking into consideration the dynamic dimension of thought-processes, it translates a quality of the libidinal economy that is necessary intermittently for establishing thought-processes, an economy on which they are founded. This paves the way for reflection on the specific libidinal economy of the superego, an economy that does not have the qualities of the reversibility and instability of the object-related and narcissistic cathexes arising from a resexualizable desexualization. The hypercathexes specific to the superego are not resexualizable because they have not arisen from a desexualization. As the Oedipus complex with its three aphorisms had already announced, the superego is the object of an ambivalence that is translated by acts of elimination, by "murders of the father"; the resexualizations that follow are the consequences of these murderous acts. In the course of the oscillations of daily life, it is more or less partially put into abeyance, more or less eliminated. The efficiency of the superego is the object of a murder, the Oedipal "murder of the father." But the *processual economy* that characterizes it offers a degree of stability, of materiality, upon which anaclisis and the transposition envisaged earlier can be based. This foundational processual libido can be eliminated by a murder, hence, the fragility of the functions of the superego and the introduction of the reassuring notion of frame.

A final proposition is deducible concerning the act of murder. This processual libidinal economy, which is the object of murderous intent, has the characteristic of being foundational for human thought through an act of murder, which it carries out against drive extinctivity. Everything depends, then, on the destiny of this "murderous" operation, on whether it is a destructive murder or a foundational murder of human thought.

References

Bleger, J. (2012/1967). *Symbiosis and Ambiguity: A Psychoanalytic Study*. London: Routledge.

Bouvet, M. (1967). *Œuvres psychanalytiques I, La relation d'objet. Névrose obsessionnelle, dépersonnalisation*. Paris: Payot.

Cervantes, M. de (1607). *L'Ingénieux Hidalgo Don Quichotte de la Manche*. Paris: Seuil, 2001.

Chervet, B. (2009). L'après coup; la tentative d'inscrire ce qui tend à disparaître. *Revue française de psychanalyse*, 73 (5): 1361–1441.

Chervet, B. (2013). L'appel au père et le meurtre fondateur, *Revue française de psychanalyse*, 5: 1510–1515.

Chervet, B. (2014). Le présent, une qualité psychique. Éléments pour une métapsychologie de la conscience. *Revue française de psychanalyse*, 78 (4): 1078–1094.

Chervet, B. (2017). La saturation de la conscience dans les rêves, les séances, les sciences. *Revue française de psychanalyse*, 81 (4): 1177–1194.

Erasmus (1509). *In Praise of Folly*. Dover: Thrift Editions.

Foucault, M. (1961). *Histoire de la folie à l'âge classique*. Paris: Gallimard, 1998.

Freud, S. (1890). Psychical (or Mental) Treatment. *S.E. 7*. London: Hogarth, pp. 283–302.

Freud, S. (with Breuer, J.) (1895). *Studies on Hysteria. S.E. 2*. London: Hogarth.

Freud, S. (1900). *The Interpretation of Dreams. S.E. 4–5*. London: Hogarth.

Freud, S. (1904). Freud's Psycho-analytic Procedure. *S.E. 7*. London: Hogarth, pp. 249–254.

Freud, S. (1911). Formulations on the Two Principles of Mental Functioning. *S.E. 12*. London: Hogarth, pp. 218–226.

Freud, S. (1914). On Narcissism: An Introduction. *S.E. 14*. London: Hogarth, pp. 69–102.

Freud, S. (1915). The Unconscious. *S.E. 14*. London: Hogarth, pp. 166–215.

Freud, S. (1917). A Metapsychological Supplement to the Theory of Dreams. *S.E. 14*. London: Hogarth, pp. 222–235.

Freud, S. (1920). *Beyond the Pleasure Principle*. *S.E.* 18. London: Hogarth, pp. 1–64.

Freud, S. (1923). *The Ego and the Id*. *S.E.* 19. London: Hogarth, pp. 3–66.

Freud, S. (1932). *The Acquisition and Control of Fire S.E. 22*. London: Hogarth, pp. 187–193.

Freud, S. (1937). *Constructions in Analysis*. *S.E. 1*. London: Hogarth, pp. 257–269.

Freud, S. (1940). *An Outline of Psychoanalysis*. *S.E. 23*. London: Hogarth, pp. 139–207.

Freud, S. ([1950]1895). *A Project for a Scientific Psychology. S.E., 1*. London: Hogarth, pp. 281–397.

Green, A. (1975). La psychanalyse, son objet, son avenir. *Revue Française de Psychanalyse*, 39 (1–2): 103–134.

M'Uzan, M. de (1978). La chimère et la bouche de l'inconscient. In: Duparc F. (Ed.) *L'art du psychanalyste : autour de Michel de M'Uzan* (pp. 235–242). Lausanne: Delachaux et Niestlé, 1998.

Ogden, Th. (2004). The analytic third: implications for psychoanalytic theory and technique. *Psychoanalytic Quarterly*, 73 (1): 167–195.

Rabelais, F. (1534). *Gargantua and Pantagruel*, trans. M.A. Screech. London: Penguin, 2006 (*La Pléiade* Fourth Book, Chapter 56, p. 670. Paris: Gallimard).

Viderman, S. (1970). *La construction de l'espace analytique*. Paris: Presses Universitaires de France.

Winnicott, D.W. (1953). Transitional objects and transitional phenomena. *International Journal of Psycho-Analysis*, 34: 89–97.

Chapter 7

Saturation in dreams, sessions and sciences

Having explored clinical situations and proposed a theory of thought based on the operation of après-coup, it is now possible to make a contribution concerning the function of dreams. This detour via dreams and the theory of dreams is the approach that Freud followed each time he made a theoretical advance. It belongs to the epistemology of psychoanalysis. The detour via the theory of dreams is to the evolution of metapsychology what the dream is to the process of becoming conscious. This approach follows the biphasic process of all mentalization, the interval period being precisely that of dreams.

In the development of the psyche, the result that can be attained is involved in establishing what is most regressive. This overdetermination prevents us from considering the genetic point of view as linear. Each stage is realized in two stages that start from what is potentially most elaborate and follows the retrogressive path in order to construct what is regressive. This approach permits the emergence of manifest results.

Each of the three registers of the theory of the drives corresponds to an investigation of a new clinical field through which each of them is expressed more specifically. This is what led to the differentiation between the three major productive nosographical categories of psychoanalysis: the transference neuroses, the narcissistic psychoneuroses and the psychoses. At each of these three "steps" (Freud, 1920, p. 59) of theorization Freud made a detour via dreams, which improved the theory of dreams and the metapsychology of the new clinical field explored.

My approach to the operation of après-coup as an operation of thought and human desire does not escape this epistemology of the detour via dreams. My contribution concerns the mission of the dream-work to saturate thought along the internal path.

I have already pointed out that human thought articulates various modes of thinking: thinking in images as in the dream-work, sensual thinking as in endogenous feelings; verbal thinking, in particular that of the session; and abstract thinking as in monosemic scientific formulations.

Beyond the specificities of each of these modes of thinking, they can all be used to fulfil a function, that of *saturating* the internal side of consciousness, the internal screen on which psychic life is presented. It is this capacity to register

DOI: 10.4324/9780429198953-7

psychic life and to inform the subject about it, to give him an endoperception of it, that makes consciousness our sixth sense-organ.

The dream-work tries to saturate consciousness from the inside, a saturation that is prolonged in the session. The same happens each time a great scientific discovery is made and is experienced as a triumph over the lack. Every new discovery is first the object of an idealization, which is followed by a second period of renunciation and mourning for this idealization. The therapeutic effect of analysis is the result of these two periods.

Freud had the intuition of this third function of dreams, the anti-traumatic function. This completed, in 1920, the two first functions, wish-fulfilment and as the guardian of sleep. The notion of the endogenous saturation of consciousness makes it possible to clarify this anti-traumatic function. We can also infer Freud's intuition of it when he wrote in 1938, "a dream, then, is a psychosis," before adding, "a psychosis of short duration, no doubt, harmless, even entrusted with a useful function, introduced with the subject's consent and terminated by an act of his will. Nonetheless it is a psychosis" (Freud, 1940, p. 172).

Saturation permits denial of a part of reality, that of the difference between perception and representation, and the production of a neo-reality in the place of that which is denied. The operation of après-coup can be used in the service of this saturation, for example for the recurrent dreams of traumatic neurosis.

Lack and tangible reality

The operation of après-coup can therefore not be considered as reality-testing. It is a stage in this reality-testing due to the fact that it plays a role in denying a reality, which, to be recognized, must first be denied. This reality is the extinctive regressivity of the drives and its link with sensory realities that give rise to neither traces nor representation. These sensory realities belong to the category of lack.

The difference between the sexes is the prototype of the two categories of sensory realities: the tangible, which gives rise to traces and representations, and lack, which gives rise to neither traces nor representations. We will see in the following chapter how the difference between the sexes combines two differences: masculine/feminine and endowed/unendowed. Only the reality of being unendowed belongs to the category of lack. The pair masculine/feminine belongs to the category of the tangible. Deprived of representable sensory realities, the extinctive tendency must utilize traces and representations belonging to tangible reality.

In 1937, Freud made the following clinical observation. A session construction revealing the traumatic dimension is not followed by recollections of the traumatic experience but ultra-clear details relating to it (Freud, 1937, p. 266). These details belong to the category of the tangible. The famous example, recalled earlier, of the forgetting of the name of Signorelli, is a demonstration of a process comprised of two deferred effects, the first one supports the denial, the second includes the traumatic reality. More recently, Jean-Luc Donnet (2006) has spoken of the *après-coup au carré* (i.e., to the power of 2 in arithmetic) with reference to the transference acting out as Freud formulated it in the Wolf Man (Freud, 1918).

The term *construction* of 1937 denotes this double après-coup: one producing an imaginary formation that accomplishes an unconscious wish and has an anti-extinctive function, the other producing a judgement of existence and meaning based on renunciation. Together, they constitute reality-testing. This is, in fact, a double test of renunciation; initially of extinction and then, subsequently, of the fulfilment of a wish. We can find the same difference during the session work between the process of something becoming conscious and the act of becoming aware of it.

In his 29th lecture, Freud (1933) argues that the dream is the product of a work of the mind that requires a turning away from the real external world, fulfilling a necessary condition for the development of a psychosis. He adds that this diversion is consciously willed and reversible, hence "a harmless psychosis." Then he adds that it disappears when relations with the external world are resumed. He makes no comments on waking, even though it links dreams and sensory perception, which are the two stages of reality-testing (p. 16).

The statement of 1938 to the effect that the dream is a psychosis becomes even more explicit. It establishes the existence of a harmless psychosis, which may be normal and beneficial depending on the circumstances in which it takes place. The loss of reality and reality-testing depend therefore on the dynamics of falling asleep and waking.

Freud's assertion that there exists a wish to sleep and a voluntary resumption of the relationship to daytime reality on waking draws attention to the processes involved. These processes border the sleep-dream system to which they belong. Falling sleep and the place accorded to psychic reality and the processes underlying the dream-work at the expense of object-cathexes and secondary processes have often been the subject of commentaries, in particular, on regression. The same cannot be said for the question raised by waking.

In the first case, it is a matter of putting into abeyance the cathexis of the perception of the reality of the object and of effecting a de-objectalization that is equivalent to a loss of reality in favour of a regression to the narcissism of sleeping-dreaming. The superego is involved in the wish to sleep and in the acceptance of this wish. It is based on parental messages inviting their children to "go to bed." It regresses to the status of dream censorship.

In the case of waking, it is a question of reestablishing the object-cathexes of sensory perception kept in abeyance during sleep. This dynamic is a form of reality-testing that is activated from the inside and from the outside. The reality-testing consists in the creation of a difference by the introduction of an imperative of re-cathexis.

The same reflections have been made on the initiation of regression at the beginning of the session and on the recathexis of the sensory perception of objects on leaving the session. Specific phobias have been observed as well as sub-confusional and uncanny states.

Contrary to what Freud's statement cited above suggests, these psychic acts are not governed by a voluntary active pole. To a large extent, they elude conscious decisions and belong to the *psychic activities of passivity* that are established under the aegis of the superego. The latter watches over the mutation by the double reversal of the work realized on the economy; first, on the regressive path, and then on the progressive path in order to direct desire towards the objects.

It is probably this efficiency of the superego that Freud was referring to when he spoke of a voluntary decision. The notion of waking unconscious guilt as developed by Braunschweig and Fain (1975) with its pivotal value between day and night must be taken into account in order to establish the metapsychology of falling asleep and of waking, and of the nycthemeral cycle. As far as waking is concerned, it is necessary to introduce the notion of nocturnal unconscious shame. It is the consequence of the regressive contact with what is refractory and what is beyond it. The trend towards the infinite extension of cathexes also requires the waking state to be able to deploy themselves in an endless state of ecstatic pleasure.

In order to limit the tendencies to erasure, which are opposed to every process of becoming conscious, the mind has at its disposal various mechanisms, such as the stimulus barrier and the act of falling asleep. When a high degree of differentiation is reached, the state of abeyance offers the possibility of deferring the process of falling asleep. Without this state of abeyance, we would be in a rapid state of oscillation, almost immediate and frenetic, between phases of falling asleep and waking up.

This being so, a mechanism related to sensory perception has an increasingly important place in the metapsychology of psychic functioning, namely, denial. It is linked to sensory perception, while in everyday language it concerns the rejection of any form of reality. Its conceptual theorization is initiated as soon as one takes into account a regressive extinctive attraction. It implies a transpositional link between this extinctive attraction and perceivable sensory reality that leaves no traces. This beyond becomes a new reality whose management involves the denial of sensory perceptions.

Perception and perceptual activity: Judgement and reality-testing

The extinctive tendency obliges thought to follow a process consisting in two après-coups with two deferred effects. The first is at the origin of a saturation by representable contents, while the second integrates the traumatic reality denied by the first. Such a procedure of two après-coups recognizes that extinctive regressivity is a reality. Reality-testing is a function that includes a period of idealization and denial in order to gain access to a de-idealization by means of the lifting of denial. The real recognition of, and consideration given to, the extinctive attraction of the drives depends on this test and not on the nomination of its existence alone. Negation makes it possible to speak of the traumatic reality without taking its traumatic quality into account at the heart of psychic functioning.

This saturation of consciousness along the endogenous path thanks to a psychic production has an interesting consequence. The reality thus perceived imposes itself as the only reality that exists. This aim is easily attained at night. For the dreamer, there is only one reality, that produced by his dream; he does not know it, the question does not arise.

Oneiric reality imposes itself in the form of perceptual identity, which is not a sensory perception; it is a hallucinatory endogenous perception. As I have pointed out in previous chapters, we need to refer to it with another term, that of perceptual activity (Chervet, 2009). This perceptual activity belongs to the hallucinatory sphere; it imposes itself in the form of perceptual identity and is subjectively taken for sensory perception.

At night this may seem quite simple, but it is much less so if we take the process of falling asleep into account, and also the process of waking, which is usually neglected. The apparent simplicity depends, then, on the quality of the temporary denial concerning sensory perception. During the day, things are more complicated, for perception continues.

In the session, endogenous reality is formulated out loud extemporaneously, hence the possible double saturation by the external sensory path (sound) and by the internal hallucinatory path. They are both combined in the production of perceptual material that emanates from perceptual activity and reaches consciousness from the inside and from the outside, and which has the function of fulfilling an unconscious wish, that the reality announced is the only one that exists.

Outside the session, people sometimes "talk to themselves out loud," which affords a similar delusion. Between the two are all our illusions, which always consist in taking our wishes for reality, both external and internal.

This mechanism of saturation is at the basis of all beliefs and ideologies, of all the systems that use the conviction characteristic of hallucinatory activity to impose the reality of the perceptual material against all reality-testing involving perception and perceptual activity; hence, the impossibility of relying on tests based on some kind of *sense of reality* (Freud, 1911). The notion of *judgement* and its corollary, the *lack of judgement*, are no longer things in themselves, but they depend totally on the context. Thus, an analyst would be totally lacking in judgement if he were to ask his patient to evaluate the meaning of, to reflect on, his associations. He would be impeding the first deferred effect of free associativity with its irrational and imaginary logics from establishing itself; this would be in total contradiction with the fundamental rule of analysis that he is supposed to uphold.

Reality-testing consists in recognizing the existence of several realities, as well as their entanglement and tricky discrimination. The judgement of meaning pertaining to perceptual activity as well as to the discrimination between sensory perception and perceptual identity are possible only in several stages and evolve according to the procedure of a double après-coup. This demolishes all the theories that argue that under certain conditions we could have access to the world by means of pure perception, such as *heuresthesia*, as well as those that argue that perception is a pure psychic creation. *Heuresthesia* considers that there exists a "possibility of gaining access to objectifiable knowledge or competence via perception without exercising conscious or voluntary control." According to this theory, "synesthesia fertilizes the mind."

In fact, perception imposes itself and we can deny only what belongs to lack by putting into abeyance a part of tangible perception that will be used to produce hallucinatory perceptual material in order to respond to the traumatic aspect of lack. What we perceive is thus always a mixture of perception-perceptual material that is tricky to disentangle.

The definitions of perception, perceptual activity and the representative field can now be even more rigorous. The correlation between the extinctive tendency with perceptions without traces defines perception proper. It retains its traumatic quality and is destined to remain perception. The correlation between the instinctual drive tendency to invest itself with the sensory perception of the tangible forms the basis of the *representative field*. And the correlation between perception without traces (lack), extinctive regressivity and hallucinatory perceptual identity can be called perceptual activity.

The mechanism of saturation is thus inseparable from the denial that it underpins. The dream is the guardian of sleep, thus of the process of falling asleep that is based on an ordinary and reversible denial, the denial of objects, and more particularly the erotic aspect of objects. This denial concerns the traumatic experience of terror when faced with a lack, emanating from a quality of the drives, their *extinctive tendency*. The denial of the sensory perceptions resonating with this extinctive regressivity allows for psychic work to be carried out on the latter, which serves to anti-cathect this extinctive tendency. It is an operation of restraint, the first foundational operation of psychic life.

Saturation thus combines a denial of a part of perceivable sensory reality, the lack, and the imposition by hallucinatory perceptual material of another part of reality, that which is tangible.

The differentiation between perception and perceptual activity is not straightforward, especially if we add that unconscious psychic reality tends to be transposed onto external perception, hence the most ordinary confusion in which we live, that of our daily animism exacerbated in the form of transference in the analytic situation.

Denial uses this detour of transposition. When there is a denial of a perceivable external reality, it is the endopsychic value of this reality that is concerned, and ultimately the elementary drive quality. Either this reality is anti-cathected by a psychic work of restraint or it must itself be denied.

We live on a daily basis with such an animistic imbroglio and a mixture of these various heterogeneous and incompatible solutions. Our topographies are in fact fragmented according to plural logics. The structural exclusivity of those that are called neurotic and psychotic meets its limit here.

Dreaming

Although the theory of dreams is considered as the basis of psychoanalysis, it was first a detour of Freud in the course of his research into the aetiology of hysteria and the theory of the neuroses (the *neurotica*) and a method of treatment adapted to the so-called transference neuroses (*psycho-analysis*). The case of Dora written in 1901 and published in 1905 (Freud, 1905), initially had the title "Dreams and Hysteria."

At the end of the 19th century, the differentiation between organic and mental illnesses was undergoing a major overhaul. The theory of degenerescence was crumbling, and the use of hypnosis introduced a new criteria of reality, reversibility. Hysteria presented all the symptoms of neurological illnesses, but hysterical disorders were reversible under hypnosis.

At that time, no one was able to say what was happening during hypnosis. Only Charcot offered a theory of the genesis of hysterical symptoms, a chronological process in two stages, with an official first stage, the trauma, and a second manifest stage, the symptom, and an interval period of *psychic incubation*, or *psychic elaboration* that Freud named a *period of latency*. In the previous chapters, I have recalled the participation of Charcot, Breuer and then Freud in the matter of the *psychic elaboration* and the *operation of après-coup*.

Freud took Charcot's *biphasic* theory and Breuer's notion of *retrogression* very seriously. In 1895, he studied this process in relation to the case of Emma, and, in 1897, he called it *Nachträglichkeit*. But having suggested that the trauma lay in early sexual seduction, in a *shocking shock*, he turned his attention entirely to the interval period. He sought to improve the method involving the backward path of remembering by using the spontaneous speech of the patient.

A whole new field of investigation of human thought was thus opened up, henceforth bi-directional and oscillatory. If the chronological onset of the trauma in two waves involves symptoms and bisphasic human sexuality, the psychic work of elaboration of the interval period follows a regressive trajectory before producing progressive material. Regression makes it possible, beginning with recent material, to realize a transformation of the traumatic regressive economy of old material. Each night, dreaming transforms this regressive economy and produces an economy of cathexis, a bonus of desire that can reveal itself by a manifest content, a dream. Hence Freud's interest in the regressive psychic activities of *passivity*, remembering, free association and, of course, even more clearly, dream-thoughts, equivalent to those under hypnosis.

The theory of dreams thus arose from this detour, in the image of dreaming that is itself such a detour. This path of the detour is one by which many discoveries have been made, and are then said to be fortuitous – the list is infinite, the most well known is that of penicillin. The *fortuitous* path is called by epistemologists *serendipity*, with its opposite, *zemblanity*. Serendipity is the fact of finding and discovering something quite different from what one is looking for. It is typical of the analytic treatment that uses the detour of transpositions. *Zemblanity* is defined by the fact of realizing unfortunate or, above all, expected discoveries; it is a matter of looking for and finding what one already has; a search that goes round in circles. Between the two, there is the immense field of the day-to-day work of every researcher.

This contextualization of *The Interpretation of Dreams* renders obsolete the so-called solipsism of the theory of dreams. This judgement overlooks the link that dreaming has with language and objects, through formal regression, the putting into abeyance of disagreeable daytime verbal thoughts and the denial of the erotic otherness of objects realized on falling asleep. Such an opinion arose under the influence of the fact that the sleep-dream system must isolate itself in order to accomplish its missions. In fact, putting the libidinal cathexis of objects into abeyance plays a part in the work of restraint realized towards the extinctive tendency. The specific scene in which they are deployed together is the erotic scene with sensual regression, including the refractory quality that characterizes it.

To elaborate his theory of dreams, Freud begins, in the first chapter of *The Interpretation of Dreams*, by reducing the infinite imaginative scope of the multiple theories of dreams put forward since Antiquity to the image of the dreamwork that obliges the abundant materials of the dream to pass through the eye of the needle of condensation. This is what quantum physicists call *decoherence*. The theory of decoherence was introduced by H. Dieter Zeh in 1970. *Quantum decoherence* is a theory capable of explaining the transition between the rules of quantum physics and the rules of classical physics as we know them at a macroscopic level. The major problem is that quantum physics admits superposed states that are absolutely unknown at the macroscopic level. The basic idea of decoherence is that a quantum system must not be considered as isolated, but rather as interacting with an environment. It is these interactions that are held to provoke the disappearance of the superposed states. There is an analogy with condensation in the dream-work.

This reduction of multiple and superposed states was realized by Freud in favour of simple statements apt at accounting for the phenomenology of dreams. In this way he founded a theory of dreams that had its place within a theory of global psychic functioning, a theory of thought. Subsequently, on several occasions, he would deconstruct himself the coherence of his theory, opening it up to other possibilities.

Interpretation also follows these two lines of reasoning: undoing the coherence of the manifest content of the dream and reducing the vast field of associations to "selected facts" alone (Bion).

These two processes can be found at the heart of all scientific research; undoing a coherence in order to open up the field of possibilities, and then reducing this field in the name of heuristic clarity.

This detour of Freud via dreams assumed a place of reference in his process of research and theorization. We can thus read a succession of affirmative statements about them in his writings: the dream is the hallucinatory fulfilment of a wish (1900); it is the guardian of sleep (from 1900 to 1914); the narcissistic system of sleeping-dreaming is equivalent to returning to the maternal womb; the dream-work has the mission of processing daytime traumas (1916–1917); it is subject from within to the reductive tendencies of the drives which endanger it, hence, the existence of "traumatic" dreams that do not fulfil a wish (from 1917 to 1920); the dream is an "attempt "at the fulfilment of a wish (1933, p. 29); and finally the dream is a psychosis (1940, p. 172).

Gradually, the emphasis was placed on dreaming rather than on the dream: the verb rather than the noun. Freud points out that the unconscious expresses itself with verbs; hence the importance accorded to the unconscious psychic act of dreaming, to psychic action, to the *dream-work* and to its unconscious operations, to their functions, their aims and purposes. The dream is the result of this work, presented on awakening on the internal screen of consciousness.

Dream functions

The psychoanalyst only has access to the accounts and memory of the dreams of his patients; he does not have access to the contents or to the dreaming itself. Thus, the functions of the dream work have to be inferred and the psychoanalytic interpretation of dreams depends on consideration of these functions.

Dreaming is "egoistic"; its internal missions are crucial. It is only secondarily, and when it fails partly, that the dream becomes a relational transaction through its narration or its utilization for other ends, artistic for instance.

Dreaming has its starting point in language, by a formal regression of words into forms that compose together a rebus. Then their transcription into thing-presentations, and then into manifest images, fulfils the function of limiting the regression to the space of images, of impeding *sensual regression* to continue its course as it does in erotic scenes. The act of dreaming thus fulfils its function as the guardian of sleep by excluding sensations that would awaken the sleeper, whether these sensations are derived from sensuality or sensoriality. Thanks to the cathexis of the field of images, both forms and thing-presentations, the sleep-dream system protects the somatic body by an anti-cathexis of regressive tendencies towards organ erotogenicity and negative tendencies that could free themselves from the somato-psychic pivot. This work requires restraint that arouses painful tension, hence a *masochism of renunciation* with regard to extinction. This restraint goes hand in hand with another task, namely, the mutation of the regressive libido into a cathectic libido that is realized under the influence of the life drive. This cathectic libido seeks to extend itself infinitely, which is another path of extinction. There is thus a double restraint. A second operation of renunciation participates in this process, towards the extinctive tendency by infinite extension. It allows the cathectic libido to follow the progressive path towards the mind and then, on awakening, towards objects. The libidinal regeneration of narcissism and the bonus of desire towards objects is brought about in this way. This process acts as a real lock on the two possible paths of extinction, by reduction and by extension. Freud (1924) called it "libidinal sympathetic excitation" (p. 163). But as early as

1900 he had emphasized the constraint imposed on the dream work of having to respect the *veins of onyx*, to use his fine expression, namely, the physiology of the organs and the physiology of psychic processes themselves. He considered, then, that the dream has diagnostic powers owing to its proximity and nocturnal sensibility to somatic states.

The telling of the dream is a second transcription in words that is added to the secondary elaboration in images, dramatized in waking scenarios. The dream reconnects with language, which, in fact, had never left it but was held in abeyance under the cover of formal regression. The dream unites two heterogeneous realities, language and the drives, via the long process of après coup.

In its turn, the work of theorization requires a supplementary stage of reduction of the infinite number of manifest contents. Freud arrives at a very ideal and succinct formula, expressed in the affirmative: the dream is a wish-fulfilment. Arriving at such succinct formulas by abstraction is a goal of all the sciences. This requires a series of reductions that also serve as condensations, the final formula containing latently the infinite number of the materials concerned.

The abstract formula offers great efficacy in anti-cathecting extinctive tendencies. When it is created, the abstraction fulfils this function through the process of saturation; a truth-effect arises from this that is not only an effect due to knowledge.

In psychoanalysis, this reduction towards theoretical abstraction is preceded by three stages; the condensation of dreams, where an infinite number of waking thoughts pass through the eye of a needle; a reopening of thoughts through free association; and finally the interpretative reduction that frees psychic work from recourse to great quantities of materials. This dynamic of reduction can be completed by supervision, which activates it again between the account of the supervisee and the comments of the supervisor. We could illustrate this reductive dynamic by the two accounts that Freud gave of one of his dreams, in 1900, and then in 1927.

In 1933, to the unconscious process of dreaming a nuance was added: the dream is an *attempt at the fulfilment of a wish* (Freud, 1933, p. 29). Between 1900 and 1933, the dream work became uncertain. We can deduce another formulation: the result of the dream-work is all the more unpredictable when it is successful. The more the dream-work fails, the more it is reduced to a mere anti-traumatic repetition. This traumatic type of dream realizes a further wish, that of dreaming. We can find this desire in "the dream within the dream" (Chervet, 2007).

The act of dreaming consists in successfully transforming the regressive libidinal economy and in promoting along the progressive path a *bonus of desire*, such as is felt after a good night's sleep. The dream memory may be forgotten more or less quickly or give rise to a narrative. This extension of the dream is an appeal addressed to another person in order to counter the attractions left open by the stumbling blocks of the dream-work. It is this need that gave birth to fortune-tellers and psychoanalysts. The power of traumatic negative forces astonishes and frightens us. It summons up the most precious qualities of the subject, his creativity and his realizations, as well as his moral qualities as a human being, such as modesty, disgust, solidarity and compassion, acquired through the resolution of the Oedipus complex. Negative tendencies are thus opposed by another tendency, that of cathexis, that continually gives fresh impetus to our thought in different ways. A third parameter is nevertheless required since negative tendencies and cathectic tendencies both strive towards extinction. This is why the death drive and the life drive cannot simply be opposed to each other. One strives towards extinction through reduction and destruction; the other has the same aim but through infinite extension and frantic dilution. A third term must be opposed to extinctivity. This is the role of the superego in daytime functioning, of the censorship in dreams, and of the stimulus barrier at the level of the drive source. It is a matter of an *imperative of renunciation* on which libidinal regeneration, narcissistic registration and mourning of the object depends.

Dreaming, searching: Psychoanalysis as a science

Psychoanalysis is often identified with a *science of dreams*. This indeed was the title of the first French translation of *Die Traumdeutung*, although this word means literally *The Interpretation of Dreams*.

This shift of meaning, or this reorientation concealing the term interpretation in favour of an apparent scientific certainty, reveals that psychoanalysis obliges us to revise the traditional definition of the notion of science and to take interpretation into account as an integral part of science. The debates on the theme of whether or not psychoanalysis is a science – in the classical sense of a sum of knowledge – conceals the difficulty introduced by interpretation, even though it is a component of thought. It is necessary to turn the question round. Does not psychoanalysis oblige us to think about a new definition of science that integrates the act of interpreting, and even the act of dreaming, the dream being a first interpretation of the unconscious tendencies under the effect of the imperative of renunciation?

The mere fact of considering that all science is a psychic production, here a theory, prompts us to understand the notion of science as having a double identity intertwining knowledge and theory. But Freud went further by considering that all psychic productions participate in a concealment, on the model of the specific distortion of the dream-work, or of the *double meaning* of the incidental speech of the session. Theories are speculative productions akin to imaginary fantasies (i.e., Edgar Allan Poe's 1848 essay *Eureka*), but as theories they also have a function concerning the need of the mind to attenuate traumatic experiences, to provide causal explanations and solutions to avoid them. Dreaming is to be considered as an obligatory stage in the process of knowledge and discovery, as a stage in taking into account the reality of lack, which initially must be denied by dreams. The dream is a concealing regressive psychic act, which, from the point of view of traditional science, is in the service of misrecognition. But it is an obligatory regressive detour with consciousness as its aim. It has a liberating role that allows the dreamer upon awakening to take into account the reality of traumatic experiences and perceptions of lack. By opposing the negative tendencies, the dream-work regenerates daytime cathexes; these may serve to produce knowledge and conscious theories, which play a role in supporting the dream's function of misrecognition. As for interpretation, it is first used in order to complete the dream-work when it stumbles. And through the new gain in awareness that it permits, it participates in the object-orientation of desire and in the misrecognition of traumatic reality. An interpretation of this first interpretation is necessary so that experiences of lack can be recognized as reality.

From the point of view of scientific knowledge, chapters V and VI in *The Interpretation of Dreams*, "The Material and Sources of Dreams" and then "The Dream-Work," could easily satisfy our need for objective knowledge. We could simply retain a positivist theory of dreaming with knowledge about the material of dreams, the memories of the day before and childhood memories; about somatic sources converted into nocturnal sensations; about primary and secondary processes, and about the four mechanisms involved in dream-production, *condensation, displacement, productions of the dream-work* and *considerations of representability*, and, finally, *secondary revision.*

Chapters IV and VII, respectively, "Distortion in Dreams" and "The Psychology of the Dream-Processes" could therefore be described as speculative, even imaginary and hazardous. In fact, they deal with the function of dreams and consider the phenomenon of dreaming within a context that includes the existence of negative attractions, those that kindle repression and the multiple defence mechanisms that all have a function of restraint vis-à-vis extinctive tendencies. The dream-work proves to have an aim and a function: the aim is libidinal regeneration and the function is the use of the negative aspirations inherent to the drives. When this work is successful, the libidinal regeneration ignores the extinctive tendencies that were taken into account by the dream-work in favour of the production of the libido.

The definition of a dream can now be unfolded. It is an interpretation, in the musical, theatrical or artistic sense of the term, of an unconscious wish that is thereby veiled which will be the object during the sessions of the first stage of interpretation. This representation of the unconscious wish itself conceals the extinctive attraction, which will be interpreted subsequently. It is these two stages with two interpretations that form the basis of psychoanalytic construction.

Depending on whether or not the analyst takes this participation of denial into account, two conceptions of analytic treatments can be outlined. For one, dreaming is sufficient; for the other, liberating object erogeneity linked to the pain of renunciation is the aim.

To return now to saturation. Frequently, we move from nocturnal reality to diurnal reality without noticing it, while waking up presents an important semiology. Perceptual identity is confronted on waking with the sensory perception of the external world. Generally, both realities are blended and mixed with different degrees of animism, without our knowing it.

Sometimes we have doubts, perceptual activity insists on remaining the only reality, and it continues to impose itself and to saturate the internal side of consciousness. The subject does not want to leave his regressive tendencies via his internal objects. He insists that reality only exists in the form of his own construction. Such a semiology of waking is observable in the session, when the patient has to stop free associating at the end of the session.

We have seen above that science is no longer only a sum of objective knowledge that decreases our ignorance; rather, knowledge reveals lack to us. Unless, that is, we are dominated by over self-estimation worthy of the Dunning-Kruger effect that Aristotle had already highlighted as ultracrepidarianism, according to which the least qualified people in a domain have the tendency to overestimate their skill, while the most competent are accessible to doubt and modesty.

Scientific knowledge is imbued with perceptual material that is necessary for the mental functioning of the scientist/researcher. Science participates in concealing the existence of a part of reality over which we are completely powerless.

Scientific work attempts to realize our wish to reduce our condition of helplessness vis-à-vis the primal scene of our drives, a scene that is constituted by laws of both material and psychic matter. When a discovery is made, there is a sense of bridging a gap in knowledge. But we have to admit that it neither eliminates the primal scene nor its experiences of exclusion nor its negative attractions.

We can thus understand the jubilation of Archimedes' Eureka pertaining to the density of bodies, thanks to the discovery of the pressure exerted on his body immerged in water, as well as that of Einstein imagining himself chasing a wave of light, or in a lift in free fall, not to forget the apple falling on Newton's head, an event that exceeded the capacities of the dream-work, obliging him to elaborate the matter on waking – perhaps in order to be able to sleep again?

These formulations are all sources of elation and truth-effects. Just like dreams, they fulfil a wish, namely, for the world to be a unique and complete entity, entirely representable and objective, that can be understood by means of a few abstract formulas that explain it! In psychoanalytic terms this translates as the wish that the primal scene at the origin of the drives could be entirely represented by a formula that overcomes all exclusion and every negative attraction, like the formula of "Trimethylamine" that suddenly emerged at the end of Freud's famous dream of Irma's injection and that found its extension in an equally succinct formula: the dream is a wish-fulfilment. This formula was followed up in 1901 by another formula stipulating that in the dream: "a thought expressed in the optative has been replaced by a representation in the present tense" (Freud, 1901, p. 647).

Research thus has the unconscious motive of suppressing the effects inherent to the primal scene, the feelings of exclusion, and to bring elements of restraint with regard to negative attractions; it is moved by the wish to successfully deny this reality that evokes terror!

This saturation of consciousness by a mathematical discovery is expressed in one of the last statements made by Grigori Perelman in an interview with the newspaper *Komsomolskaya Pravda* on 28 April 2011. Grigori Perelman was a brilliant Russian mathematician. Among other matters, he resolved one of the seven great Millennium problems: the Poincaré conjecture. He received, and refused, the prize of the European Mathematical Society in 1996, then the Fields Medal in 2006, then the Clay Prize in 2010 amounting to one million dollars. The statement evoked seems to be of rarely equaled pretension, but it is sustained by the truth-effect linked to the saturation experienced: "Why have I spent so many years trying to resolve the Poincaré conjecture? I have found a way of detecting voids ... Voids are everywhere. They can be detected and this gives us many possibilities ... I know how to control the universe. Tell me, then, why would I need to chase a million dollars?"

Sleeping/keeping vigil faces us with two truths, which clash without either of them dissolving. "God does not play dice with the universe," Einstein affirms, an assertion that is answered by Mallarmé's statement, "A throw of the dice will never abolish chance"; nor the sense of lack or emptiness.

Recourse to the abstraction of scientific formulas is the consequence of the impossibility of depicting lack in images, whether perceived along the sensory path or experienced endogenously. There will always exist an untraceable perception, that of lack, thus a missing trace through which the extinctive tendencies will be felt. It is only in dreams and delusions that a single world can exist momentarily, that of representation and perceptual identity, that of perception being denied.

The fact that a reality exists that cannot give rise to traces and images is at the origin of another psychic production, theorization. It is possible to explain how lack was produced; hence, the theories of its origin, which, for their part, can be depicted by scenarios. The most well known of these infantile theories is that of castration by cutting. It explains the absence of a penis in girls by an act of castration carried out by the father. In the "Wolf Man" case, Freud mentions the existence of an *unconscious concept* (Chervet, 2015), the "small detachable part," a concept that makes it possible to gather together many occurrences around this unique quality, some of them being observable (faeces, baby), others constructed (penis). This concept nourishes theories reinforcing perceptual activity.

We can find the same depiction of excision in Lewis Carroll illustrated by John Tenniel, on the subject of the Cheshire cat that suffers a gradually erasure of all the parts of its body until its smile is finally removed by the erasure of its mouth. All that remains of it is the word "smile." Lewis Carroll shows in this way the limits of representing things through images.

All quests and appetites for novelty, whether it is a case of art or of scientific research, seek to produce contents that participate in this aim of denying the reality of lack in order to suppress terror, and of making it a consequence.

Einstein's interviews show us how this logic is involved in his activity of research: "Words or language, whether written or spoken, do not seem to play any role in my mechanism of thought. The psychic entities which seem to serve as elements of thought ... are, in my case, of visual and some of a muscular type. Conventional words or other signs have to be sought for laboriously only in a second stage" (Einstein, in Hadamard, 1959, p. 75, translated from the French).

His response to the psychologist Max Wertheimer is still more illustrative, when the latter questioned him "about the concrete events in his thoughts" that had led him to the theory of relativity." "During all those years," he replied, "there was a feeling of direction, of heading straight towards something concrete. It is of course very hard to express that feeling in words. But I have it in a kind of survey, as it were, visually." (Wertheimer, 1945, p. 184, cited by Holton, 1988, p. 387, translated from the French). Here we can recognize the attraction of the aim to be attained and the search for a saturation of consciousness by means of vision.

Einstein's way of working also shows us the impossibility of separating images from language. Having had difficulties with language since early childhood – he only began to speak at the age of four and only really acquired language around the age of twelve – he had recourse to an alter ego in mathematics – his first wife, initially, Mileva Maric, and then his colleague and friend Marcel Grossmann, a Hungarian mathematician.

Thus, just as with dreaming, thinking in images is in no way independent of language. And further, we should recall that saturation can also be achieved by words and abstraction, thanks to a reduction of images into hypercathected succinct formula.

The *supervision* specific to the training of psychoanalysts, with, in the background, the reminiscence of the trio, Anna 0 – Breuer – Freud, also functions according to such stages ranging from an abundance of materials to succinct, "short" phrases. Saturation is based on condensation, and even on this tendency to ever-greater "succinctness" due to abstraction.

Between images and language, between dreaming and speaking, a continuity can exist by means of the attempt to fulfil a wish hallucinatorily. This upsets common sense. True, it is more difficult to sustain such a wish-fulfilment through speaking than through dreaming, but words can nonetheless also be used for such an aim. Freud recognized this in 1923, when he wrote: "When a hypercathexis of the process of thinking takes place, thoughts are *actually* perceived – as if they came from without – and are consequently held to be true" (Freud, 1923, p. 23). Henceforth, a hypercathexis of the process of thinking may permit words to be "taken as true." A hallucinatory *saturation* of words can participate in the creation of neo-realities against a background of a denial of reality. The myth of access to truth through the use of language in enunciation and interpretation collapses. A new fact has to be taken into account, the usual participation of denial in mental functioning.

There exist, therefore, several concomitant and successive realities, including the denial of the fact that there are incompatible realities. The wish for only one to exist, called truth and created by the subject, is acted each night by dreaming.

I have already pointed out that speaking in the session pursues the same mission as dreaming, the wish that there were only one world, that of perceptual activity of the subject, at the expense of that of perception. It is a matter of creating a world exempt from what specifies perception, that is to say, what is not representable or traceable, the experiences of lack. The denial thus pertains to the perception of lack, which is evoked particularly by the difference between the sexes and to a lesser extent by all differences.

According to the same logic, at the moment when they are found-invented, scientific formulas are accompanied by the same hope of saturation. The truth-effect arising from this saturation is only momentary.

The discontinuity between dreaming and speaking, that which we adopt on waking, without thinking about it, requires a new mental act that results in the recognition of the existence of two realities. Verbal thinking is the vehicle of a renunciation, a mourning of this wish for oneness, synthesis and completeness. What stands in contrast to thinking in images and verbal thinking is therefore *mourned thought*.

Scientific formulas also attempt, as does the dream memory for a few hours after waking, to maintain such a saturation against lack, by presenting itself as the *truth*. But they do not have the power to prevent, in the shorter or longer term, the return of the feeling of disappointment and helplessness inherent in the human condition. The case of Gregori Perelman, or other mathematical geniuses such as Alexandre Grothendieck, who both withdrew from the world, shows us that a solution for attempting to maintain the imposition of perceptual identity is that of anachoretism.

Earlier I said I intended to follow the example of a dream characterized by Freud as a successful dream in *The Future of an Illusion* in 1927: "The dreamer may be seized with a presentiment of death, which threatens to place him in the grave. But the dream-work knows how to select a condition that will turn even that dreaded event into a wish-fulfilment; the dreamer sees himself in an ancient Etruscan grave, which he has climbed down into, happy to find his archaeological interests satisfied" (1927, p. 17).

This account is accompanied by a note referring to *The Interpretation of Dreams* where the dream has already been discussed. The return to *The Interpretation of Dreams* reserves a surprise for us. The original dream probably dates back thirty years. It was one of Freud's own dreams – at the time he was 40 years old – very well known under the name of "Anatomical preparations." It is a very long contorted dream, full of details, in which there is insistent reference to tiredness of the legs, depicted by the laborious form of the dream itself, which does not progress.

What a difference from the schematic dream of 1927!

In 1900, the interpretation required a long associative process by means of which it is deduced, while in 1927 it is formulated at the beginning of the dream in a few succinct words. The fear of 1900, that his legs would not carry him for long, that he could not advance in life, that he would have to go to his grave young, is replaced by a presentiment of death, dealt with by an effect of rejuvenation, the joy of climbing down into a grave to make archaeological discoveries. From the disappointment linked to an unsatisfied desire in 1900, Freud passes over in 1927 to a disappointment inherent in the extinctive nature of every drive, of life itself.

Freud was then 71 years old. The dream had benefited from the long work of elaboration of its author over the last thirty years, in particular from recognition of this drive quality that is so difficult to apprehend and which he calls the death drive, but which is, in fact, the extinctive regressivity of every drive, whether of life or of death. The dream-work succeeded in turning the pain of getting old round into its contrary, that is in transforming the successive experiences of lack into a young man's sense of jubilation at discovering marvels. The threat of castration that is attendant upon the desire to penetrate the past is reversed into an unlimited and infinite bath of rejuvenation. This jubilant reversal of an idealization of the act of discovering continues to deploy itself within finiteness, that of a grave!

Dreaming had thus continued in a veiled form during all these years towards a *schematizing ascetization*, an abstraction that offers a much better response to the extinctive tendencies. The dream-work no longer has difficulty in sustaining its function of denying implacable reality, and associativity no longer needs a large quantity of materials. Interpretation is accessible, succinct and efficient. The desire to deny this reality and to plunge into the bath of rejuvenation of dreams is assured. The dream is then waited-for and hoped-for, and it is sustained by the desire to rediscover for an instant an illusion of youth.

This is what the first lines of the "Dedication" in Goethe's *Faust* sing to us:

> YE wavering shapes, again ye do enfold me,
> As erst upon my troubled sight ye stole;
> Shall I this time attempt to clasp, to hold ye?
> Still for the fond illusion yearns my soul?
>
> (...)
>
> Tear follows tear, my steadfast heart obeying
> The tender impulse, loses its control;
> What I possess as from afar I see;
> Those I have lost become realities to me.
>
> Goethe, "Dedication," *Faust*, 1808, Part I

References

Braunschweig, D. & Fain, M. (1975) *La nuit, le jour: Essai psychanalytique sur le fonctionnement mental.* Paris: Presses Universitaires de France.

Chervet, B. (2007). Le rêve dans le rêve. *Libres Cahiers pour la Psychanalyse*, 14: 133–146.

Chervet, B. (2009). Perception et perceptif dans le rêve et l'animisme. In: *L'animisme parmi nous, Monographies et débats de psychanalyse*. Paris: Presses Universitaires Francaises.

Chervet, B. (2015). Aux origines de l'irrationnel: Le concept infantile, *Revue Française de Psychanalyse*, 79 (5): 1747–1752.

Donnet, J-L. (2006). L'après-coup au carré. *Revue Française de Psychanalyse*, 70 (3): 715–725.

Freud, S. (1900). *The Interpretation of Dreams*. S.E. 4–5. London: Hogarth.
Freud S. (1901). On Dreams. S.E. 5. London: Hogarth, pp. 633–685.
Freud, S. (1905). Fragment of an Analysis of a Case of Hysteria. S.E. 7. London: Hogarth.
Freud, S. (1911). Formulations on the Two Principles of Mental Functioning. S.E. 12. London: Hogarth, pp. 218–226.
Freud, S. (1918 [1914]). From the History of an Infantile Neurosis. S.E. 17. London: Hogarth, pp. 7–122.
Freud, S. (1920). *Beyond the Pleasure Principle*. S.E. 18. London: Hogarth, pp. 1–64.
Freud, S. (1923). *The Ego and the Id*. S.E. 19. London: Hogarth, pp. 3–66.
Freud, S. (1924). The Economic Problem of Masochism. S.E. 19. London: Hogarth, pp. 159–170.
Freud S. (1927). *The Future of an Illusion*. S.E. 2. London: Hogarth, pp. 1–56.
Freud, S. (1933). *New Introductory Lectures on Psycho-Analysis*. S.E. 22. London: Hogarth, pp. 1–182.
Freud, S. (1937). *Constructions in Analysis*. S.E. 1. London: Hogarth, pp. 257–269.
Freud, S. (1940). *An Outline of Psychoanalysis*. S.E. 23. London: Hogarth, pp. 139–207.
Goethe, W. (1808). *Faust*. Oxford: World Classics.
Hadamard, J. (1959). *Essai sur la Psychologie de l'invention dans le domaine mathématique*. Paris: Blanchard.
Holton, J. (1988): *L'invention scientifique: Thémata et interprétation*, trans. P. Scheurer. Paris: Presses Universitaires de France.
Wertheimer, M. (1945). *Productive Thinking*, ed. Michael Wertheimer. New York: Harper and Brothers.

Chapter 8

Après-coup and bodily erogeneity

Sensual regression and the castration complex

When Freud directed his attention to Charcot's theory concerning the operation in two stages involved in the formation of hysterical symptoms, he put forward the hypothesis that the first stage of the trauma was of a sexual nature.

His research into the aetiology of the psychoneuroses oriented him towards the sexual factor. This allowed for the first nosographical differentiation between the psychoneuroses and the actual neuroses; early sexual seduction for the first and a misuse of sexuality for the second. But he also introduced into this differentiation a "psychical mechanism" responsible for the psychical elaboration of somatic sexual excitation (Freud, 1893), an active mechanism in the first group, but absent in the second. In the case of Emma, he considered that a symptom of adolescence linked to a post-pubertal experience of sexual arousal harked back to a traumatic sexual experience in childhood; the recent scene I of the shop assistants was linked to the earliest scene II of the shopkeeper. He subsequently modified this "neurotica" dominated by an overly systematic reification. The sexual experience involved was a repressed phantasy. The symptom was now seen as a posthumous effect of this material repressed in childhood that manifested itself in adolescence – the repressed material pertaining to infantile sexuality.

From thereon, Freud was able to broaden the notion of sexuality to childhood and to multiple vicissitudes other than that of the erotic scene. Then he differentiated the polymorphous nature of childhood sexuality from the category of infantile sexuality insofar as it is inherent to repression and a rich source of infantile amnesia (Freud, 1905). He clarified his early intuition and reinforced it permanently by highlighting "the diphasic onset of sexual development" (Freud, 1923c, p. 141), the "diphasic onset of sexual growth" (Freud, 1926, p. 37).

The diphasism of human sexuality and the two stages of the operation of après coup

A first efflorescence of sexuality takes place during early childhood in the form of polymorphous sexuality and concerns the whole body. The operations of desexualization and resexualization establish the oscillation between sensuality and sexuality. Each stage of development, from orality to genitality via anality, is based on a part of the body and grounds an erogenous zone. In fact, each of the parts of the body becomes an erogenous zone, but those of the passages inside/outside are more sensitive to resexualization; in fact, a first early stage in the sexual cathexis of all the organs that constitute organ erotogenicity (Freud, 1914). This is anti-cathected by the primary repression based on early maternal care. A part of organ erotogenicity will be desexualized and will form the basis of primary narcissism with bodily sensuality. This creates a map of erogeneity that depends on the singular history of the process of desexualisation. It is outlined with its nuances and disturbances.

This stage of infantile sexuality is characterized by the "primacy of the phallus" (Freud, 1923a, p. 142), that is, by a denial of castration recognized in the difference between the sexes. Its fate is to undergo repression under the impact of the regressive attraction emanating from primal repression. Little by little, this negative attraction shatters the denial and obliges the child to feel the difference between the sexes and to elaborate a mature sexuality through the resolution of the Oedipus complex. This is what happens during the second flowering of sexuality in puberty.

This regressive attraction has its origin "beyond" primal regression, in the extinctive regressive tendency of the drives. The necessity of neutralizing the involvement of this extinctive tendency is the reason for this organization in two stages.

Repression preserves infantile sexuality in the dynamic unconscious in the form of infantile amnesia, where it can be used according to primary types of logic.

Throughout life it will have an important role in the function of dreams of processing traumatic impressions by means of saturating consciousness, whose nature can also be described as *phallic*. It will also find its place in erotic life. The preliminaries will exalt it during sensual regression. This form of expression denotes the regressive path followed by the sensuality arising from the acquisitions of childhood towards organ erotogenicity until organ pleasure is obtained. It consists in making possible a resexualization of sensuality by putting into abeyance the assets of the educational culture of the body. It finds its end-point, its lock and limit, in orgasm, revealing the refractory state of sensibility (Chervet, 2020).

These two stages are ideally separated by a period Freud called the period of latency, a term that he would also use to designate the unconscious psychic elaboration that occurs between stage 1 of the trauma and stage 2 of the symptom. This period is dominated by a desexualization from which post-Oedipal tenderness and firmness emerge. This desexualization remains a site of conflict, which has a bearing on the establishment of the superego. Our moral, ethical and aesthetic requirements stem from it. Disgust, modesty, compassion and indignation towards cruelty are manifestations of the irreducible conflict through which the propensity to eliminate the superego ("murder of the father") and to resexualize the narcissistic functions ("incest with the mother") is expressed.

In this context, adolescence becomes the period when the possibility of following the extinctive tendency to its regressive limit is established. It is possible thanks to the previous elaboration of infantile sexuality, which has the function of concealing it. After *Beyond the Pleasure Principle* (1920), the phallic quality of infantile sexuality took on the significance of opposing extinctive attractions. The unconscious of the infantile amnesia created by repression offers a preservative negativity. Its timelessness is opposed to the limited duration of the extinctive tendency of the drives. Repressed infantile sexuality can return; it has not disappeared. But as it is repressed under the impact of extinctive attractions, it takes over the traumatic quality while at the same time attenuating it.

By means of this attenuation, it acquires great usefulness at the heart of regressive psychic activities. It makes possible the formal regression of dreams through the contents of infantile amnesia and the sensual regression of eroticism via the infinite variations of the preliminaries. This mature/infantile articulation implies a process of renunciation that remains fragile. The renunciation concerns the refusal to feel the extinctive aim of regressive longings. This consideration has major consequences, since it is responsible for the resolution of the Oedipus complex, that is, for the mourning of the cathexes of Oedipal objects and for modifications of the qualities of the drives. The source and the pressure are no longer infinite abundance and constant force. They become uncertain, wavering and intermittent. They are the result of psychic work that is subject to variations and stumbling blocks. This work is the task of the subject and grounds him, but he does not master it actively. Sensual regression is part of the regressive psychic activities of passivity, the voluntary active pole then being in abeyance.

This was how the terms of latency and the act of putting into latency were introduced not only into the theory of dreams, but also human sexuality in the form of a period of latency. They link the day before and the following day by means of the dream-work, and erotic satisfaction and the rebirth of desire, by a refractory period and a work of libidinal sympathetic excitation between renunciation and extinction.

In the case of dreams, thoughts are put into abeyance the day before; in fact, they are submitted to a regressive attraction emanating from unconscious wishes that attract them into a state of abeyance owing to their correlation with extinctive regressivity. Then they follow the path of formal regression, which allows them to enter into contact with instinctual drive impulses and to represent them. This economic path requires a work of distortion that has the function of opposing the extinctive tendencies, a distortion that culminates in the production of a manifest content oriented along the progressive path, the dream, and in a bonus of desire arising from libidinal regeneration. A similar cycle occurs at the level of the body by means of a sensual regression that exalts organ erotogenicity to the point of ecstatic enjoyment (*jouissance*). This conceals the *little death* of orgasm and the refractory period, which serves as reality-testing towards the existence of the extinctive tendency. Flight into abstinence aims to avoid this reality-testing.

The two stages of the castration complex

The castration complex is opposed to the advent of the erotic subject. It expresses a phobia of sensual regression, which, in general, concerns certain parts of the body. It thus limits the effects of disorganization linked to the attraction of extinctive regressivity. This conflict results in a regression to various forms of auto-eroticism permeated with infantile sexuality. This solution is that of the decathexis characteristic of falling asleep in favour of the hallucinatory regressive pole with the aim of libidinal regeneration reoriented towards cathecting objects on awakening.

This dynamic in two stages is part of the nycthemeral cycle and of the oscillation between night and day of mental activity, not in terms of a *complex* but of a *process* guaranteeing the processing of the internal traumatic dimension of the psyche. This process produces very variable deferred effects depending on the involvement of the superego or its elimination.

The correlation between the castration complex and the ordinary phobias of childhood accounts for the conflictual issues of the Oedipus complex involved in this process. The message of a threat of castration has the function of impeding transgressive regressions, resexualizations of the primary and secondary narcissisms (incest with the body and with the Oedipal object). It is not opposed to regression but demands a work of regression that makes it possible to approach instinctual drive regressivity while keeping it anti-cathected. This ethical task is incumbent upon the superego, the dream censorship and the stimulus barrier.

In the field of object-cathexis, this conflictuality is expressed by the oscillation between infantile object-cathexis and mature object-cathexis. It is the imperative of mourning and resolution, thus of the future of the superego, that is at stake here.

At the level of narcissism the castration complex is reflected by anxieties of loss of love and separation characteristic of narcissistic object-relations. The clinical manifestations are depressive inhibitions, melancholia, feelings of inferiority, character disorders, and so on.

The conflictual issues of castration are also noticeable at the level of libidogenesis through its vicissitudes. Deficiencies in dynamism and psychic vitality appear, as well as deficiencies pertaining to libidinal qualities.

A generalized conception of castration emerges with a central conflict between the forms of logic used in denial and its resolution under the aegis of the superego.

When the subject goes to sleep, the superego, now in abeyance, regresses to the state of censorship, which makes the dream-work possible. The regressive awakening of the traumatic dimension requires the intervention of the stimulus barrier under the cover of sleep. When these links between stimulus barrier, censorship and superego come undone, the operation of après-coup is disorganized and we witness clinical situations involving the emergence of clinical symptoms *in quick succession* and others marked by recurrent *fits and starts*.

The contribution of 1920 throws light on yet another dimension present in the identifications already approached clinically in 1916 with melancholia, namely, the *defective* dimension. This term underlines the fact that identifications can work towards defeats of mentalization. They impose a castration that is *already there*. The subject finds himself at grips with a *reduction* imposed in the establishment of mental functions, or with the progressive concretization of a castration at the heart of the psyche pertaining to its economy, dynamics, topographical organization and field of cathexis.

Such *defective identifications* are at work in the ordinary anti-Oedipus, in destiny neuroses, clinical pictures dominated by the negative therapeutic reaction and the reduction-compulsion. They produce amputations and degradations.

The question of *castration* concerns its significance regarding elimination of the superego and extinctive regressivity. Within clinical material, the *clues of castration* express the vicissitudes of the psychic work required to process traumatic regressivity. The initial shock that determines the deferred effect is defined by the traumatic power of regressivity, by attacks on the constitutive processes of psychic work and by the effect of perceptions called *castration*, which are used to transpose the extinctive quality of the drives.

Things seen and heard

Freud made a connection, then, very early on, between the formation of symptoms, human sexuality and the nycthemeral cycle, which includes the dream function. The operation of après-coup gradually has access to universality. It becomes the operation par excellence of thought and human sexuality; the operation that signifies that the extinctive regressive quality of the drives is recognized and taken into account. It governs the establishment and advent of erogeneity. Its temporal discontinuity is induced by this regressive attraction, which manifests itself by impressions of being threatened with disappearance and erasure. The extinctive tendency demands to be taken into account by a regressive period of psychic work. Subsequently, the libido will be oriented along the progressive path. The threat linked to this extinctive attraction and its execution by an erasure will be expressed by the two stages of the castration complex that are the *seen and* the *heard*. The perception of the absence of the penis on the lower abdomen of the girl offers such an objectification of extinctive regressivity with an interpretation of the absence as an act of enacted castration. As for what is felt concerning the threat, it is objectified through hearing educational messages of *caution* and *demand*.

Later, Freud noticed that there is no specific representative content in the unconscious of traumatic neurosis. Deprived of substitute forms of logic, this clinical picture had a traumatic impact on the metapsychology of 1900.

The mnemic dimension, however, is present in the form of reminiscences, of psychic acts that serve as memory without recollection, without remembering. A similarity exists between the effects of *what is seen* involving current perceptions of lack and others from childhood, in particular that of the lack of the penis on the lower abdomen of the girl; and, equally, between the effects of *what is heard* linking internal feelings and maternal messages of caution and paternal messages of demand. *What is heard* originates in the transposition on to the discourse of certain early endogenous impressions of threat arising from the extinctive tendency.

What is seen and heard thus constitute deferred effects constructed from early impressions thanks to the mechanism of transposition. They link the endogenous impressions of threat and disappearance emanating from the conflict in the first mental operations with the verbal messages of the parents and with the sensory perceptions of lack transmitted by any perception of differences.

Neither seen nor heard

The meaning of the things *seen* and *heard* depends on several factors; the impact of the imperative of resolution, the imposition of alienation on the defensive system of another and the defective tendencies. This conflictuality finds expression in all sorts of disjunctions between the messages seeking resolution, the alienating messages and the defective messages. This disjunction often occurs between the messages arising from *what is seen* and those arising from *what is heard*.

A hesitation always exists as to whether *what is heard* precedes *what is seen* or vice versa, which produces contradictions in the theory. These are linked to the fact that the resolutive dynamic is always linked with another dynamic dominated by the elimination of the imperative of resolution. This elimination requires a denial, which may concern *what is heard*, the message, or *what is seen*, the observation, or both. It is a matter of suppressing *feelings* about an internal threat recognized in verbal messages, and feelings about an internal lack recognized in some perceived external reality or other. So several instances of what is seen and heard will be necessary before they acquire the psychical value of transmitters of the reality of castration/extinction.

This conflict between denial and the recognition of this value gives an impression of confusion in certain texts of Freud from 1922 to 1925 bearing on the castration complex, the resolution of the Oedipus complex and the difference between the sexes. At the origin of this impression is a frequent equivalence in Freud's writings between boy = resolution and girl = denial. Thus the *boy's Oedipus* complex takes into account the threats and reality of castration, while the *girl's* is marked by denial; but these two forms exist both in boys and in girls.

In the session, the conflict between the *imperative of resolution* and the *propensity towards non-resolution* are reflected by a misuse of hate, which is then utilized in the service of non-resolution. A real *transvaluation* of the significance of affects occurs. Guilt is associated with the attempt to build independence and shame with the object-related orientation of sexuality. Hate is turned towards the imperative of resolution, hence the risk of the setting-up of a perversion. Pain then serves to sexualize hate as in "A Child is Being Beaten" (Freud, 1919).

The double meaning of the "negative" transference is expressed here: one that uses hate positively in the service of the construction of the object and the subject: "*the object is born of hatred*" (Freud, 1915a); and the other pertains to the defective transference of which Lacan speaks under the name of a transference of *énamouration*, whose consequences are harmful for the subject without his realizing it.

Guilt, shame, hate and pain sometimes prove to be favorable to reduction, amputation, destruction and mortification, instead of being values that ensure the maturation of the psyche, forming the basis of ethics. This transvaluation concerns the parent and the analyst. It is inherent in every process of identification. Indeed, identification has two sides: identifying through the recognition of loss, and identifying so as not to experience loss. A distinction may be drawn, then, between identifications with and without renunciation. According to the logic of transvaluation, the object that serves as a support for messages is hated. It is a matter of eliminating it. On the other hand, the object/support that uses a child for its own defensive needs is loved. The defective significance of this love then remains inaccessible to the child.

Diphasism and the physiological factor

Freud constantly referred to the mechanisms and processes that the operation of après-coup uses as being the very physiological structure of the mind. I have emphasized how he brought together in the name of the isomorphy of one and the same processual structure the formation of symptoms, the nycthemeral cycle with the dream function and human sexuality. The notion of fractality applies to the operation of après-coup.

Its onset depends on the identificatory history of a subject even if its components do not originate in his history. This history has an essential function of permitting the expression of the potential psychic processuality until it is operative. The picture emerges of a genetics of the mind open to uncertainties, stumbling blocks, unpredictability, creativity, and also morbidity. The psychoanalytic notion of overdetermination denotes this complexity of a potential already-there waiting to become operative.

The operation of après-coup and its components are potentially already-there, but they must become operative by means of an identification with another person. In order to express itself through multiple unforeseeable emergences, this potentiality requires the detour via the external world of perceptions.

The operation of après-coup is thus involved in the biological structure of human sexuality, in fact, in its epigenesis. Biological potential needs the psychical operation of après-coup to become biologically and psychically operative. Ideally, the biology of sexuality appears to be organized in two stages. Consequently, the diphasic operation of après-coup seems to belong to biology, whereas, in reality, it has made the detour via the mental life of another person to become the psychic operation par excellence of the subject.

Having ceased in 1917 to use the term *Nachträglichkeit*, Freud resorted to other expressions that placed particular emphasis on this diphasic aspect. The *diphasic onset*, the *diphasic character* specific to the human race, is said to be "the biological determinant of man's predisposition to neuroses" (Freud, 1925, p. 37). Freud adds that "the period of latency is a physiological phenomenon" (ibid., note 1). In advance of epigenetics, he further adds: "It can, however, only give rise to a complete interruption of sexual life in cultural organizations which have made the suppression of infantile sexuality a part of their system" (ibid). Without naming it, he introduces the superego and the variations between personal superego and cultural superego.

This passage condenses all the texts of this period, which are an extension of the *Three Essays on the Theory of Sexuality* (1905) and in which he conceives sexual development in terms of a genetic programme of stages (Freud, 1923a), then the Oedipus complex as a physiological process that unfolds by itself on the model of losing one's milk teeth (Freud 1924) and finally the difference between the sexes as an anatomical reality that imposes consequences on the mind (1925).

At this period, he had already stressed the fact that dream mechanisms depend on a physiological factor specific to the mind and that therefore elude psychoanalytic treatment: "On the mechanism of dream-formation itself, on the dream-work in the strict sense of the word, one never exercises any influence; of that one may be quite sure" (Freud, 1923b, p. 114). We recognize here the psychic mechanism of 1895.

In so doing, Freud gave a major place to the *physiological* constraint on psychic processes from which the subject seeks to free himself by the *factor of phantasy*, which offers, on the contrary, a sense of freedom. The unpleasure linked to the reality principle promoted by the physiological factor, inasmuch as it is an end wall erected against the traumatic reality of negative regressions, is thus attenuated. The factor of phantasy pertains to the pleasure principle and its function of concealment. It is generally linked to the *historical factor* considered to be responsible for the alienation and passivation imposed on the subject. The physiological factor thus remains unknown (Freud, 1932). A dialectical tension appears between these three factors and the randomness of chance.

This explains why, in *Beyond the Pleasure Principle*, Freud drew on biological findings, those of cells and protozoa, to elaborate the third quality of the drive, its *extinctive regressivity*, and the existence of psychical operations subject to an imperative of registration in which it is possible to recognize the physiological factor of the mind.

The metapsychological elaboration of unconscious realities required such a detour thanks to a transposition on to an adequate external material. Freud clearly formulated this psychic law in 1922. This mechanism of transposition became indispensable for the *admission to consciousness* of ideas: "anything arising from within (apart from feelings) that seeks to become conscious must try to transform itself into external perceptions" (Freud, 1923c, p. 20).

For affects, that is to say the qualitative indicator of psychic work, their admission to consciousness depends on the bodily conversion of the quota of economy that corresponds to them or on its repression. The same is true for the libidinal production that attends all psychic work. It is accessible to consciousness thanks to the experiences of regeneration and the bonus of desire. Conversion is a form of transposition at the basis of the erogenous body and feelings. In "The Neuropsychoses of Defence" (Freud, 1894), Freud proposed a new term, that of *conversion*, to denote the fact that a "sum of excitation is transformed into something somatic" (p. 49).

The transposition produces a *metaphorization* thanks to an identification, thus a misrecognition through substitution. These metaphors are the first links with consciousness. They will subsequently have to be undone in order to make way for access to knowledge, in fact for a *recognition* that needs concepts in order to be accomplished.

This detour of transposition introduces historicity and involves the qualities of the supports of transposition. This ensemble transposition-identification is akin to Bion's normal projective identification. This concept maintains a confusion between transposition, which is the ordinary projection used in phobia and animism, and projection proper, which is based on a denial. In this case, that which is denied returns from the outside. In the case of animistic transposition in phobia, the chosen object stands in correlation with an unconscious thing-presentation, which is thus kept repressed. In the case of projection, an internal tendency is eliminated by a stable denial of external perceptions. This denial risks being shattered at any time by other perceptions correlated with those denied. In the first case, the subject retains the subjective feeling that what causes his fear is endogenous anxiety; in the case of projection, external reality is accused of persecution and destructive intentions.

Randomness and the field of phantasy give transposition an apparent imaginary pliability that it barely has in reality. Psychic development depends on it entirely. And the operation of après-coup, determined by the physiology of psychic operations, becomes operative only by taking such a detour via the processuality of another person.

The category of the infantile of the years 1900 to 1905 expresses the factor of phantasy, the narcissism of 1914 the historical point of view, and the processual of 1920 to 1923 the physiological point of view. Many psychoanalytic studies prioritize the historical factor with the hope of getting free of it. On the other hand, external reality is off-putting and phantasy is attractive because it distracts. This exclusion of the constraint of the reality principle can also be found in the priority accorded to the *process* (*Proceß*) of a more or less continuous temporal unfolding at the expense of the process (*Vorgang*) of psychic operations, which are marked by discontinuity. The translation from German to French proves favourable to the concealment of restrictive laws. *Proceß* proceeds from the pleasure principle, unlike *Vorgang*, which introduces an internal reality that may be called extinction, or after transposition on to the body, castration.

This unpleasure leads us to consider the introduction of a physiological factor as a reification. The *transitional*, on the contrary, unites them without demanding discrimination. It accepts the element of confusion induced by the factor of phantasy. The notion of the *first me/not me possession* is closely akin to those of *transposition, pre-conscious* and *mixed blood.*

When Freud (1926) broached the *physiology of anxiety* in *Inhibitions, Symptoms and Anxiety*, he defined affect as a *mnemic symbol* of early experiences from which elementary physiological operations are derived by phylogenetic inheritance. The symbol of affect reflects the biological necessity of dealing with internal threats by transposition on to external danger. The expression *castration anxiety* stems from this approach, which theorizes a scene of castration and reifies it in the past.

The early transposition as a foundational act of the mind raises the problem of the link between *primal repression* and the stimulus barrier as a physiological factor. To be efficient, the primal repression has to rely on a psychic environment itself involving repression. Primary identification is an identification with the *model* of mental functioning on which the infant draws support. This model identification is the first form of relating. It inaugurates what will become the transference of authority, the point of leverage for all psychic development. This transference is active in the choice of an analyst and continues throughout the analysis.

The existence of primal repression requires us to integrate a primal imperative with the theory that supports the realization of the first psychical operations under cover of the stimulus barrier. The latter ensures a denial of external perceptions of lack that are in danger of stimulating extinctive yearnings too acutely. The imperative of transposition makes it possible to cling to tangible sensory perceptions for anti-traumatic purposes. They will subsequently be co-opted as ideational representatives, which will enable the mind to depend less on the presence of sensory perceptions and to realize psychic work in the absence of them. The restraint realized by the combination of the stimulus barrier and the imperative of transposition allows for the capture and then registration of the instinctual drive impulses in the id in the form of thing-presentations. This implies a very early transposition of unconscious tendencies and processes on to tangible external perceptions, and then on to internal materials, perceptual traces that are supposed to offer the same qualities of consistency as perceptions and their stability. This transposition *from the beginning* is opposed to extinctive regressivity, which becomes the first repressed material. Anti-traumatic clinging to external representable perceptions, as can be observed in the traumatic neuroses, is, in fact, a mechanism used to respond to extinctive regressivity and to the perceptions of lack that give rise to neither traces nor representations.

The outline emerges of a function for traces and tracing, and a model of psychic functioning that links somatic reality with that of traces. This allows for the creation of an intermediary between the extinctive quality of the drives and the sensory reality of lack, namely, the instinctual id and its major function, the libidinal regeneration of the psyche and desire. Within the id four factors are combined: the *constraint* of extinctive regressivity, the *imperative* of transposition, the *operation* of the double reversal that transforms the regressive quality into cathectic libido and the *aim* of orienting the cathexes along the progressive path towards objects. This activity was called by Freud libidinal sympathetic excitation. It is this activity that is realized by the operation of après-coup in the guise of the accomplishment of dreams.

What do we call *castration* in psychoanalysis?

The question of *castration* and of *the traumatic factor* was totally renewed in 1920 by Freud's third contribution to his drive theory. Castration was henceforth no longer conceived only as a punitive threat to an incestuous transgression, as apprehended by the castration complex and the primal phantasy of castration by the father. It was no longer linked only to anthropology and the organization of social life through the prohibition of incest. It was henceforth considered as obeying the characteristic rationales of psychic life. From the psychic point of view, incest is a consequence of the murder of the father, which amounts to eliminating the imperatives of psychic work. This murder of the superego induces a sexualization of narcissism, which leads to a suppression of psychic functions. This suppression is called castration.

The new conception of the traumatic factor, as an intra-drive quality, gives intelligibility to the diphasic organization of the psychic work of the operation of après-coup and its regressive/progressive oscillation. The transposition of extinctive regressivity on to the external perception of lacks conceived in terms of castration bestows on these perceptions the traumatic quality of the drives; then the apprehension of these lacks, by means of a causal theory, makes it possible to treat extinctive regressivity in an endopsychic way.

The notion of *castration complex* condenses elements as diverse as a *phantasy*, thus a wish-fulfilment; an *anxiety*, thus a threatening message; a *theory*, thus an explanatory interpretation; and a *perception*, thus an external reality that has acquired a traumatic value through transposition.

We can now differentiate between *castration-phantasy*, *castration-anxiety*, *castration-causality* and *castration-reality*. The latter offers a *support for the transposition of the extinctive regressivity* of every drive. It has the particularity of being without tangible materiality, therefore without trace or representation. It remains in the order of perception.

Castration is present in many myths. Through the act that it denotes, it has a foundational value. Concerning the act, we have the famous passage in the Bible: "In the beginning was the Word" (John, 1:1), rendered by Goethe (1808) as: "In the beginning was the Act," and then by Freud as: "In the beginning was the Deed" (Freud, 1912–1913, p. 161).

The various versions of Genesis all involve such an act of cutting and extraction that concerns masculine genital organs as a whole; it is frequently reversed into an act of generativity according to the denial of all loss characteristic of myths.

This two-way logic is inherent to the etymology of the word *sex*. *Secare* and *sexion* associate the meanings of cutting and ecstatic pleasure. By virtue of what is refractory the final obstacle of the orgasm links up with the inaugural cut of the myth. The sense of a *lack of enjoyment* is explained by the myth and compensated for by generativity. The message is thus transmitted through words that sexuality contains something that *cuts* it. The term *guilty* contains the idea of being cut off and the desire for sexuality exempt from any cut. Ignorance of the fact that the drive contains what works towards its own disappearance is thereby sustained. The reality of the negativization transmitted by language (the *little death*) is thus pushed back by an idealization of sexuality itself and of its generativity.

To sustain this idealization it is necessary either to suspend all earthly sexuality or to direct it towards procreation alone, or to complete it with all sorts of adjuvants paving the way for the painful awakenings of tomorrows that leave one disenchanted.

Freud did not escape this myth of an absolutely narcissistic primal state reducing the difference between the sexes. The absolute completeness obtained by the union of masculine and feminine makes it possible to deny one of the two poles of the difference between the sexes, the difference between endowed and unendowed.

In 1915, Freud was planning to write an academic metapsychology in which regression was dominated by the longing to return to an inaugural foetal narcissistic state. He rectified his position almost immediately and then rejected it in his study of melancholia. In 1919, he regarded repression as an *elementary traumatic neurosis* and reintroduced conflictuality into his ternary topography in the form of *drive duality*. He was still trying to follow the path of the phantasy of a primordial state of oneness with Eros. But he left this phantasy to Plato and the poets. The operation of après-coup renewed its ties with drive functioning whose elementary quality is to be traumatic. This extinctive regressivity of the drives is transposed on to the absence of a penis on the girl's lower abdomen, an absence that is thought about in terms of castration and absolute ecstatic enjoyment. The difference between endowed and unendowed, that is, between tangible sensory perceptions and sensory perceptions of lack calls for psychic work in several stages. This work utilizes the other difference between masculine/feminine to accomplish itself.

The psychoanalytic use of the term *castration* is different from animal, medical and anthropological castrations. These merely offer displacements and analogies for the *castration complex*, which pertains strictly to the penis and its various substitutes, the erogenous zones and, more particularly, the genital zones, in fact to the whole body insofar as it is entirely erogenous. It is the locus of sensual regressions to organ erotogenicity and drive conversions. As Freud (1914) wrote: "We can decide to regard erotogenicity as a general characteristic of all organs, and then may speak of an increase or decrease of it in a particular part of the body" (p. 84).

For the unconscious, castration does not exist; it has the status of a *disappearance* into a so-called primal attractive scene, a scene of absolute ecstatic enjoyment depicted by this disappearance. In this sense, negative hallucination fulfils such a wish. It is frequently used in dreams, myths, fairy tales and stories for children and in the religions. This is the case of the Cheshire cat in *Alice in Wonderland*, and of anchoritism. This explains why the perception of castration does not necessarily trigger signal anxiety but may give rise to a quest involving the reversal of psychic values. It then becomes the goal to be attained.

The castration complex concerns the penis and its substitutes due to the fact that the penis is a tangible, visible and representable object, and the locus of sensations arising from the regressive attraction to organ erotogenicity. Unlike many other parts of the body, the penis cannot undergo complete desexualization; and its total resexualization, which would make it disappear, is a phantasy arising from the interpretation of the absence of a penis on the girl's lower abdomen. Little boys verify its presence with their hands and their eyes; little girls, verify too the tangibility of their lower abdomen. The tangible aspect of touching prevails over the object touched. The unconscious thing-presentation of the penis becomes the reference for all the other unconscious ideas. This was what Freud sensed when he stated that the libido is masculine in essence, a statement that gives rise to reproaches based on the affirmation *I know, but all the same.* These resistances refuse the approach of abstraction, which consists in conceiving of the penis as the tangible part of the body that can be perceived by the senses and that serves as an elective support for the transposition of the emergence of cathexes. When such resistances are operative, the support is taken for the drive impulse itself. The penis is both an organ of conversion of this emergence and the *visual* representable element on to which the realization of this emergence is transposed. Erection is the figure that proves the genesis of cathexes. The vagina has a different destiny owing to the fact that it is known through sensations rather than through sight. Its thing-presentation will be formed much later since it depends for both sexes on the sensual/sensory experience of intercourse. Its early recognition depends on the endogenous sensations that are converted through it, and therefore remains quite vague for a long time. In this way the vagina acquires a prototypical significance in relation to conversion and sensual regression. The vagina is thus associated with sensations and with the sensuality/sensoriality bipolarity, while the penis is the representative of the existence of cathexes.

Without overlooking the differences between the masculine and the feminine discussed above, the genital zones fulfil the double function of being tangible perceptions, thus capable of furnishing representations, and of being areas of sensual conversion. Their sensibility, which is more exacerbated than that of other parts of the body, lies in the fact that desexualization is much less complete at their level. They thus remain much more sensitive to sensory regression driven by extinctive attractions via organ erotogenicity and more subject to all sorts of phantasies of threats. *Disappearing* opens up for them the supreme paths of ecstatic enjoyment and idealization. The doublet of representation/sensual conversion makes it possible to respond to the other pole of the difference between the sexes, that is to say to the pair endowed/unendowed. The perception of this lack calls for a theorization of causality that promotes infantile sexual theories in terms of scenarios of castration.

The *castration-phantasy* is full of the Shreberian hope (Freud, 1911) of being able to attain an experience of ideal and infinite ecstatic enjoyment, as ascribed to the female sex, and also, via the desexualized path, an experience of ideal, deistic love – the hope of being the auto-erotic narcissistic locus of infinite ecstatic enjoyment and the generativity of a demiurge. These veins of ideality are considered to be achievable by cutting off the penis. Castration then acquires a mystical value (Abelard and Heloise).

Castration-anxiety combines a sensation of menace, of imminent danger without a definite object, a message and a signal. It appears as the aim of the menace and is referred to as the consequence of a misuse, a transgression, an alienation, a demonic pact working towards the loss of the one it haunts, of a compulsion that through repetition becomes a *reduction compulsion*. Castration anxiety has the role of a warning and a summons to modify a harmful orientation of psychical activity. It summons the superego.

Castration-causality is found in all infantile sexual theories and in the castration complex. They all interpret the absence of a penis on the lower abdomen of girls as a consequence of a precise act following a transgression or a heavenly quest, or a refusal to alienate oneself to the defensive needs of a parent. The loss of love abandons the child to the fate of castration. It is integrated into a conception that attempts to deny castration as a reality in itself. Infantile sexual theories nourish the hope of escaping this destiny. It suffices to avoid the cause in order not to suffer the effects. In these theories, castration becomes a consequence rather than a cause of the theorization.

Castration-reality is an irreducible sensory perception insofar as it cannot give rise either to traces or to ideational contents. It obliges us to recognize the category of irreversibility, while the factor of phantasy promotes endless reversibility. The extinctive quality of the drives is transposed on to perceptions of lack, destruction, amputation, deterioration, degradation and, in a continuous and infinite way, on to all perceptions of differences. All these perceptions constitute castration-reality. This being so, the traumatic quality extends to all tangible sensory perceptions associated with perceptions of lack. They are considered as responsible for traumatic experiences and taken over by phobic causality; hence, the attempts to avoid them and to protect oneself by means of preventative and exorcistic measures. External castration-reality is the object of a denial in favour of a stable cathexis of the link of causality that attributes the traumatic quality to a tangible reality.

Causality

Rationally, the castration complex is an aberration, but psychically it is a necessity. It is the prototype of the irrational. I have already pointed out that it is present in each of the three organizing knots of the drive (infantile sexuality, narcissism, libidogenesis) and that it expresses the conflictuality that affects all psychic work. Recognition and denial of castration coexist in it. Several truths exist alongside each other without cancelling each other out: castration exists; castration is a phantasy; castration has been carried out on girls; the absence of a penis is not the result of castration but a fact. The affirmation that a woman is castrated is thus both true and false. A woman's body presents a lack of a penis, which was not removed. But this lack is the object of a transposition of the possible effects of the extinctive tendency of the drives.

The processing by the psyche of the traumatic dimension transposed on to this lack obliges us to conceive of a theory to interpret it, according to which what is missing should be there, was there, has been removed, has been displaced to another invisible place (up, down, in front, behind, inside, outside), that it will reappear, come back, grow again, etc. These theories postulate that it is possible to make it appear or reappear, that it is simply a matter of finding the adequate method. The initial shock of disappearance is followed by a deferred effect of resurgence. Our therapeutic and reparative aspirations are marked by such theories.

The anti-traumatic function of this theorization allows the two apparently incompatible truths to be united. The true/false dilemma is dissolved. An infantile sexual theory is false in terms of content, but true as a process of theorization responding to a necessity. The operation of après-coup transmits the existence of discontinuity at the same time as it produces continuity. As an enacted theory, it reveals and affirms what it seeks to deny.

The establishment of female sexuality and male sexuality follows this double logic characteristic of the operation of après-coup. The first moment of resolution of the Oedipus complex, entering the period of latency, links the two stages of the castration complex to the penis and to the erotogenicity of what is visible. It is dominated by the difference endowed/unendowed, conceived as the result of castration. The second stage of resolution of the Oedipus complex, that of post-puberty, concerns the pair vagina/penis and the erotogenicity of the pair visible/invisible.

Drive regressivity is linked by means of transposition to the lack perceived on the girl's body, and thus to her sexuality. Deprived of a penis, she is thought to be without desire. When the latter appears, it is experienced from the angle of the castration complex as the path of the possible disappearance of the penis. The prolonged repression of the vagina permits this amalgam between interior erotogenicity and castration. The other orifices follow the same logic, hence the numerous popular insults and expressions linking their instinctual drive demands to castration.

The association femininity/castration reinforces the repression of a vaginal impulse considered as dangerous and contagious. Time is needed for this theory to abandon its anti-cathecting function and to free access for both sexes to the feminine. The connection regressivity/vaginal erotogenicity will produce all the phantasies of disappearance in the female body, whether this disappearance concerns the part or the whole. A woman's desire and ecstatic enjoyment are felt to be a bottomless craving with incommensurable attracting power. They are depicted by images of whirlwinds, chasms and other forms of suction by the void, nothingness but also infinity.

This association castration/femininity produces yet other theories, in particular that which considers that female desire is free of all danger of castration since it is assumed to have already taken place. After the theory of a contagious castration comes that of a liberating castration *once and for all*.

A theory has been put forward suggesting that women have no castration complex or superego. This theory is based on a feminine neo-identity that mixes defiance and a bypassing of psychic laws. I am referring to the *passionarias* such as Antigone, Joan of Arc, Juliet, the suffragettes, and so on. These women take up a male cause to which they devote themselves body and soul, defying all dangers and prohibitions in the name of realizing the ideal of an other that subsumes all vulnerability.

In fact, the establishment in two stages of the pair masculine/feminine concerns both boys and girls, since it is due to the drive regressivity that is hypostasized by the doublet endowed/unendowed. What is *endowed* applies to each of the poles of the pair masculine/feminine. It expresses the existence of the instinctual drive surges and specific cathexes of each person. What is *unendowed* reflects the extinctive tendency and the phenomenon of disappearing, which is the major issue involved. In reality, the unendowed precedes the endowed, which is the result of a first transformation of regressivity into a surge of cathexis. Castration and its traumatic quality become a mere experience of lack from the moment the pair masculine/feminine is formed.

Denial of castration and the vicissitudes of extinctive regressivity

In 1937, Freud was astonished to discover that human beings are not all bisexual. He linked the necessity of making a *choice of gender* to drive duality and to a *tendency to conflict*. A portion of the libido serves to establish narcissism by means of desexualization, but the latter cannot be total since the extinctive regressive quality is not reducible. It remains active even when it is immobilized and neutralized with the help of the denial of sensory perceptions of lacks. Denying the lacks does not do away with the extinctive tendency, this irreducible reality that psychic activity can use in the service of psychic libidogenesis, but without suppressing it. The rebirth of desire is its most significant consequence.

The bisexual object-choice is an attempt to achieve narcissistic completeness. This requires a denial of the fact that each element of the difference masculine/feminine is faced with the other difference endowed/unendowed, thus with the extinctive tendencies transposed on to the reality of lack, called castration. In addition, each of the sexes lacks the embodied experience in its own body of the sensual regression of the other sex. An attempt to remedy this is made by means of identification but this cannot be totally successful, in particular due to its navel, identification with the homosexuality of the other sex. This lack orients object-choice, impedes a complete desexualization of the drives and keeps open the experience of sensual regression until it reaches its latch, orgasm, and its limit, the refractory.

Many constellations involve denial, for example those of phallic narcissism, phallic masculinity (show-offs) and phallic femininity (the vamp, the virago). All these clinical constellations reveal themselves frequently during an analysis, as neo-identities that had hitherto remained latent. They are typical deferred effects of the relation to castration authenticated as a traumatic event, while its real significance is linked to extinctive regressivity.

Denial is used each time we go to sleep. It is part of ordinary psychic work. What makes it auspicious or harmful to psychic work is its chronicity or reversibility. The dream is a normal psychosis because it is ephemeral and reversible; preliminaries are momentary perversions bringing diversity and intensity to erotic life. Dreams and preliminaries are useful for psychic functioning insofar as they take extinctive tendencies into account and use them in the service of psychic and somatic life.

The emergence in two stages of the erogenous body and the process of libidinal sympathetic excitation

The relationship (*rapport* > *faux-ami*) with castration described above reflect the relations between the psyche and the negative drive quality, the extinctive tendency that is involved in the variations of tension and in the qualitative differences at the heart of proprioceptive sensibility. These *feelings of lack* cannot give rise to direct traces. At the same time, extinctive regressivity makes use of all the sensory differences perceived on contact with objects and transmitted via language. By definition, perceptions of differences combine the perception of tangible realities giving rise to traces and ideational material and the perception of the lack inherent in all differences, which does not give rise to any traces or ideational material.

Compared to perceptions with traces, *perceptions without traces* take on the value of a *failure to trace* and of a *missing trace*. Actually, they exist only through their comparison with perceptions with traces. Every difference felt and perceived induces this interplay between what is tangible and what is lacking.

I have already mentioned the classical illustration where a tangible element is sought after owing to feelings of lack: the child, whether a boy or a girl, who moves his hand towards his lower abdomen during his activities. His gesture attests to excitation dominated by the feeling of a danger of disappearance. Touching amounts to verification and assurance. This act seeks to counter the extinctive attraction. The educational intervention of adults serves the same purpose. Erroneously, they interpret the child's act in terms of masturbation or a need to urinate, when in fact it is a matter of stimulating psychic forms of auto-eroticism at a moment when they are deficient. The reference to somatic need attests to the intuition that this deficiency concerns the physiology of psychic processes. In so doing, adults support the child's appeal to what is tangible in order to respond to feelings without any possible representation. They help the child to set up an anti-cathexis of the extinctive tendencies.

The transposition on to the two categories of perceptions, with and without traces, of the elementary extinctive tendencies, of the primordial operations of registration and of the emergence of cathexes, furnishes preconceptions of the future erotic scene and of the sexual scene attributed to the ex-parents who have become lovers. The imperative of registration ensures the restraint of instinctual drive impulses by virtue of the conversion that grounds the body and the erogenous zones. These primordial operations must tame, in fact, reduce the elementary drive tendencies and transform them into drive impulses registered in the id. A path of cathexis is then necessary in order to oppose the regressivity that is still active in them. The conversion onto the body and the transference of cathexes onto language and onto external objects creates and offers instinctual drive vicissitudes. The first registration creates the body of organ erotogenicity, which is anti-cathected at an early stage by the narcissistic mother/baby system and becomes available only after a long period of desexualization through education. This is how the paths that will serve for the future sensual regression are formed. Based to begin with on sensoriality, sensual regression later opens the body to erotic life. By virtue of the operation of après-coup, organ erotogenicity becomes the organ erogeneity of eroticism.

The introduction of a drive duality characterized by a regressive tendency to return to the inorganic and inanimate state produces an important theoretical change concerning how we think about body erogeneity. It is no longer the consequence of a mere surge of cathexes towards the body but becomes the result of psychic work. At the beginning of his work, Freud spoke of a mysterious *leap* of the somatic into the psychic, a mutation of *somatic sexual excitation* into *psychic sexual libido*: "once the somatic sexual excitation has reached threshold-value, it is turned continuously into psychic excitation (Freud, 1895, p. 108). His drive organization of 1915 is in keeping with this conception of a leap at the junction of the somatic and the psychic. Although in 1915 he envisaged successive waves, he did not envisage discontinuity at their source. This conception began to be challenged after 1920 by the introduction of a tendency to return to an earlier state, and even to the inorganic and inanimate state. In 1933, he reiterated his definition of the source but with a formulation that leaves the nature of the excitation in abeyance: "The source is a state of excitation in the body" (Freud, 1933, p. 96). But taking into consideration the "effort to restore an earlier state of things" (ibid., p. 106), to "do away with life once more and to reestablish the inorganic state" (ibid., p. 107) obliged him to introduce a rhythmical and oscillatory dynamic impelled by variations.

The same was true of instinctual drive tension; in 1915 it was presented as being constant and continuous, while after 1920 it gradually became discontinuous and uncertain, the locus of a conflict of ambivalence. The discontinuity of cathexes thus became the basis of the notion of time.

This conflict is located between two scenes, a scene of origins (*scène originaire*) producing libidinal impulses and a primal scene (*scène primitive*) with their extinction as its aim. It is expressed by the "noises" of the body, by the symptoms of sexuality (Freud, 1915b). These endogenous noises are transposed onto sounds emanating from places of exclusion, in particular the parents' bedroom. These sensorial sounds become indicators of the existence of an internal instinctual drive scene from which the subject is excluded even though he is the subject of it. We do not command either the birth or the rebirth of our libidinal regeneration and we can only exert influence more or less on the vicissitudes of our desire. Sensorial sounds become the indicators of the sensual noise expressing the conflict at the level of the work of restraint and registration that take place at the drive source.

This experience of exclusion calls forth forms of auto-eroticism as well as imaginary theories and *ideational material* that will be vested in the objectifiable generic scene of exclusion, namely, the sexual scene of the parents when they become lovers. The *primal phantasy* of the primal scene shows that it is a generic scene onto which all children transpose their experience of being excluded from their instinctual source.

The usual definition of the primal scene offers *ideational material* of combined ex-parents/lovers. Children build a relationship to the sexual bond of their parents, to the image of their sensual feelings.

This definition arose from the *transposition* onto an external reality, the parents' bedroom and its locked door, of unconscious mental operations that take place in the child. This transposition extends, of course, to the inaccessible sexual and sensual bodies of the parents. The result of these operations establishes him as the subject of his unconscious. They are the locus of negative attractions, which can undermine their accomplishment and disturb their function of libidogenesis.

In fact, two entangled scenes emerge: one in which the subject feels he disappears, the primal scene, and another, generative of his drive source, the scene of origins. Multiple images are derived from them, which can be brought together under the generic image of the *beast with two backs* used by Shakespeare and Rabelais. These images and scenarios are formed out of the child's feelings. They are scenes metaphorizing his processuality from which his feelings have arisen. He attributes them to his ex-parents, phantasized lovers, who are supposed to experience them in their bedroom of exclusion. He thereby derives his excitation from their scene and dramatizes his feelings and sensations in representative scenarios, in so-called primal scene phantasies. All the infantile sexual scenarios the child needs to oppose this negative attraction at work at his libidinal source find their origin here. The variations in his vitality, his liveliness and the availability of his desire depends on them. What characterizes all these scenarios is the feeling of exclusion and privation of an internal origin, which the child displaces onto this relational space. The attraction by what is excluded retains a strong valency, hence the temptation to cross all the boundaries of restraint, to exceed the laws of sensual regression, to free oneself from their prohibitions and to rush headlong into what is transgressive. The search for toxic flashes and strong emotions stems from this. On the other hand, the child will constantly represent and phantasize about this primal scene, spying on it out of curiosity, sometimes spending his life leaning on the door of his exclusion, with his eye stuck to the empty key hole, or denying its very existence. All these solutions make use of the bedroom scene of the parents in order to oppose the real internal primal scene that occupies the drive source. The extinctive tendency that manifests itself in it needs to be checked by the obstacles of thought processes, therefore by a restraint and a renunciation that feeds masochism.

This explains that the pictures we have of the primal scene can take on multiple forms that easily exceed the diversity of the erotic positions offered by the Kama-Sutra. Plausibility has no place. Thus the entire Kleinian phantasmagoria turns the bedroom, the bed and the bodies of the couple into fragmented heaps, into bloody butcheries, into invasions perpetrated by some Alien, into irresistible longings for some other parallel and moving world.

Some children are incapable of developing these pictures on the basis of such a transposition of their processual operations, a transposition that is enacted in all their games of penetration, interlocking, dislocation, hidden/found alternations, multiple comings- and-goings, entrances and exits, turnstiles and swings, in short, everything that produces sensory excitation. The child is seeking the scene in which his sensual excitation has its origin. Unhappy children, those who lack a capacity to play, are living *in* the primal scene. Their sexual sympathetic excitation is very reduced; this is the case, for instance, with autistic children who are absorbed by a lock or a hinge that they are constantly manipulating. What dominates are games that are reduced to repetitive acts: making holes, dislocating, destroying, making things fall, making things disappear, engulfing, collapsing. These scenarios evoke nightmares and serve to combat the terror and fright of the subject's disappearance into his own aborted primal scene.

Conversely, the development of sphincter control and motricity along with the management of the future erogenous zones leads the child to appropriate his erogenous body, to put his own latches on his body, to turn it into a primal scene for the other. Games of exclusion thus become part of the future preliminaries of the erotic scene under the banner of games of seduction, rivalry and jealousy.

The child proves to be subject to a double internal exclusion. He is excluded from his own negative tendencies, to which he opposes his restraints, and he is excluded from his own psychic processes that constitute him. His auto-eroticisms, his dreams and all his psychic activities that unfold in a state of passivity allow him to appropriate that part of himself where he is not master in his own house. Sometimes he experiences them as very attractive internal places, and sometimes as strange or bizarre objects that haunt or even persecute him.

His own primal scenes also become objects of exclusion for others. Likewise, the scenes of the body of the other, his auto-eroticisms, his thoughts, his dreams, everything that appeals to the *desire for the desire of the other*, all the intimate private scenes become primal scenes of exclusion with an attracting power. Children are covertly permeated by the activities adults are engaged in, whether it is reading, reflecting, driving, listening, conversing, admiring a landscape, savouring a dish, a wine or appreciating an aesthetic object, or whether they are engaged in some act of body care behind the locked door of the bathroom or the toilets. A major turnaround occurs when the child is able to close the toilet door (Fain, 1988).

There are an infinite number of scenes in everyday life in which the child feels excluded from the sensuality of others. Cannibalism is then employed to reduce the weight of exclusion. It promotes centrifugal and centripetal identifications: drinking, eating, reading, second-guessing the other, etc., and being drunk, being read and second-guessed by the other, etc. Common language, sweet words and insults all speak to us of these multiple identities arising from the desire to be the object of the sensuality of the other. All games based on imitation have their source here, *aping* the other until he is exasperated. And when the attraction insists at the risk of taking possession of the child, he becomes infernal, unstable, impossible. His compulsion drives him to *disturb* the adult, to disrupt his solitary activities. He calls for, makes demands on, awakens these others so that they become his "locks." Cruel and harassing forms of behavior also have their origin in this feeling of being excluded from the desire of the other, from his narcissism, from his inaccessible drive source.

The primal scene proper is beyond representation; it is intrinsically linked to terror. It is defined by this negative attraction that is unrepresentable as such. This negativity at work can only be felt. The automatic anxiety of terror is its prototype. Thus it elicits in counterpoint an intense palliative activity of representation, which has the function of restraint, registration, anti-cathexis. All these so-called representations of the primal scene are in no way the primal scene itself. They all belong to the scene of origins.

Here then we have a scene of origins that brings together the exclusion from the parents' bedroom, the multiple representations of the beast with two backs, the source of the drive, the sensual body and the erotic partner. This scene of origins is attached to the primal scene of extinctive drive regressivity, which is felt to be an attraction beyond the latches of erogeneity, beyond the obstacle of the masochism of renunciation.

The door lock depicts the oscillations between the movements of desexualization and those of resexualization, embodied particularly at the level of the erogenous zones by the comings-and-goings. Libidinal sympathetic excitation, mixing games of coming-and-going between inside and outside and the see-saw of desexualizations and resexualizations takes place. Each erogenous zone articulates a negative regressive primal scene and a scene of origins that grounds its erogeneity.

Insisting as their nomination does, on the object-related part alone of the dynamic of primal phantasies is to overlook the fact that the body of flesh is a production of the psyche, realized by a conversion of the libidinal economy on to the soma. The body is a protective lining of the soma. It is worth insisting again on the fact that the establishment of this process of libidinal resourcing, as well as of that which is responsible for the registration of instinctual drive impulses as sensual feelings, require the presence of another person, hence the historical vicissitudes and specificities of this other.

The picture emerges of a physical primal scene and a sensuality that is capable of following a regressive path until organ erotogenicity that is anti-cathected by sensuality. Transposed onto the bodies of the parents who have withdrawn into their closed bedroom, organ erotogenicity enters into connection with the ecstatic enjoyment of the couple. The heart of the primal scene, its unrepresentable negativity, finds in the orgasm of the lovers and the refractory period the limit to the regression of organ erotogenicity. The child has the preconception of the conflict ecstatic enjoyment/orgasm of which he will become the subject through the conflict that concerns his own drive source.

The countless *ideational contents* that are formed on contact with the extinctive tendency are primal scene phantasies and infantile sexual theories. These *ideational contents* anti-cathect the unique quality of the primal scene, that of being a place of disappearance. It is important, therefore, not to confuse the primal scene and *ideational contents* of the primal scene. The primal scene is heterogeneous with any discourse that claims to account for it. Words make it possible to express the feeling of disappearing, the experience of lack or difference, but they cannot express lack. Through the very act of nomination, the primal scene undergoes an anti-cathexis of restraint.

We have recognized the role of conversion. It grounds the body, which proves to be a product of the psyche that is different from the soma and the germ plasm. Erogenous body and erogeneity are deferred effects of the operation of après-coup. Depending on the vicissitudes of the work of this operation, it is possible to think about the stumbling blocks and the differences of erogenization of the zones whose destiny is to become erogenous. Freud speaks of the "somatic damage to the sexual function" (Freud, 1933, p. 94) against which anxiety is generated *anew* (ibid.).

Hypochondria is the prototypical clinical picture of the disturbances of organ erogeneity. It is situated between tumescence and tumefaction. The body-care market finds its reasons for existing in the sensibility to the reductions of erogenization. The psychoanalyst also receives requests for treatment centred on body transformations, which are unorganized body dysmorphic disorders. Child psychoanalysts also have to deal with requests from parents envisaging surgical interventions on their child's body instead of a work of mentalization. This is the clinical domain of the traumatic body. The body feels that it may lose its erogenous sensibility and the oscillatory variations of its sensuality as a result either of libidinal decathexis or of a disorganization of the libidinal source. When everything falls to pieces, the subject clings to his body.

By grounding the erogenous body, the process of restraint and conversion at the origin of erogenization has a function of protecting the soma. Freud called this process at the somato-psychic junction libidinal sympathetic excitation. The primary masochism of renunciation is the most significant expression of this. It is this process that fulfils the function of a latch and limit for extinctive tendencies. Dreams limit the regression to representations thanks to a saturation that anti-cathects the attractions emanating from organ erotogenicity. Eroticism moves towards organ erotogenicity thanks to the sensual regression of organ erogeneity. This makes jouissance possible but it remains refractory to the tendencies to extinguish organ erotogenicity. Orgasm is a reversible "little" death.

I have already referred to Freud's conception of a leap from the somatic to the psychic sphere and have made it depend on a work of the mind. I have also shown how the operation of après-coup is the locus of an imperative of registration that is realized by means of various substrata, including the body thanks to conversion. *Where there is soma, body must come into being.* This primary conversion does not consist only in a leap from somatic drive activity to psychic drive activity. It is carried out under the aegis of a superego imperative sustained by language. Conversion expresses verbal thoughts at the same time as it registers drive impulses. Conversion is a language of the body. United at the heart of the conversions are the drive qualities that escape all organization and the language code. Thus emerge the various modalities of thought that are words, images, bodily experiences, feelings and affects.

Bodily conversion is a double transposition, that is, of language-based material in the body producing a *language of the body* and of drive motions producing *somatic tumescences* linked to the sexualization of the erogenous zones. The leap of *libidogenesis* is completed by the regression of language in the body. Drives and languages meet and initiate an intermediate field, the mind, that permits an infinite number of variations and combinations.

The first bodily conversions have a history; they are realized within the mother/baby unit, the ensemble: operative mind of the mother/potential mind of the baby. They blend and merge sensoriality and sensuality. The transposition of the unconscious psychic operations and libidinal cathexes is effected on to the sensoriality arising from the desexualized and encoded gestures of maternal care; these are linked to language and are vehicles for transmitting parental tenderness and firmness; hence, the emergence of a sensuality linked to language and amalgamated initially with sensoriality. Later, when the child is directly at grips with the extinctive regressivity of his drives, a differentiation occurs between sensoriality and sensuality. This will make bodily erogeneity operative thanks to the sensual regression towards organ erotogenicity. Sensual regression reveals the latent erogeneity. This is why erotic life belongs to the regressive psychic activities of passivity.

The parts of the body do not all follow the same vicissitudes and do not have the same sensibilities to this sensual regression towards organ erotogenicity. Those known as erogenous zones retain a greater regressive potential based on their so-called educated, desexualised functions. They are zones linking the inside and the outside, where issues of penetration, in fact, contacts between sensoriality of an external origin and erogenous sensuality, are enacted. Their encounters stimulate the regressive attractions of the body, and thus the sensual regression towards sexuality. There then emerges a cartography of erotogenicity that is very different from that of tenderness, involving care, cuddles, caresses and all the interventions concerning the body that can be a source of unpleasure, whether it is a matter of medical care, accidents, rough treatment, physical punishments or abuse. The history of sensuality is just as much a question of identifications as it is based on real events. It implies a memory of the body, made up of memories and reminiscences.

This process in two stages turns organ erotogenicity, which is anti-cathected during the first stage, into organ erogeneity thanks to the sensual regression that takes place originating in sensuality. A particular field of culture is then opened up, namely, eroticism. The erotic scene frequently begins with a verbal amorous discourse, which makes way gradually for the actualization via preliminaries of organ erogeneity, while language is put into abeyance. This sensual regression has the aim of ecstatic enjoyment, which culminates in orgasm, the expression of a restraint that is responsible for a minimum level of tension that brings into play the masochism of the renunciation of extinction and renews libidinal sympathetic excitation. Metaphorically speaking, the body is attached to the bedroom of drive duality, a place where the genesis of the drive impulses unfolds. This bedroom is equipped with a lock, primary masochism. The long unfolding of the operation of après-coup has to take place before this lock becomes the latches of the erogenous zones (Chervet, 2010). The erotic sensual regression of lovers puts locks on their intimacy, allowing the latches placed on their erogenous bodies to be removed. The bodies get ready, particularly through their erogenous zones, to let themselves be filled with erotic sensibility and to put in abeyance all the functions acquired through education and civilization, to experience a more or less slow resexualization towards organ erotogenicity. A similar trajectory unfolds with the language that opens the amorous discourse, that of the scene of seduction, and follows a regression to words with a double meaning, words that thereby come increasingly closer to the erogenous zones, and which sing, by becoming metaphors, the sensual scene, the thoughts and feelings that gradually inflate the lovers. Erotic satisfaction includes the success of this work of eroticism; and the affect of love is the consequence of its achievement.

The foundational conversion of a bodily sphere whose erogeneity becomes available subsequently through sensual regression makes the body the support and the object of the first act of restraint, which opposes drive extinction by the registration of sensual feelings. This restraint grounds sensuality, which takes over the anti-cathecting function of the first act of restraint. The role of every parent, *the other of processuality*, becomes clearer: it is one of participating in anti-cathecting this organ erotogenicity, of supporting its expression in terms of sensitive sensuality, of permitting its future regression towards erotic erogeneity. The renunciation of the parents as supporting objects allows for the search for other objects with which sensual regression can be cultivated.

Sensual regression creates the regressive path of experiences back to the drive source without succumbing to the attractions of the primal scene. Its establishment requires a long process realized in two stages in keeping with the operation of après-coup. Generally, psychoanalysts have experience of the modifications of the map of body erogeneity produced by psychoanalytic treatments.

References

Chervet, B. (2010). Les fantasmes originaires et l'avènement de l'érogenéité: Les zones érogènes, les loquets des corps. *Revue française de psychanalyse*, 74 (4): 981–1006.
Chervet, B. (2020). Le rêve et l'épreuve du refractaire. *Revue Française de Psychosomatique* 57, 2020. 11–34.
Fain, M. (1988). Les "ouatères" et leurs verrous. In: *L'enfant et sa maison*. Paris: ESF, pp. 113–117.
Freud, S. (1893). On the Psychical Mechanism of Hysterical Phenomena. *S.E. 3*. London: Hogarth, pp. 27–39.
Freud, S. (1894). The Neuro-psychoses of Defence. *S.E. 3*. London: Hogarth, pp. 45–68.
Freud, S. (1895). On the Grounds for Detaching a Particular Syndrome from Neurasthenia Under the Description "Anxiety Neurosis". *S.E. 3*. London: Hogarth, pp. 90–117.
Freud, S. (1905). *Three Essays on the Theory of Sexuality*. *S.E. 7*. London: Hogarth, pp. 123–243.
Freud, S. (1911). Psychoanalytic Notes on an Autobiographical Account of a Case of Paranoia. *S.E. 12*. London: Hogarth, pp. 1–82.
Freud, S. (1912–1913). *Totem and Taboo*. *S.E.* 13. London: Hogarth, pp. 1–161.
Freud, S. (1914). On Narcissism: An introduction *S.E. 14*. London: Hogarth, pp. 69–102.
Freud, S. (1915a). Instincts and Their Vicissitudes. *S.E. 14*. London: Hogarth, pp. 109–140.
Freud, S. (1915b). The Unconscious. *S.E. 14*. London: Hogarth, pp. 166–215.
Freud, S. (1919). A Child Is Being Beaten. *S.E. 17*. London: Hogarth, pp. 177–204.
Freud, S. (1920). *Beyond the Pleasure Principle*. *S.E.* 18. London: Hogarth, pp. 1–64.
Freud, S. (1923a). The Infantile Genital Organization. *S.E. 19*. London: Hogarth, pp. 141–153.
Freud, S. (1923b). Remarks on the Theory and Practice of Dream Interpretation. *S.E. 19*. London: Hogarth, pp. 109–121.
Freud, S. (1923c). *The Ego and the Id*. *S.E.* 19. London: Hogarth, pp. 3–66.
Freud, S. (1924). The Dissolution of the Oedipus Complex. *S.E. 19*. London: Hogarth, pp. 173–179.
Freud, S. (1925). *An Autobiographical Study*. *S.E.* 20. London: Hogarth, pp. 7–74.
Freud, S. (1926). *Inhibitions, Symptoms and Anxiety*. *S.E.* 20. London: Hogarth, pp. 75–174.
Freud, S. (1932). The Acquisition and Control of fire *S.E. 22*. London: Hogarth, pp. 187–193.
Freud, S. (1933). *New Introductory Lectures on Psycho-Analysis*. *S.E.* 22. London: Hogarth, pp. 1–182.
Goethe, W. (1808). *Faust*. Oxford: World Classics.

Chapter 9

The missing trace and feelings of lack

The introduction of heterogeneity between a reality with representation and a reality without representation increases the gap often felt between theory and practice, which evokes a quip of Albert Einstein: "Theory is when you know everything and nothing works. Practice is when everything works but no one knows why. In our lab theory and practice are combined: nothing works and no one knows why."

A potentialization exists between the traumatic experiences of the sensorial differences perceived by the psyche and the differences linked to the regressive attraction emanating from the traumatic dimension of all drives. In the same way, the felt differences of endogenous origin are transposed on to those of external origin. This double correlation comprises libidinal sympathetic excitation, which carries out psychic work in favour of the libidinal cathexes of the psyche, the body and objects. However, the perception of external differences cannot provide a trace or representation to oppose the extinctive attraction. This results in an obligation to accomplish a work of thought and an experience of lack, which is peculiar to the human condition.

The heterogeneity that exists between the extinctive tendency of the drives and the various registrations established according to the various language codes explains the discontinuity that we find at the heart of the operation of après-coup. The leap in nature between drive and language is at the origin of the diphasic character of the operation of après-coup with an unconscious interval period of psychic work.

From the angle of the stages of representations (conscious and unconscious), the operation of après-coup builds an apparent rational continuity that attenuates discontinuity but does not remove it. An irrational leap exists between the experience of the initial extinctive attraction (the first stage) and the result, the deferred effect (the second stage). The same leap appears between the latter and psychoanalytic interpretation.

This leap is often used to deny psychoanalysis a status of science. In fact, rather than inferring a distortion of the scientific approach by psychoanalysis, we need, on the contrary, to recognize that this leap reflects the existence of the two heterogeneous realities mentioned above, the drive and language. We must relinquish a conception of rational continuity, which exists only in the enunciation

DOI: 10.4324/9780429198953-9

of the theory, and turn towards a conception that integrates the irrational as a reflection of this leap (Neyraut, 1997) that produces the gap between theory and practice (Donnet, 1985).

We will now examine the nature of the two realities grounding the underlying dualism and turn our attention towards the metapsychological implications involved in the operation of après-coup as it runs through the preceding chapters.

As soon as hysterical symptoms were investigated, a hiatus was recognized. In *The Interpretation of Dreams* it was situated between the *regressive* moment of the figurative transformations of latent thoughts according to formal regression and the *progressive* moment of the representative transformations promoted by an imperative in the service of bringing the unconscious into consciousness. These transformations constitute an apparent continuity of stages. But the mutative leap of the psychic economy between the regressive path linked to language and the progressive path giving rise to drive impulses enhances the importance accorded by Freud to the concept of *distortion*. I have already pointed out that he regarded this concept as his sole and unique discovery (Freud, 1923). The distortion that affects dream materials is due to the fact that extinction is not representable and that it has to be countered by psychic work.

This leap of distortion helps us to understand the fact that the theory of thinking and the interpretation of its formations can never be based on rational deduction alone. Nor do they depend on romantic free inventivity. The difference of nature that exists between latent thoughts, instinctual drive impulses and the manifest content requires us to take into account the associative context in order to understand how the two heterogeneous realities are involved.

Another discontinuity exists between the various formations, all originating in the operation of après-coup, that form the basis of the components of thought, namely, between representations, affects, emotions and the erogenous feelings of sensuality, but especially between the feelings arising from experiences involving tangible materials and those pertaining to experiences of lack. We are presented with two types of differences: those that are internal to the category of the tangible contents that form the basis of small differences and those between the category of what is tangible and the category of lack. It is a matter of traumatic difference in the strict sense of the term. This brings us back to the double difference encountered in the last chapter, that of the difference between the sexes, masculine-feminine and endowed/unendowed.

The apprehension of these differences that exist between representation and endogenous feelings, but more particularly with feelings of lack, requires rational inference and imaginative speculation. My metapsychological approach towards the *work of the operation of après-coup* integrates, therefore, these two logics. "We must call the Witch to our help after all!" (Goethe, *Faust* 1 (The Witch's Kitchen), Scene 6, v. 2365), which may be construed as the Witch Metapsychology. As Freud (1937a) writes: "Without metapsychological speculation or theorizing – I had almost said, 'phantasying' – we shall not take another step forward" (p. 225).

Two opinions are expressed with regard to speculative imagination. The first, arising from the Enlightenment, asserts suspiciously that *imagination is the mad woman in the house* (N. de Malebranche) and the second ironically that *imagination is more important than knowledge* (Einstein).

Transposition, cooptation and mentalization

I have emphasized the participation in the realization of the operation of après-coup of sensory perception and the transposition on to it of unconscious elements. Bringing the unconscious into consciousness requires the detour by such a transposition on to sensory perception of drive qualities and of the operations involved in psychic work.

The terms we use to refer to phantasies illustrate perfectly this utilization of transposition and perception. The formulations chosen to denote these phantasies are derived from this stage of transposition, which is a source of metaphors. The regressive attraction exerted over the ego by the id is transposed into a phantasy of seduction of the child by the adult; the operations that occur at the drive source, and which are responsible for libidogenesis, are transposed on to the sexual scene of the parents into a phantasy of a primal scene of ecstatic enjoyment and a scene of origins, of procreation; the intervention of the imperative of renunciation, which stops extinctive regression and establishes masochistic restraint and psychic registrations, is transformed into a phantasy of castration by the father. This last phantasy is a veritable appeal to the paternal function insofar as the latter implies the renunciation of extinction, of the sexualization of narcissism and of infantile auto-erotisms.

The three primal phantasies thus fulfil unconsciously a function of anti-cathexis towards negative tendencies. They participate together in setting up an oscillatory mode of psychic functioning with the aims of libidinal regeneration along the regressive path and objectalization along the progression path.

This notion of transposition is at the basis of what we call transference onto the body, language and the object. Without it, psychic functioning could not be established or deployed; nor could it be the object of resumptions and restorations through analysis. It is the mechanism whereby a potentiality becomes operative. It is a fundamental postulate conceiving it as present *from the beginning* of life.

The wooden reel game is the prototypical example of all children's games. The transposition of the psychical operations capable of managing absence onto the wooden reel-string ensemble, the movement back-and-forth of the arm and the emission of sounds marking the rhythm of the disappearances and returns, is the path along which the processes of separation are established. The child thus relinquishes the need to disappear with the object who has gone away. This is how the lost object is created. Later, mourning takes up this same "game," but realizes it with recollections of the person who has died in order to turn him or her into an object that is lost permanently. The result is an internal appropriation. It consists in an identification in the form of representation that contains implicitly the quality of what has been lost. The centrifugal transposition is thus followed by a centripetal cooptation. Transposition and cooptation are at the basis of all identification relating to impressions of loss. These representations are used by the hallucinatory saturation to oppose loss, but they will never be able to suppress continuously the moral pain linked to what is lost for perception. They can do so momentarily.

Something is brought by perception that is absent from representation. The latter carries within it the impression of what has been lost that governed its advent. Perception brings another difference, between perception with traces and perception without traces. This awakens extinctive regressivity, which itself is transposed onto perceptions without traces. The traumatic experience as well as the lack can thus be considered as having an external origin.

This traumatic effect scarcely exists between ideational contents owing to the fact that there are no differences of nature between them. The traumatic difference between perceptions with traces and perceptions without traces obliges the mind to utilize perceptions with traces, the "related memories" (Freud, 1937b), to respond to those without traces. Given the discontinuity of perception and cathexis of perceived objects, perceptual traces are co-opted as mnemic traces, and then as ideational contents in order to be utilized in the absence of perception.

Along the regressive trajectory, a link is created between the perception of external differences and the internal discontinuity of the feelings of terror due to the tendency to extinction. A link is established between the perception of lack via that of differences and the feelings of lack arising from the psychic work of restraint. The feeling of lack thus has its roots in an extinctive tendency and in what is refractory to extinction. It will be enriched by the renunciation of absolute narcissism and the mourning of Oedipal objects.

The correlation between the extinctive tendency and perceptions without traces defines perception proper, namely, that which retains its traumatic quality as such. In order to be mitigated, the traumatic quality is associated with perceptions with traces that are adjacent and contiguous with perceptions without traces. These perceptions are subject to a hallucinatory intensification in order to obtain a saturation of consciousness via the internal path and to ward off feelings of lack. As I have already said, the complex "perception without traces-extinctive regressivity-hallucinatory perceptual identity" may be called *perceptual activity.*

One way of answering the questions raised by this mechanism of transposition is to postulate an *imperative of transposition* that imposes itself at birth, without which the primal anti-cathexis of the extinctive tendency could not take place.

The clinical experience of traumatic neuroses, the recurrence of traumatic dreams and the compulsion to repeat resulted in the recognition of the third quality of the drives, namely, the regressive tendency of every drive to reestablish an earlier state of things, even back to the inorganic and inanimate state. Perception is not only a path transmitting sensory stimuli, but it is also utilized by the psyche ordinarily for anti-traumatic purposes. Here we are touching on an essential function of perception, namely, of providing an anti-traumatic solution. There is a necessity of anti-traumatic clinging to perception; hence, an imperative of awakening.

Economic issues prove essential in this anti-traumatic utilization of perception. The operations involved have the aim of limiting libidinal regression and of preparing its mutation into cathexis. The tendency to extinction menaces this mutation. It is conceivable that this work on the economy takes place without any ideational contents through operations that can be accounted for only at the level of abstraction.

Perceptions without traces are felt to be a traumatic *failure to trace*. They have to be processed by an activity of thought that does not have any specific contents at its disposal. Where the trace is missing, the psychic work on the economy becomes strictly processual. Where traces exist, the same economic function is concealed by their utilization.

This is the case for the baby in whom thing-presentations have not yet been formed. The difficulty of realizing such an elementary act of restraint preliminary to economic mutation explains the recourse to the anti-traumatic mechanism of clinging to a tangible materiality, that of one's own body and of the external world. The function of the ego at the level of the body and of the object is to furnish psychic work with materials that can be used at discretion. It achieves this by virtue of the pairs transposition-conversion and transposition-cooptation.

It is thus not improbable that such operations without content unfold at night. This may explain the absence of dream memories even though libidinal regeneration has occurred. The utilization of latent thoughts and waking residues is perceivable when difficulties are encountered in carrying out these economic operations.

This utilization of perception as well as transposition on to perception have major consequences. The "either/or" of aetiology – either sensory stimuli or drive impulses – makes way for the "both/and" of the impact of stimuli as well as the transposition of unconscious elements onto sensory perception.

An important change took place in the conception of the ego and of its relations with the id. While Freud was able to assert that "for the ego, perception plays the part which in the id falls to instinct" (Freud, 1923, p. 25), the need to take into consideration "traumatic" attractions beyond the pleasure principle allowed him to see that the ego is obliged to differentiate itself on account of this "traumatic" drive quality (Freud, 1933, p. 94), and not only under the impact of external stimuli against which it can defend itself by means of the stimulus barrier.

To respond to the *anxiety generated anew* (p. 94) that is produced by the traumatic attraction, the ego utilizes sensory perceptions, clings to them and transposes the internal unconscious operations and tendencies onto the external sensory perceptions. By virtue of this transposition, it turns the internal origin of the traumatic anxiety linked to the extinctive attraction of the drives round into an external danger and uses the stimulus barrier to respond to this traumatic situation. Alarm signal anxiety henceforth replaces the automatic anxiety, which is "generated anew." This capacity to use sensory perception through clinging and transposition forms the nucleus of the ego.

Though tangible perceptions offer a materiality of restraint through the traces that they furnish, this anti-traumatic solution entails a traumatic awakening due to the existence of perceptions without traces, which occur through the perception of all differences. A *missing* trace is transmitted via perception.

Differences as such do not give rise to tracing but to facilitations, feelings and *early impressions*, or to denial that allows for immobilization. The use of the material tangibility of traces is completed by the use of the stimulus barrier and of the denial that arises from it. The relation to perception proves to be twofold.

We were able to follow this dynamic in the previous chapters in relation to the difference between the sexes. Due to the fact that the genital erogenous zones are those most concerned by regressivity, they offer these two logics of transposition, onto their common materiality (the pair masculine-feminine) and onto their essential traumatic difference with the effects of lack (the pair endowed/unendowed).

The transposition of the extinctive tendency occurs spontaneously onto absences, disappearances, destructions, erasures and the lacks inherent in all differences, that is, onto sensory perceptions that do not give rise to traces. There exist, then, perceptions of lack that cannot be used for the purposes of anti-traumatic clinging, but which, on the contrary, potentialize their effects with those emanating from the extinctive tendency, the tendency of drives to return to an earlier state, even back to the inanimate state. This double correlation, from the inside towards the outside and from the outside towards the inside, and its potentialization, results in certain sensory perceptions being described as traumatic. They are attributed with an intensity that has its origin in the tension created by the tendency to reestablish an earlier state of things, even to the point of extinction, and the counter-restraint sustained by the imperative of registration.

By means of these transpositions all the interactions present in the process of libidinal sympathetic excitation are realized. This last utilizes all the stimuli emanating from perceptions with and without traces, their correlations with drive qualities and the operations of restraint grounding the masochism of renunciation. The process of libidinal sympathetic excitation has the aim of bringing about the libidinal regeneration of the cathexes of the body, the mind and objects. When it succeeds, it conceals the extinctive tendency involved in the underlying conflict. Consequently, only the feeling of lack attendant upon the regenerated cathexes attests to the existence of this reality. This sensation is attenuated to a large extent by libidinal availability and the promotion of a bonus of desire. Otherwise, symptoms operate a return of lack through a lack of mentalization. All modalities of registration are accompanied by such feelings of lack due to the restraint that initiated them. The same may be said also of all experiences of absence that have the common feature of furnishing sensory perceptions with lack.

By virtue of differences, *perceptions with traces* and *perceptions without traces* are reunited. Among the perceptions with traces, it is further necessary to distinguish between those related to what is visible, which can be transformed into images and representations, and those related to what is invisible, which give rise to sensual sensations.

The denial of perceptions of lack proves very useful initially in order to allow psychic operations to unfold and the pleasure principle not to be disturbed by extinctive tendencies. Subsequently, what was initially denied will be taken into account and the pleasure principle will be confronted with what is beyond it.

The stimulus barrier offers this possibility of denial and is gradually replaced by the process of falling asleep. But of course this denial does not eliminate endogenous feelings; it limits their stimulation by the sensory perceptions of lack. This is where the anti-traumatic utilization of perception comes into play, with clinging to the perceptions of tangible realities that are adjacent in the time and/or space of the experience of traumatic feelings. The recollection of an accident with a traumatic colouring occurs by means of elements that are linked to the scene of the accident and adjacent to the traumatic impressions; otherwise, there is a repetition of the newly generated anxiety, accompanied by a panic attack, nameless dread and an experience of terror that are repeated as such.

These adjacent elements are traces derived from sensorial perceptions. If the traumatic attraction permits it, and under cover of the denial offered by the stimulus barrier, they undergo differentiations in the form of mnemic traces and thing-presentations that can be utilized by psychic work as inner materials. Sensorial perceptions are thus co-opted as inner contents by identification. The thing-presentations created in this way can take charge of the drive impulses. This first stage of mentalization remains totally unconscious until a second stage is set in motion by a new awakening of the regressive attraction. This second stage is that of the dream-work linked to language via latent thoughts. When it fails, symptoms appear.

This ensemble in two stages defines mentalization. At the heart of thought, then, we find a mixture of ideational contents, affects, feelings, emotions and bodily sensations of internal origin (erogenous and sensual, pleasant and unpleasant) with all the variations that are met with in ordinary psychic functioning and in the various entities of psychopathology.

The fact that the traumatic attraction eventuates in no trace or specific representation obliges the mind to utilize "related memories" (Freud, 1937), which contain impressions of lack and attempt to cover them over by exacerbating the intensity of tangible materials. A saturation is thus obtained that keeps the impressions of lack apart.

The missing trace concealed by the intensification of ideational contents, affects and erogenous feelings is a challenge for metapsychology, just as the passions and desire have intrigued thinkers of all times and today intrigue the neuroscientists and biologists of the brain (Changeux, 1983, Vincent, 1986).

What we call the libido or desire has always been the object of quests that never succeed in grasping it, even though we sense their presence very concretely through their effects of conversion and phantasying, conferring upon desire a concreteness that can nonetheless not be hypostacized or represented as such. The thing-presentation of the penis is the phallic prototype of desire, from which the sensibility devolved upon the invisible vagina is lacking. In short, the confrontation of the difference representation-sensibility, linked to the pair masculine-feminine and to the pair penis-vagina, with the difference endowed/unendowed, impregnates representation and sensual sensibility with a feeling of lack. Neither representation nor sensibility escape this reality of a *missing trace* that is felt painfully. Extinctive regressivity remains irreducibly active.

Tangible traces and missing trace

A question arises concerning traces and the phenomenology of tracing. Are they the consequence of the stimuli of external reality alone, conceived by certain authors like Francis Pasche as a constant bombardment or Denise Braunschweig and Michel Fain as a primary raw brutality, evoking an economic state of the drives with a correlation between stimuli and impulses?

Freud also envisaged a constant influx of very powerful stimuli imposing themselves on the surface of the mind, thought of as a sensitive vesicle, obliging it to differentiate itself as a cortical layer and a space of reception without memory. The metaphor of the "mystic writing pad," with its sheets of paper allowing for tracing and erasure, and its wax slab, a place of memory, accounts well for Freud's conception (Freud 1925).

However, at the end of this text, Freud points out that the presence of endogenous perceptions is lacking in the model to which he has just referred with the aim of establishing the incompatibility between memory and consciousness. The "pad" of the mind is not made of wax but is the site of drive impulses that have their own impacts. In this text Freud gives priority to stimuli of external origin. In fact, our sixth sense, the internal side of consciousness, is absent from this model. It is a receptive screen on which ideational contents, in images or in words, can present themselves, as well as all the sensations of internal origin, affects, emotions and feelings, which are all bodily feelings, thus sensual, involving the process of conversion. The exploration of anti-traumatic solutions leaves, on the contrary, more and more room for endogenous perceptions, which present themselves on the inner side of the screen of consciousness.

While in 1900 the sensory realities of the past could potentially be recovered along the regressive path, in 1920 the representable part of sensory perception became the object of a possible fixation used in order to respond to negative traumatic aspirations of an endogenous origin linked to the extinctive regressivity of the drives. The latter can manifest itself spontaneously or be awakened by sensory reality without traces, which enters into correlation with it. Sensory reality is no longer defined only by its constraints on the mind, or by its imprinting effects and by the traces it procures, but also by the utilization that the mind makes of perceptual traces for anti-traumatic ends.

Even if reality in itself exists while remaining unknowable, it is accessible through the prism of this anti-traumatic utilization that confers upon it a psychic function, that of participating in the denial of another category of perceptions, both sensory and endogenous in the form of sensations, neither of which can give rise to traces and specific ideational material. This situation and this function can only be inferred. Only psychic work can respond to it with the help of traces and ideational material arising from perceptions with traces. The term *lack* designates the feelings experienced when the terror of the traumatic factor has been transformed by the regressive work of distortion. In a context where the extinctive tendencies dominate, the traces adjacent to the traumatic scene cannot be differentiated as thing-presentations. They are destined to be repeated as such.

A theoretical question arises. What about the erasure of traces and unconscious registrations? Freud never ceased to assert that they are subject to timeless conservation and that they escape the wearing-away processes of time. And yet clinical situations of negativism on a long-term basis (schizophrenia) or extemporaneously (autism) seem to plead in favour of the existence of an erasure; of course, clinical pictures of insanity too. The hypothesis of erasure goes hand in hand with that of the impossibility of using them. The traces are created by the impact of the perception of differences on regressivity or in response to extinctive attractions. Their differentiation into two poles, one accessible to drive activity, the other dominated by the principle of the code of language, allows for the elaboration of a psychic response to this regressivity. The stereotypies of autism attest to the active presence of a code principle attached to traces and sensual facilitations that have a history. But the clinical experience of autism also shows that these differentiations can be annihilated at any moment.

Whatever conceptions of perception are being considered, they are in keeping with the Freudian postulate that perception occurs passively, since the active role of the human being is to protect himself from certain disturbances induced by perception. The stimulus barrier has this function as a shield (Pasche, 1971), which will subsequently be taken over by denial and falling asleep. We know, moreover, that deafferentation produces major disturbances, which confirms the importance for psychic functioning of utilizing perceptions for anti-traumatic purposes. Denial can be only momentary. Perception is thus not an activity of the mind, but its utilization is indispensable for it.

Another hypothesis thus presents itself. Tracing proves necessary to curb the extinctive attractions of the drives. Perceptual traces offer materiality to intrapsychic transpositions, as do the external tangible realities for the transpositions on the sensory perceptions. Psychic needs differentiate traces subsequently as mnemic traces and ideational contents. The psyche thus frees itself from the obligatory presence of tangible sensory perceptions.

I have already stressed that perceptions of lack do not give rise to traces. Psychic work can therefore never be completed and psychoanalysis cannot be a theory of representation. Other modes of registrations have to be produced by the psychical apparatus.

At the level of *tracing*, two poles may be distinguished, that *without traces*, linked to perceptions of lack, that is unable to give rise to either traces or ideational contents, and that of *perceptual traces* arising from tangible materials such as the subject's own body, objects and language.

The first pole is that of the *missing trace*, the other that of *tangible traces*. They find expression in opposite affects, which may be extreme: on the one hand, traumatic terror, and, on the other, the jubilatory assumption of an ideal registration that would put an end to all extinction. Such a longing is destined to failure and to endless quests. Every content reintroduces difference, and the absence of content is correlated with the extinctive tendency. We have seen that in the erotic sphere, these two tendencies leading to extinction come up against the limit of what is refractory.

Theory provides us with expressions of the missing trace that can be observed in the session in the form of transferences: onto the body, with the sensual temptations of the session; onto the object, with the search for an ideal model of psychic functioning; and onto language, with the quest for a content that would overcome the traumatic factor.

As soon as the process of reducing regressivity is stimulated by a perception without traces or by impressions arising directly from the extinctive tendency, distress occurs, which covers over feelings of terror related to a more or less extensive threat of disappearance. The creation of returns of the repressed causes materials to emerge from the shadows of repression, which serve as a recourse. The need for psychic materials is obvious. The traces of infantile amnesia are then elicited and differentiated as double registrations in the service of this work of economic reduction. This brings us back to the question of diverse forms of memory and to the need for memory as it appears in the dream-work.

Thus, while tracing is partly bound up with the sensory impact of external reality, its differentiation as registration is driven by the processual needs activated by traumatic experience *without traces*.

This appeal to tracing and to the construction of mnemic registrations is involved in the same way in the birth of writing and in the utilization of the act of writing as a transposition of, and support for, operations of registration. The invention of numbering and writing was driven by a desire for conservation and by the sensation of the instability of memory, hence a need to form memories. We find again the anti-traumatic function of the act of tracing and of the materiality of what has been traced, invoked by the need to fend against experiences of erasure. This is true for all the arts. The creation of artistic works provides their author and other human beings with new materials that can be used, thanks to novelty, to fulfil the anti-traumatic function in relation to the missing trace. Novelty is offered to the shared illusion of being able to find/create the missing trace. The authentic artist renews his gift with new materials of illusion. Every work remains forever unfinished and infinite.

Likewise, the production of a sign as a manifest trace relating to a code does not make it possible to resolve the absence of a specific thing-presentation of the perception without traces. Words do not fall within the sphere of the various forms of drive representation (*représentance*).[1] This takes us back to the gap between regressivity and code. The missing trace persists and the extinctive attraction insists.

To return now to the difference between ideational material and feelings. The mechanism of repression relates to ideas that can only be unconscious due to their "incompatibility" and the attraction of primal repression. The conception of primal repression is variable depending on whether authors adopt wholesale the three steps of the theory of the drives (Freud, 1920), infantile sexuality, narcissism and the regressive character of the drives, that is, their tendency to return to an earlier, and even inorganic state of things. The notion of incompatibility referring originally to aesthetic and moral values needs to be revised by taking into account the domination of the regressive attraction of the said ideas. It is this regressive quality that defines the adjective "incompatible" – that is, with consciousness – and that requires a specific psychic work called *distortion* (Freud, 1900, 1923) and a connection with a preconscious registration in order to gain access to consciousness.

With regard to ideational material, work takes place within the double registration of thing- and word-presentations, with an oscillation that is favourable to formal regression, and then to the orientation of the drive economy along the progressive path. Unconscious thing-presentations are elaborated when they come into contact with drive impulses of which they become vehicles in the form of ideational representatives (*Vorstellungsrepräsentanz*), while preconscious ideas maintain close relations with the hypercathexis specific to language. These ideational representatives and preconscious ideas fulfil the function of "intermediate links" (1923, p. 21) involved in the process of becoming conscious. This double registration explains how ideas can exist unconsciously without being conscious: "An idea," Freud writes, "may exist even if it is not perceived; a feeling, on the other hand, consists in the perception itself."[2]

Psychoanalytic treatment has the aim of facilitating the construction of thing-presentations thanks to the regressive path and of reinforcing the links between the preconscious idea and language thanks to interpretation. It allows the diphasic process to unfold and relies on the dreams of the interval period. This brings us back to the two dynamics, regressive and progressive, of the operation of après-coup, and the leap between drive impulses with their thing-presentations promoting desire, and language with its formal regression producing a rebus created from preconscious ideas.

The double registration and oscillation between the two offers quite an easy apprehension of the operation of après-coup with regard to ideational material. Its different stages are the first transposition of unconscious drive impulses onto a sensory perception of representable tangible realities, the formal regression of the perceptual traces linked to language back to the thing-presentations originating in the mutation of drive impulses, and lastly the progressive orientation of the libidinal economy and the promotion of contents that can be presented to consciousness thanks to the intermediate links of the *Pcs*. The discontinuities thus readily have their place within a continuity of stages. According to this model, interpretation could be conceived both as a deduction and as an inference; this, in fact, is not the case in the clinical constellations discussed in the preceding chapters illustrating the operation of après-coup.

Let us recall Freud's first article on the forgetting of the name Signorelli (Freud, 1898). It offers a continuity of discontinuous stages thanks to the intermediate links. On the other hand, the second text (Freud, 1901) introduces a radical discontinuity, a real leap between the symptom, the forgetting of the name of the painter and the drive tendency awakened by the news of the suicide of a former Turkish patient suffering from an incurable illness. The link between the forgetting of the name and the suicide is the act of suppression; the leap resides in reversibility, which is present in the case of the act of forgetting whereas the suicide implies irreversibility.

This discontinuity is explainable by the rupture in nature between extinction and registration. The work of après-coup articulates these two incompatible and totally heterogeneous realities. It transforms a hiatus into a functional discontinuity that has a value of continuity. That is why its metapsychological elaboration proceeds from theoretical construction with the concepts of *extinctive regressivity*, promoting various forms of regressions, and *imperative of registration*, which refers to the principle of the code specific to each language. Necessity and purposes are thus united.

It is this gap that is at the origin of the form of the operation of après-coup, according to two stages with an in-between period.

Expressions of lack

As perceptions of lack and experiences emanating from the extinctive tendencies and the sensations originating in the psychic operations involved in their processing are not directly representable, their expression and registration has to follow other paths. For the formations stemming from these other paths, the apprehension of the work of après-coup is more subtle.

Certain questions raised by metapsychology have been touched on several times above. What can be said about this "something" (Freud, 1923, p. 22) that could become a verbalizable bodily experience as soon as the attractions beyond the pleasure principle impede its advent in the form of affects, emotions, feelings and erogenous sensual sensations? What is the role of language in their emergence in consciousness?

The *missing trace* obliges the mind to think, feel, imagine, construct and invent, to accuse, suspect, sublimate, speculate, theorize and interpret, and to this end to utilize traces linked to other perceptions of tangible realities, those that give rise to ideas that Freud calls "related recollections." The intensity and "ultra-clear" (Freud, 1937b, p. 266) nature of these recollections, which make up for the lack of a specific idea, attest to their involvement in the saturation that attempts to fulfil the function of anti-cathexis inevitably left incomplete by the missing trace.

Thus, all these psychic experiences aroused by the missing trace are accompanied not only by a sensation of lack specific to the human condition, but also by an attempt to intensify the solutions that they offer to conceal this sensation. The gap between the more or less successful saturation by dreams during sleep and the reintroduction of feelings of lack on awakening is the basis of the diurnal side of reality-testing on awakening, the nocturnal side being based on the gap between the saturation and the feelings due to the regressive attraction beyond the pleasure principle.

With regard to the *missing trace*, psychic functioning is obliged to find other means than that of differentiating psychic registrations on the basis of specific tangible traces. I have mentioned several of them in the preceding chapters.

One solution consists in utilizing ideas arising from other perceptions and traces *adjacent* to the missing trace. However, these will never correspond or respond adequately to the lack of a specific trace; hence, the sense of a *lack of tracing* and a *lack of thinking* and the quest for a perception capable of filling this lack.

A *compulsion to trace* and the production of *perceptual material* are thus an attempt to postpone every *lack of tracing* by saturating perceptual consciousness from the inside. Ideational contents then become "ultra-clear" and undergo a *multiplication* in number and in intensity. This utilization of the quantitative factor, and its illustration by the multiplication of an idea or image, can be named with the term *medusage*, from the name of the figure of Medusa (Freud, 1940a).

The creation of the fetish offers another prototypical illustration of this saturation. The traces from which it is created are found on the path of regression that leads to the traumatic perception. They serve as a check and limit. The defensive solution consists in modifying the value of the trace utilized for the creation of the fetish. The value of the mother's penis is attributed to it with conviction (Chervet, 1994).

Another solution is the exaltation of registration, in the form of conversions, feelings of pleasure arising from psychic work realized with tangible traces. Aestheticization depends on this mechanism.

Yet another solution lies in the production of theoretical links and interpretations transforming *perception without traces*, the *missing trace*, into a lack of tracing and a lack of perception. A quest for the perception and trace that are missing ensues. Theory asserts, then, that something should exist where something is missing.

Another very important solution was explored in the last chapter, that of the sensual regression of erotism. The refractory realizes a negative saturation, without content, in fact, a sensual neutralization. The other pole is that of ecstatic enjoyment, which is a positive sensual saturation, also without content.

Sensual feelings are bodily expressions of the conversion of erotogenic organ cathexes anti-cathected by sensuality. The latter arose from a desexualization of part of the sexual cathexes of organs. The sensitivity of sensuality is linked to the extinctive regressivity of the drives that required this transformation. When the processing of regressivity falters, the sensitivity of certain bodily regions is exacerbated, testifying to the attraction of the sexual organ and the attempt to install the anti-cathexis. Freud concluded his text on the splitting of the ego with such a clinical remark about a man who presents "an anxious susceptibility against either of his little toes being touched" (Freud, 1940b, p. 224). This particular sensitivity to active extinctive regressivity is felt as a threat of castration.

Affects, also originating in a bodily conversion, are specific qualities of the work that the psyche realizes during the various experiences that it has to manage (for instance, sadness over loss, joy in connection with reunions, etc.). They also reflect the intensity involved in the conflict between extinction and registration. In terms of intensity, the quantitative aspect of the quota of affect turns out to belong to the qualitative aspect.

Conversion occurs both for affects and feelings and for erogenous sensations. As Freud (1923) writes: "The distinction between *Cs. and Pcs.* has no meaning where feelings are concerned; the *Pcs.* here drops out" (p. 23). And just before, he says: "Actually, the difference is that, whereas for unconscious *ideas* connecting links must be created before they can be brought into the *Cs.* with *feelings*, which are themselves transmitted directly, this does not occur" (pp. 22–23). This "directly" depends on the mechanism of conversion, but it does not necessarily occur. The libidinal economy that is supposed to be converted, this *something*, which ought to have become a feeling, has to find other vicissitudes that are included in formulations, such as unconscious sensations and unconscious feelings.

The word *directly* does not mean that feelings do not undergo a work of distortion; they can be immobilized, suppressed, displaced on to other scenes, turned into their opposite, amalgamated and accumulated. They can also be the subject of an enunciation without language being indexed by their sensitive qualities. Language becomes autonomous. The notion of truth is upturned. By means of saturation and negation through a disembodied nomination, language is able to impose itself for real, without any link either to the body or to affects.

We come up against the question here of truth and distortion, as well as that of a view of feelings as a royal path of truth owing to the fact that they are supposed to gain access directly to consciousness. This conception is accepted as such by certain psychoanalytic currents that overlook the fact that the quota of affect does not escape the work of distortion that makes possible its advent in consciousness by virtue of bodily conversion, as well as its concealment and its transformations.

Basically, the psychoanalytic world tends to be divided into a psychoanalysis of emotional experience, which has the aim of working-through such experience but which confers upon it the quality of being a direct expression of truth, and a psychoanalysis that argues that endogenous feelings are memory and associative material subject to the effects of distortion that are necessary for their access to consciousness. For the emotional current, affect is the *naked truth* of the subject! For the psychoanalysis of interpretation, feelings have a value of reminiscence that has to be interpreted. Those who adhere to a form of psychoanalysis centred on emotional experience have the tendency to consider that the latter not only reflects the truth of a subject, but also the immediate match between affects and feelings and the reality of the world and of the other. Feelings are then considered as the royal path of direct access to the truth of the other, to the point of becoming the chief criterion of reality-testing. "If I feel it, it means it's true." "If I feel despoiled, persecuted, loved, etc., it is because I am despoiled, persecuted, loved, etc." The world is then recognized in the image of affects. In the session, by means of a hysterical identification, the analyst can attribute to the patient the feelings that he ought to have; he may misconstrue the patient's effective reality. Admittedly, this modality is built on the sense of ordinary anticipation that every adult has towards a baby or a child. In the best of cases, this anticipation has attracting effects vis-à-vis the development of the child, which is a way of tracing out his future path for him.

This modality is obviously part of the transference conviction in the session. For the patient, depending on his history of identification, the analyst is supposed to feel the same thing as him or, on the contrary, understand nothing of what he is experiencing. The fact of feeling is used as evidence, justification and affirmation of the absolute truth of the feeling. "I am sure I was abused as a child because I feel it"; "I love him, so he/she loves me." There is confusion between the inner experience and what is happening in the outer reality, whether past or present.

The fact of describing sensations and feelings that do not reach consciousness as unconscious emphasizes that their economy continues to be operative along other paths than those of the returns of the repressed typical of ideas. Their effects are particularly significant when we think of the unconscious guilt that is active in the clinical constellations of the negative therapeutic reaction and in the vicissitudes of inevitable degradation, but also in the destructive conduct of nations and the group psychology that are involved in the decadence of civilizations.

Another consequence of the fact that the missing trace is irreducible has often been mentioned, namely, that of theorization. In order to confront extinctive regressivity and the missing trace, scenarios are conjured up which dramatize causal theories explaining lack in terms of some sort of disappearance, whether or not it is deemed reversible or definitive. I have pointed out that the motivations for the third primal phantasy lie here. During an experience with a traumatic tone, the immediate shock is very quickly accompanied by such accusatory causal theories. A long work of latency will be necessary before it is possible to emerge from the tendency to repeat as such the scene of the "closely related recollections" (Freud, 1937b, p. 266) on which the traumatic experience has been hooked, and also the need to designate (or accuse) someone as being responsible for the traumatic event.

It is the task of infantile sexual theories to provide the function of calming the affect of terror linked to experiences of lack by proposing causal logics linking these endogenous feelings and sensorial perceptions of lack with the hope and illusion of being able to avoid what awakens this effect. Causal logic is operative well before it can be formulated, for instance, in stranger-anxiety and in the creation of infantile phobias. Thought is theorizing.

Feelings of lack are at the origin of the interpreting and theorizing dimension of thought. The psyche cannot do without theorizing and interpreting thought. Theorizing thought cannot furnish a complete and finished conceptualization unless this theory is accompanied by a denial of feelings of lack. This interpretative component of thought corresponds to the need for the psychical apparatus to process the traumatic dimension without the possibility of using traces or thing-presentations from this reality.

The connection between the perception of a lack and the psychic acts required to oppose the extinctive tendencies is at the origin of a prototypical theory according to which a perceived lack is the consequence of an act of suppression. A first theory emerges that responds to the terror of disappearance. This work of theorization can also be instigated directly by the effect of the elementary drive tendency. The transposition on to sensory perceptions of lack, the search for or creation of such perceptions (traumatophilia) permits the production of similar theories by means of which an external reality is made responsible for feelings of lack. This theory henceforth concealed the involvement of endogenous feelings. In this sense, every phobia is in itself the manifestation of an implicit theory.

The extinctive tendency can only be represented by scenarios of suppression and destruction, thus by the subtraction applied to a tangible object that is apprehended by sensory perception and representable. In the field of mentalization, the fulfilment of the wish to be invisible depends on negative hallucination, which is so exploited by mysticism and idealization. Negative hallucination is at the basis of the assumption of the ideal. Every materialization realized in the name of the ideal amounts to a lowering of the ideal. The concrete realization always falls short of the ideal. Sublimation is also caught up in this conflict between producing a tangible object and transmitting the assumption that is at the basis of the sublime. The ideal itself is empty of any content. Incompletion is the compromise utilized by many artists. I have already mentioned how Lewis Carroll portrays an act of suppression by means of a gradual erasure perfectly illustrated by John Tenniel. All the parts of the Cheshire cat's body are gradually erased until its smile is finally wiped off by the erasure of its mouth. All that remains of it is then the word *smile*. Lewis Carroll thereby shows the limits of what can be represented through images, but also the possibility of transmitting the essence itself of every living being by erasing its materiality, by suppressing its incarnation.

By transposing itself on to the perceivable lack in every experience of difference and comparison, extinctive regressivity calls for ideals and their dimension beyond any form of materiality. The perceived lack becomes a figure of the attained ideal.

On the other hand, the psychic system of *transitional phenomena* as described by Winnicott (1953) seeks to escape the judgement of attribution involved in every comparison, whether intentional or not. It establishes an equivalence between me and not-me, and between all representable sensory realities. It denies perceptions of the differences that exist between them that are capable of arousing feelings of lack. It thereby attenuates not only this resonance with ideals, but also the feeling of lack that accompanies them, and it establishes the pleasure principle of the ideal ego.

The extinctive tendency is obviously directly induced when scenes of absence, destruction and disappearance are perceived. But the significance of the disappearance proves to be twofold. It has the value of castration and idealization. For Schreber and Abélard the absence of a penis is evidence of access to supreme, divine ecstatic enjoyment.

The differences perceived by sensoriality induce and are correlated with the extinctive regressivity of the drives that is transposed at the same time on to external tangible sensory realities, facilitating the management of this tendency. This is how the ordinary and temporary phobias of childhood are produced.

This twofold correlation between the extinctive tendency of the drives and the sensory perceptions of differences forms the process of libidinal sympathetic excitation as it can be perceived in childhood through games of excitation. Hence, the tendency to attribute to the stimuli of external reality the origin of feelings of excitation as well as those of lack. The seducer is outside, and so are the reasons for lack. This appeal to phobic logic does not originate solely in practical reasons, such as the transformation of endogenous anxiety into external fear whose objectifiable object can thereby be avoided. The reality called difference gives rise neither to traces nor to representations. While the elements involved in a difference can be represented (the masculine and the feminine), the difference in itself is not. This is what Lewis Carol shows us. The void is a figure of the difference felt by a feeling of lack involving the two meanings of suppression, castration and spiritualization or transcendence.

Extinctive regressivity is thus involved in the psychoanalytic conception of mental functioning in two ways: as a concept belonging to the metapsychological corpus of mental functioning and as a reality involved in the constraint to produce an ideal theory. What specifies the process of theorization is being able to imagine and infer the underlying processes responsible for phenomena. Without speculation, neither science nor progress is possible.

This calls into question the overly radical dichotomy between clinical practice and theory. Theories also belong to the clinical realm. Prioritizing clinical practice over theory is a theory that announces that it would be possible to do without the theorizing component of thought, of disregarding its function and of ignoring the extinctive dimension that induces it. Theory is a clinical object with a particularity: it can be developed without referring to the ideational material arising from sensory perception due to the fact that it is elicited by the perceptions of lack arising from perceptions without traces both of endogenous and of external origin. Lack is at the origin of abstraction. Take, for example, the case of the zero in mathematics, which belongs, like all the other numbers, to the category of signs, even though it designates a reality that is heterogeneous to the other numbers and to countable realities. The sign zero transmits a denial of the reality of zero.

All the lacks felt and perceived are projected onto the two sides of the screen of consciousness in the form of sensations and impressions. These can be approached via adjacent ideas, but they can also follow paths that are independent of any substratum of trace or idea, such as affect, erogeneity and abstraction.

Contrary to immediate intuition, abstraction maintains very close relations with other materials known via bodily conversion and erogenous facilitations. The solution of abstraction teaches us that at the basis of all language, irrespective of the substratum it uses, there is an abstract reference that can be designated with the name code. Every path towards becoming conscious is related latently to this principle of the code. The registration on the internal side of consciousness of abstract concepts, affects and sensual feelings can succeed only if the principle of the code is effective. From the point of view of the code, theorization is to signs what affect is to the body.

This brings us back to the reasons for the fundamental rule of psychoanalytic treatments. Freud had the intuition of this imperative of encoding without theorizing it completely. It is implicit in his notion of hypercathexis as a cathexis sustained by language, depending on the secondary process and the superego. Every conscious expression depends on this cathexis. We get a glimpse here of a specific quality of consciousness. It can only take in what presents itself to it with certain qualities, those provided by its links with the code. Only what is organized by the principle of the code can become conscious (Chervet, 2014).

It is this independence of theory in relation to traces and ideational material that is denoted by the term *abstraction*. It is a question of stepping back from immediate perception, which is what dreams do every night thanks to images and to their utilization by primary process mechanisms. Abstraction is the direct reflection of unconscious psychic operations, which are only known to us by inference from the sensations generated by them.

Theories can become perception when they gain access to a secondarized formulation, and especially when they are hypercathected with the aim of producing a saturation of consciousness. They play a part, then, in *perceptual activity* and in the clinical experience of conviction.

Even when psychic work utilizes ideational contents, as is the case for the dream-work, all sorts of unconscious theories are enacted by the scenarios themselves, particularly theories that create equivalences typical of the primary process. When saturation dominates, the differences of content are blurred in favour of the equivalence in nature and intensity. The definition that Freud (1915) gives of the primary process, "no negation, no doubt, no degrees of certainty" (p. 186) is the basis of such a principle of equivalence and timelessness. According to this logic, every feeling of lack is a rupture of the illusion of equivalences.

Though a denial can be supported by the use of abstraction, theory does not have the monopoly of it. The constructions formed by the mind participate in this aim thanks to *intensity*, *multiplication* and *performance*, by means of ideas (for instance, the *still image* of the fetishist who constructs a neo-reality, the penis of the mother); by means of sensoriality (for instance, via the quest for extreme sensations); or by means of the transformation of the body (body-building and carnal art, etc.).

Extinctive regressivity and the imperative of renunciation: The masochism of renunciation

The heterogeneity between the extinctive tendency and psychic registrations raises yet other implications, in particular that of drive duality and that of the superego whose theoretical elaboration is a consequence of the first, just as its advent in the psyche depends on the resolution of the Oedipus complex.

The decisive role for the operation of après-coup of the tendency to reestablish an earlier state of things, even going back to the inanimate state, requires us to reexamine the pair life drive/death drive and the triad life drive/death drive/superego. As Freud (1933) wrote: "The instincts rule not only mental but also vegetative life, and these organic instincts exhibit a characteristic which deserves our deepest interest ... For they reveal an effort to restore an earlier state of things (p. 106) ... according to our presumption, an instinct must have arisen which sought to do away with life once more and to reestablish the inorganic state" (p. 107).

Having recognized the regressive character of the drive, Freud quite easily inferred the operative nature of a death drive working silently towards the reduction and extinction of everything that is living. What most defines the death drive is this silent, indirect operation, its lack of direct representability. The death drive is in itself silent and it tends to reduce everything that is living to silence.

The regressive quality to the point of extinction did not raise the same difficulties for Freud for each of the elementary tendencies. Admittedly, he does not confuse life with Eros, the life drive. But the expression *life drive*, as well as the hope that there is some power in the human being that sustains life unfailingly, plays a role in attributing to Eros conservative capacities, in identifying it with the first self-preservative drives and in bestowing on it functions characteristic of narcissism relating to the ideal ego, to His Majesty the Baby.

Attributing Eros with functions relating to narcissism leads to a conception of life resulting from the amalgam of two opposing tendencies, Eros and the death drive, Thanatos. Melanie Klein envisages the situation more in terms of a struggle between the two against a background of anxiety. For Freud, Eros is supposed to oppose the extinctive tendencies, to bring the existing elements together into ever-greater unities and to keep them united. But life is made up of the variegation of their amalgam.

This ego-based conception of Eros is, however, not the only one Freud put forward. Regularly, he returns to the fact that the tendency towards extinction concerns all the drives. The two fundamental drives are both seen as being haunted by extinctive regressivity, but along different paths.

An ambiguity and a difficulty had infiltrated the theory, and Freud was aware of it. On several occasions, having developed his conception of the death drive, which integrates without difficulty a regressivity going back to the inorganic state, he returns to the difficulty of thinking about a regressivity extending back to the inanimate state for the life drives. With Eros, Freud admits his embarrassment, especially as the solutions of the poets do not help him to resolve it. In fact, he attributes, in turn, two qualities to Eros, an extensive tendency and another of binding (Green, 1999), both of which are involved in what defines it, the formation of ever-greater unities. Then, with a certain remorse, he points out that the definition that applies to the drives, of striving to establish an earlier state of things, even back to the inorganic and inanimate state, ought also to apply to the life drives.

His developments on the two drives and on life are thus interspersed with remarks showing his lack of satisfaction to the extent that they do not completely comply with his fundamental definition of every drive, in particular Eros. He could not resolve himself to make an exception of the sexual drives.

In 1920, at the end of *Beyond the Pleasure Principle*, he wrote: "But we still feel our line of thought appreciably hampered by the fact that we cannot ascribe to the sexual instinct the characteristic of a compulsion to repeat which first put us on the track of the death instincts" (1920, p. 56).

More clearly still in 1933, the same remark appears again in his writings. Having recalled the definition of the drives according to which they all strive to restore an earlier state of things, even back to the inorganic state, he once again remarks that he has not succeeded in applying this characteristic to the life drive: "The question, too, of whether the conservative character may not belong to all instincts without exception, whether the erotic instincts may not be seeking to bring back an earlier state of things when they strive to bring about a synthesis of living things into greater unities this question, too, we must leave unanswered" (Freud, 1933, pp. 107–108).

Each of these citations is followed by the search for a literary or other production that might contain a conception of Eros evoking analogically the portion of truth that corresponds to this definition. It is above all Plato and the *Banquet*, through the mouth of Aristophanes, that he draws on, with the phantasy of a primordial bisexual state that was lost through section and is sought after through the desire for the other sex. On this view sexuality is driven by the wish to rediscover the wholeness and completeness of the beginning. While this phantasy fits well with the tendency to reestablish an earlier state of things, in this case, a Whole, it leaves to one side the aim of this tendency of restoring an inorganic state. This is why, both in 1920 and in 1933, Freud abandoned this path and returned to a conception of Eros as the basic principle of life, according to the classical tradition instead of an instinctual Eros characterized by the famous regressive tendency back to the inanimate state.

Could clinical experience help us to formulate a conception of the life drive that integrates the general definition of the drives? There is a propensity in every human being to die for his ideals, to subsume his instincts of preservation in the name of some ideal. Some characters, mythical or real, embody this tendency to devote oneself body and soul to a cause. Clinically, certain traits of character, such as defiance, a readiness to risk everything at any cost, certain extremely reckless forms of behaviour or ones related to Russian roulette, call for an interpretation involving an ideal, a cause defended irrespective of any sense of self-preservation, and always in the name of life, in general in the name of a better life, a utopia. It is not difficult to find such prototypical characters in all ideologies and beliefs, whether they be political or religious, and obviously in literature too.

I have already mentioned on several occasions the occurrence of mysticism. Unlike the preceding characters, the mystic does not seek death. He cultivates denuding in order to be able to approach his ideals, a principle of life, as closely as possible. True, it is possible to discern the importance of unconscious guilt that is active in this attempt to gain access to immortal life. It is also easy to infer that this unconscious guilt has its origins in the realization of psychic operations that play a part in sustaining life. We will see in the next chapter how these operations of life can be approached from the angle of the term *foundational murder*.

It is now possible to recognize that a drive tendency is involved in the wish to make the world evolve concretely with reference to a principle, an ideal that would have the consequence of eliminating conflicts, doing away with misery, ensuring peace and expunging war and of establishing love, equality, sharing, solidarity, community and fraternity, aims whose goal is to absorb differences and their effects. They are all related to a wish embracing the world as a whole and all use the principle that motivates them as a lever for an ever-greater extension.

We can recognize here the ideas I developed earlier concerning the psychic work required by transpositions onto the tangible and onto what is without traces, but also my thoughts on the ideal that remains outside representation and whose principle is to be emptied of all content.

These *visions* of the world attempt to escape the constraint of this psychic work by building a world exempt from differences. The drive that impels them is thus one of rediscovering an earlier state that preceded any feelings of lack and which preceded life, which can be reached again by the assumption of an ideal. The ideal is to be understood as a regressive longing. By denying differences, the psyche tries to establish at the heart of life a situation akin to this fundamental tendency towards assumption that defines the life drive.

In fact, this tendency does not depend on life, but is active within everything that is living. These visions of the world, these *Weltanschauungen* (Freud, 1933, 35th lecture) include strictly the most elementary definition of the drive given in 1920 as a tendency to return to an earlier state of things, and even to the inorganic state, as extinctive regressivity. But if the horizon of this return is the same for the death drive, the inorganic, inanimate life, the path along which it is reached proves to be different. In the case of the death drive, it is the path of reduction that is employed, whereas in the case of the life drive it is the path of assumption. While in the first case it is a question of extinguishing what exists, in the second it is a matter of attaining an ideal. In both cases, the aim is to do away with the differences inherent in every living being at the origin of feelings of lack.

This brings us back to Freud's suggestion that the death drive and the life drive be defined by this regressive tendency to extinction as he argued in *Beyond the Pleasure Principle*, and again in his *New Introductory Lectures* until the end of his life. The life drive is expressed by elation (Grunberger, 1971) and ideality (Chasseguet-Smirgel, 1973), and by the ever-renewed attempt to hypostacize the ideal. It thus impedes the reduction to zero of the death drive. Likewise, the death drive participates, through its reductive tendency, in establishing a restraint on the propensity of the life drive to dissolve into the evanescence of an absence of content (Viderman, 1977).

In fact, this tendency to attain the ideal can only be realized by means of a transposition onto the body and objects. Its realization can only occur via a desire for an object that serves as a support for the realization of the ideal. The state of being in love, and the hypercathexis of the object that defines it, is one of the possible occurrences. The experience of ecstatic erotic enjoyment with orgasm and the refractory moment gives a concrete foundation for my conception according to which the death drive and the life drive limit each other through their respective pretensions of reduction and assumption. Extinctive regressivity proves to be common to both drives. On the contrary, the refractory moment requires further reflection.

Even more clearly than creative inspiration, sexuality is the prototypical experience of these two tendencies to reduce tension, via elimination and assumption, tendencies that are expressed in the scene of union of the sensualities of two bodies. Creative inspiration also finds expression through union, that of a drive impulse and a material element.

In erotism, desire and the quest for satisfaction combine two aspirations, assumption and reduction. Assumption seeks to attain the immateriality of desire through a concrete *union* exalting ecstatic physical enjoyment, and reduction finds its expression through orgasm. As for the advent of the refractory factor, it bears witness to the extinctive regressivity common to both tendencies and to the intervention of a contrary principle that is opposed to this negative tendency and prepares the rebirth of desire and its future registration in the body.

The refractory factor impedes theory from contenting itself with a homeostasis between the tendencies of the two drives, of life and death. It invites the hypothesis of a renunciation of the path leading to extinction under the aegis of an imperative that is completed by those of restraint, libidinal regeneration and registration. The masochism of renunciation has two aspects here: the tension of restraint and what is refractory to extinction.

In the chapter on erogeneity, I discussed the double interpretation of the lack of a penis. According to the theory of its disappearance, it may be the object of a suppression or of a transcendence to the point of erasure. Both of them can easily be combined, the first becoming the alchemical path of the second. I applied the same logic to the smile of the Cheshire cat. While the first solution is familiar to us through the castration complex, the second calls to mind the psychic operations involved in mysticism, in the delusion of Schreber and in creative inspiration.

A double regressivity thus emerges, through the reduction of tensions to the inorganic state for the death drive and through the assumption of an ideal to the point of erasure for the life drive, both of which may be described as traumatic.

These two forms of regressivity impede any form of narcissistic stable closure because they reopen the traumatic dimension. That of Eros corresponds to the anti-narcissism of Francis Pasche (1965), turned towards the ideal. *Extinctive regressivity* is thus *double*, through *reduction to the inorganic state* for the death drive, and through *assumption to the point of erasure* for Eros, both of which are involved in anxiety and may be described as traumatic. *Inorganicity* and *erasure* are combined in every theory of anxiety and constitute the two tendencies of the id that permeate the unconscious: *exhausting the subject, being dissolved by ideality.*

The conception of an amalgam between the two drive tendencies raises the question of the work that realizes the various amalgams forming the variegated nature of life. The existence of the refractory moment insists on the fact that the two asymmetrical forms of regressivity, one silent, the other noisy, simply oppose each other according to a principle of homeostasis. They are both placed under the aegis of a third term, an imperative of restraint that opposes them. The *double restraint* that arises from this grounds psychic tensions and primary masochism, *a masochism of renunciation*. The refractory moment expresses the renunciation of extinction. This imperative has the aim of resolving tensions and of satisfying object-related erotic desire.

What emerges is a double heterogeneity. The first is between the life drives and death drives, which is the small difference. It is minor because it reflects only the difference between the paths of extinction. They share the same aim. The second is major and fundamental; it concerns the difference between extinction and registration. It is this double difference that is transposed on to the difference between the sexes.

Metapsychological reflection has an impact on these imperatives that are called on to constitute the superego, and on what promotes their efficiency and the psychic operations pertaining to the tendency to reestablish what is inanimate. These operations have the value of a *murder* bearing on each of the two tendencies. The act of *murder* may promote what is psychical or, on the contrary, impact on the imperative and liberate the double regressivity and the extinctive tendencies. With regard to the superego, the murder may be described as annihilating or, on the contrary, foundational.

The assertions of the Oedipus complex, the murder of the father and incest with the mother can be formulated in an abstract and extended manner. Castration is the symptomatic deferred effect of the annihilating murder of the superego; on the contrary, the Oedipal resolution is the accomplished operation of après-coup that reveals the involvement of a foundational murder of the superego.

Other questions arise. What is the origin of this murder that best defines the subject insofar as he is the author of what grounds him, but also the agent of what tends to make him disappear?

The notion of *resolution* is consubstantial with the Oedipus complex; it denotes both its decline and the institution of the superego, an agency that regroups all the sporadic imperatives and sees to it that all psychic work is carried out in relation to the overall context. All the results of the operation of après-coup are judged by its yardstick. Psychic work *must* reduce the double regressivity and orient the psychic economy along the progressive path towards consciousness. This *reduction* consists in utilizing the extinctive qualities of the two fundamental drive tendencies. The imperative uses them in the service of mentalization. Freud called the economy of the superego hypercathexis. He described it as a neutral and displaceable, characteristic of the superego and specific to language. It is a processual libido. The leaps and mutations from one extinctive economy into an economy of the pleasure principle and an economy of resolution are realized by virtue of such contributions of the processual libido. It is linked to the *principle of the code* represented by all languages. Its presence alone makes becoming conscious possible. I have put forward the hypothesis that the nature of the code is a quality of consciousness.

In a nutshell, the process of mentalization that is the operation of après-coup consists of two opposing tendencies with the same purpose, *extinction* and an *imperative of resolution* utilizing this opposition to reduce the double regressivity into a result of life through a series of renunciations. Its means of action is the act of murder, while its ideal aim is resolution in the form of erotic desire.

Notes

1 Translator's note: a general category including different types of representation (psychic representative, ideational representative, representative of the drive, etc.) and which implies the movement, activity of representation.
2 Translator's note: this citation (translated here from the French) appears in a note in Freud's (1922) "Préface à Raymond de Saussure, *La Méthode Psychanalytique*, in the *Oeuvres Complètes,* XVI, p. 160, but it does not feature in the "Preface to Raymond Saussure's *The Psychoanalytic Method"* in the *Standard Edition*, Vol. 19, pp. 283–284).

References

Changeux, J.-P. (1983). *L'homme neuronale*. Paris: Hachette.
Chasseguet-Smirgel, J. (1973). *La Maladie d'idéalité: Essai psychanalytique sur l'idéal du moi*. Paris: Harmattan.
Chervet, B. (1994). Dandysme et confection de fétiche ou comment habiller un vide. *Revue Française de Psychanalyse*, 58 (2): 401–414.
Chervet, B. (2014). Le présent, une qualité psychique. Éléments pour une métapsychologie de la conscience. *Revue Française de Psychanalyse*, 78 (4): 1078–1094.
Donnet, J.-L. (1985). Sur l'écart théoretico-pratique. *Revue Française de Psychanalyse*, 49 (5): 1289–1305.
Freud, S. (1898). The Psychical Mechanism of Forgetfulness. *S.E. 3*. London: Hogarth, pp. 287–297.
Freud, S. (1900). *The Interpretation of Dreams. S.E. 4–5*. London: Hogarth.
Freud, S. (1901). *The Psychopathology of Everyday Life. S.E. 6*. London: Hogarth.
Freud, S. (1915). The Unconscious. *S.E. 14*. London: Hogarth, pp. 166–215.

Freud, S. (1920). *Beyond the Pleasure Principle. S.E. 18*. London: Hogarth, pp. 1–64.
Freud, S. (1923). *The Ego and the Id. S.E. 19*. London: Hogarth, pp. 3–66.
Freud, S. (1925). A Note Upon the 'Mystic Writing Pad'. *S.E. 19*. London: Hogarth, pp. 227–232.
Freud, S. (1933). *New Introductory Lectures on Psycho-Analysis. S.E. 22*. London: Hogarth, pp. 1–182.
Freud, S. (1937a). *Analysis Terminable and Interminable. S.E. 23*. London: Hogarth, pp. 209–253.
Freud, S. (1937b). *Constructions in Analysis. S.E. 23*. London: Hogarth, pp. 255–269.
Freud, S. (1940a [1922]). Medusa's Head. *S.E. 18*. London: Hogarth, pp. 273–274.
Freud, S. (1940b [1938]). Splitting of the Ego in the Process of Defence. *S.E. 23*. London: Hogarth.
Green, A. (1999). *The Chains of Eros: The Sexual in Psychoanalysis*. London: Routledge.
Grunberger, B. (1971). *Le Narcissisme: Essais de psychanalyse*. Paris: Payot.
Neyraut, M. (1997). *Les raisons de l'irrationnel*. Paris: Presses Universitaires de France.
Pasche, F. (1965). L'anti-narcissisme, *Revue Française de Psychanalyse*, 29 (5–6): 503–518.
Pasche, F. (1971). Le bouclier de Persée. *Revue Française de Psychanalyse*, 35 (5–6): 859–870.
Viderman, S. (1977). *Le Céleste et le sublunaire*. Paris: Presses Universitaires de France.
Vincent, J. (1986). *Biologie des passions*. Paris: Odile Jacob.
Winnicott, D.W. (1953). Transitional objects and transitional phenomena. *International Journal of Psychoanalysis*, 34: 89–97.

Chapter 10

The foundational murder and the superego

In this last chapter I will attempt to describe more precisely the operations underlying the operation of après-coup. The first is an operation of restraint that concerns the extinctive tendency. Because of the missing trace, linked to the fact that the sensorial reality of lack gives rise to neither traces nor ideational contents, this operation requires a first stage during which unconscious processes are transposed onto tangible sensorial realities, the body and external realities; this sets up the first restraint against extinction. Then, an internalization takes place thanks to the traces, endogenous sensations and production of ideational material. The use of the contents arising from the sensorial realities that served for the transposition leads to animistic thinking, which is a metaphorization of unconscious processes. Another operation differentiates external realities from the internal processes. This stage is a renunciation of the fact that the tangible realities used by the transposition are ideal objects excluding all experienced lack. It allows for the recognition of differences, especially of the external reality of lack and the inner extinctive tendency. These different stages constitute reality-testing.

All of these operations are often described as a "double reversal," involving a "turning round upon the subject's own self" and a "reversal into its opposite," both preceded by an anti-traumatic transposition onto tangible realities, founding primal repression.

These operations involved in the realization of the operation of après-coup constitute thought-processes and are at the origin of all the psychic productions that can be brought together under the generic term, human thought.

The processes involved in dream-work show us that they are not created by each person's history of identifications but rather that their realization is determined by it, hence the possibility of intervening and modifying their efficiency thanks to the transference and the psychic work carried out within a psychoanalytic treatment. These improvements are made by removing the obstacles and alienating withdrawals specific to each patient that are repeated during the session; but also, thanks to the call to continue the accomplishment of the psychic functioning. This work allows each patient to regain a degree of freedom and availability. The transference is completed by an identification with the mental functioning of the analyst as transmitted by his interpretations and constructions.

This restorative identification is only truly effective if the work of de-alienation takes place concomitantly.

We have discussed the genealogy and mode of action of these processes. Their establishment and the unfolding of the work they perform follow a dynamic in two stages, that of the operation of après-coup, which generally requires a recurrent series of first and second stages in order to reach an outcome. The operation of après-coup does not happen all at once but requires partial stages, some of which may be symptomatic. The need for several nights of sleeping and dreaming as well as the need for a series of sessions teaches us that this diphasic process is only achieved through a work of repetition and working through. It is not easy to assess when this process is completed. One can feel it is over, when in fact it is not. This reality-testing often remains undecidable.

The work of registration

During the first stage the processes are transposed on to sensory perceptions of tangible realities capable of affording sensations and ideational contents. These tangible material realities are the somatic body and the objects of the outside world. Unconscious processes use these tangible realities and differentiate them into traces and thing-presentations in order to register the drives in the mind in the form of cathexes. The quality of the work of these processes is reflected in sensations and affects. The cathexes and their qualities are oriented towards consciousness, the body and objects. They form the basis of all thought-contents. The transposition onto the somatic body and onto "others" in the outside world is transformed thanks to the operation of après-coup into libidinal cathexes of the body and objects. The sensual and erotogenic body, as well as objects themselves, are thus grounded. This brings us back to the teleology of psychic work with the imperatives that support its outcome.

Freud called this first stage of processuality, consisting of the work of transposition, restraint, registration and cathexis, libidinal sympathetic excitation, without specifying the operations that are involved in it. Instead, he theorized in an innovative and brilliant way those involved in dream-work, displacement, condensation, representability and secondary revision.

The mechanisms involved in the process of libidinal sympathetic excitation are carried out every night under the guise of the dream-work, which conceals them. Only their result, libidinal regeneration, is accessible. This libidinal sympathetic excitation is more directly recognizable in the erotic scene, which exalts sensual regression in two ways; one strives towards reducing tensions to zero and the other seeks infinite extension. The exaltation of the extension of ecstatic enjoyment has a limit, orgasm as a reduction of tension. Erogenous sensitivity comes up against the lock of refractory sensitivity, which turns out to be a form of reality-testing. The elementary drive tendency to extinction, common to these two modalities, is confronted with another reality that is heterogeneous to it, an imperative of registration that promotes psychic work. It is this ordeal that is avoided by the majority of religions through abstinence and mystical assumption.

The first mission of thought-processes is to counter the extinctive tendency of the drives by establishing a restraint and registration of the drives in the id and by cathecting them in the body and objects. Part of these cathexes will be desexualized and provide the grounding for narcissism, together with sensibility and psychic contents. To carry out this project, unconscious processes are transposed onto external reality and use the classic mechanism of anti-traumatic clinging to tangible perceptions. This clinging is accompanied by a denial of perceptions of lack. This allows for the development and differentiation of the immense field of ideational contents, affects and sensations, in particular those of a sensual and erogenous nature. These first operations at the source offer almost infinite possibilities to the psyche to carry out the condensations and displacements characteristic of the primary process.

The work of lack

Thought-processes must take into account these extinctive attractions, a reality that is at first immobilized during the first stage of the operation of après-coup due to the denial of the perception of the external realities of lack. This immobilization sets up primal repression. Their dynamics unfold during a second stage using the materials made during the first stage from tangible realities. These materials are obviously not specific to the extinctive tendencies; on the contrary, they are heterogeneous to them.

There are therefore two realities that are heterogeneous to each other, one of which serves to conceal the other, but also serves to take it into account on the psychic level. The importance that Freud gives to the mechanism of distortion (*Entstellung*), to the point of using this term in the title of chapter 4 of *The Interpretation of Dreams* (Freud, 1900), and then of considering it as his only and authentic discovery (Freud, 1923a), is thus explained. These two heterogeneous realities, the extinctive tendency and the imperative of registration, are carried over into the reality of sensory perceptions and, in particular, that of the anatomical difference between the sexes. The expression "difference between the sexes" uses the name of the material supports of transposition, the two sexes and their difference, to denote the theoretical complexity that combines the two modalities of extinction and the imperative of registration that opposes it. We have already discussed the fact that this difference breaks down into two pairs of differences. A first pairing links two terms of tangible reality, the masculine and the feminine. The other pairing links the two heterogeneous realities, what is tangible and what is missing, the endowed and the unendowed. The absence of a penis on the female body is the prototype of the reality of lack that correlates with the extinctive tendency, while the presence of the penis is used by that ensuring registrations. The existence of representations and sensibility is proof of the operative nature of the imperatives of restraint and registration.

The two paths of anxiety meet and combine here, one leading to the inorganic and the other exalting the infinite. The work that the mind must carry out to counter these two modalities of extinctive tendency may be called the work of lack. To accomplish this, it uses a reality that is heterogeneous to it, that of ideational contents and sentient experiences, in order to saturate consciousness and deny the very existence of lack. Finally, it theorizes the threat of their disappearance and their absence in terms of castration.

The extinctive tendency, through reduction to the inorganic (death drive) and infinite extension (life drive), is transposed onto perceptions of unrepresentable realities, disappearances as a result of absence and destruction, but also disappearances as a result of assumption, abstraction and transcendence. These perceptions are accompanied by various sensations, such as fright, terror, anxiety and distress, but also elation, fervour and trance.

Human thought is thus composed of two dimensions, that which refers directly to what is tangible, visible and sensitive, and that which uses the contents resulting from tangible realities to account for what is perceived and felt as a lack. A distinction is therefore to be made between the work of registration and the work of lack.

Lack and reality-testing

Because the foundational operations of human thought use the materiality of the somatic body and the world of things to establish themselves, a stage of ignorance of these transpositional supports precedes any access to their recognition. The relationship to sensory reality is further complicated if we take into account that the reality of lack, as perceived through differences, requires specific psychic work that uses materials derived from the perception of tangible realities. *Reality-testing* therefore turns out to be particularly complex and uncertain, whereas it is implicitly involved when we speak of knowledge, science, scientific knowledge and research, including psychoanalytic research.

The difficulty in accomplishing the psychic work required by the internal extinctive experience presents various stumbling blocks. One of them is to resort to destructiveness, another is to make everything equivalent (the post-truth of the 21st century), instead of being able to bear the experience of ordinary feelings of lack (modesty and humility). This is how the follies of grandeur unfold, which are, in fact, follies of exhaustion.

These solutions bypass the process of reality-testing and rush to define what is reality and what is not. Causal theories are urgently produced in order to provide representable scenarios that are supposed to explain the existence of lacks. False links are thus established between the traumatic extinctive tendency and the sensory perceptions of lack, interpreted as the result of destruction. Theories of the destructive drive find their origin here.

Another solution consists in creating an equivalence between sensory perceptions of external realities and psychic productions in the mode of perceptual identity. The perceived lack becomes a production of the mind, identical to that experienced. There is then only one reality, as in dreams, that created by the mind. Scenarios of lack then have to fulfil unconscious desires. The dream of the butcher's wife (Freud, 1900, pp. 147–149), also called the dream of the beautiful butcher's wife (Lacan, 1998, p. 365), is a very fine illustration of this. Other solutions also rely on equivalence. For example, the reduction to a factual quality of the differences perceived in the external world in order to neutralize any correlation between them and the drive tendency of extinction.

Reality-testing follows a temporality in two stages, that of the operation of après-coup. The tendency to extinction induces a state of latency, and the imperative of restraint and registration constrains requires a regressive work of latency. This diphasic process has the value of recognizing the extinctive tendency and the obligation of having to carry out a work of lack. Likewise, both individual and group integration of any novelty requires, insofar as it creates a difference, a similar diphasic process of elaboration. Major scientific journals like *Science* or *Nature* know that when erroneous information with a strong emotional or imaginative impact is disseminated as scientific fact by the media to the general public, it then takes about 10 years to rectify it.

The creation of equivalences and causalities

Equivalence came to light with the 21st century, to be precise in 2002–2003 with the notion of "post-truth," in a highly charged traumatic context (the attack on the Twin Towers). It had been used to support suspicions, accusations and justifications for the Iraq War (the third Gulf War waged by Bush and justified by Iraq's so-called biological weapons). Since then, the notion of post-truth has taken on a mass dimension and has been enriched by a constellation of terms relating to negationism, such as "alternative facts," "fake news," "hoax," "brain-washing," etc. How can we fail to think that this negativistic logic has also extended to scientific and psychoanalytic research. Freud (1933a) had already mentioned it in his 35th lecture, "The Question of a *Weltanschauung*" from the standpoint of nihilism.

Having been used 2,000 percent more often than the previous year, the term *post-truth* was voted 2016 Word of the Year by the editors of the *Oxford Dictionary*, to the point of describing the beginning of the 21st century as a "post-truth era" and "post-factual era." All these formulas spread in 2016 during the referendum campaigns on the United Kingdom's membership in the European Union (Brexit), and the American presidential elections; and more recently in Europe, where they gave rise to the establishment of committees responsible for verifying information. A general atmosphere of suspicion of propaganda has spread based on facts of enunciation at the expense of any other reference system.

The *Oxford Dictionary* defines the term *post-truth* thus: "that which refers to circumstances in which objective facts have less influence in shaping public opinion than appeals to emotion and personal opinions."

These notions had already appeared in the past under other terms, such as lie, error, fiction, hoax, falsification, imposture, usurpation, mystification and, of course, propaganda. The mental functioning to which it testifies had remained in abeyance as virtuality in the name of a certain degree of moral guilt and an ideal of truth. The revelation of a psychic mode of functioning that had hitherto been repressed is commonly observed in analytic sessions. It is one of the functions of interpretation to reveal unconscious identities that had been completely unnoticed hitherto but involved in the symptomatology.

Falsification was particularly used in the 20th century by propaganda and by anticipatory novels in the form of plausible fiction. George Orwell's novel *Nineteen Eighty-Four* and Newspeak naturally come to mind here.

The virtuality of this equivalence was at the heart of the debate that animated French psychoanalysis between the recomposition of a past (Pasche, 1974), the registration of which is to be consolidated from indices of reality, based on traces and endogenous sensations form part, and the construction of a past (Viderman, 1977), the advent of which is realized as a response to a need for restraint. Two theories of "returns" and two theories of the unconscious, both present in Freud, are then defended, that of a productive unconscious and that of a historical unconscious.

The equivalence is dialectized with the process of differentiation to which any scientific approach refers. Awareness is the basis of the latter. The causalities and equivalences thus created must first be made conscious and then subjected to the test of awareness of the function they fulfil, that of opposing the regressive attractions (Lambertucci-Mann, 2018).

This allows us to appreciate the "beautiful differences" that were so dear to Freud (Letter to Groddeck dated June 5, 1917, in Groddeck (1977)).

The production of causalities and equivalences is therefore part of the work of lack and of psychic responses to the question of *differences*. The creation of infantile causal theories attempts to deny the existence of differences per se with conceptions that support the fact that those differences have been produced. As for equivalence, it attempts to neutralize the effect produced by the differences by reducing them.

Both of these methods support the narcissism of small differences by attenuating the traumatic factor inherent in all differences. They are part of the *complex of differences* and participate in the *work of lack*.

Equivalence is particularly used by the psychic functioning that we call collective psychology, mass psychology or group mentality. These constellations are busy suppressing the traumatic effect by denying differences. But equivalence is also at the basis of analytical listening for a completely different purpose. Evenly suspended listening accords equal attention to all the patient's associations, which from this point of view become equivalent. This approach is taken up by analysands. By its very method, psychoanalysis therefore offers support for equivalence and the latter offers them the possibility of avoiding the conflicting issues of shame, guilt and moral pain that result from the difference made between Oedipal cathexes and object-cathexes. Equivalence tries to escape the psychic work of renunciation and mourning.

Frequently the session is extended to the outside world. This becomes a huge continuous session. A unique world is promoted according to the model of the dream. On waking, a conflict arises between preserving the equivalence or differentiating among infantile, Oedipal and object cathexes. As pointed out above, this psychic dynamic characterizes the collective dimension and its use of denial. The facts of words, sensory realities and endogenous realities remain undifferentiated. Let me emphasize that for the psychoanalytic method, this way of evading the issue is a technical strategy, a detour that, on the model of the martial arts, uses as a means to achieve its aims the path opposed to the desired goal. The fundamental rule and listening erase differences and remove renunciations in order to better make their necessity felt from within.

If we add to this tactic the relativism that accompanies the notion of interpretation and that of the unconscious, we can easily see how psychoanalysis can participate in this confusion, and how it can be used for such a goal! It is about making all facts equivalent by placing them under the tutelage of one and the same reference, enunciation. All facts are then enunciated facts that all become equivalent.

A three-step process emerges. The facts are first relativized in the name of the subjectivity of all perception; they become potential errors to be rectified. Then an equivalence is established between facts and discourses; indeed, the facts of perception only gain access to psychic material through the involvement of language. They thus also become facts of discourse. The interplay between monosemy and polysemy testifies to the two identities specific to all reality. Finally, the fact of speech is imposed as being the unique proven fact, the truth.

The second step, that of equating facts and discourse, is overdetermined by the goal of the third, that of imposing a conviction. In so doing, it is in fact a question of denying the differences between the various categories of facts, those of perception, deduction and enunciation. By this denial of differences, it is a question of denying lack and the extinctive drive tendency.

Reality-testing and the recognition of differences

Such a process bypasses all reality-testing, which is replaced by a conviction.

The term *reality-testing* appeared in Freud's writings in 1911 in "Formulations on the Two Principles of Mental Functioning" (Freud, 1911a), and was deployed in 1916–1917 in "A Metapsychological Supplement to the Theory of Dreams" (Freud, 1917). It is therefore one of the great institutions of the self. Previously, reality-testing on waking up was presupposed. Analysis was supposed to perfect it thanks to its main tool, interpretation. Making conscious was equivalent to becoming conscious. The purpose of interpretation was to reveal an unconscious reality and, by taking it into account, to achieve recognition of external reality and the difference between psychic reality and sensory reality. Interpretation was a wake-up call. But from 1923 (Freud, 1923a) onwards, the automaticity between enunciation and becoming conscious was called into question. Language was essential but no longer a sufficient guarantee. By its very nature, it helps to support denial. This deconstruction continued in 1925 and 1926 (Freud, 1925, 1926) by questioning the function of interpretation and its relationship to judgement. To illustrate this development, it suffices to compare what Freud states in "'Wild' Psycho-analysis" (Freud, 1910) and in "The Question of Lay Analysis" (Freud, 1926). In 1910, technical errors were of little importance compared with the truth of the content of the interpretation, which always prevailed despite the resistances and clumsiness of the analyst. In 1926, he had his impartial interlocutor exclaim: "Interpret! A nasty word!" and he continues, "I dislike the sound of it; it robs me of all certainty. If everything depends on my interpretation, who can guarantee that I interpret right? So after all everything is left to my caprice" (Freud, 1926, p. 219).

In 1923 he recognized that the hypercathexis of words can be used to impose a reality built on the basis of denying another part of reality. We are familiar with Freud's play on words between truth and reality, when he asserts that, in the case of a hypercathexis of thought, thoughts are held to be true (Freud, 1923a, p. 23). Then in 1937, the upheaval in thinking about interpretation continued with the link made between construction and conviction, and therefore between theory, belief and ideology. Finally in 1939, the differentiating function of language and its role in reality-testing was reaffirmed, even though the theorization of reality-testing test was not completed. He emphasizes that differentiation requires a period of abeyance or latency. Reality-testing takes time and an initial submission to unconscious psychic realities. It is only in the future that the discrimination between realities can become clear.

The gap between 1900 and 1939 relates to the notion of loss of reality. In 1900, the unconscious brought new realities that relegated conscious realities into the background. In 1915, the unconscious took hold of psychic realities thus rendered unavailable. In 1924, loss was approached through the denial of sensory realities and the regressive pull of extinctive tendencies. Symptoms, as well as distortions and neo-constructions, then have the role of replacing what is lacking and of saturating consciousness so that the lack cannot return. This dynamic of loss and construction is specific to dreams, psychoses, beliefs and ideologies. It also concerns analytical treatment through the castration complex, with its threat and reality. The last words of the unfinished work *An Outline of Psychoanalysis* (Freud, 1940) concern castration as a loss and the role of the superego in the work that this requires. The superego can be seen as the agency that guarantees the consideration of all realities, including that of extinctive tendencies. The stumbling blocks of reality-testing are therefore to be correlated with fluctuations of the superego and the operations of renunciation that characterize it.

This debate about reality-testing is obviously not restricted to psychoanalysis. Many citations could be used to show this; for example, the most recent one by Cédric Villani (2011) (Fields Medal):

The mathematician looks like a character from Arthurian legend, condemned by a strange fate to admire the world only through abstract reflection. Unable to face blinding reality, he scrutinizes this reflection down to the smallest detail, caresses it and explores it with his thought and logical reasoning. ... For the mathematician, who seeks to get to the bottom of things, even familiar gestures are imbued with an unfathomable, disheartening mystery. But mischievous mathematics makes a reflection of it so improbably beautiful, so apparently understandable, that the mathematician, the willing victim of a magnificent lie, falls each time in love with the reflection he explores.

(pp. 114–115)

This citation puts subjectivity and the needs of the researcher's mental apparatus at the forefront. Science emerges as the progeny of hysteria, with the notions of truth, reality, lies, delusion, reasoning, logic and the state of love. Mathematical objects are neither objects that are accessible by direct sensory perception nor productions relating to psychic reality such as phantasies. They attempt to account for concreteness, which should also be recognized in the operations specific to the reality of the mind, a reality not to be confused with what we call psychic reality. In "The Acquisition and Control of Fire," Freud (1932a) differentiated three realms: the realm of phantasy (desire), the realm of history (identifications) and the realm of physiology (psychic processuality and its laws). The psyche has its cunning tricks of phantasy to cover up the fact that it is grappling with physiological and historical necessities.

Created by the mind, metapsychological objects become real by finding their place in the field of reality while retaining their dimension of virtuality. They represent the materiality of psychic processes accessible only through their tangible effects. At the same time, they fall within the field of the unknowable in itself and of pure theorization and speculation.

Freud took up a position on this point very early on. Reality, whether it is the reality transmitted by the sensory organs or that which is projected from the inside onto the internal screen of consciousness, our sixth organ of the senses, belongs to the register of the unknowable. Within the mind there are two modes of reality, the psychic reality characterized by the infinity of its imaginary possibilities, which escape any reality index, and the reality of the mind that is subject to the limitations of its laws and the necessities which it must obey. Let us recall the famous Freudian metaphor of 1931 about incompatibility: a man cannot urinate and have an erection at the same time (Freud 1932a, pp. 192–193).

The fact that all reality is unknowable does not prevent science from existing, even if its discourse can be conceived as metaphorical and evolutive. Discrimination between realities is necessary. Freud never ceased to differentiate them; for example, inorganic, organic, psychic and germinal realities. Other differentiations can be proposed by following the notions of tangibility, virtuality and lack, but also those of deductibility, inference, contradiction, incompatibility as well as those of theorization, speculation and abstraction. There is no science without a process of theorizing, and without the precession of a process of theorizing, imagination and speculation. Psychoanalysis modifies the definition of science by integrating, through the recognition of this precession, interpretation and speculation. It is in this way that it can share the status of a scientific subject with other fields. Science includes interpretation and speculation.

These remarks simply take up in a more contemporary way the classical, Platonic and Aristotelian elements of knowledge conceived as the result of an interpretation; interpretation of things perceived by the sense organs for Plato; interpretation linked to linguistic enunciation for Aristotle. Psychoanalysis offers another approach based on the interpretation of unconscious wishes, a fundamental drive tendency and procedural requirement. Various realities can then be understood: the unconscious, psychic reality, the reality of the mind and the realities of the external world, the body included.

None of these interpretive approaches call into question the existence of realities. Kant underlined that approaches to reality are marked by the prism of the subjectivity of the researcher. Then Bachelard included the researcher-observer in the reality approached. It depends on the conditions of observation, in which the observer is included. Scientific statements designate realities that exist in a context of observation; hence, an infinite number of approaches are possible. This is exactly what the psychoanalyst experiences in his daily work.

On the other hand, the point of view asserting that reality does not exist outside the observational context, or even that perception is created by the subject, posits that unknowable reality does not exist independently of the context. It can then be argued that this reality is created by observation itself, by sensoriality or by denomination. If we take this one step further it is the observer who creates the observed fact. The perception or deduction of facts is then only a construction that depends solely on the mind of the one who provides a theory-fiction of them. This point of view ascribes a primary role to unconscious phantasy and to the perceptual identity produced by hallucination.

This was not Freud's position; he believed in the existence of perceptions, realities and facts independent of observation, even though they are inherently inaccessible and unknowable in themselves.

Psychoanalysis includes the instinctual drives and unconscious psychic processes, but also the mechanism of denial and the psychic work of distortion required due to the extinctive tendency and its effect of lack.

It is therefore possible to distinguish truth from reality. Truth is a myth that seeks to establish the world on the basis of psychic registrations alone and denies the existence of a missing registration, that of the extinctive tendency. Truth is libidinal in essence, while reality includes tendencies that are dissimilar to libido. Like dreams, myth transforms all realities into libidinal realities, and it makes lack the fulfilment of an unconscious wish.

The conception of a demiurge researcher is based on the search for a truth stemming from a libidinal conception of the psychic life that seeks only to register and fulfil and is free from any extinctive tendency. This quest for truth often calls upon the effect of beauty to reinforce the truth effect; hence, the aestheticization that we have already encountered with the citation from Villani. The poet asserts it even more simply: "Whatever is created by the spirit is more alive than the matter" (Baudelaire, 1851). Indeed, matter contains reality, which produces its own disappearance.

This aestheticization is an attempt to make people forget extinctive reality by proposing a world comprised of a single reality instead of the two heterogeneous ones considered above. The reality of lack presents itself again, along with the use of tangible reality either to deny the latter or to take it into account. On a pragmatic level, we are reminded here of the gap between psychoanalytic work in direct contact with the associations of a physically present patient and the work of applied psychoanalysis realized in an article or a book. This distinction evokes another between psychoanalysis and psychotherapy. The latter supports the libidinal dimension against the reality of lack, while the former takes into account the function of libidinal cathexes vis-à-vis extinctive reality. The perception of aesthetic human creations makes it possible to alleviate the work of lack and the demands linked to the perception of differences.

An evocative example is that of the poetic names given to quarks by physicists. They are taken from James Joyce's great work, *Finnegan's Wake*. The quarks have been divided into six "flavours." The English names remain the most used: Up, Down; Strange, Charm; Beauty (Bottom), Truth (Top).

The same logic applies to the names given to spaceships, for example those for missions to Mars: Spirit, Phoenix, Opportunity, Curiosity, Insight, Perseverance, Ingenuity, etc.

Libidinal cathexis and perception

The complexity of the relationship to perception did not escape Freud. The notion of perceptual identity inherent to the theory of dreams bears witness to this; later Winnicott's formula of the "found-created" also alludes to it.

I have already discussed the mechanism of transposing unconscious realities onto sensory perceptions of external reality and the body, and also that of clinging to perceptions of tangible reality. I added a distinction between *perception* and *perceptual activity*. The first is transmitted through the sense organs, which give immediate awareness of the world without any real internalized knowledge of it. As for *perceptual activity*, it arises from the capacity of the mind to create *perceptual identities* through hallucinatory activity, to the point of no longer being aware of the gap that exists between sensory perception and hallucinatory perception. Confusion frequently exists, especially when waking up and falling asleep. This confusion is at the root of animistic thinking (Botella, 2005). The reference to day and night is not sufficient to distinguish with certainty the perception of sensorial stimuli passively received by the sense organs and the perceptual activity entirely created by the use of traces and ideational material. The contents produced in the mode of perceptual identity are liable to saturate temporarily the internal face of the screen of consciousness. As in dreams, they are accompanied by the conviction that there is only libidinal reality. Perceptual activity limits and attenuates, and even removes and eliminates, any experience of lack. This is the most subtle capacity of the psychic apparatus. With the dream of the butcher's wife (Freud, 1900, pp. 147–149), I recall how the psyche is able to use lack to accomplish a hallucinatory wish-fulfilment. Hysterical identification is based on a common unconscious wish, an Oedipal wish, and on the ability through hallucination to fulfill this wish by evoking a lack.

Reality-testing thus turns out to be very uncertain. Several types of realities overlap on both sides of the screen of consciousness. Psychic reality has no tangible material substrate and is involved in various functions, such as hallucinatory wish-fulfillment and the anti-cathexis of the extinctive tendency. Perceptual identity finds its place between the sensory field related to external reality and a libidinal field forming the basis of truth. "Phantasy" has an intrapsychic function that gives thought-processes a materiality value.

These remarks show that the notions of facts and reality have been completely called into question by psychoanalysis. But this increased complexity has also been supported by other sciences; for example, quantum theories with the notion of decoherence.

We must admit that what we call perception is an amalgam that is tricky to deconstruct. The work of differentiation carried out by reality-testing remains a mystery. Any epistemological reflection on science, and therefore on psychoanalysis, must take into account the existence of such differences, but also the fact that they are submerged in necessary amalgams produced by the psyche.

Our experience of analysis teaches us that sensory perceptions induce an awakening of the unconscious internal world that is capable of taking possession of them in order to remain unconscious. We also know that the decrease in perceptions promotes an awakening of regressive psychic contents.

In a more complex way, the internal psychic world needs to carry out psychic work in order to co-opt perceptions encountered by chance, in the form of ideational material and sensations, while unconscious tendencies and processes are constantly being transposed onto the external world in order to use it to differentiate themselves. This transposition onto perceptions of tangible reality serves as a restraint on extinctive tendency, while the perception of lacks via differences awakes it; hence, the clinging to the tangible perceptions and the denial of differences.

Awakening is the site of a conflict between all these realities, between a quest for the object of the drive and the advent of the lost object. To escape this conflict, one solution is to cathect daytime objects with passion. They become transference supports of a quest for the object of the drive and the object of the ideal. Another solution is to hate the world of objects on waking up. External realities are renounced to avoid renouncing drive qualities. With hate, another stumbling block appears for the superego, destruction and eradicating murder.

Destructiveness and the fluctuations of the super ego

"Man has within him a lust for hatred and destruction. In normal times this passion exists in a latent state, it emerges only in unusual circumstances; but it is a comparatively easy task to call it into play and raise it to the power of collective psychosis," of "psychoses of hate and destructiveness" (Freud, 1933b, p. 201).

This sentence cited by Freud was written by Einstein, but it could have been written by a psychoanalyst. It postulates a constitutional destructive impulse, a need to destroy that must be countered by psychic activity and is always ready to take advantage of the shortcomings of the latter in order to flourish. This conception postulates a Manichean struggle and a process of constantly taming this need to destroy.

Einstein wrote it in his letter to Freud in 1932 in order to seek, in the name of the United Nations, his participation in reflecting on a crucial question: "Is there any way of delivering mankind from the menace of war?" a question underpinned by pragmatic concerns: can humanity be saved from its destructive and ultimately self-destructive tendencies? Einstein regarded destructiveness as a basic instinctual drive disposition against which it was necessary to set up an international, supra-state political organization tasked with arbitrating conflicts between states. The creation of this organization, Freud writes, involves "the unconditional surrender by every nation, in a certain measure, of its liberty of action, its sovereignty that is to say" (Freud, 1933b, p. 200). Note the introduction of the notion of renunciation in response to the vicissitudes of destructiveness within groups.

We are familiar with Freud's text, *Why War?* in response to Einstein, in which he turns resolutely towards the individual psyche; hence, his doubt concerning the possibility of an international organization preventing wars. Since such an organization can only be run by human beings, their mental functioning would have to be exempt from any affective factors, and further they would have to subordinate their instinctual life to the "dictatorship of reason" (ibid., p. 213). They would have to be, as it were, supermen, thus inhuman, a Nietzschean notion derived from an idealization based on a denial of reality that requires psychic work to be undertaken regularly. This reality that makes men human is the extinctive tendency of the drives, which stands in correlation with the perception of castration and finds expression in feelings of terror, anxiety and lack. The work of lack is never definitive, and, according to the words of the poet, it "is never acquired by man" (Aragon, 1944). It is regularly required and marked by fluctuations. We have already encountered this idealization in the expression "love of truth," frequently set in contrast by Freud with "the recognition of reality" and best illustrated by Josef Popper-Lynkeus's (1899) short story "Dreaming like Waking." Freud's commentaries, in his two short texts of 1923 (Freud, 1923b) and 1932 (Freud, 1932b) give a good account of the seduction that such an ideal promising infinite assumption can exert.

In *Why War?* Freud does not directly discuss the conception adopted by Einstein, but he differentiates the destructive tendencies and the drive that "is at work within every living creature and is striving to bring him to ruin and to reduce life to its original condition of inanimate matter. Thus it quite seriously deserves to be called a death instinct" (Freud, 1933b, p. 211). In a quandary, he did not envisage destruction via the path of idealization that expresses a tendency to infinite extension to the point of extinction, a tendency that can define the life drive (Chervet, 2021). Every quest for the Grail that is not transformed into a wish for expansion is self-defeating and, for the masses, a way of destroying civilization and the world.

Freud states that the destructive drive arises when the death drive is turned outwards onto objects with the help of the musculature, while another portion of the death drive remains within the organism. But he says nothing about the risk of harm that determines this turning round of the drive, or about the positive functions of the death drive maintained within. Nor does he envisage a turning round of the life drive towards the outside in connection with the harm produced by infinite expansion.

In 1920, in *Beyond the Pleasure Principle*, he recognized that the two basic drives, the life drive and the death drive, are characterized by their tendency to return to an earlier state, even back to the inorganic, inanimate state. This tendency to extinction is easy to understand where the death drive is concerned. It occurs by means of reduction and retraction. For the life drive, the logic is different because the term *Eros* refers to the propensity to create ever greater unities, thus an expansive tendency. Consequently, the earlier state could easily be thought of as a primitive integrity. But Freud did not follow either Empedocles, for whom Love seeks to restore Spheros disturbed by Strife, or Plato and his primordial hermaphrodism that desire seeks to restore. If we cease to attribute Eros with conservative qualities that belong in fact to narcissism, the life drive can be defined as an infinite extensive tendency that also leads to extinction, and not to preservation. Writing in water leaves no trace of registration. Clinical situations involving idealizations and passions are the pathological manifestation of this.

Each of the two elementary drives has an effect on the other. The death drive prevents the infinite extension of the life drive by stabilizing psychic contents, and the life drive impedes the reduction of the death drive by favouring an evolving dynamic. This results in a logic of reciprocal restraint with the production of materials that are both stable and evolving. Two stumbling blocks emerge: immobility and evasion. It is necessary, therefore, to reflect on this twofold work of restraint. Clinical experience controverts the solution of a homeostatic equilibrium between the two modes of extinction. As Freud (1937a) points out himself, the development of sexuality is not completed with the solution of bisexuality. Drive duality results in an obligation to make an object-choice. This was why Freud (1923a) introduced into the theory an agency responsible for choices and renunciations, namely, the superego.

As Eros has neither a function of preservation nor of registration, a measure of restraint is necessary towards the reduction of the death drive and towards the extension of the life drive, by using the qualities of reduction and extension of each of the elementary drives. The extensive lability of the libido must be reduced and registered as psychic libido within the id, the great reservoir of the libido; a portion of this sexual libido will have to be desexualized into narcissistic libido; then Oedipal object-cathexes will have to be mourned in order to enrich object-related desires.

Life results from such renunciations of extinction. These renunciations have the significance of *foundational murders* (Chervet, 2015).

Under the guise of this imperative of renunciation, a double restraint is thus set up. It is responsible for a libidinal tension that grounds the economy of the id. This tension produces primary masochism, the *masochism of restraint*. It subsequently becomes erotogenic by means of a bodily conversion that replaces masochistic tension by the pleasure of desiring.

Thanks to masochistic restraint, extinctive regressivity is changed into various forms of regression, the formal regression of dreams, the sensual regression of erotic life, the incidental regression of sessions. The tendency to extinction explains the need for the psyche to submit regularly to such regressions of mentalization, nocturnal and diurnal. This masochism at the origin of psychic life is unsustainable in the long term. Such growing tension would promote extinction. Even the anchorites who take up the challenge add auto-sadism to it. Primary masochism must open itself up to other fates; for example, that of sadism, which offers the solution of sexual ecstasy with a regression to refractory sensitivity that resists extinctive tendencies; but also that of desexualization, which produces all the modes of psychic registration. Denise Braunschweig (1971) derives the recognition of reality from the sublimation of masochism. Sublimating the masochism of restraint helps to recognize the reality of extinctive regressivity and lack; sublimating sadism, the discovery and knowledge of external realities.

At the heart of this economic tension, the traumatic tendency to return to an earlier state constantly manifests itself. The turning round of the drive towards the outside allows for the anti-traumatic utilization of the perceptions of tangible material objects and perceptual traces. The first anti-cathexis, brought about by an immobilization of the libidinal economy made possible thanks to the stimulus barrier, is then replaced by dynamic psychic work producing psychic contents. It now becomes clearer how the stimulus barrier operates. Thanks to a fixation to the perception of tangible realities, it denies the perceptions of lack and immobilizes the drive tendencies to extinction. The two phases, immobilization and the production of cathexes, belong to the operation of après-coup.

The orientation of the elementary drives towards the outside is induced by an inner necessity that finds its way by relying on the sensations produced by the mother's ministrations in infancy. This dynamic of transposition is at the origin of the transference in analytic sessions. Psychic processes can only become operative through transposition, by being supported by those of another person and by identifying with them. This is the chief role of the *Nebenmensch* (Freud (1950 [1895]. This identification is that of the "father in [the subject's] personal prehistory" (Freud, 1923a, p. 31). It is an identification with the model of the processuality of another human being.

All transference is thus the vehicle of two elementary tendencies, reduction and extension, and ambivalence towards the superego imperative to carry out the psychic work required by these tendencies towards extinction. It contains the potentiality not only of future renunciations but also resistances to them. What is involved here is the conflict between respecting or eliminating the superego imperative.

Destructiveness and cruelty appear in this context of ambivalence towards the work required by the extinctive tendencies. Destructive acts then take place towards objects and the subject's own body. It is a matter of destroying in order to stop the inexorable disorganization due to retraction or expansion. In these threatening contexts, these destructive acts can occur in the service of conservation and safekeeping. The act of destruction therefore has the function of preserving life by destroying an extraneous person or a part of one's own body. It becomes a drive of mastery or fundamental violence (Bergeret, 2007).

Anyone who refers to masochism is also referring to sadism. Sadism is another vicissitude of the orientation of the extinctive tendencies towards the outside, along the path of sexuality. But it does not form a symmetrical pair of opposites with primary masochism. There exists a precession of the masochism of restraint, which is the first mode of the masochism of renunciation. It is the basis of everything that is called thought and mentalization. The restraint to which it is linked has the function of countering the extinctive tendency.

In his text on war, Freud points out that the harm to sexuality occasioned by the process of evolution of culture can stir up catastrophic reversals for humanity. As Freud (1933b) writes: "It may perhaps be leading to the extinction of the human race, for in more than one way it impairs the sexual function" (p. 214).

The evolution of civilization calls for a destructive reversal owing to this impairment of sexuality. Einstein's response therefore depends on the place left to sexuality by the evolution of civilization. The superego must assume responsibility for an oscillation between civilization and eroticism, just as it has integrated that between night and day.

Instead of dwelling on an external political authority governing groups and masses, Freud focuses on the internal politics of the mind governed by superego imperatives. The advent of moral conscience, thus of judgement and the superego, comes about as a result of a re-internalization of the elementary tendencies transposed initially on to external perceptions. The politics of the mind is governed by an agency responsible for two reversals that result in qualitative modifications of the drive. These two stages of the operation of après-coup take into consideration the traumatic extinctive tendency. Destructiveness is the sign of a stumbling block in the advent of the second stage.

Consequently, Freud was able to set aside the question raised by Einstein. The concern about how to prevent war was replaced by another: "Why do you and I and so many other people rebel so violently against war? Why do we not accept it as another of the many painful calamities of life? After all it seems to be quite a natural thing, to have a good biological basis and in practice to be scarcely avoidable?" (Freud, 1933b, p. 213).

Freud was thus raising the question of the origin in the superego of the rebellion that made Einstein and himself "pacifists": "We cannot help doing so. We are pacifists because we are obliged to be for organic reasons" (p. 214). Further on he adds: "This is not merely an intellectual and emotional repudiation; we pacifists have a constitutional intolerance of war, an idiosyncracy magnified, as it were, to the highest degree" (p. 215).

With the term *organic reasons* he is referring to the "process of evolution of culture" arising from a renunciation of the direct satisfaction of drive aims, an inhibition of aims, thus an imperative of cultural development that is at the origin of the emergence of moral conscience and the advent of the superego. Pacifism and rebellion against destruction prove to be gains resulting from the resolution of the Oedipus complex, as are modesty, disgust and remorse, all signs of a superego that is the heir of this resolution. In his remarks on pacifism, Freud speaks of a superego that, once acquired, is held to be stable to the point of becoming constitutional and not subject to variations and stumbling blocks. But the end of his letter is intriguing due to the movement that emerges in favour of the cultural ideal. He expresses the hope that "the rest of mankind will become pacifists too" (Freud, 1933b, p. 215), that is, that they will resolve their Oedipal complex and establish their superego. An uncertainty appears, then, concerning this aim. Freud then asserts in the form of a credo: "whatever fosters the growth of civilization works at the same time against war" (ibid.)

This profession of faith idealizes the process of acculturation and overrides the assertion made a few lines before that cultural development may lead to the extinction of the species.

Thus, by attributing cultural development alone with the capacity of protecting mankind against war, Freud very clearly places priority on the superego imperative turned towards the cultural ideal, and he neglects the unconscious guilt towards the drive produced by all cultural development. The notion of impairment for sexuality leads us to recognize that a real superego ensures the oscillation between civilization and eroticism. The superego must support access to an erotic life, which offers, through orgasm, a specific satisfaction of the extinctive tendency that has just died on the shore of what is refractory. It ensures the oscillation between sensual regression and cultural gains by means of desexualization.

This affirmation of an established pacifism and this ideal attributed to cultural development reveal an incomplete conception of the superego. The latter is, in fact, subject to oscillations that are favourable to its various functions, progressive and regressive. It contains an imperative to mourn idealizations, which is the object of hate, and of a murder for the benefit of the extinctive tendencies. Thus, we find again, formulated in metapsychological terms, the assertions of the Oedipus complex, an inaugural murder that gives free rein to incestuous longings and leads to partial or total castration. Sexualization and castration are the consequences of the elimination of the superego, of its murder.

Destructiveness is thus the sign of a disorganization of the mind following a reversal of the demand for mentalization, an eviction on which group and mass destruction is based. It reveals either a failure in the very establishment of the superego or its temporary elimination; hence, Melanie Klein's and Lacan's formulations concerning the archaic superego and the obscene and cruel superego. In preserving the term *superego* in these formulations, they follow the oscillatory and regressive logics of the superego in order to designate occurrences where the aim is to eliminate some of its functions by means of murder. It would therefore be more exact to speak of obscenity and cruelty in situations where the superego has not been established or has been eliminated. This fragility of the superego forms the background against which the forms of destruction enacted by groups and masses are exalted. It is in this sense that Freud denounced an illusion, one of a superego that can offer a stable dictatorship backed up by reason. This is an idealization that has not been mourned.

In fact, the superego offers capacities for regression that make it possible to realize all the regressive forms of psychic work, in particular the regressive psychic activities of passivity, for example the dream-work thanks to censorship, the work of libidinal sympathetic excitation and libidinal regeneration thanks to the stimulus barrier and the work of setting up the operation of après-coup thanks to the fundamental rule.

Casting a glance back to the formulations prior to 1920 allows us to compare post-1920 destructiveness with the 1900 notion of castration and to bring destructiveness into relation with the indestructibility of unconscious desire, which can then be understood as an anti-cathexis against extinctive tendencies. Repression takes on a new intelligibility. It is a compromise, a preservative mechanism of reduction, just as putting something into dormancy brings about a reversible disappearance.

Castration is evocative of mythical figures, of terror and conjuration, the castration of Uranos by Cronos and the apotropaism of Medusa's head (Freud, 1922).

At the level of theory we have a constellation of concepts: castration anxiety and its complex, with its two stages and its theories; the reality of castration as a perception awakening the traumatic feelings related to all differences; the enactment of castration in the form of numerous acts of destruction – ever since Oedipus's eyes – all referring in the unconscious to one and the same prototype, the loss of the thing-presentation "penis" representing every libidinal cathexis. All acts of destruction are correlated in the unconscious with this prototype. The erasure of the penis in the unconscious portrays maximal sexual enjoyment with its strong attracting power. Schreber (Freud, 1911b) enacts such a transformation giving access to absolute sexual enjoyment. His delusion calls to mind Tiresias's evaluation concerning women's sexual enjoyment compared to that of men. These are infantile sexual theories linking disappearance and sexual enjoyment. According to these theories of denial, cutting or severance is the precondition for gaining access to supreme sexual enjoyment and erasure the sign that such enjoyment is ongoing. This correlation between sexual enjoyment, extinction and castration is present in the use that Lacan makes of the term *jouissance*.

This threat of a loss of cathexes becomes a reality in *Beyond the Pleasure Principle* (1920) through the tendency to return to an earlier state, even back to the inorganic state. It now becomes possible to follow the kernel of truth contained in castration theories. They are based on the reality of a regression leading to extinction, an extinctive regressivity that is characteristic of every drive. The term *castration* takes account of the transposition onto the body of this regressive tendency towards extinction, recognized in the difference between the sexes, that is, in the absence of a penis on a girl's body. Sexual theories are therefore a response to frightening extinction (punitive castration) and to the powerful regressive attraction until extinction (extreme sexual enjoyment). This theorization of castration is derived from a foundational murder of mentalization.

Metapsychology must theorize the suppression of cathexis, the destruction of objects to be cathected or already cathected, whether they are external objects, the subject's own body or psychic objects, and the extinction of cathexis itself, at its source.

Painful acts of destruction, but also sadism, are vicissitudes of hate. However, the sadist and the masochist form a couple. They enjoy satisfactions that they both bring each other. Sadomasochism abandons all destructive purposes. This couple is built on the primary masochism that precedes the development of the sadomasochism couple.

Hate appears in two guises: hate for what is new and creates differences and hate aimed at defending what has been acquired. Hate is, in fact, awakened by any difference introduced by a new object insofar as this object requires an activity of cathexis, which involves a deconstruction of what has been acquired in order to integrate what is new. The seductive effect of what introduces new differences goes hand in hand with the tendency to resexualize all the already existing cathexes. Every seduction calls into question the narcissistic equilibrium, requires psychic work and triggers hate. This ordinary hate becomes murderous when the refusal to carry out the work of integration of the new differences dominate. It then turns into destructiveness and supports an accusatory theory and a denial of what gave rise to it.

Destroying a tangible object can be conceived as an act whose aim is to fulfil an anti-traumatic function. The destruction covers over the extinctive aim and fuels the theory that what is lacking has been destroyed. The key issue at stake concerns the work of restraint at the drive source, work that is of foundational importance for cathexes and their registration within the psyche.

Given the absence of any representation of lack, the cathexis of its reality continually tends to disappear, hence the resumption of thought-processes that have the function of countering the attraction to extinction. The focus of our considerations is then on the imperative of restraint and registration on which every act of mentalization is based, restraint that is at the origin of the masochism of renunciation.

This imperative to carry out a work of mentalization is the object of a conflict that is experienced in the form of guilt, guilt about not carrying out this work, and, contrary to unconscious guilt towards the drive, is linked to the realization of this work. It is this superego-related guilt that Freud (1916) is concerned with when he considers the sense of guilt of criminals. Such a scenario is familiar to children who seek punishment for a minor misdemeanor, thereby concealing a psychic work that has not been carried out at the level of their Oedipal cathexes. On the other hand, it is drive-related guilt that foments the negative therapeutic reaction, mental degradations and also cultural breakdowns.

I have referred on several occasions to group and mass psychology. Mass psychology offers regressivity and hate, vicissitudes outside mentalization. Acts of mass destruction permit modes of extinction that have no common measure with private acts of destruction. A lone individual can commit serial crimes, but not genocide, which can only be generated by mass idealizations and theorizations. Genocide is based on the belief that the total eradication of a people, in whole or in part, can permanently exterminate feelings of lack, which then return from the outside through those eradicated.

The above remarks help us to think again about notions such as attacks on linking, the drive for mastery, fundamental violence, and other theorizations inspired by Melanie Klein, for whom drive duality is a constant war between two noisy entities, one that generates children while the other devours them. At the heart of such conceptions, anxiety is the sign of the defeat of Eros. This model moves away from Freud's conception of the drives as a regressive tendency leading to extinction, which is involved in experiences of terror and anxiety. It is necessary therefore to distinguish between destruction, decathexis, erasure and the extinction that precedes every cathexis.

Destruction is a solution found by the psyche when the work of renunciation of drive extinction, a foundational work of the mind, is defective; in fact, when the oscillations between the various progressive and regressive psychic activities do not occur satisfactorily, between the dream-work, the session work, the interpretive work, the work of mourning, the work of culture and so on. This defect is our common lot, hence the irreducible tension between superego-related guilt and drive-related guilt, both of which are turned into guilt towards the object. This conflict confers on the superego and its imperatives a great deal of fragility and unpredictability, which have repercussions on the result of the operation of après-coup. When this operation unfolds satisfactorily, the best sign of its success is the unpredictability of the content of its result. This is the case for dream-contents and the quality of the bonus of desire on waking up.

The embedded operation of après-coup and the foundational murder

Unpredictability is the most precious quality of a successful operation of après-coup. It is the reflection of the production of a *bonus of desire* free of any content and open to diversity. The uncertainty of this bonus justifies the existence of psychoanalysis. The operations for which the processual imperative is the guarantee still need to be explored more deeply, while taking into account the fact that this uncertainty stems from the imperative itself. There is nothing less certain and stable than the superego!

The unpredictability and irrationality of the different kinds of logic involved in the operation of après-coup lie in the fact that they are subject to realities of a radically heterogeneous and incompatible nature, the extinctive regressivity of the two elementary drives, on the one hand, and the imperatives of restraint and registration, as well as elaboration and resolution, on the other. These imperatives are related to an ideal of mental functioning oriented by the teleology of psychic life, that is, the capacity to present its psychic formations on the screen of consciousness and to produce a bonus of desire that is open to the multiple vicissitudes linked to the infinite diversity of the world. The complete accomplishment of this operation depends on the imperative of *resolution* specific to the superego. Freud likens this resolution of the Oedipus complex to the terms destruction and decline to which he attributes a biological determination with the metaphor of the loss of milk teeth. But he also recognizes the fundamental ambivalence related to carrying out this resolution. The operation involved is a *murder* that is foundational as soon as it concerns the drive qualities that it utilizes and transforms. This murder is the specific operation of the superego, one which grounds hypercathexes. It plays a role in the unfolding of the operation of après-coup by means of the diverse imperatives that intervene throughout this operation and which are required to unite and work together under the aegis of the agency of the superego.

Depending on whether this murder occurs under the aegis of the superego imperative and concerns the drive or whether it concerns the imperative itself and gives free rein to the extinctive regressivity of the drives, several vicissitudes will emerge.

The first concerns the creation and growth of psychic life; such a murder is then foundational for the mind, for drive functioning itself, for thought and desire.

The second, that which avoids psychic work and the imperatives, results in eradications and annihilations, even leading to a disorganization of the drive source itself.

Another vicissitude is that of the murder of the object supporting transposition. Here we can recognize the eliminating murder classically described as Oedipal, but also that of *Totem and Taboo* (Freud, 1912–1913) concerning the *primitive father* with its cycle of guilt: expiation, reparation, re-erection, obedience after the event. This murder combines the two aspects of the eliminating murder and the foundational murder. This orientation of the murder towards the *other* of transposition has consequences for the place accorded to the object in analytic work and in the theory. A relationalization of metapsychology may appear. The wish realized by theory is then to never separate from the object. Thinking about psychic life undergoes a shift towards intersubjectivity. The support of transposition is taken for the drive impulse and the imperative of registration, the object for the model. Within this line of theorization, the object is already-there and no longer an identity that has to be acquired and that depends on a mode of cathexis described as object-related.

The ambivalence between the foundational murder and the eliminating murder is transferred onto objects that serve as supports for transposition. Each parent is a transpositional support for the ambivalence of resolution discussed above. He or she becomes in turn a seducer of transgressive resexualization and a firm and tender parent promoting the growth of his or her child, and assumes the double identity of an imperative promoter or liquidator. The foundational murderous act is in conflict with the Oedipal murder.

Another solution for avoiding the imperatives to carry out psychic work concerns the value of castration, depending on whether it is recognized as a loss of reality, as a figure of ecstatic enjoyment or denied as a reality. In this last case regressive work does not take place. The productions utilized to reinforce denial are regressive reminiscences cathected in the progressive direction. Their main aim is to support the progressive orientation and not to modify the regressive economy. The tendency to extinction becomes a discharge through the body and the external world. There is then neither restraint nor regression nor a period of latency. The operation of murder seeks to establish a state of continuity ensuring the denial of the perceptions of lack. The operation of après-coup is replaced by monophasic psychic work that utilizes mnemic materials without modifying their economy. In "Constructions in Analysis," Freud (1937b) stresses that such a solution is involved in beliefs and private delusional beliefs, in constructions and collective ideologies. He points out that psychoanalytic interpretation can also be used with the same aim. All these progressive productions serve to saturate consciousness in such a way that the regressive attraction is not felt. The denial of external lack completes this saturation.

The complete fulfilment of the operation of après-coup is the mark that castration, that is to say feelings of lack that are noticeable through sensoriality and their correlation with the feelings of the tendency to extinction, have truly been taken into account at a psychic level. The mere turning round of regressive longings into progressive discharges cannot be equated with an accomplishment of the operation of après-coup. It is only the oscillation of the psychic work related to the resolution of the tendencies to extinction by a modification of the regressive economy that is the mark of the reality of the *foundational murder*. Feelings of lack as well as feelings of satisfaction arise from this.

How is the ambivalence between the two kinds of murder resolved? How is it decided on which side the scales will tip? The intensity of the attractions towards extinction is matched by the power of the imperatives. In the best of cases, it is the long path of psychic registration that prevails, and then gives way in the face of somatic extinction. The identificatory history of each of us intervenes in very varied ways in the solutions to the conflict between these two vicissitudes. The choice is never unequivocal. Psyches are organized into fragmented topographies.

The foundational murder promotes libidinal regeneration and cathexes of the body and the external world thanks to libidinal sympathetic excitation. It is active in the desexualization of a portion of the drive cathexes and allows sexual libido to be turned into narcissistic libido. We can also find it at work in the mourning of Oedipal objects in favour of libidinal object-cathexes. It is operative during each of these stages and whenever a new object is cathected. It is involved in the appropriation of each element within psychic functioning as a whole. It grounds the partial and global aspects of thought. It is required by the various imperatives that form the basis of the multiplicity of part-cathexes, and by the superego that brings them together under its aegis into a whole that is not a unity. This is what gives the operation of après-coup its fractal configuration and an embedded constellation.

Castration has its place at the heart of this conflict of ambivalence concerning renunciation, between the eradicating murder and the foundational murder. The threat of castration acquires its significance from being a call to recathect the imperative of resolution. The *call to the father* in the primal phantasy of *castration by the father* has its positive significance here.

Thus the resolution that establishes the superego and psychic processes is an oscillation that involves renunciation and cannot be reduced to all or nothing, nor to what is partial or what is completed. This oscillation rests on two imperatives, an *imperative of regression* permitting the economic generativity and regressive psychic activities of the hallucinatory and sensorial pole and an *imperative of progression* leading to the mourning of libidinally cathected objects. These two imperatives are the seat of a conflict between accepting not to follow transgressive extinctive logic and renouncing resolution by avoiding the imperatives and denying the sensory realities that recall the tendencies to extinction. Renunciation and murder are the objects of the same ambivalence.

Foundational murder and renunciation

The foundational murder is the key operation of renunciations. It is operative at all levels of the processuality involved in thought; hence, the connection between thought and unconscious guilt and the tendency of superego demands to be reversed. The emergence of unconscious shame follows from this. The non-transgressive outcome of this reversal through unconscious guilt is the nycthemeral oscillation of day and night. On the other hand, hypersomnia is a clinical sign of unconscious shame.

The uncertainty hanging over the realization of the operation of après-coup obliges the mind to find materials it can use to help it carry out the economic and foundational operations that are inherent to it. It will draw help from the perception of tangible materials and, above all, from the tracing that goes with them. I have mentioned several times the role of perception and of the stimulus barrier in this function of tracing. As perception is inevitable, except during sensory deafferentation, which is not viable for any length of time, the work of the stimulus barrier is indispensable for limiting continuous amounts of stimuli and fostering tangible realities that give rise to traces at the expense of the realities of lack, which remain without traces. Perceptual traces can be transformed into memory traces and thing-presentations, which acquire a high degree of plasticity and pliability, making it possible to overcome the dilemma between imprint (*everything is written*) and erasure (*writing in water*).

The clinical experience of tattooing and scarifications, irreversible traces and scars created voluntarily, expresses the conjurative and apotropaic interest that exists between tracing and the missing trace. The traumatic sources of the ordinary use of makeup, concealed behind the reversibility of games of seduction, can also be found here.

All psychic work has its place within the operation of après-coup, which constitutes the common reference of all the modalities of work. This operation is obliged to realize itself according to two specific *moments* of work: first, a regressive work of restraint and registration and, subsequently, a progressive work of presentation and awareness. The results of the psychic work are *overdetermined* by the imperative to accomplish the operation of après-coup, by the identificatory history that made it possible for the processes to be established and by the contingency of the sought-found circumstantial realities that are used in order to achieve these two moments.

I have already emphasized the need for a transposition onto a supporting object and onto the value of the response of this object. The detour via another human being (*Nebenmensch*) capable of responding to terror and distress outlines the trajectory of the advent of the object. The other helping person of primary care generously lets him or herself be used as an object supporting processuality. The detour via this processual object and the identification with the model of its processuality are at the origin of the object itself. The notion of a primary object is wrong from the point of view of metapsychology. It considers the result acquired before its realization and objectalizes prematurely the *other of processuality* in order to assert the certainty of its presence and to deny its absences, its shortcomings and failures, as well as the vicissitudes of its advent.

The purpose of psychic work is neither the object nor language, but rather consciousness and the availability of cathexes. The realization of this purpose requires the utilisation of the body, the object and language, the three spaces of transposition and transference. The object arises from this detour of transposition: language, from the obligation to encode; the erotogenic body, from the conversion of affects and endogenous feelings. The object is therefore the definitive form of the *other of processuality* as a *by-product*.

For mentalization to occur, it *must* therefore be supported by the operative processuality of another person. Indeed, the role of primary identification is the appropriation of an ideal model of functioning.

This need for the operative force of another processuality is so important that when the infant does not find it, he looks for it in the concrete materiality of this other in relationship to whom he is alienated, or in that of another perceivable reality of tangible consistency, onto which he will cling desperately in order to find a bit of this reliability and tangibility that he needs.

Children with autism show us how the *other of processuality* can be replaced by a piece of hard matter, plastic, wood or string, which are then animated by the child himself through stereotyped frenetic contact. The attempt to save the primordial processual operations from imminent extinction is directly noticeable here. They hang on the thread of stereotypy and the consistency of matter, the laws of which function as a code.

The most fundamental feeling is not distress but terror, which is destined to become the tragic experience of *feeling that one is disappearing from oneself*. Distress is a secondary affect expressing the lack of means a subject has to deal with this traumatic terror he experiences due to the extinctive tendency. Our clinical work will vary depending on whether we consider distress or terror as first; our conception of psychic life and metapsychology will not be the same either. The response to distress is the vehicle of a processuality on which processual identification can rely in order to overcome the experience of terror. In concrete reality, the gap between terror and distress is thus not so great as in theory.

Processuality has a value of material consistency. But it is *more* than materiality, just as mourning is *more* than a repression. So what did Freud mean when he wrote of the "destruction" of the Oedipus complex?

The extreme recourses show us not only the force of negativization stemming from extinctive regressivity, but also the varying power of the repercussions promoted by the processual imperative involved in the elaboration of all clinical formations, even the most desperate ones. This power to realize a work of psychic registration, and the uncertainty of its outcome, is present in all the clinical pictures encountered.

Responsible and not guilty; the cunning tricks of psyche

One of the vignettes presented in chapter 4 offers us a very particular occurrence of this combination. Through her treatments and her sessions, Mrs. X used medical and psychoanalytic institutions to reanimate her suspended biological functions. She instrumentalized their protocols to achieve her aim of having a child. She teaches us something that is both ordinary and strange, namely that a subject can seek, find and use a processuality provided by an institution without constructing or appropriating the psychic processes that would make her independent of it. Freud (1923c) describes the case of the painter Haizmann and religious institutions. Mrs. X combines medical and psychoanalytic institutions.

This possibility of using the functions of a superego assumed by an institution is, in fact, a very frequent occurrence that needs to be taken into account when evaluating the endings of psychoanalytic treatments with regard to the capacity to do without the institutional basis. It is very difficult to differentiate between what is appropriated by an individual and what is borne by the external institution. The success of the notion of *setting* is the best reflection of this tricky differentiation.

Very often, it is only subsequently that such an evaluation can be made. Humans created institutions because they know how difficult it is to construct and sustain internal processualities.

This occurrence is also ordinarily accessible in the state of love, which has the capacity to reveal the potentialities of a subject. It also exists during the honeymoon periods of some analyses. A precipitated transference leads to an apparent recovery, even though we know that the work still remains to be done. While this interplay between the outside, delegation, support and appropriation is a familiar one, the evaluation of the role played by each of them can only be made retrospectively.

The fact that it is possible to use an equivalent or external stand-in for the superego without constructing an individual superego, whether personalized, cultural or interpersonal, obliges us to think about our place in the institutions that surround us, psychoanalytic included. And it is when these are lacking that their role is recognizable.

With Mrs. X, we are witnesses to a compromise of *responsibility*. An act can be accomplished without appropriating the means permitting it, and thus without having to bear guilt for the foundational murder; the question remains of the guilt concerning this lack of appropriation, thus concerning the superego itself.

Processual identification can occur with or without appropriation, with or without renunciation. Our acts can be overdetermined by this appropriation or carried out without it. They then become behaviours.

Guilt about responsibility is linked to this appropriation. Hence the temptation to avoid it by instrumentalizing institutions. Guilt then appears for not having taken responsibility. Guilt navigates between Scylla and Charybdis.

From this we can conclude that processual identification, whose ideal outcome is the establishment of the superego, can lead to an identification with or without a renunciation of the drive tendencies to extinction, which is reflected by an absence of mourning of the object and the institution that served as a support. Identification is a regressive form of the impersonal superego. It presents itself to us with its *power* and its *uncertainty*, its materiality and its fragility, its plasticity and its lability. Resistances against the operation of après-coup are confronted with the resistance (solidity) of the operation of après-coup. Therapeutic work consists in changing this conflict of resistance into dynamic and productive consistency.

A preconception of processuality exists, which explains Mrs. X's approach. No one suggested to her that she should see a psychoanalyst. Someone who is devoid of efficient processuality may in spite of everything be able to recognize its existence in another person or in an institution. Mrs. X found support in one of her sisters who was in analysis. She was thus able to embody her precession transference without leaving behind her childhood constellation.

Elementary processual operations are already there in the form of preconceptions, capable of being transposed on to external realities without necessarily becoming intrapsychic realities. Our profession requires us to be these transpositional supports. Can we facilitate their appropriation? It has to be admitted that sometimes processuality only exists during the time of the sessions. The dilemma between acquisition and influence continues, as do questions concerning the interminability and efficiency of the foundational murder. How can the latter be integrated as the content and agent of interpretation?

The foundational murder and posthumous events

Throughout this book one notion has remained in the background, even though it appeared in Freud's work at the same time as he described the operation of après-coup. It is involved in the production of unconscious formations and in the constructions that use the repressed as materials and that confer upon them their portion of historical reality. It is the notion of *posthumous* that I am particularly interested in here, for it is not a matter of murder or resurrection but rather of repression. Admittedly, repression is analogous with a murder in that it entails a disappearance. Repressing is a way not only of avoiding extinction and of conserving, but also of remaining in a state of incompletion with regard to the imperative of registration.

The portion of truth in Freud's choice of the term *posthumous* is therefore to be sought in its content. Repression is directed towards the operation of murder and also the return. Although Freud did not say that the content concerned processual operations, he warned us against the error of sexualizing repression as Fliess had done. For Fliess, repression rested on an alignment between bisexuality and biological sex.

Freud's reminder is important at the theoretical level and also from the standpoint of therapeutic work. The psychoanalytic act – interpretation and construction – is not a sexual act. The word *posthumous* refers to the pair inhume/exhume. The principle of therapeutics cannot therefore be sexuality, even if it is the content of the inhumation/exhumation. The psychic act rests on the activity of processes and on their specific operation, the foundational murder.

While the superego is responsible for the desexualization that establishes narcissism, it is first involved in the restraint that is opposed to extinction. Through its action it plays a role in the creation of instinctual drive impulses, in the desexualization promoting narcissism, and in the mourning of Oedipal objects. The notion of posthumous helps to clarify the fact that the aetiology of a symptom is not only sexuality, but also the processes involved in it.

The notion of posthumous followed the same fate as that of the term *après-coup*. It disappeared on a manifest level while remaining implicit in the conception of biphasic psychic functioning, and in the fact that the work carried out during the second stage makes use of the contents of the first stage.

This notion also has its place in phylogenetic thought through the murder of the father and its effects of overdetermination in civilization. The texts of Freud that give the murder of the father a role in the birth of social life, culture, morality, group mentality and civilization all deal with psychic processes themselves.

The word *posthumous* has two etymological sources. One arises directly from the roots of the word, the other from homophonic contagiousness. The Latin word *postumus* means last and was altered by *humus*, giving rise to posthumous. But it is the evolution of meaning that I am interested in. The meaning of *postumus* changed from last to last born. Then, through condensation, *postumus* referred to *the last child born after the father's death*. Posthumous therefore refers to the subsequent result of a repression related to the father's death. This term refers, certainly, to a content but first and foremost to psychic operations themselves, those that we have already discussed from the angle of murder, the elimination of the superego imperative and the foundational intervention of this imperative in the quality of the drives. Freud retained these two meanings by thinking of the operation of après-coup as a generative process, with a repressed first murder and then a second promoting a manifest result. In order to serve as a foundational act for registrations, the murder carried out by psychic processes must occur in two stages. The first is repressed and the second brings about a return of the first, transformed by virtue of the interval period between them. This detour via the etymology of the word *posthumous* enacts a process provoked by any contact with the reality of death, namely, that of psychically inducing an investigation that serves as restraint. Freud's work can be read as a long and meticulous investigation into murder. Beginning with the myth of Oedipus, the plague of Thebes requires an investigation, which is the deferred effect of the murder. It is also the means by which healing occurs. At the end of his life Freud investigated the murder of Moses. Later, Lacan followed this same logic with "The Purloined Letter" of E. Poe.

With the murder of the father and the subsequent investigation, an entire line of thinking in Freud's work emerged, that of phylogenesis. In 1900, it was the Oedipus complex with the murder of the father of personal history, a murder that opened wide the path of transgressive regression towards incest and its inevitable outcome, castration. Freud discusses this murder under the auspices of the universality of the generic processes of human thought. In 1911–1912, it was the primal Father of *Totem and Taboo* who was the object of murder with the genesis of social organization and civilized morality under the effect of guilt. The murder of the father and his restoration are repeated in turn. In 1923 and 1924, murder was involved in the process of mourning the father; hence, the resolution of the Oedipus complex and the establishment of its heir, the superego. Freud introduced a nuance of great importance. Murder is foundational for identifications and concerns the parents (Freud, 1923a, pp. 31–32). The paternal became an agency and murder an impersonal internal operation. In 1938, Freud offered us his "historical novel" *Moses and Monotheism* (1939). In this text, the act of murder and its repression are more important than the object of the murder. What makes its return are consequences, remains and fossils attracting the act itself. Freud gives circumcision as an example; we may add stigmata and crucifixion. It is this foundational murder that is responsible for the guilt linked to the spiritualization of the mind.

Moses and Monotheism is the novel that bears witness to the dynamic of après-coup in Freud's own work, a novel that reveals and recognizes murder as a crucial mental operation that is involved in all psychic acts and that takes place in several stages punctuated by repression and posthumous events. Freud thought of monotheism as the deferred effect of a two-stage operation that required two murders.

Psychoanalysis comes across as a theory of thought based on foundational acts of murder, which may turn into eliminating murders. The theoretical language used by Freud accounted for this well before murder became an object and an element of metapsychology.

Our study of the operation of après-coup has enriched our understanding by showing that the operation of après-coup conceals a series of murders that are consubstantial with its realization. The term *murder* denotes the processual operation par excellence, the primordial psychic act. This grounds the first act of restraint, establishes narcissism and promotes the desire for objects. In fact, it unfolds in several stages and registers what is irreversible in the psyche. This quality is specific to the superego.

The aim of the superego imperative is to promote the regression-progression oscillation and, above all, to index the realization of both of them with a degree of irreversibility. The libido of the superego is a libido conveying such irreversibility. Murder acts through the intermediary of this libido of renunciation of irreversible effects.

Reversibility, timelessness and irresponsibility belong to the factors of phantasy and imagination in psychic reality. But this is a fundamental part of the psychic operations that are characterized by irreversibility, temporality and responsibility. Oscillation occurs between these two registers, offering a fortunate attenuation of the extinctive tendency, the traumatic reality that is expressed in the tragic dimension of human life.

We have seen that processuality in two stages and the two murders that characterize it have the particularity of already being there as a potentiality, and further that their realization requires that it has its place within a contingent historicity. The potentiality that is already there is a mixture of the biology of the mind and the identificatory inheritance. A theory of psychic transmission emerges in which biology and the historical inheritance of identifications are interwoven. A collective history enacted in the past changes into psychic potentiality, which itself changes into a new reality with the support of a new singular history. The history of the two murders inherent to the operation of après-coup organizes transmission. This is Freud's legacy to us.

But what becomes of the libido specific to these operations of murder required by superego imperatives when it is not *used* by psychic work? Illness and horror then risk becoming the masks of terror. We are thus faced with new enigmas. What is the future that the current operation of après-coup, that in which we are living now, is preparing for us? What traumatic past is it in the process of modifying so that it can once again give us this bonus of freedom, which will have to open itself to disappointment once it has travelled the path of illusion and been obliged to give it up over and over again?

References

Aragon, L. (1944). Il n'y a pas d'amour heureux. In *La Diane française*. Paris: Seghers.
Baudelaire, C. (1851). *Fusées; mon cœur mis à nu*. Paris: Gallimard, 2016.
Bergeret, J. (2007). *La violence fondamentale: L'inépuisable Œdipe*. Paris: Dunod.
Botella, C. S. (2005/2001). *The Work of Figurability: Mental States without Representation*, trans. Andrew Weller. London: Routledge.
Braunschweig, D. (1971). Psychanalyse et réalité: À propos de la théorie de la technique psychanalytique. *Revue Française de Psychanalyse*, 35 (5–6): 655–828.
Chervet, B. (2015). *Le meurtre fondateur: L'acte psychique par excellence*. Paris: Presses Universitaires de France.
Chervet, B. (2021). L'envie et l'infinie extension de la pulsion de vie. *Revue Française de Psychanalyse*, 85(3): 679–699.
Freud, S. (1900). *The Interpretation of Dreams. S.E. 4 and 5*. London: Hogarth, pp. 1–621.
Freud, S. (1910). 'Wild' Psycho-analysis. *S.E. 11*. London: Hogarth, pp. 221–227.
Freud, S. (1911a). Formulations on the Two Principles of Mental Functioning. *S.E. 12*. London: Hogarth, pp. 218–226.
Freud, S. (1911b). Psychoanalytic Notes on an Autobiographical Account of a Case of Paranoia. *S.E. 12*. London: Hogarth, pp. 1–82.
Freud, S. (1912–1913). *Totem and Taboo. S.E. 13*. London: Hogarth, pp. 1–161.
Freud, S. (1916). Some Character-Types Met with in Psychoanalytic Work. *S.E. 14*. London: Hogarth, pp. 218–226.
Freud, S. (1917). A Metapsychological Supplement to the Theory of Dreams *S.E. 14*. London: Hogarth, pp. 222–235.
Freud, S. (1920). *Beyond the Pleasure Principle. S.E. 18*. London: Hogarth, pp. 1–64.
Freud, S. (1922). Medusa's Head. *S.E. 18*. London: Hogarth, pp. 273–274.
Freud, S. (1923a). *The Ego and the Id. S.E. 19*. London: Hogarth, pp. 3–66.
Freud, S. (1923b). Josef Popper-Lynkeus and the Theory of Dreams. *S.E. 19*. London: Hogarth, pp. 261–263.
Freud, S. (1923c). A Seventeenth-Century Demonological Neurosis. *S.E. 19*. London: Hogarth, pp. 72–105.
Freud, S. (1925). Negation. *S. E. 19*. London: Hogarth, pp. 233–239.
Freud, S. (1926). *The Question of Lay Analysis. S. E. 20*. London: Hogarth, pp. 183–258.
Freud, S. (1932a). The Acquisition and Control of Fire *S.E. 22*. London: Hogarth, pp. 187–193.
Freud, S. (1932b). My Contact with Josef Popper-Lynkeus. *S.E. 22*. London: Hogarth, pp. 219–224.
Freud, S. (1933a). *New Introductory Lectures on Psycho-Analysis. S.E. 22*. London: Hogarth, pp. 1–182.
Freud, S. (1933b). Why War? *S.E. 22*. London: Hogarth, pp. 195–215.
Freud, S. (1937a). *Analysis Terminable and Interminable. S.E. 23*. London: Hogarth, pp. 209–253.
Freud, S. (1937b). *Constructions in Analysis. S.E. 23*. London: Hogarth, pp. 255–269.
Freud, S. (1939). *Moses and Monotheism*. London: Hogarth, pp. 1–138.
Freud, S. (1940 [1938]). *An Outline of Psychoanalysis. S.E. 23*. London: Hogarth, pp. 139–208.
Freud, S. (1950 [1895]). *Project for a Scientific Psychology. S.E. 1*. London: Hogarth, pp. 281–397.

Groddeck, G. (1977).*Ça et moi: Lettres à Freud, Ferenczi et quelques autres*. Paris: Gallimard.
Lacan, J. (1998). *Séminaire V, Les formations de l'inconscient*. Paris: Seuil.
Lambertucci Mann, S. (2018). Vicissitudes des transformations psychiques. Le travail de déformation. *Revue Française de Psychanalyse*, 82 (5): 1237–1299.
Pasche, F. (1974). Le passé recomposé. *Revue Française de Psychanalyse*, 38 (2–3): 171–182.
Popper-Lynkeus, J. (1899). Traümen wie wachen (Dreaming like waking). In: *Phantasien eines realisten*. Vienna: Alpha Buchhandel.
Viderman, S. (1977). *La construction de l'espace analytique 2: Le céleste et le sublunaire*. Paris: Presses Universitaires de France.
Villani, C. (2011). La matematica è stata un amante difficile. *La Recherche*, 457: 114–115.

Index

abstraction 27, 117, 126, 172, 193, 223
acoustic hallucinations 89–91
adolescence 182–183
affect 2, 11, 36, 50, 190, 219–220
amnesia, infantile 182
analytic après-coup 63–65, 75, 111–113, 136; *see also* clinical situations
analytic object 64
animism 23, 58, 64–65, 79–80, 100–101, 121, 158, 159, 168
anti-cathexis 10, 36–37, 39, 42
anxiety 7, 38, 39, 46, 61, 63, 190, 210–211; automatic 62; castration- 16, 190, 194
après-coup 2, 5–8, 12, 14, 23–24, 26, 31, 80, 88, 95, 115, 145, 165, 189, 192, 198, 203–207, 216–217, 251–255, 259; amount of 37–38; analytic 63–65, 75, 79, 111–113, 136; biphasic operation 71, 74, 81–82, 124–125, 127, 130–131, 148; castration 34–35, 184–185; castration-anxiety and 16; complexity of 122, 128; connection with the superego 75; double reversal 146, 166, 191, 231; elusiveness of 122, 126, 128; French conception of 66; Freud's conceptions of its operation 47–51; in Freud's process of theorization 41–43; Lacan's conception of 55–56, 57–60; moments 134; palliative 108–111; renunciation 138, 139; *see also* renunciation; resolvent path 66; return 15–17, 135–136, 140; sequential dreams 91–93; sexuality and 38–41, 187–188, 195; shock 28–29, 36–37, 39, 57; stage 1 135–137; stage 2 137; temporalities 138–139; theorization and 75–76; translation 18, 21–22; unconscious guilt 35
association(s) 33, 111, 125; free- 79, 80, 116, 131, 136, 157
associative remembering 29, 41
automatic anxiety 62
avoidance 38

belief 44–46
Berger, D. 18
beyond the pleasure principle 58, 62, 116, 119, 134–135, 144–146, 159
bidirectionality of thought 145–147
Bion, W. R. 62, 189; *Language of Achievement* 63; "O" 152
biphasism 71, 74, 81–82, 124–125, 127; of thought 147–148
Bleger, J. 156, 157
Braunschweig, D. 35, 166, 213, 245
breakdown 63–64; fear of 65
Breuer, J. 28, 30, 136, 154, 169

Carroll, L. 176, 221
castration 31, 35, 36–37, 40–42, 45, 52–53, 60, 77, 101, 119, 121, 124–128, 132, 176, 182, 196, 248–249, 252–253; -anxiety 16, 190, 194; -causality 194; denial of 196–197; -phantasy 194; in psychoanalysis 191–194; -reality 194
castration complex 34, 184–185, 191, 193; things seen and heard 185–187
cathartic retrogression 30, 135
cathexis 23, 38, 44, 47, 63, 78, 130, 137, 139, 153, 249; anti- 10, 36–37, 42; de- 77; hyper 57, 83, 132, 140, 147, 151, 158, 161, 223, 229; libidinal 64, 241–242; object- 184; sexual 39–40

causality 14, 31, 56–57, 128, 130, 135, 194, 235–237; castration- 194; *see also* deferred effects
Charcot, J.-M. 28, 29, 56, 134–137, 150, 154, 169
childhood sexuality 181
children and childhood: memories 31–32; play 64, 81; sensuality 201
chimera 64, 158
clinical situations 73, 84–90; analytic après-coup 63–65, 75, 78–79; biphasism and repetition 81–82; countertransference 95–97; deferred effects 80; deferred effects of defective identifications 104–108; dream of the dropped baby 82–83; enactment of "successive analyses" 82; fundamental rule 79–80; palliative operation of après-coup 108–111; sequential dreams 91–93; session animism 101–102
compulsion 194
condensation of dreams 172
confidentiality 73
consciousness 1–2, 4, 130, 137, 152, 158, 223; saturation 174–177, 178; speech and 2–3
continuity 131–132
conversion 151, 189, 202–203, 218–219
cooptation 209
counter-shock 116, 129
countertransference 71, 73, 95–97, 113, 136
coup 18, 129
Cournut, J. 51

dandyism 98–99
Darwinism 145–146
death drive 50, 61–62, 173, 179, 224, 226–228, 244
decathexis 77
decoherence 170
"deferred" 19–20
deferred effects 30, 33, 37, 43, 45, 49, 56, 65, 74, 78, 87, 89, 117, 122, 147; of defective identifications 104–108; neo-identities 97–98; perceptual saturation 98–99
deferred obedience 44
denial 23, 35, 44, 46, 48, 53, 71–72, 75–78, 121–122, 131, 132, 138, 139, 168, 186, 197, 248–249; of castration 196–197; reversible 42; role in the sleep-dream system 78–79, 212, 214; sensory perception and 77, 166; symbiosis 157; temporary 42
desexualization 182–183
desire 1–3, 5, 8–11, 42, 44, 48, 72, 73, 93, 119, 125, 146, 153, 169, 201; erotic 120; overdetermination 9–10; return of the repressed 6; unconscious 7
destructiveness 243, 246, 248–250, 255
Diderot, D., *The Indiscreet Jewels* 120
difference 27, 101, 125, 126, 207, 222, 236; perception of 6–7, 76–77; recognition of 237, 241; between the sexes 7, 16, 35, 48, 56, 76–77, 98, 101, 102, 119, 164, 192, 194, 233
diphasism 188; of human sexuality 181–184
discourse 52, 79, 80
distortion 5, 18, 29, 46, 48, 75, 103, 121, 131, 148, 207, 216, 219
distress 61–62, 255; *see also* anxiety
Donnet, J.-L. 51, 65, 164–165; *L'enfant de ça* 66–67
double transference 88
dreams and dreaming 2, 3, 10, 29, 40, 42, 72, 82–83, 124, 133, 150, 168, 169–170, 173–174, 178–179; anti-traumatic function 164; childhood memories and 31–32; condensation of 172; distortion 75, 148, 207; functions 78, 171–173; as guardian of sleep 171; interpretation 4, 73, 133–134, 173–174; "murder" 87–89, 94–95; novelty and 6–7; as psychosis 164–165; quest for 116; saturation 158, 163–164; sequential 91–93; "Three Fates" 32–34; wish-fulfillment 172, 177; *see also* interpretation; memory
dream-work 1, 2, 7, 31, 61, 72, 75, 78, 80, 81, 87, 89, 94–95, 101, 121, 125, 127, 131, 134, 159, 163, 172, 174; decoherence 170; quantum decoherence 170; wish-fulfillment 165, 175; *see also* interpretation
drive(s) 1, 2, 4–6, 11, 29, 37, 39, 40, 46, 47–48, 52, 55, 100, 122, 126, 128, 198; conversion 151; death 50, 61–62, 173, 179, 224, 226–228, 244; duality 198; infantile sexuality 22, 31, 48, 128, 129, 153, 181–184, 188, 216; intra- 118–119; life 61–62, 173, 224–228; registers 83, 163; regressivity 10, 16–17, 41, 43–44, 57, 63, 66, 78, 135, 145, 195; renunciation 5; theory of the 122–123, 129–130; thing-presentations

55; working-through 22–23; *see also* extinctive tendency; regression and regressivity

early impressions 139, 211
ego 39, 44, 55, 72, 210; ideal 52–53
Einstein, A. 76, 176–177, 243
Emma 14, 16, 28, 29, 46, 83, 134, 169; scene I 135–136, 137, 140, 181; scene II 135–137, 139–140, 181
encoding 150, 152
endogenous impressions 40
endogenous perception 76
English translation of Freud 19–20
equivalence 235–237
Erasmus, D. 120
erogeneity 44, 202–205, 226; *see also* sexuality
erogenous body, emergence of 197–205
erogenous zones 203–204
Eros 50, 61, 224–225, 244–245
erotic desire 2, 120, 136, 203
ethics 73
evenly suspended attention 79–80, 157–158
extinction 5, 36, 190; renunciation 8
extinctive regressivity 1, 16, 17, 22–23, 44, 46, 48, 50, 60, 64, 75, 84, 122, 123, 126, 128, 129, 132, 135, 146, 147, 182, 197, 217–222, 224–229; *see also* drive(s)
extinctive tendency 7, 94, 97, 100, 101, 116, 119, 121, 166, 168, 222

Faimberg, H. 51, 65
Fain, M. 51, 166, 213
father complex, deferred obedience 44
fear of breakdown 65
feelings 220–221
femininity, castration and 196
Ferenczi, S., *Thalassa* 49
fetishism 45, 46, 83
Fliess, W. 28, 154, 257
forgetting and forgetfulness 1, 147; of the analyst 71–72; Signorelli 34, 41–43, 53, 164, 165, 217; *see also* memory
formal regression 2, 4, 29, 41, 47, 48, 55, 62, 63
fort-da 140
foundational murder 245, 251–252, 256, 257–259; renunciation and 253–255
frame 155–157, 159–161
France, concept of après-coup in 66

free association 78, 80, 157
French translation of Freud 17–19
Freud, E. 15–16
Freud, S. 2, 3, 5, 8–10, 12, 14, 15, 26, 47, 54, 64, 65, 78, 81, 83, 94, 117, 118, 124, 126, 128, 132, 141, 164, 169, 179, 192, 198, 210, 219, 223, 235, 250, 257; "'Wild' Psycho-analysis" 238; "The Acquisition and Control of Fire" 157, 239; *Beyond the Pleasure Principle* 40, 43, 183, 188, 225, 226, 244, 249; "A Case of Paranoia Running Counter to the Psychoanalytic Theory of the Disease" 23, 38–41, 139; *Civilization and Its Discontents* 17, 44; conceptions of the operation of *après-coup* 47–51; "Constructions in Analysis" 157, 252; *The Ego and the Id* 47, 143–144; Emma 14, 16, 28, 29, 46, 83, 134, 137, 169, 181; English translation 19–20; extensive conception of après-coup 50–51; "Formulations on the Two Principles of Mental Functioning" 144, 237; French translation 18–19, 21; *The Future of an Illusion* 44, 178; *Group Psychology and the Analysis of the Ego* 43–45; "Heredity and Aetiology of the Neuroses" 16; *From the History of an Infantile Neurosis* 36–38, 49; *Inhibitions, Symptoms and Anxiety* 190; *The Interpretation of Dreams* 4, 5, 29–30, 31–35, 134, 144, 148, 170, 174, 178, 233; "A Metapsychological Supplement to the Theory of Dreams" 159; *Moses and Monotheism* 40, 258–259; *nachträglich* and *Nachträglichkeit* in 15–16, 30, 31–35; "The Neuropsychoses of Defence" 189; *An Outline of Psycho-Analysis* 115, 157–158, 238; *Phylogenetic Fantasy: Overview of the Transference Neuroses* 49; process of theorization 41–48; "A Project for a Scientific Psychology" 28, 134, 157; "Psychical treatment" 150–151; *The Psychopathology of Everyday Life* 41; "The Question of Lay Analysis" 238; restrictive conception of après-coup 49–50; Schreber case 40, 248; "Sexuality in the Aetiology of the Neuroses" 30–31; *Studies on Hysteria* 4, 28, 55, 149–150, 157; theorizations 26–27; theory of the drives 122–123; *Three Essays on the Theory of Sexuality* 188; "Three Fates"

32–34, 41; *Totem and Taboo* 78, 251, 258; *Why War?* 243–244, 246–248; "Wolf Man" case 176
fright 61
fundamental rule 30, 57, 73–75, 79–80, 134, 136, 149, 153, 157, 223

generalized reminiscence 138
genius 12
God 152–153
Goethe, W. 20, 26; *Faust* 179; *West-Eastern Divan* 18
Graben 18
Green, A. 51, 61, 64; *L'enfant de ça* 66–67
Grothendieck, A. 178
guilt 27, 33, 34, 72, 186–187, 192, 250; responsibility and 256; unconscious 12, 35, 78, 166

hallucinations 7; acoustic 89–91; negative 77–78, 193, 221; perceptual activity 167
hate 87, 100, 106, 186–187, 249; sexualized 48–49
Hegel, G.W.F. 159
heuresthesia 168
Hugo, V. 65
humour 35
hypercathexis 83, 132, 140, 147, 151, 158, 161, 223, 229, 238
hypnosis 157, 169
hypochondria 202
hysteria 4, 135, 145, 149, 151, 154, 169

id 5, 11, 23, 29, 47, 55, 97, 139, 146, 191, 210
ideas 216
identification 61, 157, 187; defective 185; neo-identity 97–99, 196; primary 190; processual 256; projective 189
imagination 208
imperative of registration 3, 21–23, 36, 46, 48, 58, 97, 116, 117, 119, 123, 126, 128–130, 139, 140, 198
imprint 139
incest 33, 191
incidental thought 80
infantile amnesia 182–183
infantile sexuality 22, 31, 48, 128, 129, 153, 181, 184, 188, 216; primacy of the phallus 182–183; repression 182–183; *see also* sexuality

interpretation 3–4, 6, 10, 26, 42, 73, 87–88, 113, 131, 133, 135, 170, 173, 174; post-Kleinian 62–63; resolvent 5; substitutive 5
interval period 28–29, 48, 66, 137–138, 169
intra-drive 118–119

jealousy 23
jouissance 121
judgement 167–168

Kant, I. 240
Klein, M. 61, 63, 224, 248, 250
knowledge 8, 52, 53; dreams and 173–174; scientific 175
Kohut, H. 66

Lacan, J. 4, 8, 18, 23, 48, 52, 66, 136, 187; conception of après-coup 55–56, 57–60; on language 60; *le nachträglich* 54–56
lack 8, 10, 26, 38, 39, 42, 44–46, 52, 74, 76, 77, 119, 125, 126–127, 132, 148, 158, 164, 168, 173, 176, 209, 211, 214, 233, 252; expressions of 217–223; of judgement 167; perception of 27; and reality testing 234–235; *see also* castration; desire
language 2, 53, 78, 89–90, 132, 146, 147, 149, 152, 158, 177; conversion 151; dreams and 4; Lacan on 60; metapsychological 18; psychic function 5; translation 18–19; *see also* speech
Laplanche, J.: *The Language of Psychoanalysis* 54; *Problématiques VI* 21
latency 29, 48, 56, 57, 116, 130, 134, 183; *see also* period of latency
Le Guen, C. 51
libidinal cathexis 241–242
libidinal regeneration 42, 73–75, 78, 117, 118, 174
libidinal sympathetic excitation 10, 64, 171–172, 191, 201–204, 206, 222, 232
libido 5, 42, 94, 120, 121, 147, 161, 171, 193, 196; castration complex 184; hypercathexis 57; processual 78
life drive 61–62, 173, 224–228
listening 73, 80, 82; to listening 65
Little Hans 41

Malraux, A., *Anti Memoirs* 115
Marty, P. 62
masochism 18, 83, 87, 104, 105, 245, 246; of renunciation 10–11, 44, 48, 144, 171, 224–229; of restraint 11, 64, 117, 125, 129, 144
mass psychology 250
maternal reverie 61, 64
memory 15–16, 27, 28, 30, 49, 57, 117, 134, 138, 146–147, 213, 215; associative remembering 29; dreams and 31–32; processual 9, 40, 84, 118
mentalization 211–213, 221, 229, 254–255
metaphors 189, 208
metapsychology 44, 46, 51, 66, 115, 124, 151, 207–208; process 153–155
mise en abyme 36, 119, 124
missing trace 217–218
mnemic traces 138, 145, 209
modes of functioning 83
moment 134
mourning 138, 139, 149–150
"murder" 17, 22, 78, 87–89, 94–95, 119, 161, 258, 259; foundational 245, 251–256
mysticism 152, 226

nachträglich and *Nachträglichkeit* 14, 28, 30, 65, 124, 130, 136, 145, 169; in 'A Case of Paranoia Running Counter to the Psychoanalytic Theory of the Disease' 38–41; in Freud 15–16; in 'From the history of an Infantile Neurosis' 36–38; in The Interpretation of Dreams 31–35; in Lacan 54–56; Lacan on 54; "return" 15, 16–17; in 'Sexuality in the Aetiology of the Neuroses' 30–31; translations 18–19, 21
narcissism 22–23, 44, 48, 122, 123, 128, 139, 159, 171, 191, 196; castration complex 184; primary 39–40, 47, 182
Nebenmensch 140, 157, 245–246, 254
negative hallucination 77–78, 221
negative tendencies 5, 172–173
neo-identity 97–99, 196
neo-reality 29, 31, 38, 46, 78, 83
neuroses: symptoms, positive and negative aspects 49; traumatic 62
neurotica 48, 133–135, 181
Neyraut, M. 51
nocturnal unconscious shame 166
Nordlinger, M. 21
novelty, dreams and 6–7

"O" 152
object-cathexis 184
occult science 45
oceanic feeling 26–27, 43
Oedipus complex 6, 47, 59, 108, 182–186, 188, 195, 258; "murder of the father" 17, 88–89, 161, 191; principle of resolution 130
Oeuvres completes de Freud (psychanalyse) (OCF.P) 18–19
One, the 52
Other, the 52, 60
other of processuality 204, 254–255
overdetermination 63, 82–83, 106, 113, 117, 138, 187; of thought and desire 9–10

pacifism 247
pain 11, 44, 64, 116, 187; unconscious 78
palliative operation of après-coup 108–111
Pasche, F. 213
perception 27–28, 38, 76, 152, 167, 168, 176; of difference 6–7, 76, 237, 241; endogenous 76; libidinal cathexis and 241–242; sensory 76, 77, 166, 192, 213; with traces 211–212; transposition 208–211; without traces 197
perceptual activity 7, 77, 135, 167, 168, 175, 209, 223
Perelberg, R. 51
Perelman, G. 175–176, 178
period of latency 2, 28, 29, 42, 135, 169, 182, 188
periods 15
Pfister, O. 9
phantasy 8, 9, 36, 37, 48, 75–76, 181, 188, 189–190, 192, 208; castration- 194; primal scene 199–202; retrospective 37–38
phobia 189, 221
phylogenesis 49
play 64, 81; sexuality and 200
pleasure principle 8, 57, 62, 75, 95, 138, 139, 144, 156, 188; beyond the 58, 62, 116, 119, 134–135, 144, 145–146, 159
Poincaré conjecture 176
Pontalis, J.-B., The Language of Psychoanalysis 54
Popper-Lynkeus, J., "Dreaming like Waking" 243

"posthumous" 257–259
post-truth 235–236
preconscious 28–29, 152
pre-verbal traumatic impressions 40
primal scene phantasy 199–202, 208
primary destructivity 62
primary narcissism 39–40, 47, 182
principle of resolution 130
"process" 159–160
process 153–155; analytic 156; thought- 155–159
processual libido 78
processual memory 9, 40, 59, 84, 118
processuality 255–257, 259
projection 23, 110–111, 189
Prozeß 153–155, 189–190
psyche 120
psychic activities of passivity 125, 136, 147, 155, 166, 169, 179, 203, 248; regressive 42–43, 72, 77, 79, 80, 116, 121–122, 145; sensual regression 183
psychic matter 1–4
psychic registration 7, 15, 17, 22, 46
psychic work 2, 5, 7, 11, 15, 17, 20, 22, 29, 37, 40, 46, 47, 49, 50, 58, 64, 75, 77, 84, 103, 110, 111, 115, 116, 118–119, 124–125, 130, 135, 136, 160, 168, 183, 185, 254; modalities 120–121
psychoanalysis 9–11, 50, 55, 56, 143, 163, 173, 219–220, 240–241; castration 191–194; confidentiality 73; ethics 73; frame 155–157, 159, 160–161; fundamental rule 30, 57, 73, 79–80, 134, 136, 149, 153, 157, 223; interpretation 3–5, 6; *see also* interpretation; mass 250; as a science 206–207; transference 37; *see also* transference
psychoneuroses 181
psychopathology 49
psychosis, dreams as 164, 165

quantum decoherence 170
quest 152–153

Rabelais. F., *Gargantua and Pantagruel* 120
reality 27, 39, 48, 176, 242; castration- 194; neo- 29, 31, 38, 46, 78, 83; principle 138, 144, 156, 188; tangible 164; -testing 74, 132, 133, 148, 158, 164–168, 182, 234–235, 237–239
reduction 78, 194

registration 5, 39, 116, 123, 131, 135–136, 147, 152, 232–233; imperative of 3, 21–23, 36, 46, 48, 58, 97, 115–117, 119, 126, 128–129, 130, 139, 140, 198
regression and regressivity 11, 15, 20, 21, 37, 46, 47, 51, 53, 79–80, 122, 130, 138–139, 140, 160, 169, 216–217, 248; drive 10, 41, 43, 57, 66, 78, 145, 195; extinctive 1, 16, 17, 22–23, 44, 46, 48, 50, 60, 64, 75, 84, 122–123, 126, 128, 129, 132, 135, 146, 182, 197, 217–219, 221, 222, 224–229; formal 2, 4, 29, 41, 47, 48, 55, 62, 63; imperative of 253; sensual 171, 198; temporal 29, 134; of thought 147; work 159; working-through 22–23
regressive attraction 5, 9–10
religious feeling 116
remembering 29–30, 135, 137, 169
reminiscence 9, 49, 56, 57, 61, 74, 82, 88, 117, 118, 186; generalized 138; processual 84; sensory 89; *see also* memory
renunciation 5, 17, 57, 59, 74, 78, 83, 94, 97, 130, 138, 139, 165, 173; of extinction 8; and foundational murder 253–255; imperative of 208; masochism of 11, 44, 48, 144, 171, 224–229
repetition 81
representation(s) 27, 76, 77, 83, 207
representative field 168
repression 9–10, 57, 182–183, 192, 216, 248
resignification 66
resistance 1, 7
resolvent interpretation 5
responsibility 256
restraint 16, 17, 44, 116, 118–119, 125, 130, 140, 146, 152, 170, 249–250; masochism of 129, 245
retrogression 29, 137, 154
return 15–17, 135–136, 140
reversible denial 42
Roland, R. 26, 43
Rosenberg, B. 64

sadism 246
sadomasochism 104–106
saturation 158, 163–164, 166–168, 172, 174–178, 218
schematizing asceticization 179
school phobia 84–89

Schreber, D. 40, 248
science 143, 175–178, 239–240; interpretation and 173; occult 45; psychoanalysis as 206–207; theories 3–4, 7, 8–9
secondary elaboration 47, 118, 130–132, 155, 172
semiology 82; of waking 174–175
sensory perception 76, 77, 166, 192, 210–211, 213
sensuality 64, 77, 146, 182, 201, 218–219
sequential dreams 91–93
serendipity 169–170
session animism 101–102
sexuality 2, 31, 34, 38–39, 48, 50, 88, 192, 225, 244; après-coup and 187–188, 195; childhood 181; diphasism of 181–184; emergence of the erogenous body 197–205; erogenous zones 203–204; hate and 48–49; organ erotogenicity 171, 182, 184, 192, 193–194, 198, 202, 203; period of latency 2, 28, 29, 42, 135, 169, 182, 183, 188; sadism 246; trauma and 181
Shakespeare, W. 33, 65, 199
shame 187; nocturnal unconscious 166; unconscious 78
shock 28–29, 30, 36–37, 39, 41, 46–48, 57, 63, 125, 129, 134–135, 138, 169; counter- 116; *see also* trauma
signifier 52, 55, 59, 60, 123; *see also* Lacan, J.
sleep-dream system 106–108, 170, 171, 176; role of denial in 78–79, 212, 214; waking 165–166, 174–175
Sodré, I. 51
speech 55, 59–60, 73, 80, 132, 151, 158, 177; consciousness and 2–3; incidental 79
Squiggle technique 63
studia humanitatis 143
substitution 46, 61, 189
substitutive interpretation 5
superego 6, 8, 30, 44, 47, 49, 81, 83, 147, 148, 161, 183, 188, 244, 246–248, 256, 259; après-coup and 75; castration and 184–185; psychic activities of passivity 43, 72, 77, 116, 122, 125, 136, 145, 147, 155, 166, 169, 183, 203, 248
symbiosis 157
Symbolic, the 17, 55, 60
symptoms 29, 30, 46, 56; neurotic, positive and negative aspects 49

temporal regression 29, 37–38, 134
temporary denial 42
terror 255
theories and theorization 3–4, 26–27, 33, 73, 75–76, 117, 121, 172, 173, 221, 222; of *après-coup* 18; of causality 14, 31, 56–57, 128, 130, 135; Darwinism 145–146; of dreams 169–171; drive 122–123; Freud's process of 41–48; Kleinian 61–64; scientific 7, 8–9; of thought 143–145
thing-presentations 1, 17, 36, 53, 55, 113, 117, 118, 126–127, 132, 137, 139–140, 146–147, 149, 171, 216
thinking and thought 1–2, 3, 8, 11, 35, 45, 47, 49–50, 88, 143–144, 163; abstraction 223; bidirectionality of 145–147; biphasic operation 147–148; double nature of 149–150; free-association 79, 80, 116, 131, 136, 157; in Freud 150–153; ideas 216; imagination 208; incidental 80; mentalization 211–213, 221, 229, 254–255; mutation 155; overdetermination 9–10; -process 155–159; "process" 153–155; regressive 146; reminiscence 9; representations 27, 76, 77, 83, 207; work 150; *see also* association(s); perception
third primal fantasy 121
thought *see* thinking and thought
"Three Fates" 32–34, 41
traces and tracing 1, 30–31, 76–77, 84, 91, 101–102, 119–121, 126, 127, 139–140, 146, 164, 168, 176, 190–191, 197–198, 210–218, 254; imprint 139; mnemic 138, 145, 209; thing-presentations 17, 118; *see also* memory
Traduire Freud 19, 21
transference 6, 37, 50–52, 57, 73, 80, 84, 87, 113, 135–136, 141, 246; counter- 71, 95–97, 136; double 88; neurosis 49
transitional space and object 64
translation 4, 18, 19–20; "après-coup" 18–19, 21–22; "deferred action" 19; *nachträglich* and *Nachträglichkeit* 18–19; "process" 153–154; psychopathology of 20–22; *see also* interpretation
transposition 158, 168, 186, 188–190, 208–211
transvaluation 187
trauma 7, 10, 14, 27, 28, 36–37, 39, 42, 43, 45, 48, 53, 56, 57, 72, 93–94, 118, 121,

128, 134, 136, 169, 181, 206; castration-anxiety 16
truth 8, 52, 53, 177, 178, 219–220, 240–241; post- 235–236

ultracrepidarianism 175
unconscious 3–4, 6, 28–29, 47, 53, 97, 143, 149, 150, 152; concept 176; guilt 12, 78, 166; pain 78; processual memory 9; shame 78

Vienna 10–11
Villani, C. 238–239, 241
Vinci, L. 9–10, 117
Vorgang 153–155, 189–190

waking 165–166; semiology of 174–175
Weltanschauung 44, 77, 226
Winnicott, D. W. 57, 62–64, 221
wish-fulfillment 45, 165, 172, 175, 177
word-presentations 147, 151, 152; *see also* language; speech; thing-presentations
work 150; psychic 159; regressive 159; *see also* dream-work; psychic work
working-through 22–23
writing 215

Zeh, H. D. 170
zemblanity 169–170